CAMBRIDGE
IN ENGLISH LE

Edited
D. E. C. YALE
Fellow of Christ's College and Reader
in English Legal History at the University of Cambridge

PETTYFOGGERS AND VIPERS
OF THE COMMONWEALTH

THE PUBLISHER WISHES TO THANK
THE MANAGERS OF THE MAITLAND MEMORIAL FUND
FOR THEIR GENEROUS SUBVENTION TO SUPPORT
THE PUBLICATION OF THIS BOOK

Historians have long recognized that members of the lower branch of the legal profession, the ancestors of the modern solicitors, played an important part in early modern English society, but difficulties in establishing their identities and recovering their career patterns have hitherto left them virtually unstudied. Attorneys, solicitors, clerical officials, and court holders were the most numerous groups of legal practitioners of their day and the lawyers most often in direct contact with ordinary people who were seeking legal remedies. Based on source material in both local and national repositories, this book aims to reconstruct their professional and social history. It examines changes in the size, education, work, and organization of the profession over the course of the period. It considers the social origins of practitioners, the material rewards and possibilities for social mobility offered by a legal career, and the role of lawyers in the life of the localities. Finally, it evaluates the nature and quality of the legal sevices they provided for the public. The work charts the massive sixteenth-century increase in central court litigation and offers an explanation of it largely in terms of social change and the decline of local jurisdictions. It also comes to the surprising conclusions that litigation was relatively cheap and that social groups other than the landed gentry constituted the majority of those who used the courts. At the same time, it argues that the period witnessed a major turning point in the relationship between the legal profession and English society. The number of practitioners in the lower branch who were associated with the legal institutions of London grew to such an extent that by 1640 the ratio of lawyers to population was not much different from that in the early twentieth century. Although this tremendous growth in the amount of legal business and the number of legal practitioners created some serious administrative problems, the commonly held view that the lower branch in this period was largely untrained, dishonest, and uncontrolled is no more than a myth. The potential for social mobility offered by a legal career changed over the period and should not be exaggerated, but by the mid seventeenth century members of the lower branch were well established as responsible and respectable members of the middle ranks of local communities, especially in towns.

PETTYFOGGERS AND VIPERS OF THE COMMONWEALTH

The 'Lower Branch' of the Legal Profession in Early Modern England

C. W. BROOKS

Department of History, University of Durham

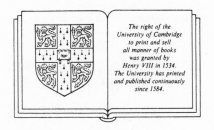

*The right of the
University of Cambridge
to print and sell
all manner of books
was granted by
Henry VIII in 1534.
The University has printed
and published continuously
since 1584.*

CAMBRIDGE UNIVERSITY PRESS

CAMBRIDGE

LONDON   NEW YORK   NEW ROCHELLE

MELBOURNE   SYDNEY

PUBLISHED BY THE PRESS SYNDICATE OF THE UNIVERSITY OF CAMBRIDGE
The Pitt Building, Trumpington Street, Cambridge, United Kingdom

CAMBRIDGE UNIVERSITY PRESS
The Edinburgh Building, Cambridge CB2 2RU, UK
40 West 20th Street, New York NY 10011–4211, USA
477 Williamstown Road, Port Melbourne, VIC 3207, Australia
Ruiz de Alarcón 13, 28014 Madrid, Spain
Dock House, The Waterfront, Cape Town 8001, South Africa

http://www.cambridge.org

© Cambridge University Press 1986

This book is in copyright. Subject to statutory exception
and to the provisions of relevant collective licensing agreements,
no reproduction of any part may take place without
the written permission of Cambridge University Press.

First published 1986
First paperback edition 2004

A catalogue record for this book is available from the British Library

Library of Congress cataloguing in publication data
Brooks, C. W.
Pettyfoggers and vipers of the Commonwealth.
(Cambridge studies in English legal history)
Originally presented as the author's thesis
(doctoral–Oxford)
Bibliography: p.
Includes index.
1. Lawyers – Great Britain – History.   I. Title.
II. Series.
KD466.B76 1986   340′.023′42   85–26896

ISBN 0 521 30574 8 hardback
ISBN 0 521 89083 7 paperback

For Sharyn

CONTENTS

vii

Contents

LIST OF TABLES AND FIGURES

PREFACE

This book has been a long time in the making, and it is a pleasure to acknowledge here some of the many people who have helped me along the way, although I alone am responsible for all errors and interpretations.

My greatest debt is to S. H. Brooks, who did so much to make it possible for me to undertake the project, and who has always managed to combine patient encouragement with trenchant criticism. Professor S. F. C. Milsom aided my early attempts to learn something about legal history. Professor J. S. Cockburn has been a constant and valued source of friendship and advice. Mr C. A. F. Meekings kindly passed on to me some of his vast knowledge of King's Bench records. Mr Philip Styles helped me to see how the resources of local record offices could be used to illuminate the activities of attorneys. Dr J. H. Baker, Mr C. S. L. Davies, and Dr K. M. Sharpe read through earlier drafts of the work and made many valuable points about the content and the way it was expressed. I am particularly grateful to Dr P. H. Williams for his very generous help at a number of difficult stages as this project progressed from an Oxford doctoral dissertation to a book. Also I thank the examiners of my thesis, Drs G. E. Aylmer and E. W. Ives, for their careful reading and helpful comments on that work.

The research has been carried out in many different places in England and also in the United States. Financial assistance from various sources has therefore been invaluable. Grants from the British Academy and Durham University have contributed towards travel expenses. A fellowship from the Huntington Library made it possible for me to consult the Ellesmere manuscripts. I am especially grateful to the Principal and Fellows of Brasenose College, Oxford for extending my research fellowship at the college to a fourth year, which enabled me to continue my research and to benefit further from the stimulating company which I found amongst my historical and legal colleagues there. I also thank the many librarians and archivists who have assisted me, and in particular I thank Messrs Hawkins and Co. of Hitchin for allowing me to consult the account book of George Draper and the history of their firm by Reginald Hine.

Finally, and above all, two people have helped me more than I can easily say. My first graduate supervisor, Dr W. R. Prest, has for many years given friendship, encouragement, constructive criticism, and innumerable references on a scale far beyond the call of duty. I hope that this book is in some degree a small recompense. At Oxford, the late J. P. Cooper directed my research and set a scholarly example which I am very glad to have known. Anyone who knew John Cooper will remember him for the generous way in which he shared his remarkably profound knowledge of late medieval and early modern history. I benefited and learned from this quality as well as from the crucial advice which he gave me at many stages during the course of my work.

Durham   C.W.B.

ABBREVIATIONS AND CONVENTIONS

Bodl.	Bodleian Library, Oxford
Brit. Lib.	British Library, London
CSPD	*Calendar of State Papers, Domestic*
HCRO	Hertfordshire County Record Office, Hertford
Hunt. Lib. EL. MS	Ellesmere manuscripts, Huntington Library, San Marino, Calif.
PRO	Public Record Office, London
SBT	Shakespeare's Birthplace Trust, Stratford-upon-Avon

Unless otherwise stated, the place of publication of all printed books is London. In all dates the year is taken as beginning on 1 January.

INTRODUCTION

The subject of this book requires a word of explanation. Essentially, it is a study of the early modern antecedents of that group of English lawyers known today as the solicitors. Unlike the legal profession of the United States, and, indeed, that of many other countries which have been influenced by the common law tradition, English lawyers are divided into two branches which are characterized by different forms of training and regulation and by some very general differences in function. One branch of the profession, the bar, enjoys a monopoly right of audience before the superior courts. The other, the solicitors, provides a wide range of legal services to the community which include conveyancing and advocacy before inferior tribunals such as Magistrates' and County courts. Moreover, since there is a firmly established convention that litigants should not consult directly with barristers without the intervention of a solicitor, the latter also instruct members of the bar in cases which come before the higher courts.

In its modern form, the solicitors' branch of the legal profession is the product of a series of measures passed by Parliament in the 1870s and 1880s which authorized the Law Society to act as the largely self-regulating governing body of the profession. These statutes also greatly simplified its identity. After 1873, a solicitor could be defined easily as anyone who was authorized by the Law Society to practise. Before 1873, there was no such single qualification which admitted a man into the profession; many of the lawyers whom we would now call solicitors were then known as attorneys at law, men who were, technically, officers of the two main common law courts, King's Bench and Common Pleas. Going even further back into the past, to the sixteenth and seventeenth centuries, the problem of clearly identifying the ancestors of the solicitors becomes even more acute. The term 'solicitor' was then only just coming into use.

The common law attorneys again figure prominently in the story, but
the history of the attorneys is closely intertwined with that of the
court bureaucracies. Furthermore, some court officials, such as the
six clerks in Chancery and the filazers of the Common Pleas, also
offered legal services directly to clients. On the other hand, some men
who practised law had few, if any, direct links with the major
institutions of the common law such as the royal courts or the inns
of court and chancery in London. All of these practitioners come
within the scope of this book, but, apart from the fact that they had
no right of audience to plead in the central courts, the legal profession
below the bar had no clear or concise definition. For this reason, and
for greater ease of exposition, I have chosen to confer on all of these
various groups of lawyers the blanket label of 'lower branch' of the
legal profession. The expression is completely anachronistic to the
early modern period, and, although it conveys a distinction which
was in some respects clearly felt, it should not be taken to imply any
assumptions about the unity of the profession below the bar or about
the relationship, which was much less developed than it has since
become, between these lawyers and the 'upper branch' of barristers,
serjeants, and judges. Like 'armed forces', the term 'lower branch'
is nothing more than a convenient collective noun which covers
several groups of men with different functions and different forms
of structural organization.

The reasons for undertaking research on the early modern legal
profession are simple. Historians have for a long time recognized that
lawyers and law courts were important features of sixteenth- and
seventeenth-century English life, but, until recently, very little has
been written about the courts, and, even more surprisingly, almost
nothing about the lawyers, particularly those lawyers like the practitioners of the lower branch who were, in comparison with figures
such as Sir Edward Coke and Sir Francis Bacon, very largely
uncelebrated and unknown.[1] Furthermore, although historical debates within the last fifty years have generated a number of works on
the aristocracy, gentry, and smallholders, the history of the professions is still in its infancy, and so, too, in many respects is that of
those middling groups in society – the merchants, artisans, and
yeomen – to which professions such as the lower branch belong. This
book aims to make some contributions on both of these fronts, and,
as should become clear in the chapters which follow, I believe that
this period witnessed important changes in the size and shape of the

lower branch and in the relationship between lawyers, their clients, and the courts. It was also one in which even rather obscure lawyers such as country attorneys made important contributions to local administration, politics, and society.

There are at least two ways to approach the study of a professional group. One method is to concentrate on those activities of the professional which are connected with the services he is supposed to provide for other members of the community. For example, the study of doctors can be a study of the application of medical science to society, and the study of lawyers an attempt to describe the interaction between practitioners, the law, and their clients. The other way to look at professionals is to study them as a particular kind of social group, as a social category typified by certain characteristics – learning, self-regulation, and a fiduciary relationship with clients – which set them off from others such as the gentry, the merchants, or the peasantry. We can ask whether and how such groups existed in the past and try to determine what, if any, role they played in politics or the processes of social change.

This book attempts to follow both of these paths. The chapters on the organization of the lower branch and on legal education have been written with at least one eye on the consequences of these aspects of professional life for the community at large. Moreover, since members of the lower branch were vital links in the process by which litigation came into London, a number of questions have been raised in Chapters 4–7 about how the legal system operated and the pressure under which it came during the early seventeenth century. At the same time, other chapters are devoted primarily to the life-styles and economic prospects of practitioners and to their strictly non-professional activities in the communities where they lived.

In the pursuit of all of these objectives, it has been essential to concentrate attention on the lower branch in the provinces as well as on the lower branch in London. Most of what has been written hitherto about the English legal profession has been based on those lawyers who worked in the royal courts at Westminster and who were associated with the inns of court and inns of chancery in London. However, in the early modern period, the majority of the practitioners who worked in London also lived and worked in the provinces. Equally important, there were many jurisdictions within the localities – for example, borough courts, manorial courts, and quarter sessions – where lawyers could ply their trades, and these lawyers were not necessarily the same men as those who were active in London. Thus the book attempts to work within two geographical dimensions, the one metropolitan, the other provincial, and the reader should be aware of the research strategies which have been adopted in order to make this possible.

In any historical inquiry the extent to which the questions we want to ask can be answered satisfactorily depends on the quality of the surviving evidence. From this point of view, the materials available for the study of the early modern lower branch do not seem very promising. There are no known registers of practitioners which provide details about dates of admission, about the areas of the country from which they came, or about the social backgrounds of parents. Nor are there any very extensive sets of private papers of the kind which survive in large numbers from the eighteenth century, and which make it possible to depict daily routines precisely, to quantify the nature, size, and profits of practice, and to fathom more easily the attitudes of individuals towards politics or religion. Finally, since members of the lower branch were quite ordinary people of relatively moderate means, many of them remain obstinately obscure even after the most comprehensive local research.

The result of all these deficiencies of evidence is that much of what is presented here has been a matter of reconstruction; reconstruction of the membership of the lower branch; reconstitution of professional structures; and the retrieval of lost career patterns by piecing together a mass of particular details from a large number of individual biographies. The names of individual practitioners at various dates have been culled from court records and from other sources such as the papers of the early Stuart commissions on fees. In particular, thanks to the 'Rolls of Warrants of Attorney' which are preserved in the plea rolls of King's Bench and Common Pleas,[2] it is possible to compile for every English county a directory of all the attorneys who worked in these courts at any one date. Using this source, lists of the names of practitioners have been compiled for the years 1560, 1580, 1606, 1625, and 1640. Since the attorneys were the most numerous group within the lower branch, these lists are the key to the social history of the profession because the names and addresses which they provide make it possible to unlock other sources such as wills, town records, and the vast miscellaneous collections of local record offices.

However, by the early seventeenth century, there were at least a thousand men active in the profession at any one time, and over the entire period from 1560 to 1640 the number comes to several thousand. Hence, some means of reducing this large number of names to a sample group which could be investigated in greater detail had to be devised. One possible method was to look at the economic and social functions of the lower branch by taking a sample of several hundred attorneys from all over the country at various dates and then following their careers in the national and local sources. This approach offered the advantage of wide coverage, but in a study which involved quite obscure men, it had the serious practical limitation of precluding the kind of microscopic local research which might bring some unknown characters into the light. It would also have severely limited the scope of the study. Regional variations could have been treated only superficially, and, more important, essential questions about the structure of the provincial profession, about the political and bureaucratic activities of local practitioners, and about the social medium in which they moved would have been lost in vague generalizations.

Consequently, another method has been adopted; that of making case studies in three different counties – Warwickshire, Hertfordshire, and Devonshire – which aim to look at all members of the profession in these particular localities who were active in 1560, 1580, 1606, 1625, and 1640. This approach, too, has its limitations. County borders do not necessarily define social or economic entities, and lawyers, like geographical features, very often crossed these frontiers. Moreover, a larger sample would undeniably produce a more general picture, particularly as it is clear that local variations are numerous even in the limited areas which have been chosen for study. But, insofar as the right questions are asked, the case study method does at least promise the prospect of a reasonably full picture, and if the peculiarities of the areas under study are defined well enough, it should provide the means to define a series of types. In addition, the detailed studies have been supplemented by comprehensive searches for evidence in other localities, and, especially in Chapters 3, 9, and 10, an attempt has been made to incorporate as much material as possible from other parts of the country. The great value of the three-county sample is that it helps to produce a framework against which disparate pieces of information from other places can be more clearly understood.

Although to some extent based on the availability of sources, the choice of counties reflects some important regional variations. The full significance of these will emerge in due course, but for the moment some general remarks about them can serve as an introduction. One of the smallest counties in England, Hertfordshire, like the other counties of East Anglia, was by the early seventeenth century greatly influenced by the requirements of London's rapid growth.[3] In the southern part of the county there was a considerable trade in horses, and cattle were fattened for the London market. Central Hertfordshire had a mixed agrarian regime, but here too most crops were used for fattening stock. In the northern part of the shire wheat and barley were grown along with malt, which constituted an important commodity in the markets of towns like Hitchin.[4] Like its agriculture, Hertfordshire's social structure was influenced by London, since its proximity to the capital attracted many successful merchants and courtiers who were anxious to invest the profits of either office or trade in land. Thus at the top end, its social structure was so mobile that the Stones have remarked that by 1642 Hertfordshire 'had the lowest proportion of pre-1485 gentry and the highest proportion of post-1603 gentry of any county for which we have record so far...'[5]

Devonshire was a very different kind of place. One of the two or three largest, most populous, and richest shires in the realm, it was, like Norfolk and Suffolk and the other counties on the Western assize circuit, a hotbed for lawsuits. The county economy reflected its varied topography. The highland regions of central Devon were used for pasturing sheep and cattle, while the lowland valleys, particularly those around the southern coast and along the river Exe specialized in arable crops, including fruit production and feed for fattening livestock. Since the sea adjoined the county on two sides, fishing and maritime transport were significant sources of non-agricultural employment, but by far the most important industry in Devon was the production of cloth, a characteristic Devonshire shared with other counties in the south-west such as Gloucestershire, Somerset, and Wiltshire.[6] Unlike Hertfordshire, Devon had a stable gentry population composed of perhaps four hundred small landowners, but it appears that the manorial system was not strong, perhaps because much land was held on long (usually ninety-nine-year) leases.[7]

Located in the geographical centre of England, Warwickshire for all of the sixteenth century and most of the seventeenth was a county of middling prosperity with what might be described as an average number of lawsuits and an average sized legal profession.[8] The county was divided by the river Avon into the topographical features which Thirsk has described as the two basic types of the east Midlands. North of the Avon, the forest of Arden was still filled with trees in the sixteenth century; in the south the Warwickshire fielden supported a mainly arable economy. In the latter region small farms of from twenty to sixty acres produced large crops of barley, wheat, and peas, but also supported pigs, cattle, and sheep. In the fielden 'economic inequality was conspicuous', since as much as one-third of the population consisted of cottagers and labourers.[9] Perhaps only because it has been more thoroughly studied, the forest of Arden appears to have been the most rapidly changing of the two areas. In the sixteenth century the economy was mainly pastoral, but in the early decades of the seventeenth century there was a shift towards dairying and cheese production, the chief markets being Coventry and Birmingham. The Arden social structure was, nevertheless, relatively static. There were a large number of established freehold peasants whose standard of living progressed steadily, but neither the gentry nor the landless seem to have made significant gains.[10] Like most forest areas, the Arden attracted a large number of migrants so that as much as 40 per cent of the population was landless by 1660. These wage labourers supported themselves by various crafts, and, presumably, as the seventeenth century progressed became more and more involved in the production of iron and coal and in the metal industries which were growing up around Birmingham during the course of the century. This was the most important economic development in the county during the period, although its full impact was not recognized until the end of the seventeenth century.[11] The social structure of the Warwickshire gentry was relatively stable. The heralds' visitations of 1619 list 275 pedigrees, which may suggest a gentry population of 350 or so, a figure roughly in line with Everitt's estimate for Leicestershire in 1640, a county of not dissimilar size and agricultural geography.[12]

The three counties contained a variety of towns. Coventry is a classic example of a large and important medieval town which saw itself in the midst of a painful decline during the mid sixteenth century, even though it was in 1603 still among the ten largest urban centres in the county.[13] Exeter, though not even a twentieth of the size of London in the early seventeenth century, was perhaps the fifth largest town in England, and continued to prosper as an entrepôt for the Devon cloth trade, and as an administrative centre. To use the terminology of Clark and Slack, it was a major provincial capital.[14] Warwick, to some extent like Hertford, was a medium sized town in which a serious sixteenth-century decline in trade and industry was followed by the town's development by the later seventeenth century into a centre for the distribution of goods and services.[15] On the other hand, the other major west Midland town in the sample, Birmingham, was an unincorporated town which grew progressively prosperous during the course of the late sixteenth and early seventeenth centuries as the hub of the metal trade. Birmingham and its neighbouring parishes were already quite populous in the mid sixteenth century; by 1700 the city boasted some 7000 inhabitants and was fast becoming one of the the most important towns in England.[16]

The rest of the towns in the sample were smallish market towns of various sizes, but none had a population of more than around 3000. Some of them were incorporated and some were not. Of the Hertfordshire market towns, the most important was Hitchin, a manorial town with a population of about 1800 in 1603.[17] In Devon, the late sixteenth and early seventeenth centuries found towns which were perhaps in better condition than those of the nation as a whole. Hoskins has written that this period was probably the most prosperous in the history of the many chartered towns – Barnstaple, Totnes, Torrington, and eight others – which by the nineteenth century were to become notorious pocket boroughs.[18] The largest of these was Barnstaple, an assize town and centre for the cloth trade, which had a late Elizabethan population of about 3000. Even so, Torrington is frequently cited as the most important trading town in Devon after Exeter.[19]

Devon, Hertfordshire, and Warwickshire present a large variety of economies and towns, but it cannot be claimed that the counties are in any way typical of all the rest of England, not to mention Wales. At least two important areas are not included in the detailed study. The first of these is East Anglia (specifically Norfolk and Suffolk), for centuries the richest part of England and consequently a region of many lawsuits and the home of many lawyers. The second is the north of England, from which only about 4 per cent of King's Bench and Common Pleas litigation came, and where, apart from Yorkshire, lawyers associated with the central courts were relatively few and far between. It is towards these two areas in particular, the one lowland and prosperous, the other upland and backward, that comparative glances will be aimed when we look up from the microscopic study of the three principal counties.

Finally, there is one last remark about methodology which must be made at this stage. Many of my conclusions about changes in the legal profession, about the state of legal administration, and about the role of lawyers in early modern society are based on a simple statistical analysis of the volume and nature of litigation in the central courts and of the social status of the litigants. Some readers may find this a dubious endeavour, particularly when there are such obvious difficulties in the way of defining what constitutes a lawsuit and when the evidence does not readily reveal the exact type of quantitative information which one would like ideally to have. However, there are several good reasons for thinking that such an undertaking is worth while, whatever the hazards. First, counting cases in order to measure the performance of courts is nothing new. As we shall see, it was done by court officials in the reign of Elizabeth I, it was done by parliamentary commissioners who investigated the legal system in the 1820s and 1830s, and it is still done today. Second, in the absence of any quantitative signposts, it is impossible to talk in any sensible way about how 'law-minded' or how 'litigious' any one period or country was in comparison with another. Unless some attempt is made to produce a general sketch of who used the courts and why, legal history will continue to be preoccupied with tracing the genealogies of doctrine, and our understanding of the legal system will be biased by evidence assembled from general contemporary comment or surviving private papers, both of which inevitably tend to over-represent the experiences of the more wealthy sections of society.

2

LAWYERS AND THE ROYAL COURTS IN LONDON DURING THE REIGN OF ELIZABETH

I

In 1558 the English legal profession already had a long history. From the earliest years of the post-Conquest era, and probably long before, kings had made provision for the settlement of disputes between individuals and acknowledged the need for legal specialists who could aid litigants seeking redress before the royal tribunals. Prior to the beginning of the thirteenth century, most of the officials associated with the king's courts in London were still clerics, but by the end of that century the emergence of full-time lay lawyers, who were subjected to a certain degree of royal regulation and discipline, can be discerned and charted.[1]

The most important and most highly organized of the early common lawyers were the serjeants at law. By the early fourteenth century they had become a distinctive order of lawyers who usually numbered some twelve to fifteen men at any one time. The serjeants were the senior members of the legal profession below the judges. They were nominated by royal writ, their creation was accompanied by great public ceremony, and they wore characteristic robes and a cap, the coif. In addition the serjeants enjoyed the privileged professional position of having an exclusive right to plead before the court most frequently involved in civil litigation, the Common Pleas.[2]

However, there were other royal courts besides the Common Pleas, and although the serjeants could and did practise in tribunals such as Chancery, Star Chamber, the court of Wards, and the court of Requests, in these jurisdictions they enjoyed no monopoly and so had to share the business of pleading with another group of lawyers known as the apprentices at law. Early in their medieval history, the apprentices were probably men who were training to become serjeants, but by 1400 they had emerged as a separate branch of the profession, and, roughly speaking, they are the ancestors of the modern barristers. During the later middle ages and the early modern period, they earned their livings by offering in other courts the services which serjeants supplied to clients in the Common Pleas.[3] As the amount of litigation entertained by such jurisdictions increased during the course of the sixteenth century, so the number of apprentices (or pleaders or counsellors at law, as they were also known) grew accordingly.[4]

Thus by the beginning of the reign of Elizabeth, the serjeants and pleaders were well established as those lawyers who served as advisors to litigants and who argued cases before the royal courts. They usually received their training at the 'third university of England', the inns of court in London.[5] The royal judges were appointed from amongst their ranks, and, along with the judges, they were responsible for that part of the legal process which contemporaries called 'judgment' and which we would describe by using the terms substantive law or jurisprudence.

However, the processes connected with a lawsuit in the medieval and early modern periods were not limited to the argument of counsel and the decisions of judges on points of law. From their beginnings until their reform in the second half of the nineteenth century, one of the most crucial facts about the royal courts at Westminster was that, although they were located in London, they entertained cases from all over the country. Consequently from the earliest days the royal jurisdictions had been obliged to find ways to direct sheriffs in the provinces to make arrests, execute judgments, and force defendants to answer the summonses of plaintiffs. By the time of Queen Elizabeth, these tasks had been accomplished for centuries via a complicated system of judicial writs. Writs authorized the courts to act; they were the means by which defendants were forced to appear, or, alternatively, the devices used to delay appearance; they could be used to take some forms of property; they moved cases from London back to the provinces for trial before the judges at assizes; and, finally, they were the medium through which the decisions of the courts were carried out.[6]

Early modern lawsuits very often seem as preoccupied with writs as with the issues which had originally caused the dispute. Given this, it is not surprising that there were large numbers of men associated with the courts who made their livings by issuing and handling these writs, men concerned with what contemporaries called the 'practical' as opposed to the 'theoretical' part of the law. These practitioners constituted a large part of what we would call the legal profession, but, apart from a common concern with procedure, they were an extremely diverse group of men who defy easy definition or categorization. In the eighteenth and nineteenth centuries, they would become known as the lower branch of the legal profession, but in the sixteenth and seventeenth centuries such a blanket label, though convenient, can seriously mislead as to the nature of the thing it describes. In order to understand these groups of Elizabethan lawyers, we must leave behind all modern conceptions of what constitutes a profession. Instead, we must enter the world of the judicial bureaucracy, a world of clerks and under-clerks, of parchment and writs.

The reason why the early modern lower branch was so amorphous and ill defined is that there was in the world of procedure no such thing as an English legal system. Since there was no system, there is no simple definition of the lawyers who worked in it. True, all of the royal courts administered the national law of the realm. Equally, although there was by the early seventeenth century some specialization, members of the upper branch of the profession, the serjeants, pleaders, and judges, could work in all of the courts without restriction. Consequently there was a sense of unity about the substantive law. There were also some known criteria by which the jurisdictions of the various tribunals were mapped out. For example, the court of Chancery was the court of equity, which handled uses and mortgages; the Common Pleas and King's Bench specialized in debt, trespass, and other personal, real, and mixed actions. But in reality, contemporaries were well aware that it was all too easy for litigants to pursue the same suit through more than one court at the same time.[7] Equally, all of the courts with which we are concerned here were the king's courts, and they all sat in his palace at Westminster. Yet they had all arisen during different historical periods and developed along different lines without any view to the creation of a rational whole. The two busiest of the courts, King's Bench and Common Pleas, had settled down to permanent residence in Westminster Hall at different dates, the one in the thirteenth and the other in the late fourteenth or early fifteenth century. The court of Star Chamber in its mid-sixteenth-century form was largely the creation of King Henry VIII's minister, Cardinal Wolsey. The court of Wards and Liveries was established by statute in 1540. The

Exchequer was mainly a royal accounting department which over the years had evolved a small common law jurisdiction. The statute which established the court of Wards laid down the structure of the clerical bureaucracy which was to run the tribunal, but in this Wards was unique. In all the other courts, the nature of that structure was closely related to the development of procedures which had, over the years, evolved into the 'course of the court'.[8]

In Common Pleas lawsuits were begun by original writs issued out of Chancery, but the subsequent preparation of a case for hearing before the judges was handled by the officials associated with the Common Pleas itself. There were some seventeen to twenty 'filazers' who issued the writs which summonsed or forced defendants to answer the complaints of plaintiffs (mesne process). Once both parties had entered their appearances in court, the three prothonotaries recorded the 'matters in suit' and prepared pleadings. The *custos brevium*, the titular chief clerk of the court, was responsible for taking custody of writs returned by the sheriffs, who were responsible for execution of them in the shires. Altogether over thirty officials were associated with the procedural business of the Common Pleas; there were also four cryers, two pursuivants, and a porter.[9] In the King's Bench the officials included a single prothonotary, filazers, a clerk of the crown (who was responsible for the criminal side of the court's jurisdiction), the *custos brevium*, and the clerk of the exigents. In addition, procedural changes in the court which had taken place since the end of the fifteenth century produced a number of unofficial clerks whose posts arose within the office of the chief prothonotary.[10]

The bureaucracy in the Chancery and the judicial side of the Exchequer differed from that in the common law courts largely because the judicial functions of the departments had been grafted onto offices which had originally arisen in connection with, on the one hand, the king's secretariat, and on the other with his principal financial department. For instance, the six clerks in Chancery, who were responsible for much of the clerical work involved in the equitable jurisdiction, had been important administrative officials under the master of the rolls in the fifteenth century. Much the same was true of other officials such as the cursitors, but as the judicial work of the Chancery grew during the course of the late fifteenth and early sixteenth centuries, some entirely new offices were also created. By 1590, there were at least forty-one different officials in the

Chancery dealing with the clerical work connected with litigation, and, as we shall see, many of them employed large numbers of assistants.[11]

By contrast, although the Exchequer was one of the largest royal institutions, only a relatively small proportion of its officials were concerned directly with litigation.[12] Similarly, within the remaining major conciliar and prerogative jurisdictions, Star Chamber, Wards, and Requests, the clerical bureaucracies were considerably smaller than those in the principal common law courts and Chancery. For example, in Star Chamber there was a clerk of the court who kept the records, orders, and decrees, and another who dealt with process. The registrar recorded the decisions of the judges, and, as in Chancery, there was an examiner who was responsible for recording written depositions of witnesses.[13] The establishment of Requests was similar, whilst in the court of Wards, there was a single official, the clerk of the Wards, who handled most of the paperwork connected with litigation.[14]

It is convenient to lump all of these officers together, and to call them a judicial bureaucracy, but, although a useful label, the word needs to be stripped of most of its modern connotations. Here we are not dealing with formally trained men who gained their positions as a consequence of passing exams and who carried out highly defined tasks laid down by strict regulations in return for remuneration in the form of a salary.[15] The methods of appointing officials varied from court to court, within courts, and also over time. In the Common Pleas most officers were appointed by the Lord Chief Justice, but the *custos brevium* and the chirographer were appointed by royal letters patent and the second prothonotary by the Chief Justice on the nomination of the *custos brevium*.[16] In Chancery some offices were in the hands of the Lord Chancellor and others in those of the master of the rolls.[17] In Wards and Star Chamber the major officers were appointed by letters patent.[18] In all of the courts new offices were created from time to time and filled by royal letters patent, and during the late Elizabethan and early Stuart periods most office holders had to pay considerable sums of money either to the crown or to courtiers and other officials in order to obtain their positions. The fact that money was changing hands only exacerbated the already established custom that offices once granted were virtually the freehold property of the occupier.[19] In addition, although some officials received nominal salaries, all earned their incomes mainly by charging fees for each piece of work done, for each writ that was written. These financial considerations along with appointments for life (or even longer) created strongly entrenched vested interests. In some instances individual families such as the Cottons and Mills of the Star Chamber, the Hares of the Wards, and, most notoriously, the Ropers of the King's Bench dominated their courts from fifty to well over one hundred years.[20] Such long tenures need not necessarily have had deleterious effects, but they were symptomatic of the relatively autonomous nature of the offices, and this was a characteristic of the system which did cause difficulties. For example, at the end of the reign of Elizabeth, Lord Chancellor Ellesmere's attempts to introduce reforms in Chancery were thwarted in part because he did not enjoy complete control over all the officials in his court.[21] In a number of jurisdictions, including Chancery, Star Chamber, King's Bench, and Common Pleas, quarrels broke out from time to time between officials over the demarcation between spheres of work or about fees. The legal bureaucracy was hardly monolithic; internal politics and rivalries were a constant fact of life.

Once appointed, the major office holders enjoyed almost complete freedom to exercise their posts more or less as they pleased. In most instances, this meant the creation of a small empire which was organized in much the same way as any contemporary business from that of the town artisan to that of the greatest London merchant would have been. In other words, the basic unit of organization was the household of the official. If he held a minor post, he might do most of the work himself. If he had a busier office then he would be assisted by a greater or lesser number of underclerks who were recruited by himself. They were responsible to the office holder (and not to the king or the judges), and they were usually trained up by an apprenticeship which involved learning the job by helping others to do it. Moreover, although the law might lay down that particular writs were necessary, the office holders had a great deal of independence in determining what the procedures and costs surrounding the issuing of writs should be. In effect, this meant that they could alter the procedural law by altering the practices of their offices.[22] An important instance of this occurred in the early Tudor King's Bench. Traditionally, procedure in that court, like that of the Common Pleas, had been based on the original writ out of Chancery, followed by mesne process issued by the filazers, and the enrolling of pleadings by the chief prothonotary of the court. However, in the late fifteenth century, the chief prothonotary, apparently with the connivance of the judges, began to use a legal fiction based on the bill of Middlesex in order to enable plaintiffs to summon defendants without having to go either to the Chancery for the original writ or to the filazers for mesne process. The new bill procedures had a number of important consequences, among which was a significant improvement in the efficiency of the court, but they also meant that the cursitors in Chancery and the filazers of the King's Bench were left nursing grievances which lasted well into the second half of the seventeenth century. The cursitors had plenty of other business and so weathered the storm reasonably well, but the filazers of the King's Bench declined into insignificance whilst the chief prothonotary of the court established a new empire of underclerks to handle all of the business which was flooding in his direction.[23]

A more mundane illustration of the extremely personal nature of legal office holding is that at the beginning of the reign of Elizabeth, the place where the work was done was usually determined entirely by the individual who held the post. Thus in the 1580s, the filazers of the Common Pleas could be found in various sets of chambers spread around the inns of court and inns of chancery. Mr George Kemp, the secondary of the King's Bench, kept his office in Fleet Street; the *custos brevium* was established next to Ely House in the Strand. For over half a century, the Cotton family operated the Star Chamber office out of their house in Well-yard near St Bartholomew's Hospital, and customers evidently had to make their way through clothes lines containing the laundry from neighbouring houses in order to reach it.[24] The officers of the court of Wards were spread all over Holborn until 1590 when John Hare, the clerk of the court, built new chambers in the Inner Temple.[25] Hare's action was part of a general trend amongst those involved in the busiest offices. In the 1570s Sir Nicholas Bacon, the lord keeper, built a hall for the use of the twenty-four cursitors in Chancery and their underclerks. Like the six clerks in Chancery, who had long occupied their own inn, the cursitors now enjoyed a communal life akin to that of the London guilds or the inns of court and inns of chancery. They held dinners, accumulated plate and pictures, and studied writs after dinner.[26] A different kind of communal life in another new office building, that of the chief prothonotary of the King's Bench in the Inner Temple, was described vividly by John Trye, a seventeenth-century filazer.

The said office itself was of so great and large extent and the Seats, so many in it, that it looked more like a church than an office, and incited Strangers to offer up their Devotions there, when at first they came to it; it was as Large as *Westminster Hall* is broad... and containing from end to end four rows of seats...there did these Clerkes to the Chief Clark anciently sit, and were therefore called sitting, entering clerks.[27]

As Trye's picture shows, underclerks were an important fixture in the procedural underworld. Many of them were obscure men who have left little trace in the records of the courts or elsewhere, but there is no doubting that they were numerous. There must have been at least one or two connected with every legal post within the Westminster jurisdictions, and in the larger offices they were truly legion. For instance, the twenty-four cursitors in Chancery employed twenty-four underclerks. But the most notorious examples of growing numbers of clerks were found in the offices of the six clerks in Chancery. In the Elizabethan period, each six clerk was reckoned to have had at least ten clerks working under him, and these enjoyed so much responsibility that they were eventually made sworn officials of the court.[28] Nor were underclerks less common in courts other than Chancery. Bell noted an increase in the number of clerks in the Elizabethan court of Wards, and there were many underclerks in the numerous offices of the King's Bench and Common Pleas.[29]

Today, the words clerk and underclerk denote people who man typewriters and perform fairly mechanical tasks having to do with the paperwork of the firm which employs them. In one sense this was no less true of the clerks and underclerks of the early modern law courts. Their immediate tasks involved writing out writs, pleadings, interrogatories, or whatever other instrument was the product of their office. But, on the other hand, these mechanical tasks led many clerical officials and their surbordinates to become involved with activities which we would normally associate with lawyers in the wider sense. They dealt with individual clients, gave advice, organized litigation, and sometimes held other legal offices outside their own courts. In these and in many other respects which should soon become evident, such clerical officials were very closely related to another class of lawyer whom we have not considered hitherto, the common law attorneys.

Attorneyship was in a sense a natural consequence of the processes set in motion by the writs which were issued by the clerical officers of the courts. If he sued out or was issued a writ from Westminster, a man who lived in the country, whether in Newcastle or Slough, soon found himself involved in litigation which was going to be fought out in London. Pursuit of the cause would therefore necessitate costly trips to the capital and time-consuming worry over the finer points of fairly technical judicial procedures. These were considerable inconveniences. Thus from an early date kings enabled favoured individuals to save time and trouble by granting them permission to appoint an attorney to attend in their place before the courts at Westminster. By the end of the thirteenth century, the favour once granted to a few had become a right of all litigants, and from this date the men who acted as attorneys appear to have been professionals insofar as the same names appear in the court records over a number of years acting for different clients. Since litigants were legally liable for the process which was issued in their name, the courts took the appointment of attorneys seriously, and from the reign of Edward I these were recorded in the 'Rolls of Warrants of Attorney', which in the case of the King's Bench and Common Pleas were bound up with the main records of the courts, the plea rolls.[30]

By the beginning of the reign of Elizabeth, therefore, the attorneys of King's Bench and Common Pleas were as ancient a part of the legal profession as the serjeants at law or the pleaders. Similarly, as the prerogative and conciliar courts emerged during the course of the fifteenth and sixteenth centuries, these too, like the older common law courts, found it necessary to appoint attorneys. Although the exact details differed from court to court, the functions of the attorneys in every jurisdiction were essentially quite similar. They acted for defendants or plaintiffs involved in lawsuits and were responsible for helping to further the cause by keeping abreast of procedural developments and by framing pleadings so that cases could be considered by the judges.

The best illustrations of the activities of attorneys, particularly those who worked in King's Bench and Common Pleas, are their professional guide-books and manuals. For example, *The Attourneys Academy* begins with a table of the dates of the law terms and lists appearance days and days for the return of writs. The guide-books point out what most introductory paragraphs describe as the 'order of suing process' out of the courts, and explain the offices to which the practitioner should go in order to carry out each of the many procedural steps involved in a lawsuit.[31] On the whole, therefore, the learning of the attorneys was practical; it was concerned with the bureaucratic and procedural rather than the more theoretical aspects of the law. However, by the middle of the sixteenth century, their work also extended as far into the substantive law as the selection of the form of action on which cases were to be fought and the process of pleading to the issue which was to be tried by juries.

Today, we normally think of law as a set of abstract rules which can be applied to any given circumstance, but in earlier periods a remedy could be sought in the royal courts only if an appropriate form of action – debt, assumpsit, trespass, etc. – could be made to apply to it. Since attorneys were very often the practitioners first in contact with men who felt they had a grievance, one of their most important functions was to help a potential litigant to discover whether he might have a case at law and to select the form of action most appropriate to it.[32] Pleading, on the other hand, took place once both parties had come into court, and it was the mechanism by which the matters in a case were resolved into a simple issue of fact which could be decided upon by a jury.[33] Until early in the sixteenth century, pleading was done through verbal discussions between counsel and judges at the bar of the courts in Westminster Hall.[34] But by the middle of the reign of Henry VIII, these verbal pleadings had given way almost completely to written ones, and at the same time the business of pleading in cases which did not involve difficult questions of substantive law passed from the upper branch of the profession, the serjeants, judges, and barristers, to the lower. Consequently, with the aid of the prothonotaries, precedent books, and registers of writs, the attorneys of the two parties could plead to the issue simply by exchanging written papers.[35] The serjeants and barristers would be called in only in case of difficulty or in those instances where some question of law remained unresolved after the case had been returned to Westminster after trial at *nisi prius* in the country.[36]

The fact that the main functions of attorneys brought them into such close contact with laymen who were involved in or contemplating the touchy business of litigation meant that there had been, throughout their history, a good deal of royal and public concern about such practitioners. As one post-Restoration reader at the inns of court put it, attorneys were mentioned in more regulatory statutes than any other occupational group in the realm.[37] In general, during both the middle ages and the early modern periods, the emphasis was on controlling admission to practise, maintaining standards of training, and preventing excessive numbers of practitioners. In 1294, the ordinance 'De Attornatis et Apprenticiis' specified that the judges should appoint a limited number of qualified men to act as attorneys.[38] The next attempt at regulation came in the form of a statute passed during the reign of Henry IV in 1402. The preamble begins with a note of the 'sundry Damages and mischiefs that have ensued before this time to divers Persons of the Realm by a great number of Attorneys, ignorant and not learned in the law'. The body of the act then ordains that 'all the Attornies shall be examined by the Justices, and by their discretion their Names put in the Roll, and they that be good and virtuous, and of good Fame, shall be received and sworn well and truly to serve in their office....

And if any of the said Attornies do die, or do cease [practising], the Justices for the Time being by their Discretion shall make another in his Place, which is a virtuous Man and learned, and sworn in the same Manner as afore is said. And if any such Attorney be hereafter notoriously found in any Default of Record or otherwise, he shall forswear the court.[39]

In effect, 4 Hen. IV c. 18 specified that attorneys should become sworn officers in the court where they served.

Too little is known about the practices of the fourteenth-century courts to permit a judgement as to whether this statute lays down new regulations or merely reiterates those already in existence. Nevertheless, it is certain that by 1560 the procedures it mentions – some form of examination for those who applied to practise and the administration of a sworn oath to those who were admitted – had become the main formal qualifications for men who wanted to work as attorneys in the court of Common Pleas. However, although there had been some concern about the number of practitioners in the fifteenth century, and although the question of numbers was a major cause of public concern under Elizabeth and the early Stuarts, there were evidently no limits on the number who could be admitted. In 1580, there were some three hundred Common Pleas attorneys, and at any given time during the early modern period they were the most numerous single group of legal practitioners.[40]

The statute 4 Hen. IV c. 18 refers to 'all the attorneys', and makes no distinctions between the main courts then in existence, Common Pleas, King's Bench, and Exchequer, and so it seems most probable that the statute was intended to apply to practitioners in all of these jurisdictions. However, as we have seen, by the beginning of the reign of Elizabeth newer jurisdictions had taken shape, and changes had occurred in some of the older ones. Thus the history of attorneyship cannot be outlined with reference to the statute alone, but must also be traced within each of the individual courts.

Even in the other ancient common law tribunal, the King's Bench, the relationship between the attorneys and their court had by the later sixteenth century become rather different from that in the Common Pleas. In the fifteenth century King's Bench attorneys were appointed in much the same way as in Common Pleas. Furthermore, although it is unlikely that admission to practise in one court carried with it the automatic right to work in another, during the fifteenth and early sixteenth centuries some men who acted in one court also acted in the other. For example, Blatcher found in her study of the King's Bench in the 1480s and 1490s that 160 attorneys were active simultaneously in both courts while there were 105 who worked in King's Bench alone.[41] Similarly, comparisons of the names of attorneys in the Rolls of Warrants of the two courts show that as late as the beginning of the reign of Elizabeth most practitioners worked in both of them.[42] However, during the course of the later sixteenth century, major changes within the King's Bench significantly altered this picture. After 1560 most of the men who acted as attorneys in the King's Bench were not practitioners admitted according to the statute of Henry IV, but men who were technically clerks of the chief prothonotary of the court. A tax assessment of court clerks and lawyers, dated 1574, mentions that attorneys of the King's Bench were appointed at the discretion of the prothonotary.[43] In the early seventeenth century, attorneys of the King's Bench who were involved in lawsuits were usually styled as clerks of the prothonotary, not as attorneys.[44] From the late sixteenth century, the prothonotary's docket rolls, which are a kind of index to the King's Bench plea rolls, contain alphabetical lists of the names of the prothonotary's clerks. A comparison of these lists for 1606 with the names of attorneys in the King's Bench plea rolls confirms that in this year the 173 clerks were by far the most significant group of attorneys in the court. The Rolls of Warrants contain sixty-one additional names, but some of these men were clerks in other offices of the court, and most of them handled far less business than the clerks of the prothonotary.[45]

Many of the details of this change in the status of the King's Bench attorneys are obscure, but there is little doubt that it was ultimately connected with the bureaucratic revolution which accompanied the emergence of procedures by bill of Middlesex and *latitat* as the

primary King's Bench process. As we have seen, these new procedures enabled the chief prothonotary to monopolize the business of
the court, and the attorney-clerks were an essential part of the clerical
empire which helped him to handle it. In addition to fulfilling their
role as attorneys, each of them also was responsible for and profited
from issuing writs and writing up lawsuits in the plea rolls.[46]
Furthermore, the control which the chief prothonotary exercised
over the appointment of his clerks enabled him to limit their
numbers, and, evidently, to sell the offices. Throughout the period
from 1560 to 1640 there were always many fewer King's Bench than
Common Pleas practitioners, and in the late 1630s it was alleged that
the Chief Clerk earned some £500 p.a. by 'making attorneys'.[47]

A consequence of the rise of the prothonotary and his clerks in the
King's Bench was that from the point of view of attorneys, the King's
Bench and Common Pleas became increasingly insular. Well into the
reign of Elizabeth some attorneys had been active in both courts, but
by the turn of the sixteenth century, this had become exceedingly
rare.[48] On the King's Bench side the reason for this was that, since
they received fees for procedural work, the attorney-clerks had
everything to gain by not taking cases into alien courts, and, as the
jurisdiction of King's Bench and Common Pleas were largely
similar, there was little reason to do so. From the point of view of
the Common Pleas, things were more complicated. In the early part
of the Elizabethan period, the King's Bench procedures offered
litigants real advantages in terms of costs and speed of action, and
so there was evidently some drift of business away from the Common
Pleas, but this was soon resisted by the officials there. As early as
1564, the judges proclaimed that Common Pleas attorneys had been
'overmuch occupied with fruits in other courts', and ordered that,
henceforth, they should restrict themselves to practise in Common
Pleas, 'and forbear to be towards as Plaintiff, directly or indirectly
in any other the Queen's Majesties Courts here at Westminster'.[49]
The authority of this order on its own probably would not have been
sufficient to have caused the segregation of attorneys into their
respective courts which was apparent by 1600, but another factor was
at work. The control of the prothonotary and his underclerks over
the procedural work in King's Bench meant that a Common Pleas
attorney would gain little by taking cases into the King's Bench
which might have been heard equally well in Common Pleas.[50]
In fact, there appears to have been some positive hostility towards

the King's Bench attorneys. In 1615, the judges of the court enlisted the support of the king in order to force assize officials to allow 'the clerks and Atturneys of *our* Bench to appear as Atturneys for their clyents as other Atturneys of the Common Pleas doe'. Evidently, clerks of assize sympathetic to the Common Pleas were thwarting King's Bench practitioners by raising the question of whether or not the prothonotary's clerks should be allowed the same privileges as ordinary common law attorneys.[51] For at least half of our period, therefore, the attorneys in the two major common law courts comprised somewhat autonomous groups of men, and the differences between them extended both to their styles of life and to the extent to which they were ordinarily involved in politics and public life within their local communities.

The attorney-clerks of the King's Bench are an excellent illustration of the fact that practice as an attorney in the early modern period could very often merge with work in the court bureaucracies. In theory the attorneys of the Common Pleas were different because, whilst they were officers of their court, their office had functions which were supposed to be distinct from those of the clerks who were responsible for issuing writs, process, and pleadings. But in practice, even in the Common Pleas, there was a degree of overlap between the two groups of men. From at least the fourteenth century, and very probably from the beginning of the history of the courts, the officers of both King's Bench and Common Pleas, particularly the filazers, had been amongst the busiest of the men who acted as attorneys.[52] This was no less true in the sixteenth and seventeenth centuries than it had been earlier. Furthermore, many Common Pleas attorneys received their training as clerks in the offices of the prothonotaries, and some of them retained their clerkships even after they had become sworn attorneys. Apart from what can be gleaned from a study of the plea rolls, there is little direct evidence about this practice in the sixteenth century, but in 1633 the judges expressed concern about the 'Clerks of Prothonotarie offices and Attorn[eys] of this Courte who have promiscuously exercised the distinct professions of Clerk and Attorney', and declared that those who held both positions should make a permanent and binding decision about which vocation they intended to follow in the future.[53]

Although this order clearly identifies the existence of Common Pleas practices which combined the office of attorney and that of clerk to a court official, it is also important to stress that they were a good deal less prevalent in Common Pleas than in the King's Bench. In the 1620s and 1630s, there were some 120 prothonotaries' clerks, but at the same date the total number of attorneys was in the region of 1300.[54] Thus, even if, in addition to the prothonotaries' clerks, we make allowances for the filazers and their clerks, court officials and their underclerks can have accounted for only 15–20 per cent of the total population of men who acted as attorneys. Lack of information about underclerks precludes any such calculation for the Elizabethan period, but there is no clear reason to think that the percentages would be very different. So, throughout most of the period from 1560 to 1640, a large proportion, probably the majority, of the Common Pleas attorneys had no direct links with other sectors of the clerical bureaucracy. This is, perhaps, a highly technical point, but it does have practical significance. Those attorneys of the Common Pleas who were not clerks or underclerks were the only members of the lower branch of the legal profession who did not have a direct vested interest in the established procedures of the courts and the fees which went with them. The growth of this group of men who represented litigants, but who did not necessarily identify with the court officials, was one of the most important features of the profession during this period.

II

If the overlap between the attorneys and their kin in the clerical offices of the Common Pleas was only partial, in the newer equity and prerogative jurisdictions it was very nearly complete. In the court of Chancery, the six clerks, assisted by their small army of underclerks, added to the task of acting as attorneys for plaintiffs and defendants to their already considerable responsibilities for the procedural paperwork of the court. If a potential litigant wanted to undertake a suit in Chancery, he found a six clerk's clerk who would advise him on the business, see that all the appropriate writs were issued, brief counsel, and appear for him in court. Since the right to act as an attorney was one aspect of the six clerks' monopoly over Chancery business, it was, along with the others, jealously protected. No outsiders were allowed to perform this function, and so there was little or no overlap between the men who worked in the six clerks' offices, and the attorneys of the King's Bench or Common Pleas. Moreover, insofar as a rein was kept on the number of six clerks' underclerks by the lord chancellor and the clerks themselves, there was in effect a limit on the number of men allowed to act as attorneys in the Chancery.[55]

The place of attorneys in the other jurisdictions which had emerged during the sixteenth century, Star Chamber, Wards, and Requests, was similar to that in Chancery with one important exception. In all of these courts, the number of attorneys was confined to a very small number. There were two men in Wards, three in Requests, and three in the Star Chamber who had a monopoly over the business of working with clients to prepare their cases for hearing before the court.[56] The reason for the small number of attorneys in these courts, all of which became quite busy during the course of the sixteenth century, was mainly that the crown had never made any specific arrangement for the creation of official attorneys whose job it was to represent clients. The Henrican statute which created the court of Wards made no provision for attorneys. The office simply evolved, and the right of appointment was apparently in the hands of the master of the rolls.[57] In Star Chamber, by the end of the reign of Elizabeth it was customary for attorneys to be appointed by the chief clerk of the court (although his patent made no mention of the right), and they seem to have emerged as an extension of his office, since it was claimed in the 1590s that he had in the past always granted such posts to his 'own men'.[58] Similarly, in Wards, there was a tradition of keeping the offices of attorney within the clerical 'family'. Attorneyships frequently went to men who had begun their careers as clerks in another of the offices.[59]

Given these circumstances, it is not surprising that the numbers of attorneys in these courts were limited. In the beginning there was little business, and thus there was pressure not to have it spread too thin. As the monopoly over a growing volume of work became more lucrative, those with the power to create attorneys were in a position to demand money in return for a grant of the office. This was certainly the case in Star Chamber during the 1580s, and was very likely true in the Wards as well.[60] Once a man had to pay for an office, he was unwilling for the grantor to appoint more holders who would demand a share of the fees, and some men, such as Edward Latymer in Wards, went so far as to obtain indentures with specific clauses to this effect.[61]

The limitations on the number of attorneys in King's Bench, Chancery, Star Chamber, Wards, Requests, and the Exchequer had important long-term consequences. One of the most useful services provided by the attorneys of a court such as Common Pleas was that a potential litigant in the country could tell a local attorney about the business he needed done at Westminster, and the attorney would go up to London and see to the details for him. The litigant was thereby saved the trouble of travelling long distances to handle the mass of procedural work which accompanied any lawsuit. The trouble with the courts in which there were limits on the number of attorneys was that, since such courts had few practitioners, the litigant in the country would be hard put to find a link between himself and the court. His options if he wanted, say, to sue in Star Chamber were either to go up to London himself or to find another intermediary who would go there for him, and who would then do the business with the official attorneys of the court. The latter was naturally the easiest course to follow, and the need for men who could oversee business in this way gave rise to the legal practitioners known as 'solicitors'.

In the mid sixteenth century, the word solicitor had only very imprecise meanings. It did not necessarily denote a branch of legal practitioners distinct from the court officials, attorneys, and pleaders. In fact the verb form was as common as the noun, and 'to solicit' meant, simply, to handle the affairs, mainly the legal affairs, of another man.[62] At the beginning of the reign of Elizabeth, when there was relatively little business in courts such as Chancery and Star Chamber, soliciting was of little concern to the public or to the authorities. But when business in these jurisdictions expanded during the course of the sixteenth century, solicitors and the problems associated with them became more apparent. Although the laws of maintenance provided some scope for regulation, the difficulty was that soliciting was largely uncontrolled and largely open to anyone, whether trained as a lawyer or not, who cared to try his hand at it. Cases from the early Elizabethan period in which men tried to sue for fees due to them as solicitors indicate that those who acted in this capacity were not required to prove any legal qualifications.[63] From at least 1577, when William Harrison complained about 'sundry varlets that go about the country as promoters or brokers between the pettyfoggers of the law [the attorneys] and the common people', there was widespread concern about the increase in the number of solicitors who had no connection with courts or with the inns of court and chancery.[64] Here was a legal activity which was very much like that of the official attorneys but which could be, and evidently was, very often performed by laymen. Yet, at the same time, soliciting was frequently, and probably most often, undertaken by men in the recognized 'legal professions'. The attorneys of the Common Pleas 'solicited' causes in Chancery or Star Chamber. Chancery clerks and even the clerks of counsellors at law sometimes acted as and described themselves as solicitors. Finally, it was widely accepted that men at the inns of court who were waiting to become pleaders should supplement their livings by soliciting.[65]

Thus solicitors defy easy definition. Moreover, the problems in the way of describing them illustrate very nicely those which make it difficult to define what constituted the early modern legal profession as a whole. 'Soliciting' shows that in terms of the most basic functions of giving advice to clients and supervising the course of lawsuits, the 'legal profession' was completely undifferentiated. Indeed, since untrained laymen as well as trained lawyers could perform such tasks, the 'profession' lacks any definition beyond a purely functional one. But, on the other hand, the early Elizabethan profession was also highly compartmentalized, even atomized. This is an apparent contradiction, but an accurate account of the early modern lower branch necessarily lies within the paradox. Attorneys of the Common Pleas were not allowed to act as attorneys in the King's Bench. The offices of the six clerks in Chancery were a world of their own. In Wards or Star Chamber, there were carefully prescribed limits on the number of attorneys, and those who were appointed usually enjoyed already a connection with the court. Any of these men might solicit a cause in a court to which they did not belong, but there was no single, unified lower branch. There was no single piece of parchment which enabled a man to practise. Such lawyers were lawyers simply because they had gained admission to practise before a particular court.[66]

Finally, even the convenient distinction between an 'upper' and a 'lower' branch was less clear in the sixteenth century than it has become since; indeed, there is no evidence that these terms were ever used to distinguish between different types of lawyer in the period before 1700. In the early Tudor period most counsellors at law appear to have resided at one of the inns of court, but the call to the bar (hence the modern term barrister) at such an inn did not become the sole qualification for the right of audience before the royal courts until the end of the reign of Elizabeth.[67] Throughout the period from the later fifteenth to the middle of the sixteenth century clerical officials and attorneys were also members of the inns of court, and since there was in any case no formal qualification for gaining the right to plead in the courts, there was no theoretical reason why an attorney should not have acted as a pleader and *vice versa*, even though in practice it did not happen very often.[68] Similarly, although by 1600 attorneys and solicitors were the lawyers most often consulted by clients at the beginning of a suit, there was as yet no sign of the later rule against 'direct access' which prescribed that litigants should contact barristers only through a member of the lower branch.[69]

In general, the mid-Tudor legal profession was largely untroubled by disputes about distinctions between the 'upper' and 'lower' branches or about formal qualifications for practice at any level. One of the main reasons for this was that, although offices and courts appear confusingly numerous, the profession which worked at Westminster was in fact relatively small. There were usually no more than ten to twelve serjeants at law at any one time in the period up to and including the early years of the reign of Elizabeth.[70] Calculations of the number of pleaders are somewhat uncertain, but informed guess-work suggests that in 1560 the practising bar probably contained no more than eighty or ninety men.[71] This means that the early Elizabethan upper branch as a whole totalled no more than one hundred lawyers or thereabouts.

Problems of definition make it equally difficult to estimate the size of the lower branch. For example, there is the question of how many of the court officials, particularly those in Exchequer and the Chancery, should be included. The most reasonable answer for the present purposes is to count only those who earned money both by writing legal process and by acting for clients either as attorneys or solicitors. Thus the attorneys and clerks of the 'plea' side and the eight sworn clerks of the 'equity' side of the Exchequer should be included; so, too, must the attorneys active in the Duchy Court of Lancaster, but most of the other officials in these tribunals need not be. Similarly, the six clerks in Chancery and their underclerks clearly qualify. The twenty-four cursitors in Chancery and their twenty-four underclerks are a more difficult case, since it is not clear that they regularly acted for litigants, but for the sake of argument they, too, can be taken into consideration, as may the two examiners, the maker of liveries, the maker of writs concerning wards, and the two makers of subpoenas and their assistant. Then to these must be added the entering clerks and attorneys of the courts of Wards, Star Chamber, and Requests, at least another nine practitioners. Taken altogether, these clerks and attorneys of the prerogative and equity courts come to some 130 men, a figure which includes most of the underclerks.[72]

Turning to the main common law courts, King's Bench and Common Pleas, a study of the rolls of warrants of attorney for 1560 reveals the names of 178 men who were active as attorneys, most of whom worked in both jurisdictions. However, it is unlikely that all of those qualified to act had cases in the rolls during the terms that were investigated, so this total should be rounded up to, perhaps, 200 to account for absentees.[73] On the other hand, it is unnecessary to add many names to this figure in order to take account of office holders. Most of the filazers, many minor office holders, and probably the majority of underclerks are included, because they frequently served as attorneys. The three prothonotaries of the Common Pleas and a few of the other major office holders did not, but including these would not raise the total to more than 210. Some underclerks who did not act as attorneys will have escaped the count, but, judging from what later became common practice, they are unlikely to have been numerous. Thus, allowing generously for the unknowns, a minimum of 210 and a maximum of 250 is a reasonably good estimate of the size of the lower branch on the common law side.[74]

If the sub-total of 130 equity and prerogative court practitioners is added to the 210 to 250 active in the King's Bench and Common Pleas, we discover a lower branch numbering 340 to 380 men, and a legal profession at Westminster, including both branches of about 430 to 450. Undoubtedly, this is something of an underestimate. Some underclerks, but probably not very many, will have eluded the head-count. More important, there is no way to estimate the number of men who solicited causes, but who had no formal connection with any of the Westminster courts; indeed, these solicitors present the greatest single difficulty in the way of a completely satisfactory quantitative picture of the lower branch. Chapter 3 will demonstrate that such practitioners were numerous, but it will also show that many of them had connections with the legal institutions of the provinces if not with those of London. In any case, in 1560, they did not give undue cause for concern to the judges, the privy council, or the public. Moreover, the small scale of the Westminster legal world and the fact that the normal way of progressing within it was through service in particular offices and courts meant that such regulation of the legal profession as was necessary could be maintained informally through personal relationships, by face-to-face contact. Changes in social attitudes and the late-sixteenth-century increase in litigation were soon to transform this tranquil picture.

3

THE LEGAL PROFESSION IN THE PROVINCES

I

The early centralization of royal justice and the concentration of the main courts of the realm in the capital city were features of the English legal system which were unique in Europe.[1] Consequently, an account of the English legal profession must inevitably start in London. But having begun in London, it cannot stop there. The royal courts heard cases from every part of the realm. Many of the litigants for whom members of the lower branch acted lived in the country. Most of the lawyers themselves led double lives, one part consisting of residence and private practice in the provinces and the other of termly trips to London for the sittings of the royal courts. The history of the lower branch must, therefore, be written within these same geographical contours.

As the sixteenth century wore on, there was a tendency for practitioners such as the six clerks in Chancery or the officials in the court of Wards, men who were concerned mostly with issuing procedural writs, to dwell full-time in the City. But this was by no means common during the early Elizabethan years. As late as 1589, at least twelve of twenty-two officials of the court of Common Pleas had a principal residence in the country, and so too did all of the six clerks in Chancery.[2] If, even for the major office holders, work in London was mainly a term-time affair, this was all the more true for those practitioners such as the attorneys of King's Bench and Common Pleas, whose main function within the legal system was to act as links between men in the country and the royal courts. In 1560, only 10 to 15 of the some 160 Common Pleas attorneys made London their place of permanent habitation.[3] The rest went home to the country at the end of the four legal terms of the year, and it was in the provinces that they found the clients whose cases they brought up to Westminster. In general, the geographical structure of the profession was a good deal different from that of the eighteenth century (or that of today), when there was a more rigid division between lawyers who worked in London and those who worked exclusively in the provinces.[4] The best proof of this assertion is simply the fact that Common Pleas attorneys found in the plea rolls handling cases from a particular part of the country can almost always be traced back to residence in the same county or region. For these practitioners, termly trips between home and Westminster were a regular routine. All early modern lawyers spent a lot of time in the saddle.[5] Indeed, travel was such a characteristic feature of their lives that it had to be taken as a distinct possibility that death would come during an absence from home. For this reason, many practitioners stated in their wills that, in order to save expense, they were willing to be buried in whatever place they happened to be when they died.

The attorneys were, therefore, the tentacles through which the Westminster courts got out into the provinces, and it is a text-book commonplace that by the sixteenth century these courts dominated the legal system.[6] However, the extent of the reach of the mid-Tudor royal courts and of the legal profession which was associated with them must not be exaggerated. In reality it was somewhat superficial.

First, although it is admittedly notional, an estimate of the number of lawsuits commenced in the central courts per 100,000 of total population in 1560 comes to 479, a figure significantly lower than for any subsequent period in English history.[7] Second, at the beginning of the reign of Elizabeth, the regional distribution of central court litigation was biased disproportionately in terms of population towards London, East Anglia, and the Home Counties. Third, many of the suits handled by the courts involved men whose dealings crossed the territorial boundaries of the borough or shire. In Common Pleas, the most typical cases among those which originated in London involved a London businessman who was suing someone in the provinces.[8] Similarly, on the rare occasions when men from more remote parts of the country do appear in the court records, they are frequently there in connection with a case which reveals contact with someone from outside their own region. For instance, in one of the few disputes from north-eastern England which came before Common Pleas in 1560, Christopher Rawe, a merchant of Newcastle upon Tyne, was sued for debt by Richard Turnor, also a merchant, of Boston in county Lincoln.[9] It would be misleading to imply that all common law litigation took this form. Cases involving land and between litigants from the same shire or town can certainly be found. But, in general, Common Pleas business came from the wealthiest parts of the country and frequently transcended local or regional jurisdictional boundaries. In these respects, it was by and large national rather than local litigation, and there is no reason to doubt that these characteristics of the Common Pleas were shared by the other royal courts at Westminster.

Finally, and most important, there were also very distinct limits on the extent to which the London legal profession was represented in the provinces. In 1560 the London profession numbered some 350 to 400 men. Of these, there were approximately 200 common law attorneys who provided the main links between the provinces and the courts. Most of these attorneys lived in the country, but if the figure of 200 is broken down in order to discover the number of practitioners active in particular counties, it soon becomes apparent that there could not have been many of them in any single locality. For example, the plea rolls of King's Bench and Common Pleas indicate that six men were handling cases from Warwickshire in the earliest years of Queen Elizabeth.[10] Two of them, Thomas Hawes of Solihull and Richard Sparrey of King's Norton in Worcestershire, near Birmingham, are known to have lived in or near the county, but there is circumstantial evidence that at least three of the others, Christopher Barnard, Henry Warner, and Roland Durant, did not.[11] Warner probably lived in Staffordshire; Barnard had connections with Londoners; and Durant, who practised in both King's Bench and Common Pleas, handled cases from many different counties, including those as far away as Lincolnshire.[12] In Hertfordshire, the picture was much the same; the lower branch in the county was represented by only three men – Robert Brychette of Barley, Thomas Hanchette of Uphall, and John Kettle of King's Langley.[13]

Warwickshire and Hertfordshire were small counties which did not send very much litigation to Westminster. But even in those areas where litigation was heavier, there were not very many attorneys. Devonshire at this date had eight or ten resident practitioners including Anthony Copleston, Thomas Hore, Richard Calmady, Henry Luscombe, Robert Predying, and Robert Prideaux.[14] In that most litigious of all counties, Norfolk, eight practitioners have been identified, though there may well have been four or five others who handled cases in the county, but whom we cannot verify as living there.[15] There were as many as six attorneys in the large and litigious county of Yorkshire, but, by contrast, it is difficult to identify positively any practitioners from the counties of the far north, Northumberland, Westmorland, and Cumberland.[16]

If there were relatively few attorneys active in the provinces in 1560, there were even fewer of the other principal class of lawyers who worked in Westminster, the pleaders and serjeants at law. Even if the estimate in Chapter 2 that the upper branch in 1560 contained some eighty to ninety men underestimates by half the numbers of such lawyers, there could have been no more than an average of three for each English county at that date. But here again allowance has to be made for regional variations. Only thirty men from Warwickshire were called to the bar over the course of the entire period from 1555 to 1640.[17] In the early sixteenth century, an important town such as Coventry frequently found that the lawyers it appointed as recorders had to resign because pressure of work kept them in London.[18] At the close of the sixteenth century the closest counsellor upon whom the citizens of Warwick could call was a Mr Pagett of Rugby, and neither he nor the town recorder was sufficiently available to be briefed properly.[19] On the other hand, in Devonshire and also in Norfolk, lawyers had always been prominent members of the local community. Large numbers of men from Devon entered the inns of court, and in the fourteenth century nearly half of the Devonshire MPs were practising lawyers. Furthermore, the six Devon towns which had been granted charters before 1560 had recorders, positions usually held by members of the upper branch, although some of these may well have been non-residents.[20]

II

An argument that the London courts were not all-pervasive in 1560 is surprising only if the multitude of other jurisdictions in existence at this time are ignored. In fact, no institutions were more ubiquitous in early modern England than courts of law, and those at Westminster made up only a small, if important, minority of them. To begin with, there were the royal palatinate courts of Chester and Durham and the tribunals associated with the Duchy of Lancaster. Then there was the King's Council in the North, which heard cases from Yorkshire and the far north, and the Council in the Marches of Wales, which performed a similar function in the Welsh marches.[21] On the more local level, every county had quarter sessions administered by justices of the peace as well as county courts and numerous hundred courts. Towns were empowered to maintain courts of small pleas. In Cornwall and Devon, the stannary courts entertained suits between the local tin miners. Throughout the realm, nearly every locality would have come within the jurisdiction of courts associated with manors, i.e. courts baron and courts leet.[22] Last, but hardly least, the ecclesiastical courts reached deep into every rural deanery.[23] Some of these courts, particularly the county and some hundred courts,[24] had declined considerably by the mid sixteenth century, but most legal historians, writing with their sight firmly fixed on London, have been concerned almost exclusively with the common law administered at Westminster and have been too ready to dismiss local jurisdictions as either moribund or subservient to the law and lawyers of London. For example, Sir William Holdsworth wrote that by the end of the fifteenth century the central courts of common law had definitely established their supremacy over the local courts whether communal, franchise, feudal, or manorial.[25] Insofar as the royal courts had in theory established their authority to hear appeals from local jurisdictions, this statement is unexceptional. But if this analysis leads to the conclusion that local justice was either inactive or unimportant as a fact of everyday life, then it is seriously misleading. In the mid-Tudor period, the common lawyers had yet to exert fully their influence over the procedures and organization of all local courts.[26] There were literally thousands of local manorial courts where the less affluent members of sixteenth-century society could pursue minor grievances and disputes, and if these could not satisfactorily resolve the matter then there were the borough courts and, depending on where the parties lived, the regional tribunals.[27]

In short, much legal business in the mid sixteenth century went on without reference to Westminster Hall. Indeed, there is a considerable amount of evidence which shows various kinds of communal effort to restrain individuals from removing disputes from the localities. Some sixteenth-century manorial courts imposed fines on tenants who took causes which could be tried within the local jurisdiction to the common law courts in London.[28] In a number of towns, including Cambridge, York, and Coventry, citizens were threatened with disenfranchisement if they sued outside of the borough court.[29] One of the most interesting examples of attempts to restrict disputes from flowing towards Westminster in fact comes from London itself. Not only did the metropolitan government operate a comprehensive set of local courts,[30] but the ordinances of most of the city livery companies forbade their members to resort to law without the permission of the company's governing body.[31] The records of companies such as the Carpenters' and Stationers' show that the guild officials had the power to imprison recalcitrant members, that they were willing to entertain complaints brought by outsiders against brethren of the companies, and that they generally spent a great deal of time on the business of settling disputes.[32]

Another source of resistance to the removal of suits to Westminster came from landlords who owned manors, and who were reluctant to let business drift away from their seigniorial jurisdictions. In 1560, for example, Francis Russell, Earl of Bedford, complained about the removal of suits concerning copyhold land from his manorial court at More in Hertfordshire into the court of Requests. He asked the masters of Requests to 'end the same, or dismiss it to my said court, where justice shall be truly administered, for I am loth to have my tenants troubled with long and chargeable suits'.[33]

Bedford's letter introduces the question of whether these efforts to limit the intrusion of London justice into the localities should be considered a kind of feudal reaction against royal law, but in reality such a question misses the point. Manorial courts were franchise courts, but they were franchises granted by the crown, and few would have raised any objection to the right of royal courts to control their activities if called upon to do so.[34] Equally, when towns such as York punished burgesses for taking cases to the Council in the North or to Westminster, they were not resisting royal authority. On the contrary, the city fathers of York, like those of any other incorporated town, readily acknowledged that they held their court by virtue of a grant from the crown – that it was in fact a royal court.[35] But the fact that a town court or a manorial court was in this sense a royal court also meant that, within limits, it was just as legitimate as any other royal jurisdiction. Therefore, from the point of view of those who held local courts, there was no reason to allow the removal of litigation from them to other tribunals, particularly when such a transferral would inevitably result in loss of fee income to local court officials.[36] Within the network of jurisdictions which spread across the countryside there was certainly an established legal hierarchy, but there was no fully developed legal system in the modern sense. Localities were jealous of their rights, and, what is more, there was

a widespread appreciation that London justice was expensive, that
it could disrupt local harmony, and that when individuals resorted
to London they undermined the dignity of local institutions.[37] Sir
Thomas Smith may have been indulging a fantasy when he wrote
that manorial courts 'doe serve rather for men that can be content
to be ordered by their neighbors, and which love their quiet and profit
in their husbandrie, more than to be busie in the lawe'.[38] But,
judging from the laments which accompanied the decline of such
courts in the seventeenth century, his ideal was one which was widely
shared.[39] In any case, in 1550 local jurisdictions were still the centres
around which much of the legal life of the realm revolved. They were
the courts most familiar and most resorted to by perhaps 90 per cent
of the population.[40]

Excessive concentration on the Westminster courts distorts the
picture of the legal institutions and legal activities of the realm. Much
the same is true for the legal profession. If we look at lawyers with
one eye on courts such as King's Bench and Common Pleas and
another on the inns of court and inns of chancery, we lose sight of
a large part of the early Elizabethan legal profession. We know that
the number of lawyers active in the London profession in 1560 was
relatively small if considered from a provincial perspective. Yet we
also know that there were many provincial jurisdictions, and, on a
closer look, it becomes clear that lawyers of a sort plied their trades
in all of them. A return to the shires with those lawyers who practised
in London reveals a legal profession significantly different from that
which frequented Westminster Hall.

The major provincial tribunals – those in the palatinates of Chester
and Durham, the Council in the North, and the Court of Great
Sessions and Council in the Marches of Wales – all developed both
a provincial bar and a lower branch which included attorneys and
clerks whose general functions were much the same as those of
similar practitioners in London. The provincial bars were composed
of a limited number of men who had been trained at the inns of court,
who practised on the English assize circuits and at Westminster Hall;
men who were in short members of the London-based profession.[41]
However, the attorneys and clerks in these courts had little to do with
any of the legal institutions of London. Indeed, this part of the lower
branch in the provinces seems at one and the same time to have been
distinct from that which worked at Westminster and to have reflected
many of the characteristics of the insular clerical offices typical of

royal tribunals such as Chancery, Star Chamber, and the court of Wards. Disputes arose frequently before the Council in the Marches of Wales and the Exchequer Court at Chester about the number of attorneys who should be admitted to practise. In the 1580s the lord president of the Council in Wales was accused of attempting to reduce the number of attorneyships from twenty-four to eighteen so that he could take higher profits from selling them. At Chester there was trouble in the early seventeenth century when the number of practitioners was allowed to rise to nine. By the 1630s, at the latest, attorneyships in Wales were being sold for as much as £100 each.[42] Whether this ever occurred at Chester is unknown, but what is clear is that the lower branch at the Exchequer Court constituted a small clique of men whose interests were tied up exclusively with work in the palatinate, and who were reluctant to open up their 'closed shop' to outsiders. The office of attorney was frequently passed down from father to son, and there were intermarriages amongst the families of practitioners.[43] None of the attorneys engaged in work before the courts at Westminster, but several of them, like Robert Whitby of Chester, were involved in the legal business and local government of nearby boroughs.[44] Furthermore, if the inventory of the late-sixteenth-century practitioner Lawrence Wright of Nantwich is anything to go by, such a career could be quite lucrative. Wright left goods worth some £621, and his family was one of the richest in a quite wealthy town.[45]

As a consequence of an almost complete loss of the judicial records of the Council in the North, little is known of the lawyers who practised there apart from a list of attorneys which dates from 1621.[46] This shows that there were about twelve to fifteen men in practice at any one time, and a comparison of the names of these practitioners with those who enrolled before the courts in London indicates that they worked exclusively in the north, although, as at Chester, there was a tendency for work before the Council to be combined with service in local government or with activities such as court keeping. For example, one of the practitioners in 1621, Philip Penrose, had served earlier in his career as a deputy to the clerk of the peace of the East Riding of Yorkshire.[47] In addition, a dispute which arose in the later years of James I over the rights to certain types of procedural work within the Council demonstrates that the practitioners in the north, again like those at Chester, had a strong sense of corporate identity and self-interest.[48]

Whether or not the attorneys who worked before the Council in the North remained outside the orbit of the London legal profession until the abolition of the jurisdiction in 1642 is impossible to tell, but at Chester, and in Wales, there is no evidence of infiltration from outsiders in the period before the Civil War.[49] So, on the whole, from the point of view of the lower branch, these provincial courts appear to have remained centres for a small number of practitioners who had little or no direct contact with London either through the houses of court or through the Westminster jurisdictions. The one significant exception to this rule was the palatine court of the Bishop of Durham. Here there is evidence that from at least the 1620s some notable local practitioners, including the local antiquary and attorney Christopher Mickleton, combined London training and practice with work in the palatinate. But in fact the degree of insularity within all of these jurisdictions is well illustrated by a post-Restoration book of admissions to practise before the court, which contains petitions from prospective attorneys to the bishop's chancellor. Without exception, these certify that the candidates had served an apprenticeship with a lawyer who had already been admitted to the jurisdiction. One of the petitions, dated 1663, which is from a man called George Moorcroft, is particularly revealing. Moorcroft explained that he had come to Durham after having completed a four-year apprenticeship with one of the six clerks in Chancery in London, but he had been told that he could not gain admission to the palatine court without first serving as a clerk to an established practitioner there. According to his petition, Moorcroft had then spent the next three years doing just that.[50] In the closed world of the provincial jurisdictions even a London pedigree was not necessarily an assured entry to practise.

Apart from the regional jurisdictions, another group of courts which provided work for men of law were the tribunals based on tenurial relationships, those of baronies, liberties, honours, and manors. In these courts the most important 'legal' official was the steward, and, largely because of common practice during the late seventeenth century and afterwards, it is frequently assumed that such men were invariably lawyers.[51] But in the sixteenth century this was not always the case. Stewardships in some of the more important baronies and liberties were often held by important noblemen or members of the gentry. For example, the Duke of Norfolk was hereditary steward of the liberty of Bury, which had been before the dissolution of the monasteries a possession of the abbot of Bury St Edmunds.[52] Ordinarily, in such circumstances the more technical business involved in running the court was handled by a lesser official appointed by the titular steward. But even this was not invariably true. The Earl of Bath evidently sometimes presided personally over the manorial courts which constituted the local government of sixteenth-century Manchester.[53]

Nevertheless, the more typical situation was one in which a landowner who was entitled to keep manorial courts appointed a steward to preside over them. Practices in such courts varied considerably, but, according to authorities such as John Kitchin, most of them met twice yearly in a village hall or ale-house. In theory and in most instances in fact, manorial courts consisted of two distinct tribunals. The court baron was a customary court incident by prescription to every manor and was called by the authority of the lord. Courts leet were attached to some, but not all, manors, were held by the authority of the crown, and administered common and statute rather than customary law. The courts baron were concerned primarily with customary tenures and with the incidents and services due to the lord from them. Within their jurisdiction came questions concerning the transferral and inheritance of copyhold and freehold land, the customs of the manor relating to entry fines for copyholders, and by-laws regulating agricultural practice. But courts baron were also empowered to hear all kinds of actions – trespasses, debts, etc. – between lord and tenants and the tenants themselves where the debt or damages were less than 40s. Courts leet, on the other hand, were involved with keeping the peace, enforcing statutes, and seeing that the assizes, such as those of bread and ale, were carried out.[54]

The functions of the manorial steward were twofold. At the court leet, over which he presided, the steward was both the judge of matters determinable and the secretary or clerk who drew up the records of the court. At the court baron, he performed the secretarial function and convened the court, but was judge only when the court was composed entirely of copyholders. When freeholders were amongst the tenants of the manor, they were the judges about and makers of presentments of abuses against the customs of the manor. In either case the steward stood in a crucial position in the exercise of customary law. He was obliged to uphold the interests of the lord, but he also had occasionally to adjudicate between lord and tenants on such sensitive issues as the entry fines or terms of tenure of copyholders. At courts leet, he was an agent responsible for seeing that the king's justice was done.[55]

The princely households of great territorial magnates such as the

Percys and Staffords had always included trained lawyers, even serjeants at law, whom they retained to provide legal advice and to supervise manorial courts, even though the courts themselves were frequently held by deputy.[56] However, the stewards of lords of manors amongst the greater and lesser gentry were ordinarily much more obscure men. Until roughly the 1570s or 1580s, the evidence about the identities of stewards is not very good, and even then they are a highly elusive prey who come into view only under the microscope of the most localized research.[57] What is clear is that they were an extremely diverse group of men.

Some stewards, like Arthur Gregory of Stivichall in Warwickshire, were barristers whose practices appear to have been based more on local court keeping and office holding than on advocacy before the central courts in London.[58] But other barristers, like Thomas Green of Stratford-upon-Avon, combined London practice with court keeping, and so, too, did some of the common law attorneys and even some of the chancery officials.[59] Still other stewards were inns of court men waiting for the call to the bar, and there were others, perhaps numerous, who enrolled at legal inns, but who never progressed to the bar and whose training may therefore have been minimal.[60]

However, what is most interesting about the Elizabethan stewards is that many of them appear to have had no official connection with either the royal courts in London or with the inns of court and inns of chancery. For instance, of thirty-three late-sixteenth-century Warwickshire stewards, as many as twenty-four appear to have been neither common law attorneys, barristers, nor members of legal inns.[61] Some of these stewards were small landowners with only the most amateur interest in the law.[62] Others are more difficult to classify. John Wise of Coleshill in Warwickshire was steward for a number of manors belonging to the wealthy Throckmorton family and thus may have earned a large proportion of his income from such work, although his will shows that he also had agricultural interests.[63] John Jeffrey of Yardley in Worcestershire acted as a steward in local courts and was for some time a clerk of the peace in Warwickshire. In his will he described himself as a yeoman, but it is noteworthy that two of his executors were the local Common Pleas attorneys, William Booth and Thomas Smalbroke.[64] The papers of the Stuart commissions of fees show that in early-seventeenth-century Devon there were a number of men who had no apparent connection with

London but who acted as stewards and attorneys in several different local courts. One was Richard Tickett, steward of Crediton Hundred and an attorney in the Guildhall Court at Exeter. Another was Thomas Avent, steward of Plympton hundred and attorney in the town court of Plympton Erle.[65] The multiple employment of these men, and those such as Wise and Jeffrey, suggest that they may have been practising law on a more or less full-time basis, and the best way to describe them is by use of the sixteenth-century occupational label, court holder.[66]

As the examples of Tickett and Avent demonstrate, men who worked as manorial stewards sometimes practised as attorneys in town courts, and, in general, urban jurisdictions harboured a number of legal practitioners, some of whom had connections with West-minster and some of whom did not. From the early middle ages, one of the privileges which accompanied urban corporate status was the right to administer justice in both civil and criminal causes. On the civil side this meant the establishment of courts of small pleas whose jurisdictions over actions involving town residents were defined by an upper limit on the value of money or property which might be at issue before the dispute had to be taken to London.[67] The limit varied from town to town, but in the late sixteenth and early seventeenth centuries it was generally set in the borough charter at somewhere between £5 and £50.[68] From as early as the thirteenth century, legal representatives, attorneys and pleaders, were allowed to work in these courts. In the beginning most of them were probably no more than articulate and knowledgeable amateurs.[69] But at least some of these provincial practitioners had been professionalized very early. In 1550, London had long had a professional bar in the Guildhall and Hustings courts, and, although it was exceptional, the 1553 town charter of St Albans made specific provision for the appointment of town court attorneys.[70]

The methods by which these urban practitioners were appointed varied considerably. The most common characteristic was that the urban work was not open to all comers, and there were usually limits on the number of men allowed to practise. In some towns the selection of attorneys lay with the recorder or with the town clerk; in others, probably the majority, local attorneys were elected by the members of the urban governing body, the common council. Whatever the method, it is clear that in most towns of any size there was a steady stream of applicants seeking the privilege.[71]

Similarly, the training of urban practitioners had no fixed patterns. Towns rarely specified any qualifications other than that they should control admission, but in overcoming this hurdle local connections were undoubtedly useful to the prospective lawyer. For this reason, the most successful strategy for gaining an urban attorneyship may have been to begin by serving as a clerk in the office of either the town clerk or recorder. This was the case in Reading, Cambridge, and several other towns.[72] In Reading, for example, William Wylmer was admitted an attorney in the borough court, and then in 1607 he became town clerk. In 1629, his son Edward was sworn as a town attorney and promised the town clerkship. At the same time, two of the clerks of the borough recorder went on to become local attorneys. One of them, Thomas Wylliamson, was granted the post in 1607 on condition that he forsake his master's service, keep a house, and live of himself 'as the other attorneys do'.[73] This pattern of training urban practitioners within the local courts themselves was codified in the town of Canterbury in 1656, when the local authorities passed an ordinance specifying that only the town clerk, the recorder, and the town attorneys should be allowed the privilege of raising up clerks who could be eligible in the future for attorneyships.[74]

A final, but quite significant, feature of the urban jurisdictions is that towards the turn of the sixteenth century some towns passed ordinances designed to prevent borough court attorneys from practising at Westminster. For example, an order of the Ipswich town assembly, dated 1592 and repeated often afterwards, stated that attorneys 'in this Court... shall [not] practise as Atturney[s] in any Court at West[minste]r'.[75] The rationale of this restriction was evidently the need to insure that attorneys were available to serve local litigants and to encourage them to use the local court.

It is likely that Ipswich's policy towards town attorneys was fairly common. Comparisons of the names of urban attorneys submitted in depositions to the commissions of fees in the 1620s with practitioners mentioned in the plea rolls of King's Bench and Common Pleas suggests that in a number of places – Bury St Edmunds, Andover, Plymouth – town attorneys did not work at Westminster.[76] Equally, the four attorneys of the Guildhall Court at Exeter, Nicholas Trosse, Henry Ratcliffe, John Drake, and Richard Tickett, never appear in the plea rolls in London.[77] They might have acted as solicitors in cases which went to London, but in a city such as Exeter, where access to Westminster practitioners must have been easy, it is more likely that they were regularly preoccupied by local business. As we have seen already, Tickett was active in at least one other provincial jurisdiction. Trosse, who was the younger son of a late-sixteenth-century Common Pleas attorney, could certainly have had a London practice, but evidently chose not to.[78]

However, by the early seventeenth century, the urban practitioners had become a very diverse group. If the four attorneys of the Guildhall in Exeter seem to have been concerned exclusively with local business, other town attorneys such as John Rosyer of Barnstaple or Richard Skinner of Tiverton combined work in a local court with practices in Westminster jurisdictions.[79] By the turn of the sixteenth century, the number of attorneys associated with courts such as King's Bench and Common Pleas had increased considerably and, as a consequence, their presence was being felt more directly in the provinces.[80] Ordinances such as that passed by the Ipswich town assembly in 1592 were designed to stem the tide of litigation and lawyers which was rolling towards Westminster, not to establish new precedents.

The practitioners who worked before the palatinates and the regional councils, the town court attorneys, and some of the court keepers and stewards are the provincial practitioners of the early modern period most easily recognized today as men of law, but during the reign of Elizabeth they would not have been the only ones. To begin with, there were, particularly in cathedral towns, proctors and other legal functionaries of the ecclesiastical courts. The majority of these men appear to have had little to do with the municipal as opposed to the ecclesiastical laws of the realm, but it would be a mistake to draw too distinct a line between the two.[81] The Common Pleas attorney Nicholas Street of Exeter practised common law and at the same time held the post of registrar in the Consistory Court of the Bishop of Exeter.[82] At least one notary public, Samuel Jeakes of Rye in Kent, was elected in the early seventeenth century to a town clerkship, a post directly concerned with the administration of the common law.[83]

But, leaving aside these practitioners, there were still others who could offer services closely connected with the law. Most numerous of these were the scriveners, men who engaged in a wide range of activities. In London, the Company of Writers of the Court Letter, whose records date from as early as 1392, were incorporated in 1616 so that 'the Anciens and better sort [could] governe the Ruder and irregular part of the same'.[84] Scriveners were trained through apprenticeship, and from 1550 the register of the company records five or six admissions each year. The oath of the company indicates that the writing of deeds and bonds made up the main work of the scriveners, but the nature of these tasks led many of them to act also as money lenders, and at least ten of the men admitted to the company as apprentices between 1550 and 1640 are known to have practised in the courts at Westminster as attorneys.[85] Much less is known about scriveners in the provinces, but in some places there were clearly large numbers of them. For instance, in York Palliser found twenty-five scriveners amongst the sixteenth-century freemen of the city, far more than any other group of lawyers, and there were eighteen scriveners in Norwich in 1569.[86]

As the dual occupations of the attorney-scriveners of London imply, the work of the attorneys and that of the scriveners was sometimes similar. Both were concerned, or became concerned, with writing legal instruments,[87] and the scriveners' expertise in drawing deeds may imply that they were good men to consult for the interpretation of them. The close relationship between the two occupations with respect to the writing of deeds and other legal instruments is well illustrated by the fact that the first systematic treatise on the subject, *Symbolaeographia*, was written by the York-shire attorney William West.[88] Moreover, as was the case in London, some provincial scriveners combined their trade with practice as attorneys. Henry Hooper was the first of a long line of lawyers in Tonbridge Wells.[89] Another Elizabethan scrivener, Thomas Hill of Norwich, had been trained as a clerk and practised as an attorney in the municipal Sheriff's Court.[90]

It is impossible to determine with any precision how many scriveners sometimes practised as attorneys or acted as solicitors. All that can be concluded is that some did and that in an age when occupational distinctions were much less clearly defined than they have since become, the obstacles in the way of such activities were not serious. Equally, it is difficult to say whether the scriveners (or some of them) and the other professional, semi-professional, and amateur provincial practitioners should be classified as lawyers in the same sense as those who were trained at the inns of court or who worked in the royal courts at Westminster. The important fact is that there were in the provinces a number of different kinds of men who could offer legal services, and they add an important perspective to any picture of the early modern legal profession which is based purely on London. Provincial legal institutions, the manor, the hundred courts, and municipal courts, were the scenes of much legal activity, and there were practitioners in the country who were evidently capable of handling this business. At this level any attempt to define whether a particular individual was in any meaningful sense a professional lawyer must be resolved largely by a consideration of practical criteria such as the extent to which he was engaged full-time in legal activity and, perhaps, of the nature of the work itself. Legal education or qualification to practise in a royal tribunal might provide a narrow definition, but in the provinces connections with courts in London or with the inns of court and inns of chancery very often counted for little. For example, as late as 1668, it was unclear whether an attorney of the Common Pleas could demand to be allowed to represent a client in a manorial court.[91] In the provinces, as in London, gaining an admission to a particular court – a task which was by no means always easy – was the first step to practise, and very often the best way to achieve such an admission was to have been trained within the jurisdiction. Most town court attorneys and all of those who practised in the palatinate of Chester or before the Council in the North were certainly professional lawyers in the ordinary sense of the words. Yet many of these practitioners had no connections with London. As in London itself, the massively complicated and particularized nature of local jurisdictions meant that there was no single qualification which permitted a man to practise within them. To contemporaries this would have seemed perfectly right. Attorneys brought disputes to court; hence restrictions on their right to practise in outside jurisdictions insured that business would come into the court to which they belonged. Equally, local control of admissions and of numbers of practitioners meant that local authorities were in a position to regulate the activities of lawyers who acted within their communities.

The manorial stewards were even more ambiguous legal characters than the local attorneys (and sometimes of course the same man acted in both capacities). In the early seventeenth century, Sir Edward Coke stated that stewards should have legal training, but acknowledged, rather regretfully, that very often they did not.[92] The stewards were on the borderline between the lawyers and the man of affairs. Stewards who were barristers at the inns of court or attorneys working at Westminster must of course be reckoned amongst the members of the common law profession of London. So, too, should those who were members of legal inns, but who had not progressed up the ranks of membership to become pleaders (or barristers). Yet, since mere admission to a legal inn tells little about the nature of an individual's legal knowledge or practice, it would be wrong to stress too strongly the similarities between all members of this group and the 'professionals'.[93] More important, the men described as court holders and a number of the other Elizabethan stewards were members neither of legal inns nor of the lower branch of the London profession. They are such an obscure group of men that it is difficult to say much about the careers of individuals, but some account of their training can be pieced together. Some stewards, particularly those of the largest landowners, were trained up in magnate households. Others were probably no more than servants, with various degrees of practical experience.[94] For example, John Smith of Nibley, one of those more superior stewards with a background at the inns of court, castigated Lord Berkeley's high steward in Gloucestershire, Anthony Huntley. According to Smith, Huntley knew no Latin, and was a man 'fitter for ffaires and markets of Cattell and sales of wood, wherein he had good skill, then to grapple' at law with the formidable enemies of his master, the Littletons.[95] On the other hand, most lawyers of whatever variety – serjeants, attorneys, town clerks – employed clerks to assist them with their work. Thus it is possible that many stewards were trained through such service, and, as we have seen already, some town courts and the staffs of town clerks were certainly the starting points for some legal careers.[96] To attempt to determine whether such men were professional lawyers is impossible and perhaps pointless, but to leave them out of a picture of the early modern legal world would be misleading.[97]

Indeed, it is tempting to suggest that there were two legal professions (or at least two groups of legal practitioners) in England during the early years of the reign of Elizabeth, one centred on London and another whose training and activity was concentrated in the country. An accurate comparison of the sizes of the two is virtually impossible. Although we can produce figures for the number of London practitioners, the uneven survival of manorial and town court records puts any firm estimate about the purely provincial practitioners beyond reach. Even so, to conclude that they were at least as numerous as the men connected with London is more than a fair guess. In towns such as Norwich and York, there were certainly more scriveners than common law attorneys active at any single date before around 1580. The twenty-four Warwickshire stewards who had no connection with London compare favourably with the fifteen or twenty attorneys who were active in the county between 1560 and 1606. Many towns had two or three borough court attorneys.[98] Finally, nothing has been said about those men who had no connection with any court but who took up legal practice on their own initiative. Such practitioners are difficult to identify, but contemporaries complained about them so frequently that they must not be left out of the reckoning.[99] Nor can they be stereotyped easily. For instance, it was a commonplace that vicars should help their parishioners settle disputes; in the case of some, such as the Yorkshireman Edmund Cundy, curate of Wortley, this duty could turn into a considerable legal practice.[100] More sinister was the tendency for apparently unlearned men to take up as business ventures offices such as that of undersheriff or clerk of the peace, which were intimately connected with legal processes and which would have been more competently held by men with some legal training. A particularly notorious example of this comes from Suffolk in the form of two yeomen, Robert and Matthew Crisp, who apparently made careers out of dealing in minor administrative posts. They were profiteers who played fast and loose with other people's money, including that of the crown.[101]

The number of such pseudo-lawyers and the extent of their practices cannot be measured with any accuracy. Nevertheless, they, like the town court attorneys and the semi-professional court holders, were significant figures in the legal institutions of the localities. They served as town clerks, clerks of the peace, and undersheriffs. Although they were not connected with the central court or the inns of court and chancery, they must have been willing (and sometimes able) to advise countrymen about the law and, if necessary, to act as intermediaries between clients in the country and those lawyers who were associated with the Westminster jurisdictions. If these speculations are correct, then they all have some claim to being described as the precursors of the solicitors. But at the same time they are testimony to the limited size and scope of the legal profession in London at the beginning of the reign of Elizabeth.

4

THE INCREASE IN LITIGATION

I

Whether we are considering it in London or in the provinces, two points emerge from the study of the structure of the early modern lower branch. The first is that the profession was intimately tied to the clerical offices of the various courts. The other is that its primary function within the legal world had to do with the conduct of litigation. As Chapter 8 shows, practitioners in the country did certainly engage in a number of non-litigious activities. But to an extent surprising to us today, the work, public image, size, and shape of the lower branch of the legal profession were deeply involved with lawsuits. Consequently, the single most important fact about the history of the profession (and of the system within which it operated) during this period is that from the mid sixteenth century until the outbreak of the Civil War, litigation came flooding into Westminster Hall both suddenly and on an unprecedented scale. Before going on to assess its consequences for the lawyers, we must stop now to look hard and long at the nature and causes of this phenomenon.

II

Historians have long suspected that litigation increased during the late sixteenth and early seventeenth centuries, but the exact dimensions of the development have never been fully explored.[1] The problem is that evidence about litigation is either super-abundant and difficult to manage or, alternatively, completely non-existent. The multitude of jurisdictions, both lay and ecclesiastical, which operated on the national or local levels render it impossible to produce a global picture. On the other hand, there are major gaps in the records of courts as important as Star Chamber or the Council in the Marches of Wales, and virtually nothing at all survives about the litigious work of the Council in the North.[2]

This lack of evidence is hardly an issue with major royal courts such as Chancery, King's Bench, and Common Pleas, but the very success of these tribunals during the period has made their principal records some of the most daunting of all early modern documents. Since King's Bench and Common Pleas were the major law courts of the realm, any analysis of litigation must begin with them, but even Maitland was forced to conclude that the plea rolls are so unwieldy 'that we can hardly hope that much will ever be known about them'.[3] Given the nature of the records, some kind of quantitative approach is a logical first step to studying them. But the problems of defining what constitutes a case, and of counting cases as opposed to masses of procedural paperwork, mean that attempts to arrive at no more than an estimate of the volume of litigation entertained by the courts are beset by difficulties.[4]

One effective technique for measuring business in King's Bench and Common Pleas was pioneered by Marjory Blatcher. It involves comparing the fines taken by the crown in different years for the seals which were attached to the judicial writs issued by the two courts. The income from the seals is an indicator of the level of procedural activity in the courts, and Blatcher was able to put together a long series of annual totals which reflects fluctuations in the volume of business over nearly two centuries of the late middle ages and early Tudor period.[5] However, the use of the profits of the seals does have limitations. They are not counts of cases, and they do not make it possible to draw distinctions between cases in advanced stages and cases in which an action had been initiated by the plaintiff but the defendant had refused to appear, or in which there had been an out-of-court settlement. Nor do they give any indication of the relative volume of civil (plea side) versus criminal (crown side) business in the King's Bench. Finally, the accounts on which Blatcher based her study evidently do not survive as a series for the period after 1559.[6]

In fact, no single set of records will yield accurate and accessible information about the number of suits commenced in the common law courts. However, there are documents – the docket rolls of the three prothonotaries of the Common Pleas and the chief prothonotary of the King's Bench – which can be used to project a fairly accurate picture of the number of cases in the two tribunals which had reached the point where the defendant had answered the summons of the plaintiff and come into court to join issue.

The prothonotaries were responsible only for the so-called advanced stages of litigation which took place once both parties had made an appearance. Their entries in the plea rolls of the courts refer to the making of pleas, imparlances, and demurrers, the issue of writs of *venire facias* to call jurors, and the enrolment of *posteas* recording the decisions in trials which had taken place at assizes.[7] Essentially, the docket rolls are a secondary set of documents which contain very brief notes of the much more lengthy entries which the prothonotaries and their clerks made in the plea rolls, and so the dockets can serve as a kind of index to the main series.[8] Since the prothonotaries had nothing to do with the issue of writs of mesne process which so often resulted in multiple entries in the plea rolls, one great advantage of the dockets as a guide to the volume of litigation is that they exclude the mass of duplication which arose from such entries. Nevertheless, particularly in the Common Pleas, there is no guarantee that only one entry per case was made in the docket rolls in any given year, and new entries relating to old cases were almost certain to arise over the course of more than one year. For example, an imparlance in one term might be followed by a pleading in the next and a *venire facias* recording the summons of jurors in yet another a year later. Samples of cases in the Common Pleas rolls for 1606 indicate that as many as 20 per cent of all entries in that court's dockets were duplicated within one year.[9]

Fortunately, things were simpler in the King's Bench. There, mainly because of the contraction in procedure which accompanied the domination of the court by the chief prothonotary, it was rare for a formal entry to be made for a case until it had run its course through the court, regardless of whether the conclusion came in the form of a trial at *nisi prius*, a settlement out of court, or a judgment entered through the failure of the defendant to enter any plea.[10] Consequently, the King's Bench docket rolls provide a very accurate means for measuring the volume of business in advanced stages in the court in any one year.

Keeping these characteristics of the docket rolls in mind, they have been used to produce the figures for litigation in advanced stages in King's Bench and Common Pleas between 1560 and 1640 which are displayed in Table 4.1. In the case of Common Pleas, the numbers represent a count of docket roll entries for the single years 1563, 1580,

Table 4.1 *Cases in advanced stages in King's Bench and Common Pleas, 1490–1640*

	King's Bench	Common Pleas	Total
1490	500[a]	1600[b]	2100
1560	781[c]	3200[d]	5278[f]
1563		5793[e]	
1580	3805[c]	9300[g]	13,105
1606	6639[c]	16,508	23,147
1640	8109[c]	20,625	28,734

[a] The work of Blatcher and Ives suggests that an average of about 400–500 cases a year in King's Bench is likely for the 1490s. M. Blatcher, 'Touching the Writ of Latitat: An Act of No Great Moment', in *Elizabethan Government and Society*, ed. S. T. Bindoff, J. Hurstfield, and C. H. Williams (1961), p. 201 n. 1. Ives, 'The Common Lawyers in Pre-Reformation England', p. 167.

[b] Hastings, *The Court of Common Pleas*, p. 183. The Common Pleas presents difficulties because there are no complete sets of docket rolls for the earlier period. For Michaelmas Term 1483, Hastings counted 6,000 plea roll entries, but since 5100 of these were related to mesne process, this figure is not comparable with those for King's Bench. If we multiply the remaining 900 entries by 20/8 (the ratio of return-days in Michaelmas Term to the total number in the legal year as in D. Sutherland, *The Assize of Novel Disseisin* (Oxford, 1974), p. 178), we obtain a total of 2100 cases a year in advanced stages. If we then make the same 20 per cent allowance for duplication as in the other Common Pleas figures, the estimate of 1600 emerges.

[c] Three-year averages. Source for 1560 is PRO IND 1339; for 1580, IND 1346–7; for 1606, IND 1356–7; for 1640, IND 1369–70. The series for 1640 runs from Easter 1637 to Hilary 1640.

[d] Because the docket rolls of Common Pleas are incomplete for the years before 1563, exact figures for its business in 1560 are unavailable, but estimates based on a comparison of the seal profits for 1490 and 1560 indicate a volume in 1560 of something in the region of 3200 cases annually.

[e] PRO IND 20–1, 23.

[f] This total takes Common Pleas business at 4497, which is the average of the figures for 1560 and 1563.

[g] Sources for Common Pleas figures in 1580, 1606, and 1640 are PRO IND 54–6, 157–65, 353–8.

1606, and 1640 with 20 per cent having been subtracted to allow for duplication. Since the King's Bench entries are more reliable, and since no additional error would be introduced by counting clusters rather than individual years, the King's Bench figures are averages of counts of docket roll entries for three years around the dates 1560,

1580, 1606, and 1640. Neither of the sets of statistics is perfect, but they are as good an estimate of the volume of litigation as we are ever likely to get, and other kinds of contemporary evidence leave little doubt that they are of the right order of magnitude.

The figures compiled by Blatcher for the incomes from the seals and the counts of docket roll entries are quite different indicators of the level of activity of King's Bench and Common Pleas. The former measures all the business which came before them; the latter only those cases which progressed to advanced stages. Nevertheless, by combining the results of both approaches we are able to achieve a uniquely good picture of fluctuations in the fortunes of the two courts over nearly three centuries. Blatcher shows that, beginning in the decade 1360–70, income from the seals rose from £325 to a high point of £575 in the decade 1410–20. Next came a long period of steady decline which lasted throughout the fifteenth and early sixteenth centuries, and which culminated in an all-time low in 1524–5, when the seals yielded just £103. Thereafter, there was a gradual improvement in the fee income to the extent that by the end of the decade 1550–60 the seals were earning as much as they had done at the previous high point in the 1410s.[11]

Earlier work by Blatcher and by Ives and Hastings, on the actual numbers of cases in the early Tudor courts, shows the same trends as the seals material and also forms a link with the counts of cases from the Elizabethan and early Stuart docket rolls. According to these findings, at the end of the fifteenth century about 2000 cases in advanced stages were making their way through King's Bench and Common Pleas. Then, during the early sixteenth century, business dropped off, and Ives detected a distinct trough in 1524 when King's Bench apparently heard only about 100 cases.[12] But once again, as the seal profits predict, the number of cases began to pick up again after 1530, and by the opening years of the reign of Elizabeth, King's Bench had more than recovered its late-fifteenth-century position and was hearing an average of about 800 suits a year. There are no complete series of docket rolls for the Common Pleas until 1563,[13] but the 5793 cases in advanced stages in that year clearly represent a major increase in the volume of business in the court over what it was in 1490.

The crucial point, though, is that from 1560 litigation in both courts began to soar. Between 1560 and 1580 King's Bench business increased by nearly five times to just under 4000 suits in advanced stages per annum. The 9300 cases in Common Pleas represent an equally striking increase. Taken together, the two courts were hearing about six times more actions than they had been at the end of the fifteenth century.

As it happens, corroboration that the early Elizabethan years witnessed an explosion in litigation comes from evidence which, once again, can be tied in with figures for the profits of the seals. One of the earliest recorded instances of recognition of the growth in central court business arose in 1578 as a result of a dispute between the justices of the King's Bench and Common Pleas and a man called William Killigrew, who put forward a proposal to farm the queen's revenue from the seals of the two courts. The judges, and in particular Sir James Dyer, CJCP, argued strenuously against the scheme on the grounds that in 1578 business in the courts was greater than it had ever been before and was increasing yearly. Dyer claimed that 'the increase of the revenues for her ma[jes]*ties* tyme hath been 1000 m*a*rkes [approximately £667] a yere more ten [*sic*] any her noble pr*o*genitors ev*er* hadd'.[14] He then pointed out that in 1578 the King's Bench seals had earned £750 and those of Common Pleas £1300, or a combined total of £2050. Given what is known about the volume of litigation in 1580, just two years after 1578, this sum is just about what one might have predicted. As Table 4.1 indicates, between 1560 and 1580 the number of suits in advanced stages increased by nearly three times from 5278 to 13,105 per annum. Blatcher's figures for incomes from the seals in 1560 show the benches earning £171 8s. 6d. and £549 15s. 7d. respectively, a total of £721 4s. If this figure is multiplied by three, the factor for the increase in litigation, we get £2163 12s., quite a reasonable approximation on the total mentioned by Dyer. Thus the evidence about the value of the seals in the mid-Elizabethan years provides significant independent support for the reliability of calculating the volume of litigation in King's Bench and Common Pleas by making counts in the docket rolls. Equally important, the figures show that the total business of the courts, and not just the incidence of cases in which both parties had come into court, was on the increase.

Moreover, as Table 4.1 indicates, the volume of litigation continued to grow, albeit at a slightly milder rate, during the second half of the reign of Elizabeth, and then well into the early seventeenth century, although after 1600 the pace was a good deal less spectacular than it had been before that date. By 1640, a total of just under 29,000

Table 4.2 *Litigation commenced in Chancery, 1432–1558 (average number of petitions per annum)*

	Cases
1432–43	136[a]
1470–5	243
1475–85	553
1485–1500	571
1500–15	605
1515–29 (Thomas, Cardinal Wolsey)	534[b]
1529–34 (Sir Thomas More)	943[c]
1533–44 (Sir Thomas Audley)	1243[d]
April 1544–March 1547	1046
(Thomas, Lord Wriothesley)	
March 1547–Dec. 1551	844
(William Paulett and Thomas, Lord Rich)	
Jan. 1552–Aug. 1553	798
(Thomas Goodrich, Bishop of Ely)	
Aug. 1553–Nov. 1555	1300
(S. Gardiner, Bishop of Winchester)	
Nov. 1555–Nov. 1558	1082
(N. Heath, Archbishop of York)	

[a] Figures for 1432–1515 from N. Pronay, 'The Chancellor, the Chancery, and the Council at the End of the Fifteenth Century', in *British Government and Administration*, ed. H. Hearder and H. R. Lyon (Cardiff, 1974), pp. 88 9.
[b] F. Metzger, 'The Last Phase of the Medieval Chancery', in *Law-Making and the Law-Makers in British History*, ed. A. Harding (1980), p. 50.
[c] J. A. Guy, *The Public Career of Sir Thomas More* (1980), p. 50.
[d] Figures for 1533–58 derived from *Lists of Early Chancery Proceedings*, vols. vi–x.

cases were progressing through the courts, 8109 in King's Bench and 20,625 in Common Pleas. On the eve of the civil wars, there was twice as much litigation in King's Bench and Common Pleas as there had been in 1580, perhaps fourteen times more than in the 1490s.

Although the statistical evidence is often imperfect, comparisons can be made between the volume of business in King's Bench and Common Pleas and that in other courts. Thanks to the published lists *Early Chancery Proceedings*, the number of petitions (essentially the number of suits commenced) addressed to various chancellors between the early fifteenth century and 1558 can be charted with some accuracy.[15] As a glance at Table 4.2 confirms, the most notable feature of the Chancery over this period is that, unlike King's Bench and Common Pleas, it experienced no phase of early Tudor decline. Instead, business in the court progressed steadily with significant leaps forward under the Yorkists and again during the chancellorship of Sir Thomas More (1529–31). Unfortunately, after 1558 exact numerical evidence about litigation in Chancery is difficult to obtain, but it seems likely that the number of petitions may have doubled between the beginning and the end of the reign of Elizabeth, when, according to estimates by Jones, the court was hearing perhaps 1600 cases per annum which had reached advanced stages.[16] After 1600, there was a great deal of public complaint about abuses in Chancery and numerous accusations that its business was growing to exorbitant proportions.[17] But, although the evidence is perplexing and often contradictory, the truth appears to be that whatever increase there may have been was only marginal. One source even suggests that during the reign of James I the average for suits commenced was only 1464 per year,[18] which, if accurate, would indicate a decline, and it is generally agreed that there was some contraction in business during the lord keepership of Thomas Coventry (1625–40).[19] In general, by the time of James I the problems of Chancery had more to do with bureaucratic stagnation and growing procedural complexity than with any massive influx in suits.[20]

Trends in Star Chamber were somewhat similar to those in Chancery, even though its total volume of business was always considerably less. Litigation in the court grew from 12.5 cases p.a. under Henry VII to about 120 each year during the supremacy of Cardinal Wolsey.[21] After 1529, we lack figures for the remainder of the sixteenth century, but there is no reason to think that there was anything other than a gradual increase in Star Chamber work up to the reign of James I, during which the court heard an average of 325 suits (commenced) per year.[22] Virtually no Star Chamber records survive for the period after 1625, but the historian of the court, Barnes, believes that its business was stagnating by the later part of the reign of James I, and that it is unlikely that there was any further growth between 1625 and the abolition of the jurisdiction by the Long Parliament in 1642.[23]

The profiles of most of the other major courts are rather fragmentary. All that can be said of Wards and Requests is that business was probably growing during the reign of Elizabeth.[24] On the equity side of Exchequer, there was a rise in the average number of bills from 84 p.a. between 1558 and 1587 to 334 p.a. for the years 1587–1603,

Table 4.3. *Summary of the volume of litigation in various courts during the reign of James I*

King's Bench	6639 cases p.a. in advanced stages
Common Pleas	16,508 cases p.a. in advanced stages
Chancery	1600 cases p.a. in advanced stages. Perhaps 3000 p.a. commenced
Star Chamber	325 suits p.a. commenced
Exchequer: equity side	332 bills p.a. filed.
common law side	100–150 cases p.a.
Chancery courts of the palatinates of Durham and Chester	450 decrees and orders p.a.
Council in the North	2000 civil and criminal cases p.a.
Council in Wales	1500 cases p.a. in advanced stages

and, during the reign of James I, the tribunal heard an average of 332 bills each year.[25] Moving beyond London, it has been estimated that, under the early Stuarts, the chancery courts of the palatinates of Durham and Chester issued an average of 450 decrees and orders each year, which undoubtedly means that the number of cases initiated was considerably higher.[26] Sir Edward Coke claimed that the early Jacobean Council in the North, which had a criminal as well as a civil jurisdiction, heard 2000 cases annually.[27] The equivalent tribunal in Wales, the Council in the Marches, entertained about 1500 cases a year in which both parties had come into court (advanced stages), and it maintained this level right up to the civil wars,[28] even though it, like the Council in the North, experienced considerable political unpopularity.[29] Finally, although their main concerns were tithe, slander, and testamentary and matrimonial causes rather than civil litigation pure and simple, it is worth noting for the sake of comparison that litigation in the church courts also increased during the course of the sixteenth century. For example, in the diocese of Norwich, the number of cases brought before the bishop's consistory court grew from 97 in 1519 to 288 in 1569; similarly, in the diocese of Winchester, there was an increase from 36 cases in 1527 to 169 in 1566.[30]

Putting together all this information about litigation in the early modern courts leads to two general conclusions. First, in terms of the number of lawsuits they entertained, either the King's Bench or the Common Pleas was far more important than any other single court in the realm, and the two of them together certainly heard far more cases than all of the other courts combined. For example, if we add up all the known figures for litigation in other courts in the early seventeenth century, we get a total of something in the region of 6000 cases, but this must be compared with 23,000-odd cases which were being heard at that time by the benches. Second, the evidence from all of the courts shows that, while there was a general increase in litigation between 1550 and 1640, it was the reign of Elizabeth which was the most notable for the remarkable increase in the number of lawsuits. After 1603, business in King's Bench and Common Pleas grew more slowly than previously; a number of the other tribunals experienced a period of stagnation.

III

Just as the docket rolls have enabled us to outline the awesome increase in the number of lawsuits which came before the Elizabethan and early Stuart King's Bench and Common Pleas, there is another set of records which contributes details about the nature of this litigation by providing information about the people who used the courts and the business which brought them to Westminster Hall.

In both courts, once the parties to a suit had appeared in court and were about to join issue or, alternatively, when the plaintiff had reached the stage where he was about to outlaw the defendant for failing to appear, the rules of practice required that the litigant take out a writ called the warrant of attorney which recorded the name of the attorney whom he had chosen to represent him. At the end of each term these warrants were collected together and written out by a clerk on parchment. The resulting 'Roll of Warrants of Attorneys' was then bound up at the end of the plea roll for the relevant term. The form of the warrant was simple, the key words being 'A *ponit loco sue*', his attorney (who was named) versus the other party, and this formula was followed by a brief description of the form of action on which the suit was being pursued (debt, trespass, trespass on the case, detinue, etc.).[31] Like most other plea roll entries, each warrant was preceded by a marginal note recording the county in which the action was 'laid', and, luckily, the names of the parties, especially defendants, were almost always accompanied by a style designating their social status (gentleman, knight, yeoman, labourer, etc.). Thus, although the purpose of the warrants was to record the appointment of attorneys, they incidentally contain valuable information about the names, addresses, status, and causes of action of the litigants.

As a source, the rolls of warrants have one serious flaw and two very great strengths. The flaw is that they tell us only about those litigants whose cases had reached 'advanced stages'. A warrant was not required in those instances where a suit was commenced but then dropped either because there was settlement out of court before issue was joined, or because the defendant failed to appear and the plaintiff did not bother to have him outlawed. Settlements out of court in the early stages of a suit were quite common; failure to outlaw a defendant was undoubtedly less so, but the frequency of neither can be estimated with any great accuracy. Nevertheless, it is important to decide what differences there may have been between those litigants who went to advanced stages and those who did not. It is quite possible that the difference was negligible. On the other hand, since each step through which a cause was pursued cost a litigant more money, it would seem logical that richer men would be more likely than poorer men to take a case as far as possible before giving up. If this is so, then evidence from the rolls of warrants may tend towards a relative underestimation of the presence in the courts of men of lower social status, and this must be kept in mind when considering the social composition of litigants.

The first great advantage of the rolls is that they are a manageable source which make it possible to boil down the great mass of material contained in the plea rolls and to avoid difficulties which might result from re-counting multiple entries. Only two warrants were ever likely to be taken out in any given case (one for the plaintiff and one for the defendant), and possible repetitions of this kind can be accounted for relatively easily since a roll of warrants for any one term rarely ran to more than 150–200 membranes. The second strength of the warrants is that they contain an accurate account of the information required. The rules of the courts specified that precise styles and addresses should be given for defendants; otherwise the plaintiff was subject to being non-suited.[32] Procedure with regard to plaintiffs was less rigorously controlled, and in practice plaintiffs were styled only if they claimed the rank of gentleman or above. Thus the rolls enable us to say with confidence what percentage of all litigants was above the rank of gentleman and what below it. Furthermore, a detailed picture of litigants below the rank of

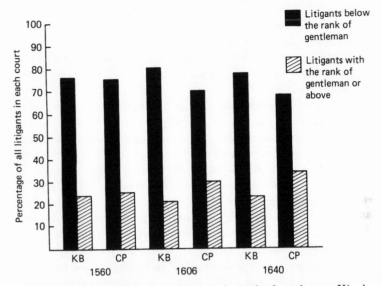

Figure 4.1. Litigants above and below the rank of gentleman, King's Bench and Common Pleas, 1560–1640. (For a complete breakdown of the social status of litigants see the Appendix, p. 281.)

gentleman can be drawn from information about those who were in court as defendants. In general, there is every reason to believe that an analysis of sample rolls of warrants for given years across the period 1560–1640 yields a reasonably reliable profile of the men and women who were using King's Bench and Common Pleas.

The results of a study of rolls of warrants for single terms in the years 1560, 1606, and 1640 are illustrated in Figure 4.1. The most striking thing about the social status of litigants as revealed by this material is the extent to which both courts were open to a surprisingly wide cross-section of the population. Throughout the period, men styled gentleman or above made up between 25 and 30 per cent of all Common Pleas and 20 to 25 per cent of all King's Bench litigants. Although the correlation between the styles men used and their occupations or wealth were not always exact, it is reasonable to postulate that the majority of men who called themselves gentlemen, esquire, or peer were in fact members of that broad category of wealthy landowners known as the gentry. At the very least, we can be confident that they were amongst the richest men in the realm, and it has long been an historical commonplace that the gentry monopolized both the common law and the royal legal institutions. So what is surprising about the figures in Figure 4.1 is that this group accounts for only a minority of all litigants. By far the majority, at least 70 or 80 per cent, of the people who used King's Bench and Common Pleas were in fact drawn from a large spectrum of the population other than the gentry.

A closer inspection of those non-gentry litigants who appeared in court as defendants reveal roughly equal numbers of men who owned or worked land and those whose livelihood probably came primarily from other sources. One-third of all Common Pleas, and 15–20 per cent of all King's Bench, defendants were either yeomen or husbandmen. If these figures are added to those for the 'gentry', it would appear that approximately 65–70 per cent of litigation involved people closely connected with the land, a not unexpected finding for a society whose primary industry was agriculture. On the other hand, 25 per cent of all Common Pleas and 30 per cent of all King's Bench defendants came from the commercial and other classes for whom land was not a principal source of income. This group of litigants includes a wide range of wealth and occupations. Most were merchants or provincial traders such as tailors, grocers, butchers, chapmen, or innkeepers. But a few university dons are included, and so too are carpenters, bricklayers, miners, and labourers. The remainder of the litigants in both courts (about 10 per cent) were lawyers (mainly attorneys), clergymen, and widows who were in court about suits relating to the estates of deceased husbands.

The relative presence of various social groups in King's Bench and Common Pleas appears to reflect fairly accurately the distribution of wealth in the nation as a whole. The gentry classes probably owned about 30 per cent of the national wealth[33] and they appear as about that percentage of litigants in the courts. It is impossible to know how well off the non-gentry litigants were, but some estimate of the range of their wealth can be hazarded. The average Exeter merchant may have earned around £100 a year in the early seventeenth century. In medium sized and smaller towns, annual merchant income was probably (on a liberal estimate) no more than £50, which is also about the right figure for the average yeoman farmer.[34] Husbandmen and smaller artisans were worth even less,[35] but in the latter category there could be considerable variation. Some men styled weavers or clothiers may have been individual workmen, but others might well have been major producers who employed upwards

Plaintiffs	versus	Defendants		Total
Gentleman and above		Gentleman and above	Below the rank of gentleman	
		176 (12%)	227 (16%)	403 (29%)
Below the rank of gentleman		317 (22%)	691 (49%)	1008 (71%)
				1411 (100%)

Figure 4.2. Social analysis of plaintiffs versus defendants in Common Pleas, 1606. Numbers in ( ) equal percentages of all cases. (*Source:* PRO CP 40/1753.)

of thirty people.[36] Thus, although it is undoubtedly true that very few of the litigants below the rank of gentleman came from that part of the population (perhaps one-third) which lived on or below the edge of subsistence,[37] it is clear that provincial farmers, merchants, tailors, and artisans could find legal representation and use the courts. Equally important, King's Bench and Common Pleas were not instruments which any one class or group used exclusively in their own interests against any other class or group. Figure 4.2 analyses the relative instances of cases in the Common Pleas in Michaelmas Term 1606 in which a plaintiff from one broad social group sues a defendant from the same or some other social group. It shows that men below the rank of gentleman were involved as plaintiffs in 71 per cent of all litigation, and that they were a good deal more likely to sue their social superiors than to be sued by them.

The extent to which there was change in the social composition of litigants between 1560 and 1640 is a complicated problem. On the basis of the raw data, it would appear that there was only a marginal shift in the relative presence in the courts of gentry as opposed to non-gentry litigants. The figures for the percentage of gentry suitors using King's Bench at the three dates in the sample remain constant at between 21 and 23 per cent. On the other hand, in the Common Pleas, there was a small, 7 per cent, increase in the number of litigants who styled themselves as gentlemen, but there were also significant differences in the profiles of those litigants who acted as plaintiffs as compared with those who were in court as defendants. Between 1560 and 1640, the percentage of gentry plaintiffs declines from 28 per cent to 25 per cent, whilst that of the gentry defendants increases from 25 per cent to 39 per cent.

However, the analysis cannot stop short with consideration of the numerical evidence. Changes in the significance of status designations, and in particular that of 'gentleman', must also be taken into account. In 1560, the use of the style 'gentleman' was confined largely to substantial landowners and only the most important townsmen. But over the next eighty years this style was appropriated more and more promiscuously by men in both rural and urban settings who had some money and social pretensions, but who were in no sense members of the elite of landed society.[38] Thus as a guide to real wealth and social position, the term 'gentleman' becomes more and more devalued the closer we get to 1640. Since men styled 'gent.' make up one of the largest categories of litigants, this development clearly has important implications for the study of litigation, the full significance of which can best be illustrated by putting the following hypothetical case. If the real wealth and status of the people who used King's Bench and Common Pleas had remained exactly the same over the period it would not be surprising to find that in 1640 a larger percentage of them were using the style 'gentleman' than had been the case in 1560. Instead, what we actually find is that there is hardly any change in the statistics for the composition of litigants in King's Bench, so the logical conclusion must be that the real presence in the court of the gentry (defined as only the wealthiest landowners and townsmen) declines over the period.

In the Common Pleas, the picture is less simple. Taking into account the change in the use of the addition 'gent.', some of the 25 per cent of plaintiffs in 1640 who styled themselves gentleman and above would probably have been in the 'non-gent.' category in 1560. Thus the relative 'real' presence of the 'gentry' in the court as plaintiffs evidently declined by more than the 3 per cent difference between the figure for 1640 and that for 1560. For the same reason, the 14 per cent increase in the figure for 'gentry' defendants must be misleading to some extent about the real social composition of defendants; for example, there may have been no change at all in the wealth of defendants. Nevertheless, the statistical decline in the status of Common Pleas plaintiffs is impressive and stands with the evidence from King's Bench to suggest that men from outside the traditional elites were finding access to the courts easier in 1640 than they had in 1560. Furthermore, although the figures for Common Pleas defendants may be misleading, if plaintiffs and defendants are considered together, there would appear to be a distinct possibility that men below the rank of gentleman were more likely to sue their social superiors in 1640. The increase in litigation involved an increase in the use of the courts by people from all ranks of society. But insofar as there was change in the social composition of litigants, it was one which indicates that a significant feature of the rise in litigation was the relative growth in the number of litigants from social groups other than the gentry.

If we turn now to the geographical origins of litigation (Table 4.4), we find that there was a predictable correspondence between the distribution of population and wealth in the realm and the extent to which the various regions were represented in the courts. Litigation in both King's Bench and Common Pleas came most regularly from London and the other economically prosperous parts of the country. In 1560, London was the home of approximately 3 per cent of the national population,[39] but at least 17 per cent, and perhaps one-quarter, of all Common Pleas suits involved at least one party who lived there, very often a great merchant who was suing someone from the provinces with whom he had business dealings. The other notably litigious area was East Anglia, which accounted for no less than 26 per cent of Common Pleas business in 1560. Like London, this was an area whose economic importance in the early modern period cannot be measured purely in terms of its population, although that was considerable. Norfolk and Suffolk were extremely rich counties whose agricultural, maritime, and industrial economies were linked to wider markets in London and the rest of northern Europe. They were also the home of large numbers of wealthy freehold farmers.[40] As a consequence of these economic and tenurial circumstances, East Anglia had long been notable for the litigiousness of its population and the large number of lawyers it produced.[41] Altogether London, the Home Counties, and East Anglia accounted for some 56 per cent of all Common Pleas litigation in 1560, and yet another 16 per cent of its business came from another notably prosperous region, the counties in the south-west which made up the Western Assize Circuit, many of which enjoyed the fastest growing economies of the early Tudor period.[42]

The major difference between the two courts was that King's Bench seems to have had a bias towards the Western Circuit, whereas Common Pleas leaned towards the Norfolk; the only apparent explanation for this is that King's Bench attorneys were thicker on the ground in Devon, Somerset, and Wiltshire than anywhere else in the country while mainly Common Pleas men worked in Norfolk

Table 4.4. *Geographical distribution of litigation in King's Bench and Common Pleas, 1560–1640 (percentages by assize circuit)*

	Common Pleas			King's Bench 1606
	1560	1606	1640	
Home (Kent, Essex, Sussex, Herts., Surrey)	13 (11)	16 (11)	15 (10)	12
Midland (Derby, Lincs., Notts., Rutland, Northants., War., Leics.)	9 (7)	13 (9)	13 (12)	11
Norfolk (Norfolk, Suffolk, Cambs., Hunts., Beds., Bucks.)	28 (25)	19 (16)	18 (14)	13
Northern (Yorks., Durham, Northumb., Westmor., Cumb.)	3 (2)	5 (4)	4 (3)	2
Oxford (Oxon., Berks., Gloucs., Mon., Herefords., Worcs., Shropshire, Staffs.)	12 (10)	13 (9)	12 (8)	14
Western (Hants., Wilts., Somerset, Dorset, Devon, Cornwall)	15 (14)	12 (7)	15 (14)	25
London and Middlesex	19 (31)	16 (43)	22 (39)	21
Lancs and Cheshire	1	4	1	
Illegible	—	2 (1)	—	2
Total	100	100	100	100

Notes: These figures are compiled from the 'Rolls of Warrants of Attorney' in PRO CP 40/1187, 1733, and 2476 and KB 27/1395. In these documents the venue of each case is noted in the left-hand margin alongside the entry. However, in the Common Pleas, the marginal venues cannot be regarded as an entirely accurate guide to the true geographical origin of the case. The common law demanded that the place where the events in a case transpired should be carefully designated so that a knowledgeable jury could be appointed. But as early as the late thirteenth century, the judges came to recognize a class of cases which could be tried in any venue the plaintiff chose. This group was known as 'transitory', because they were regarded as having 'no necessary connection with a particular locality', and they included actions such as debt. By the beginning of the seventeenth century, these rules were relaxed even further so that the distinction between 'transitory' and 'local' actions (most commonly the old real actions) became meaningless. Under these circumstances, attorneys seem frequently to have 'laid' cases in London, even if they did not originate there, because process to outlawry was quicker in London. Also, London juries may have been seen as a safeguard against those in the country, which were frequently subject to influence by one party or another. Thus, if we calculated the geographical origins of cases solely on the basis of the marginal venue, there would be a great danger of seriously overestimating the number of actions which arose from London.

In some instances, the styles of the plaintiff and defendant make it possible to tell for certain whether a case 'laid' in London actually arose there. In 1560, for and Suffolk.[43] Given that both areas were hotbeds for lawsuits, what seems most likely is that we are seeing here the consequences of two different, but equally long-established, chains of associations between the lawyers of a region and a particular court. Attorneys were trained by serving as clerks to older practitioners. Thus West Country attorneys traditionally associated with King's Bench, tended to produce even more attorneys who were tied to the same court. In East Anglia, the same process was at work, but the ties were with Common Pleas. Since there was by 1560 little substantive difference in the remedies offered by the two courts, litigation simply tended to follow the lines between the localities and the royal courts which were formed by the lawyers.

Comparing the geographical distribution of litigation in 1560 with that in 1640, the most interesting features are that there was little change in the percentage of cases which came from London, and a slight relative decline in the amount of East Anglian litigation which went into the Common Pleas. During the course of the period, while the population of England grew one and a half times, that of London

---

Notes to Table 4.4 (*cont.*)

example, 17 per cent of all cases in the sample are known to have involved at least one party who lived in London, but in 1606 this figure falls to 9 per cent, a fact that adds some weight to the view that London was becoming relatively less important as a source of central court litigation. However, this still leaves a large number of cases where the venue is given as London but where it is by no means certain that either party lived there. Fortunately, some evidence about London defendants can be derived from the way they were styled in actions of debt based on written obligations. Such a defendant was first said to be 'nuper' London, but this was then followed by a clause which states that he is 'alias dictus' his name, style, and residence as it was given in the written obligation. Thus in many cases the true home of the defendant can be discovered. This still leaves the problem about the residence of the plaintiff. It cannot easily be solved, but it is also clear that he frequently was not a Londoner. Therefore, the percentages given here have been compiled by redistributing those cases 'laid' in London which obviously did not arise there, or where the information in the 'alias dictus' clause suggests that the action originated from another county. The marginal venues are given in round brackets. The corrected venues cannot be regarded as absolutely accurate, but the fact that they generally agree with the figures for the King's Bench, where this technical problem does not arise, lends them credibility. So does common sense.

Sources: Holdsworth, *History of English Law,* v, p. 118. Sir Edward Coke, *The Second Part of the Institutes of the Laws of England* (1797 edn), p. 230. *The Practick Part of the Law,* pp. 10, 12.

quadrupled from some 99,000 to approximately 400,000 people, and its general economic preponderance over the rest of the realm became even more pronounced that it had been before.[44] Given this, the very insignificant increase in the proportion of litigation which came from London suggests that its importance as a source of legal business did not keep pace with its economic supremacy. The explanation is that litigation from areas other than London was flooding into West-minster even faster than the growth of London was generating new suits. Similarly, since the total amount of legal business was growing steadily, the 9 per cent drop in East Anglian litigation over the period does not represent any lapse in the proclivity of people from that part of the country to go to law. Rather it demonstrates that by 1640 the regional distribution of litigation was much more even than it had been eighty years earlier.

An idea of the kinds of disputes which brought litigants to King's Bench and Common Pleas can be derived from an analysis (Table 4.5) of the brief notes given in the warrants of attorney about the forms of action on which cases were being sued. The forms of action were a set of categories which the lawyers used to classify the legal remedies available in particular circumstances; by the mid sixteenth century the great majority of cases fell into one of four principal types – trespass, actions on the case, debt, and ejectment.[45]

According to the writs themselves, actions of trespass involved an alleged breach of the king's peace. In many instances this violence (*vi et armis*) was undoubtedly exaggerated, but actions of trespass did signify disputes in which the plaintiff was claiming that an active wrong had been committed against him. Trespass lay for offences such as chasing cattle, knocking down hedges, breaking a close, and mowing grass, or digging without permission in another man's mine.[46] Such cases often involved long-standing disputes of consid-erable personal or social consequence. They also illustrate the extent to which force and violence still played a large part in men's affairs during the early modern period. For example, wrangles over enclos-ures could result in actions of trespass, and the great chronicler of lawsuits, John Smith of Nibley, frequently mentions how the breaking of closes and forcible entry were commonplace tactics in the numerous property disputes of his master, Lord Berkeley.[47]

In terms of the development of legal doctrine, actions on the case were descendants of actions of trespass, but they were used to claim redress for accidental or intentional wrongs which lacked any implication of deliberate violence. As their name implies, these actions also reflected the fact that since the fourteenth century, in situations where there was no established writ which offered a remedy, the judges had allowed the legal advisors of plaintiffs to formulate a new writ to cover the specific details of the new case.[48] Consequently, actions on the case applied to a wide variety of circumstances, many of which related to business transactions or the activities of people in service trades. In general they can be classified under five headings: negligence, nuisance, fraud, slander, and nonfeasance. A carrier who misplaced or lost the goods he had agreed to carry could be sued on an action on the case. So, too, could a tailor who agreed to make a suit but failed to deliver, or a surgeon who undertook to cure a man but through negligence made him worse. An example of nuisance would be the erection of a house which blocked light from the windows of the one next door. Actions for slander arose from speaking ill of a man in a way which was likely to do him legal or financial damage. Fraud could arise from abuses of legal process, or the use of loaded dice in gambling, and actions on the case also lay for false warranty of goods sold or for selling land without sufficient title.[49] Finally, from the early sixteenth century, the judges held that actions on the case for *assumpsit* should be allowed in order to enable creditors to enforce promises made in the absence of written obligation.[50]

Of all the forms of action, debt appears to be the most straightforward. Basically, it lay in those instances where one man owed another a certain sum of money, However, there were two further factors which influenced the way in which the law of debt had developed. Under most circumstances, unless the plaintiff could show that the obligation in question arose from a written deed under seal, the defendant could answer his plea by waging his law; that is, by the production of oath helpers who were willing to swear that he did not owe the money.[51] Since few prudent businessmen would have wanted their fortunes to be exposed so openly to the possibilities of perjury inherent in these rules, it is not surprising that about 90 per cent of the actions of debt in the Elizabethan and early Stuart plea rolls are lawsuits which were based on written obligations.[52] Furthermore, so-called actions of debt on specialty were a very reliable means of seeking legal remedy. It was difficult for a defendant to deny that he had entered into an obligation which existed in writing, and the common law judges demanded proof, such as a receipt, before they would accept that he had fulfilled it. Hence the scope of written obligations and actions of debt was in practice extended far beyond the recovery of money lent or due for the sale of goods. Thanks to a legal instrument known as the conditional bond, debt could be used to secure many different kinds of obligation. The bond was a written agreement in which one man promised another that if he did not perform some specified act by a specific time, then he would owe instead a certain sum of money as a penalty. The action of debt would then be available to enforce the payment. Bonds of this kind were used to secure the payment of principal and interest on money lent and were therefore intimately involved in the extension of credit. Land sales could be guaranteed by bonds, and so too were all kinds of commercial agreements.[53] They were used to bind partners to arbitration awards, and to ensure, for example, that one party should be allowed to occupy a piece of land 'without trouble, let, vexacion, costs, entry sute, or demand' from another.[54] In short, the usefulness and range of the bond was almost limitless. It was the most significant single legal ligament in early modern society, a fact which is no less true because it has received so little attention from scholars.

Debt, trespass, and actions on the case set the scene for a number of different kinds of dispute situation. However, keeping in mind the importance of agrarian activities in early modern society, it is unfortunate that one of the few points about which they are not very enlightening concerns the percentage of suits in King's Bench and Common Pleas which directly involved questions about the possession of rights to land. During the course of the late fifteenth and early sixteenth centuries, the action of ejectment replaced the older real actions (such as *novel disseisin*) as the principal means of trying title to both freehold and copyhold land, and so we can be certain that all of the cases under that heading in Table 4.5 are definitely about real property.[55] The problem is that it is impossible to tell exactly how far land figures as the primary issue in the total number of actions of trespass, case, and debt. Many, very probably the majority of, actions on the case concerned issues such as slander, nuisance, and misfeasance where title to land or transactions about land were not immediately at issue.[56] Equally, it is obvious that actions of debt between borrowers and lenders or between the merchants, artisans, and traders who made up such a significant proportion of the litigants in the two courts were more likely to be about money and goods than

Table 4.5 *Forms of action in King's Bench and Common Pleas, 1560–1640*

	1560		1606		1640	
	King's Bench	Common Pleas	King's Bench	Common Pleas	King's Bench	Common Pleas
Debt	19% (148)	67% (3013)	46% (3054)	80% (13,206)	80% (6487)	88% (18,150)
Trespass	55% (430)	16% (719)	22% (1461)	6% (991)	5% (406)	3% (619)
Actions on the case	19% (148)	2% (90)	19% (1261)	2% (330)	13% (1054)	5% (1031)
Ejectment	—	1% (45)	8% (531)	2% (330)	2% (162)	1% (206)
Miscellaneous[a]	7% (55)	14% (630)	5% (332)	10% (1651)	—	3% (619)
Total	100% (781)	100% (4497)	100% (6639)	100% (16,508)	100% (8109)	100% (20,625)

[a] Includes, among others, detinue, covenant, waste, and breaches of statutes.

Sources: PRO KB 27/1194, 1395, 1647; CP 40/1187, 1735, 2476. Figures in brackets are estimates of the total number of cases involved from Table 4.1. Common recoveries, collusive actions for the breaking of entails, which accounted for 79, or 9%, of all Common Pleas actions in the 1560 sample, have not been included in these figures. After 25 Eliz., recoveries were no longer recorded in the plea rolls, but were moved to another set of records (PRO CP 43), so they do not figure elsewhere in the table. However, that they made up a significant part of the work of lawyers is indicated by their frequent appearance in the 1560 rolls. From sample recovery rolls in later years (CP 43/3 and CP 43/91), it is clear that these actions continued to be an important source of business.

about property. However, exact percentages can be given in neither case. Thus all that can be said with any assurance is that the actions of ejectment provide a measure of the minimum frequency of disputes about real property. The prevalence of actions such as debt and case is a reminder that not all litigation was about land, but the exact proportion of those actions which involved real property versus those which did not remains uncertain.

If we turn now to the figures in Table 4.5, several general trends are worthy of note. First and foremost, there is the persistent growth in the absolute and relative frequencies of actions of debt. In King's Bench, this must be attributed in part to the evolution of bill procedures which gave the court for the first time competence to hear such cases from counties other than Middlesex.[57] But the general rise of debt, and in particular its increase in Common Pleas, can be traced back at least to the later years of Henry VII. Statistics compiled by Kiralfy show that in 1512 debt accounted for 58 per cent of all Common Pleas business.[58] By 1560, this had grown to 67 per cent, by 1572 to 75 per cent, and by 1640 to 88 per cent. Nor does it appear that the growth of debt can be accounted for solely by a corresponding decline in the other forms of action. Up to 1606 at least, all of the forms of action increased in absolute numbers; debt simply appears to have grown faster than the others. Even after 1606, this was generally the case, but during the early seventeenth century there were also some significant changes in the relationship between the number of cases in the various categories. Debt continued to grow and actions on the case maintained their percentage and absolute numbers. However, there was a decline in both the relative and absolute frequency of actions of trespass (down by some 1493 cases) and actions of ejectment (down by 493). Actions of trespass, it will be remembered, arose from wrongs accompanied by 'a kinde, or at least with a colour of violence',[59] and actions of ejectment concerned titles to land. On the other hand, actions on the case were more likely to arise from business dealings, and actions of debt usually involved written obligations. The real level of violence involved in actions of trespass should not be overemphasized, and some of the decline in ejectment and trespass in King's Bench and Common Pleas may be due to a movement of business away from those jurisdictions to others.[60] Nevertheless, these figures do suggest that the increase in litigation was accompanied by a shift away from business about land and away from incidents where men acted first and then went to law towards disputes which arose either from all sorts of business dealings or from prior agreements which were known to be enforceable at law.

IV

Thanks to the docket rolls and the rolls of warrants of attorney, we can characterize the typical litigant in King's Bench and Common Pleas as a man below the rank of gentleman who was in court because of a debt, probably a debt on a written obligation. The only other court for which comparable evidence about the status and business of litigants is available is the Jacobean Star Chamber, a jurisdiction in many respects quite different from King's Bench and Common Pleas.

In theory, Star Chamber was a criminal court which offered remedies against wrongs accompanied by violence, and it also had an important concern with members of the legal profession who committed offences such as perjury, forgery, or maintenance during the course of their professional activities. In fact, however, even though Star Chamber had no jurisdiction over freehold titles, most of its business since its rise to prominence under Cardinal Wolsey had to do with property both real and moveable.[61] During the Jacobean period, in 80 per cent of all the cases which came before the court formal allegations of violence, fraud, forgery, champerty, etc. ultimately boiled down to disputes about property. What is more, 55 per cent of all actions involved men of the rank of gentleman and above, and in the same percentage of cases there is strong evidence that the parties in Star Chamber suits were already at law in another court. Thus by the early seventeenth century, it is clear that 'Star Chamber litigation was gentleman's business first and foremost', and Star Chamber had also become to a large extent a court whose jurisdiction was being exploited by both plaintiffs and defendants to mount collateral actions designed either to shore up or confound suits that were already in progress elsewhere.[62]

Apart from Star Chamber, King's Bench, and Common Pleas, the other major royal court was of course the High Court of Chancery. Chancery was second only to King's Bench and Common Pleas in volume of litigation. Equally important, it was responsible for administering that branch of English law which has come to be known as equity. The theoretical basis for the equitable jurisdiction was the notion that litigants should be free to petition the lord chancellor when for one reason or another it had been impossible for them to find justice at common law.[63] In practice disputes concerning some kinds of uses, trusts, mortgages, and the specific performance of contracts were all tried in Chancery. Even more common numerically were suits to discover documents or property in instances where the plaintiff was unable to fulfil the technical requirements of common law actions. Another important sphere of Chancery work was a consequence of the chancellor's power to issue injunctions which could control the behavior of individuals,[64] and in addition the court could on occasion offer relief against the very stringent legal requirement of the conditional bond that nothing less than the complete performance of the obligation should be taken to constitute satisfaction. For example, at common law a man who entered into a bond to pay a penalty of £120 if he defaulted on the repayment of a £60 debt could be made to pay the full penalty even if he was robbed on the way to pay his debt, or if he had been ill and paid it a day late, or if he paid only £59. In these and similar instances where the extremities of law were likely to result in harsh or unreasonable penalties, defendants to bonds could petition the chancellor to issue an injunction to stop proceedings at common law and then give a hearing to the case so that he could consider the special circumstances which, they believed, should in conscience release them from their obligation.[65]

As the use of injunctions to stay proceedings at law on penal bonds illustrates, Chancery cases, like those in Star Chamber, frequently occurred in conjunction with common law actions. On the question of the status of litigants, we can only speculate. Uses and trusts were frequently associated with large landed estates, so it is logical to expect that richer men were usually involved in cases where they were at issue. On the other hand, anyone, whether rich or poor, might, as a result of bad luck or an unreasonable creditor, end up in a situation where he needed to beg relief for failing to fulfil the conditions of a bond. But two further factors also need to be taken into consideration. Chancery litigation was probably a good deal more expensive than common law litigation, and richer men were more likely than less wealthy ones to be able to afford suits which involved more than one court.[66] All things considered, therefore, the most realistic guess is that a profile of Chancery litigants would look more like that of Star Chamber than that of King's Bench or Common Pleas.

Information about litigants and lawsuits in the remaining courts at Westminster and about those in the country is fragmentary, but worth trying to piece together. In almost all of them, both on the national and local level, jurisdiction was dependent on some special characteristic of one of the litigants. The court of Wards, for example, entertained all types of action, but one of the parties had to be a royal ward. The court of Requests was an equitable jurisdiction which in theory at least was only supposed to hear the pleas of poor men.[67] The Exchequer had both an equitable and a common law jurisdiction (which mirrored those of Chancery on the one hand and the common law courts on the other) but its scope was limited to causes in which one party could claim in some way to be a debtor of the king.[68]

Moving beyond London to the palatinates of Durham and Chester and the Duchy of Lancaster, we find again, as in the royal Exchequer, the existence of both equitable and common law jurisdictions. Thus the range of remedies available within the palatinates and duchy was the same as in London, but, of course, they could only be offered in those disputes which fell within the territorial boundaries which defined the competence of the courts.[69] In the same way, the geographical element was also important for the regional councils in the north and in Wales, but the specific powers of these tribunals were laid down, not by customary institutional practice, but by the instructions issued by the crown to the respective lord presidents on the occasion of their appointment. These instructions varied over time and they were subject to particularly great adjustments in the early 1600s as a result of challenges made to the conciliar jurisdictions by the common law judges.[70] But, in general, the councils enjoyed competence over criminal as well as civil matters, and their authority in civil disputes reflected features typical of both common law and equitable jurisdictions. They could not try title to land, but, like the Chancery at Westminster, they could hear actions touching property where there was an equitable issue involved, and they also heard common-law-type cases such as debt, detinue, and trespass.[71]

Finally, if we magnify the jurisdictional map even more intensely, we come to the borough and manorial courts. In the former, at least one litigant had to be a resident of the town where the court was held;[72] in the latter, both had to be tenants of the manor. In most towns, royal charters or custom established an upper limit on the amount of money in dispute before the case had to be taken to

Westminster; the exact sum varied from place to place but was usually somewhere within the range of £10 to £40.[73] In manorial courts a maximum jurisdictional limit of 40s. was enforced by a statute passed in 1278.[74] Both types of court offered remedies in debt and trespass, and most authorities agree that these local tribunals were far in advance of the royal courts in hearing actions involving misfeasance and nonfeasance, including the enforcement of verbal agreements.

This survey of the lesser royal and provincial tribunals provides only the most general insights into the types of litigants who could be found in them.[75] Given the nature of its business, Wards was probably patronized mainly by the gentry, but it is hardly worth speculating about the other Westminster courts.[76] For those outside London, it would seem reasonable to propose that the more circumscribed the jurisdiction, the larger the proportion of less wealthy litigants among its clientele. Poor men with small causes would be less willing to go to London than richer men with larger causes. The Council in the North, for example, was originally intended as an aid to the poor, and in 1609 its jurisdiction was limited to actions involving less than £40.[77] At the same time, since richer social groups such as the gentry were a relatively small proportion of the population, it is logical to expect that they would appear more often in courts with a wide catchment area than in those with a smaller one. On the basis of this kind of reasoning, it is likely that courts such as those of the Councils in the North and Wales had a lower percentage of gentry litigants than King's Bench and Common Pleas, and this was certainly the case in town courts and manorial courts.[78]

Fortunately, information about the nature of litigation in these courts is better than that about litigants who brought it into them. There was a wide range of business in courts such as Wards or Requests, but in every jurisdiction for which there is detailed information – Wards, the Exchequer of Pleas, Council in Wales, and manorial and borough courts[79] – it is apparent that, as in King's Bench and Common Pleas, debt was paramount. It is clear that actions of debt, and the ubiquity of written obligations in particular, will be a major consideration in any conclusions about the causes and significance of the increase in ligitation.

5

THE CAUSES OF THE INCREASE IN LITIGATION

I

By 1600, the enormous increase in litigation which had taken place since the 1550s began to produce concern amongst observers, both inside and outside the legal profession, that there were too many lawsuits. In the space of a mere half-century England seemed to have become an extremely litigious country.[1]

Exactly how litigious early modern society was can be gauged only by making comparisons with other periods. We know already that for two hundred years before 1550 litigation in the central courts was much lower than it was to become by 1550.[2] Going even further back into the past, during the twelfth and thirteenth centuries, much legal work may have been done in local courts, but simple comparisons of the bulk of the plea rolls leave little doubt that central court business was nowhere near the level it was to reach under Elizabeth.[3] For the period after 1640 and on into the eighteenth century, there is as yet no statistical evidence of sufficient quality on which to build a confident picture of trends in litigation. Cockburn's counts of cases heard by justices of assize remain high until the late 1660s and early 1670s, when a quite precipitous fall-off begins, which lasted well into the eighteenth century.[4] But, since cases at assize were by definition cases nearing completion, such figures may not be a reliable guide to the number of causes commenced. Statements made by court officials to parliamentary inquiries give the quite contrary impression that litigation was still buoyant in the 1720s.[5] On the other hand, literary evidence and studies of the legal profession suggest that by the middle of the eighteenth century the expense of going to law in the royal courts and changes in the attitudes of attorneys towards litigious business may have led to a decline in the number of suits generally, but in particular to a decline in the number which went

to Westminster.[6] Moreover, investigations into the volume of court
business just before the major Victorian law reforms, which were
reported in 1829 by the Parliamentary Committee on Courts of
Justice, indicate quite clearly that there was at some stage a general
falling off in central court litigation between 1660 and the early
nineteenth century.

According to the Committee, between 1823 and 1827 an average
of 72,224 actions were commenced in King's Bench and Common
Pleas each year.[7] By comparison, in 1606 the same two courts
handled a combined total of about 23,000 cases which had reached
the point where both parties had come into court or at which the
plaintiff was about to outlaw the defendant for failing to appear.
Thus, if the threefold increase in population between 1606 and the
1820s is allowed for, the raw statistics suggest that the rate of
litigation was about the same during each of the two periods.[8]
However, suits commenced and suits in advanced stages are not
exactly comparable. In any age, including our own, many more suits
are commenced than ever reach the stage at which both parties are
about to appear in court.[9] The problem is, of course, that we have
no precise way of knowing the exact number of suits commenced in
the early modern courts. But figures for the number of original writs
sued out in Chancery between 1569 and 1584, which were compiled
by a contemporary, suggest that twice as many suits may have been
commenced as reached advanced stages in the Common Pleas.[10] If
this factor of two is used as a multiplier for obtaining a minimum
figure of 50,000 for the number of early modern suits commenced
in King's Bench and Common Pleas, then it is evident that there was
very likely more central court litigation per head of population under
Elizabeth and the early Stuarts than there was in the first half of the
reign of Victoria, and this conclusion is supported by what is known
about the volume of litigation in other courts. Perhaps surprisingly,
the number of suits commenced in Chancery, which averaged about
1500 p.a. in the ten years from 1800 to 1809, was much the same
during the two periods.[11] On the other hand, common law actions
started in the Exchequer between 1823 and 1827 averaged 7400 per
annum, undoubtedly many more cases than were entertained by that
court in the early seventeenth century.[12] But against this must be
set the early modern courts such as Star Chamber, the Councils in
the North and Wales, and the palatine jurisdictions of Chester and
Durham, which were either abolished during the civil wars or

gradually atrophied over the course of the late seventeenth and the eighteenth centuries.[13]

However, in both the early modern period and the Victorian era, any conclusions about litigiousness must take into account business entertained by local courts as well as that which came before the central or regional ones. Reports on local jurisdictions collected by the parliamentary commissioners in 1831 show that town courts and surviving manorial courts had begun to atrophy quite severely by the later eighteenth century and were nearly moribund by the 1820s.[14] But, at the same time as this was happening, provincial courts of requests were becoming more common, and, particularly in large cities such as Liverpool, Manchester, and London, they handled many thousands of cases.[15] In 1830, all of these local jurisdictions entertained some 297,422 actions, and, if these are added to the 90,000 cases heard in the central and major regional tribunals at the same date, the overall litigation rate comes to 2767 suits per 100,000 of population in England and Wales.[16]

As the foregoing figures indicate, in 1830 about three-fourths of total litigation took place in local jurisdictions, and the next phase in the history of litigation, that between the late 1840s and the present, was dominated by largely successful attempts to further expand local jurisdictions and make them more accessible to the public. A statute of 1846 laid the foundations of the modern county court system, and from 1867 onwards central court litigation declined considerably as more and more cases came before local tribunals.[17] In general, the total volume of litigation continued to rise so that by 1975 some 2.2 million cases were being heard each year, 1.8 million of which were plaints in the county courts,[18] and this coincided with an increase in the level of court use over what it had been at the time of the parliamentary inquiries. In 1847, the rate of litigation per 100,000 of total population was 3284. In 1913, the equivalent figure was 4235; in 1975, 4537.[19]

Whether these figures reflect periods more or less litigious than the late sixteenth and early seventeenth centuries is difficult to determine with precision since we lack at present anything like accurate global figures for local court business in early modern England.[20] For what it is worth, a very speculative calculation of the rate of litigation in 1606 comes to some 4638 cases per 100,000 of population heard in all local, regional, and national ecclesiastical and civil jurisdictions.[21] This figure suggests a society much more litigious than that of the early

Table 5.1. *Causes commenced in central courts per 100,000 of total population*

1606	=	1351
1823–7	=	653
1975	=	560

Note: The figure for 1606 includes cases in Common Pleas, King's Bench, Chancery, Star Chamber, Wards, Requests, and the equity and common law sides of the Exchequer (total equals 54,075 cases commenced). The figure for 1823–7 includes business in King's Bench, Common Pleas, the Exchequer, and the Court of Great Sessions in Wales (total of 82,932 cases). *Parliamentary Papers* (1829), p. 202. Causes in Chancery have been estimated at 2000 p.a. *Report from Committee... into Chancery* (1811), p. 956. Population in England and Wales in the mid-1820s is taken to be 13 million. The figure for 1975 is arrived at by dividing 280,163 causes heard by the Court of Appeal, Chancery, Queen's Bench, and Family Division of the High Court (excluding probate) by 500. *Judicial Statistics 1975*, pp. 56, 103–4. Readers should note that the figures given in *ibid.*, p. 36, for rates of litigation differ from mine because the former are based on the number of people in the age group 15–64 rather than on total population.

Victorians, but hardly more litigious than our own, and, as a preliminary conclusion, this would seem to make sense. As we shall see, there is every reason to believe that the late-sixteenth-century increase in central court litigation was accompanied by a certain decline in that of the local courts which became more pronounced as the seventeenth century progressed; consequently, early modern court business was probably at its very peak in the last years of Elizabeth. At the same time, it is also true that since the mid nineteenth century actions for personal injury and divorce have brought many ordinary people into contact with the legal system.[22] On the other hand, even allowing for some decline in local jurisdictions, in the earlier period ecclesiastical courts, town courts, and manorial courts were certainly more active than they were to become subsequently. Furthermore, given the ubiquity in Tudor and Stuart times of local jurisdictions which reached down even to the village level, it seems reasonable to postulate that the average person was much more likely to have something to do with a court before 1700 than he was afterwards. What is absolutely certain is that at no time before or since have the central courts in London been more frequently resorted to. As Table 5.1 demonstrates, the number of central court cases commenced per 100,000 of population was nearly

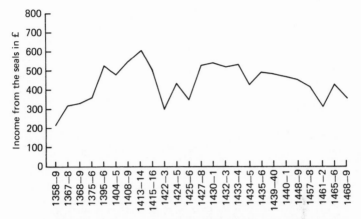

Figure 5.1. Income from the seals of King's Bench and Common
Pleas, 1368–1469. (*Source :* M. Blatcher, *The Court of King's Bench,
1450–1550 : A Study in Self-Help* (1978), Appendix.)

twice as great in 1606 as in 1823–7 and nearly three times greater than
in 1975.

Thus the years between 1560 and 1640 appear to have constituted
one of the most litigious periods in English history, if not the most.
But, paradoxically, this age had been preceded by one in which there
was a serious decline in the amount of business entering King's
Bench and Common Pleas. Any explanation of the sixteenth-century
increase in litigation must, therefore, begin with an account of the
late-fifteenth-century decrease.

II

The level of litigiousness in any society is a consequence of the
confluence of a large number of non-legal as well as legal factors.
Sociologists and lawyers who have studied court usage in recent times
agree that the number of potential disputes in any given society is
likely to increase as population rises and economic relationships
become more complex. But, whether or not such disputes end up as
lawsuits depends on a number of other conditions such as the
attitudes of citizens towards the law, the effectiveness of legal
institutions, the cost of litigation, the nature of the legal profession
and other characteristics of social structure or business practice.[23] So,
too, an explanation of the fall and rise of litigation in England must
consider a number of different variables. Some of these have to do

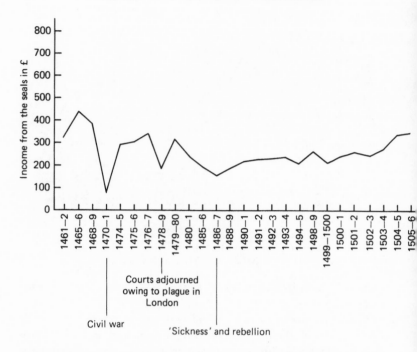

Courts adjourned
owing to plague in
London

Civil war

'Sickness' and rebellion

with broad issues of demographic and social change. Others are concerned with court procedures and with the inter-relationships among various jurisdictions on both the local and national levels.

The earliest known phase of fluctuation in the fortunes of King's Bench and Common Pleas, that between 1358 and 1448 (see Figure 5.1) is relatively easy to explain in terms of the general demographic and economic conditions of late-medieval England. The series of mortality crises associated with the Black Death of the mid and later fourteenth century probably reduced population by at least one-third, or from approximately 4.5 to 3 million people. Subsequent outbreaks of epidemic disease during the first half of the fifteenth century may have cut numbers even further to about 2.5 million, and population stagnation continued until the end of the fifteenth, possibly until the early decades of the sixteenth, century.[24] Because England previously had been seriously overpopulated in comparison with its productive capacities, the immediate consequences of the demographic disaster were in fact a short spell of economic prosperity which lasted through the reign of Richard II and into the early decades of the fifteenth

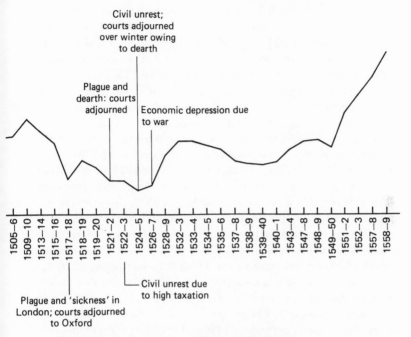

Civil unrest;
courts adjourned
over winter owing
to dearth

Plague and
dearth: courts
adjourned

Economic depression due
to war

Plague and 'sickness' in
London; courts adjourned
to Oxford

Civil unrest due
to high taxation

Figure 5.2. Income from the seals of King's Bench and Common
Pleas, 1461–1558. (*Source:* As Figure 5.1.)

century. However, this golden era did not last for long. From 1410 until at least the middle of the century, agricultural profits fell, towns complained of their poverty, and there was a slump in England's main export industry, the cloth trade.[25] One need not agree completely with the most gloomy assessments of the early fifteenth century to understand why the profits of the seals of King's Bench and Common Pleas fell from a peak of £619 in 1413–14 to £445 for the years 1448–9. Put simply, fewer people doing less business meant fewer suits at law.

However, when we consider the course of litigation during the second half of the fifteenth century, simple explanations begin to seem inadequate. The profits of the seals (Figure 5.2) continued to decline after the accession of Edward IV in 1460 and on into the reign of Henry VII, which began in 1485. A gradual recovery took place in the later years of Henry VII, and there was a quite steep climb at the beginning of the reign of Henry VIII. But the general levels of court business did not again reach those of the early fifteenth century until 1509–10, and soon after that date there were all-time lows in litigation, in 1517–18 and again between 1521 and 1527–8.

One difficulty in the way of a simple account of these developments is that the state of the economy between 1460 and 1525 is debatable. It is generally accepted that the mid fifteenth century experienced a long depression which lasted into the 1460s, but here agreement stops. Older interpretations have depicted the second half of the fifteenth century as a time of slow but gradual recovery from the mid-century slump, and there is indeed some evidence for this, since the figures for the export of cloth double between 1470 and 1510.[26] However, more recent research has cast doubt on this optimistic picture. If population recovered at all before 1520, that recovery was extremely fragile.[27] Furthermore, studies of late-medieval towns suggest that there was a general crisis in the fortunes of even the largest urban communities during the period, a crisis which reached a particularly crucial stage in the 1520s.[28] Nevertheless, all things considered, trends in litigation from the mid-1480s onwards are not incompatible with the sort of economic trends which these contrasting interpretations suggest. The general level of litigation was indeed low during this period, but between 1485 and 1510 the profits of the seals, like the exports of cloths, doubled.

This brings us to the crucial years between 1510 and 1528–9, years in which business in the two benches declined to such an extent that they have often been described as a time of crisis for the common law. However, the sudden drops in litigation during this period can in fact be attributed directly to a series of short-term social and economic crises which in many instances resulted in a loss of business for no other reason than that the courts were frequently forced to close. As a glance at Figure 5.2 will confirm, the rate of litigation in King's Bench and Common Pleas was not impervious to events outside Westminster Hall. For example, in the 1470s and 1480s falls in the profits of the seals frequently coincided either with outbreaks of disease in London or with the advent of civil war.[29] During the first half of the reign of Henry VIII, a remarkable series of such external calamities accounts for the great depression in legal business which is reflected in Blatcher's figures for seal profits.[30] At £309 10s. 7d. these were relatively high in 1515–16, but over the course of the next year, 1517–18, they plummeted to a total of £150 10s. 7d. The reason is that in this year London was hit by an outbreak of 'sickness' so severe that Henry VIII fled his capital for six months and contemporaries estimated that as many as one-third to one-half of the population died.[31] The consequences for legal business are best illustrated by making a term-by-term analysis of the profits from the seals. Michaelmas Term 1517 was adjourned early and so yielded only £12. After Christmas, the plague abated temporarily, and seal income rose to £50 in Hilary Term 1518, a figure not much less than that for the same term one year previous. However, in the spring the pestilence returned, and Easter Term profits fell to £6 3s. 8d. The court sitting for Trinity Term was begun in Oxford, but it was later adjourned back to London, and the seal incomes once again came to a respectable £50.[32] Thus the dramatic overall decline in the seal profits is directly attributable to the complete inaccessibility of the courts for two of the four legal terms.

By the autumn of 1518, conditions had apparently improved sufficiently for men with legal business to return to London. Seal income in 1518–19 rose to £228 7d., and in 1519–20 it came to £200 3s. 7d., although it seems likely that lingering fears about the unhealthiness of the metropolis may have kept business below the level of 1509–10 or even 1515–16. Certainly, in the summer of 1520 Henry VIII was once again deeply concerned about his own safety.[33] In any case, beginning in 1521 the country in general and the courts in particular were hit by another six years of plague, civil unrest, and economic disaster. The chronicler Edward Hall described 1521 as a year 'not without pestilence or dearth of corn'; the courts adjourned early in Michaelmas Term with predictably low returns from seal income.[34] As far as is known, they were open for business as usual over the next three years, from 1522 to 1525, but in 1523 Wolsey's demands for a parliamentary tax of 4s. in the pound were met by resistance and warnings from the king's commissioners for the tax that the country was too poor to pay.[35] Then, in the spring of 1525, attempts to collect the cardinal's unparliamentary Amicable Grant led to widespread protests about poverty in the countryside, general unrest, and open rebellion by 4000 men in Suffolk.[36] Given these conditions, it is not surprising that court business remained low, and further evidence that the nationwide complaints about hard times contained much substance comes from the fact that the courts were adjourned early in Michaelmas Term 1525, because of 'great dearth' over the winter months.[37] In the next year for which there are returns for the seal income, 1526–7, profits were still low, and the explanation, once again, appears to have been economic depression. Trade and the clothing industry had been hard hit by the war with France; in Suffolk cloth workers were again threatening rebellion. Only in 1528–9 does the situation seem to have eased.[38] In this year the seal incomes recovered significantly, and from this time onwards legal business in King's Bench and Common Pleas began that gradual rise which led eventually to the tremendous burst in litigation under Queen Elizabeth.

Thus the great trough in common law business between 1517 and 1528 must be seen as an aberration in which a series of short-term causes temporarily interrupted the fragile rise in business which began in the 1480s and continued with some set-backs after 1530. In sum, although the economic evidence is hardly satisfactory, there is reason to believe that the general trends in litigation over the course of the fifteenth and early sixteenth centuries were determined primarily by underlying demographic, economic, and social conditions.

III

It must be acknowledged at once that this explanation of changes in the volume of litigation over the late fifteenth and early sixteenth centuries contrasts sharply with what has become the orthodox picture of the administration of justice during the period. According to most writers, social and economic interpretations of trends in litigation are unnecessary or irrelevant because the fifteenth-century decline of King's Bench and Common Pleas was a consequence of nothing more than their own shortcomings, a symptom of their failure to administer justice effectively.[39] The inflexibility of the common law courts on points of substantive law severely limited the scope of the remedies they were able to offer within the context of a 'changing' society.[40] Furthermore, they failed in the most basic task of any legal tribunal: they were incapable of getting defendants to come into court to answer the complaints of plaintiffs. Partly this was a reflection of the proclivity of the courts to pay more attention to procedural paperwork than to taking effective action and to the ease with which outlawed litigants could gain royal pardons and so escape the most severe sanctions the legal system could impose. Partly it was due to breakdowns in law and order which arose from the incompetence of kings and the potential for disruption inherent in the magnate affinities associated with bastard feudalism. But, as much as anything else, it reflected the dependence of royal justice on the willingness of sheriffs in the localities to perform the essential tasks of delivering writs, making arrests, and selecting impartial juries. Unpaid members of the landed gentry who usually served for only a year, sheriffs were subject both to real impediments in the way of performing their duties and to temptations to abuse the office in the interests of kin or friends rather than the king's justice. In the opinion of Blatcher, for example, this combination of procedural weakness and official corruption had by the end of the fifteenth century severely crippled the common law courts. Her studies of the King's Bench records indicate that only about 19 per cent of defendants summonsed actually bothered to appear. Given this, it is hardly surprising that the business of the benches declined; no sensible person would have used them if there was the remotest possibility of finding a remedy elsewhere. Consequently there was a movement away from these jurisdictions towards those which were beginning to prove themselves more effective, namely Chancery and Star Chamber.[41] By 1530, the old common law jurisdictions were gravely in need of reform. Only after making a series of procedural innovations, and only after changes had taken place in the attitudes and behaviour of the gentry and nobility, would King's Bench and Common Pleas again manage to attract business back into court.[42]

Since it raises so many profound questions, this pessimistic view of legal administration in the late middle ages and early Tudor period must be taken seriously. However, quite apart from the fact that it is based largely on a gross misreading of the causes of the decline in litigation in the 1510s and 1520s, few of the specific arguments involved stand up to close examination.

For example, there does at first sight seem to be a possible connection between the fall in the amount of common law litigation and a rise in the number of proceedings in Chancery. In 1432–43, some 136 petitions were addressed to the lord chancellor each year, but by 1475–85 the number had grown to 533 p.a. Thus litigation in Chancery increased by a factor of five at the very time when that of the common law courts was in decline, and during the remainder of the fifteenth century, while the fortunes of King's Bench and Common Pleas were still on the wane, litigation in Chancery held steady.[43]

Up to a point, this growth in Chancery business was undoubtedly a response to gaps in the remedies available at common law.

Chancery enforced arrangements connected with the enfeoffment to use, a popular device for organizing family settlements, whilst the common law courts remained sceptical about them.[44] Until the mid sixteenth century, only Chancery offered relief to copyholders against manorial lords,[45] and the court also had the advantage of being able to provide litigants with the power to enforce the specific performance of obligations or to oblige opponents to produce documents which might be vital to the determination of a case. The common law of debt demanded the strict observance of the conditions of the penal bond, but the chancellor could consider extenuating circumstances.[46]

Nevertheless, given that all of this is true, it is a severe distortion of historical perspective to see in the development of Chancery either direct competition with the common law or a reflection of any particular failings of King's Bench and Common Pleas. Much of the chancellor's competence to hear causes which alleged riot, forgery, detention of documents,[47] and other perversions of justice was a consequence of the formalization within a single department of a jurisdiction which had long rested in the undifferentiated king's council, and so has nothing whatsoever to do with a shift in business away from the common law.[48] Some of its mercantile litigation sprang from the traditional responsibility of the chancellor to resolve disputes involving aliens; another large chunk is attributable to the use of the close rolls by merchants to register financial deals in such a way as to avoid the laws of usury.[49] A perennially important area of commercial litigation in Chancery involved claims for equitable relief from situations where one party or the other found that they were losing a case at common law. In these instances litigation in Chancery was actually in parallel with actions in King's Bench and Common Pleas.[50] Only in the field of uses was Chancery evolving a novel jurisdiction which directly threatened the older land law administered by the two benches.[51]

Even more to the point, the statistical evidence demonstrates conclusively that the late-fifteenth-century increase in Chancery business hardly compensates for the reduction in that of King's Bench and Common Pleas. We do not know the exact number of suits commenced in the two benches in the mid fifteenth century, but it is possible to produce a perfectly satisfactory conservative estimate by making the following calculation. In 1490, there were approximately 2000 cases p.a. in advanced stages in the two courts. A minimal guess is that this implies that twice that number, or 4000 suits, were being commenced each year.[52] In 1490, the profits of the seals of King's Bench and Common Pleas were £217, or about one-half the average for the decade 1450–60.[53] Therefore, in 1450 the number of suits commenced was probably something in the order of 8000 p.a. Over the same period, the number of suits commenced in Chancery increased to about 570 each year. The numbers speak for themselves; the drop in business in King's Bench and Common Pleas was ten times greater than the increase in the business entertained by Chancery. Furthermore, as was shown above, there is no reason to assume that all of the 570-odd Chancery suits in any one year can be attributed directly to a shift in business away from the common law.

Similar tests can be applied to the relationships among the various royal jurisdictions during the 1520s. Recently, great claims have been made for the importance of Henry VIII's minister, Cardinal Thomas Wolsey, as a man who appreciated the shortcomings of the legal system and who tried to use his position as chancellor to make Chancery and Star Chamber instruments for providing better justice.[54] Like other chancellors before him, Wolsey proclaimed his intention of making the equal administration of justice to rich and poor alike one of his primary objectives.[55] What made him different was a willingness to direct snide remarks at the common law and an apparently active policy of promoting litigation in the jurisdictions over which he presided.[56] One measure of his success is that the number of cases in Star Chamber rose from about 13 p.a. in the reign of Henry VII to well over 100 each year during Wolsey's tenure as chancellor.[57] However, the impact of Wolsey on the proportions of litigation shared by the various royal courts was relatively slight. It is true that common law litigation reached an absolute nadir in the 1520s, but the fact is that Chancery litigation increased hardly at all under Wolsey. The court averaged 530 petitions during his tenure as compared with 500 in the period 1508–15.[58] Only the 100-odd cases a year which Wolsey drew into Star Chamber can possibly be seen as detracting from common law business, and this number of suits commenced does not account for the fall in suits in advanced stages in King's Bench from 700 in 1510–11 to 100 in 1524, much less for the concurrent decline in Common Pleas business.[59] In short, a deflection of suits away from King's Bench and Common Pleas towards Chancery and Star Chamber cannot account for the drastic changes in their fortunes between 1518 and 1524.[60] Nor is there any strong evidence of a struggle between advocates of the progressive methods in equity and the more conservative supporters of the common law. Common lawyers worked in both types of court.[61] Some practitioners had doubts about Chancery procedures; some conservatives in the 1520s (as was the case throughout the period covered by this book) were worried about the dire consequences if chancellors too readily relaxed obligations imposed by the conditional bond; some may have thought that Wolsey had pushed conciliar justice too far. But no one in the legal profession appears seriously to have doubted that the two sets of jurisdiction should continue to exist.[62] Finally, it is worth remembering that the recovery of common law litigation after 1530 was accompanied, not by a corresponding decline in Chancery business, but by a further, large, increase in it.

At the same time, just as it is dangerous to overstress the lack of competitiveness of King's Bench and Common Pleas, so, too, is it mistaken to exaggerate the significance of procedural innovations in helping them to improve. The two most celebrated procedural developments of the early Tudor period were the emergence of procedure by bill of Middlesex and *latitat* in the King's Bench, and the further refinement of the action of *assumpsit* so that it could be used to provide remedies for breaches of parole agreements. The principal advantage offered by bill procedure was that it enabled a plaintiff to initiate an action in King's Bench without having to sue out and pay for an original writ in Chancery. Potentially, this saved expense, and in addition the first writ issued in connection with suits by bill called for the sheriff to arrest the defendant and see that he entered bail.[63] The importance of *assumpsit* was that it relaxed the strict common law requirements for written evidence of agreements between parties, and it also offered the prospect of getting a defendant to pay damages for the loss he caused the plaintiff by failing to fulfil his promise.[64]

Together, these two innovations have always been seen by legal historians as the crucial elements which rejuvenated the medieval common law and enabled it to compete in the early modern world. There is no doubting their long-term importance. *Assumpsit* forms the basis of the modern law of contract.[65] Procedures by bill of the sort pioneered by King's Bench became commonplace in both benches by the later seventeenth century.[66] Nevertheless, their impact on court usage has been seriously exaggerated. The statistics on the frequency of the forms of action demonstrate conclusively that, at the very time when it was just becoming available, actions of *assumpsit* for debt amounted to a trickle compared with the enormous flood of actions based on written obligations, and in fact the percentage of the latter increased further over the course of the sixteenth and seventeenth centuries.[67] Equally, although procedure by bill may have been cheaper (at least in the middle of the sixteenth century) than procedure by original writ, it is hard to see why it should have been any more effective in forcing defendants to appear. Both types of procedure depended ultimately on the willingness of sheriffs to execute writs.[68] In any case, it is obvious that after 1550 business in Common Pleas, which offered no new procedures in the sixteenth century, grew very nearly as fast as that in King's Bench, and, contrary to textbook generalizations, the level of litigation in King's Bench never in this period exceeded that of its sister court. One reason for this is the surprisingly mundane fact that there were always more attorneys attached to Common Pleas than to King's Bench, and attorneys were the means by which suits came to court. But, more generally, although the cheapness and convenience of the new procedures undoubtedly helped King's Bench to poach some business from Common Pleas, the relative advantages offered by bill and *latitat* were less great than has usually been assumed, in an age when inflationary pressures lowered the real costs of litigation anyway.[69]

Procedure by bill and *assumpsit* were perhaps the most important technical developments of the early and mid sixteenth century, but they were not the only ones which had some effect on litigation. For instance, between 1550 and the middle of the reign of Elizabeth, the judges gradually allowed copyholders as well as freeholders to try the titles to their land in the common law courts by using the action of ejectment.[70] The numbers of such cases were relatively small,[71] but the fact that a common law remedy was now available on matters as important as the possession of land may well have encouraged a new class of men to use the Westminster jurisdictions. More significant, however, was the passage of the statutes of uses and wills.[72] This legislation had two important effects. Enfeoffments to use now came within the cognizance of the common law, and so after 1540 cases involving uses were as likely to be tried by King's Bench and Common Pleas as by Chancery.[73] Furthermore, the new acts apparently created so much confusion and so many complications about the law relating to uses that many later commentators, including Matthew Hale and Sir Francis Bacon, thought the statutes themselves contributed to the increase in litigation.[74]

Insofar as the use had caused real property litigation to drift away from King's Bench and Common Pleas, the statutes clearly helped them to regain business, and another boost came in 1551 when the government of Edward VI once again publicly reiterated the ancient rule that Star Chamber, Chancery, and other conciliar courts should not meddle in disputes which could be settled at common law.[75] Thus by mid-century both the threat (insofar as one had ever existed) that King's Bench and Common Pleas would be by-passed by substantive innovation in other courts, and possible trespasses on their jurisdiction by aggressive chancellors such as Wolsey and Wriothesley, had been successfully thwarted.[76] However, such developments hardly explain the magnitude of the late-sixteenth-century increase in litigation. As we have seen already, the transferral of litigation to Chancery in the late fifteenth century was not as severe as has sometimes been suggested. Moreover, the statute of uses and renewed regulation of the scope of conciliar justice did not lead to a dramatic fall in the business of Star Chamber and Chancery which accounts in some magical way for the rise in that of the common law courts. Litigation increased in all of the Westminster courts during the reign of Elizabeth.

Next, we must consider the potential impact of changes in the values and behaviour of the aristocracy and gentry on the effectiveness and use of the courts. According to one traditional line of interpretation, fifteenth-century noblemen were more likely to settle their disputes by force of arms than by recourse to law, and the bastard feudal affinities which they created were regularly involved in the disruption of legal processes solely for factional or political ends.[77] However, over the course of the sixteenth century a change supposedly took place. Some of the more disruptive features of bastard feudalism subsided.[78] Great magnates were less likely to give money fees to large numbers of retainers other than officials and servants, and complaints about the abuses caused by gangs of retainers were a good deal less noisy than they had been previously.[79] Equally important, humanist writers such as Erasmus and Sir Thomas Elyot began to promote a new ideal of noble *virtu* which de-emphasized the traditional military vocation and chivalric values of the aristocracy. In place of service to the state through the practice of arms, they advocated a nobility under the crown which would serve the realm by acting in a magisterial capacity.[80] A number of historians have agreed that one consequence of these changes in attitude and behaviour over the years between 1500 and 1600 was a growing tendency for the nobility and gentry to replace violence with the resort to law as their principal means of resolving disputes.[81]

In theory such changes in the habits of the élite should have had a profound influence on the effectiveness of the courts. According to Blatcher, almost every ill of fifteenth-century judicial administration can be laid at the door of the sheriff.[82] Sheriffs were recruited from the gentry; if we can postulate a change in gentry mentality towards a greater respect for law and order, then we should be able to postulate better sheriffs and more effective courts. Unfortunately, the facts make such a conclusion easier to assert than to prove. In the first place, the case against the effectiveness of the fifteenth-century courts and against the lawlessness of the fifteenth-century nobility is far from water-tight. The most systematic evidence about the corruption of sheriffs and the weakness of the courts comes from Blatcher's statistics about the failure of defendants to answer the summonses of plaintiffs in the King's Bench, but her analysis completely ignores the crucial fact that it is only to be expected that far more suits should be commenced than ever reach advanced stages.[83] There must have been many instances in which the first writs were meant only to initiate a process of compromise. In the fifteenth century, as in the seventeenth, arbitration was a popular means of resolving conflicts.[84] Some historians would go so far as to deny that the general level of magnate violence and disrespect for law was any higher in the fifteenth century than it was in periods before or afterwards.[85] Late-medieval noblemen are known to have used the common law courts, and it is certainly the case that the magnate affinities characteristic of bastard feudalism existed in the later fourteenth century when the volume of litigation was high.[86] Furthermore, there is no doubt that law and order were threatened in the 1440s and 1450s by the medieval equivalent of gang warfare, but at least one local study shows that this was apparently not incompatible with an increase in litigation.[87] On the other hand, common law litigation continued to decline under the Yorkists and Henry VII, even though these reigns are usually associated with a return to order.

But, no matter what the situation was in the fifteenth century, the crucial point to consider is that many of the most important practical

impediments to the administration of justice remained unreformed
long after the sixteenth-century increase in litigation was well under
way. During the reign of Elizabeth, there were still complaints that
the primary sanction of the common law courts, outlawry, was so
ineffective that people who had been subjected to it did not bother to
sue for pardons from the crown.[88] At the very centre of the system, in
the courts themselves, corruption flourished. The heady Elizabethan
market in legal offices did nothing to improve administrative integrity; even the reputation of the judges was not unblemished.[89] In the
localities, retaining continued into the later sixteenth century. The
practice survived because monarchs needed the military manpower
which magnate affinities could supply, but the potential for disruption
evidently survived too. As late as 1595, Queen Elizabeth was worried
about the adverse effects retaining might have on justices of the
peace.[90] Tudor rule did little to diminish the ability of powerful men
to pervert the course of justice. In a lament which was common in the
Tudor and early Stuart period, one John Stanley of county
Nottingham protested that he could not 'count for his own' that
which had been adjudged by local juries because of the great power
and 'countenance' of his local enemy, Sir Thomas Stanhope.[91] Even
more typical were perpetual complaints and discussions about the
notorious difficulty of finding impartial juries, and instances of the
malpractices and corruptibility of sheriffs and undersheriffs were
truly legion. Queen Elizabeth's close advisor the Earl of Leicester
admitted openly during a Star Chamber trial that he regularly
committed the illegal act of writing to jurors to encourage them to
appear at cases before the justices of assize.[92] Attorneys frequently
found it necessary to chivvy sheriffs to serve writs; on occasion they
were physically intimidated by local officials who were sympathetic
to the cause of a client's opponent. Undersheriffs could be carpeted
if they arrested the friends or political allies of sheriffs, and it was
just as widely recognized amongst the later Tudor and Stuart gentry
as it had been by the Pastons and their correspondents that the
principal advantage of the office of sheriff was the power it gave to
favour one's friends and damage one's enemies.[93]

Last, but hardly least, we are bound to weigh the importance of
changes in the mentality and behaviour of the aristocracy and gentry
against the simple fact that members of this elite were not amongst
the majority of users of the courts. Most litigants at common law were
yeomen, merchants, and artisans, and the increase in litigation was

characterized by a slight broadening in the social spectrum from which the litigants were drawn.[94] We know all too little about the attitudes of these social groups towards the rule of law, but it would be fair to say that they represented those sectors of society which had always been least affected by the ties of bastard feudalism. Their interests and activities, as much as those of the aristocracy and gentry, must figure large in any account of the increase in litigation.

IV

Thus neither technical innovation nor changes in attitudes were primary causes of the massive rise in the number of lawsuits which entered the royal courts from the middle of the sixteenth century. Indeed, although developments such as the evolution of bill procedures in King's Bench were significant, it is not clear that they were necessary pre-conditions for the increase in litigation. One of the more interesting features of the phenomenon was that more and more people were resorting to law even though serious defects remained both in the remedies it offered and in its adminstration. One illustration of this point is the sustained ubiquity of the conditional bond. It was a clumsy instrument for many of the jobs for which it was used; its penalties were enforced with mechanical rigidity by the courts. But in a society where the legal means of enforcing action were weak and where men lived in constant fear of corrupt officials and partial juries, a written agreement which was exceedingly difficult to challenge, and which could bring to bear severe financial penalties (backed ultimately by imprisonment for debt), obviously provided a reasonably safe and sensible aid to doing business.[95] George Norburie summed up the grim reality about the reliability of promises in a society which often harped on the importance of honour when he wrote, 'a man's bond under hand and seale is his oathe, whereby he testifieth before all men'.[96]

And it was business which was ultimately responsible for the upturn in the fortunes of King's Bench and Common Pleas after 1550. Just as the fifteenth- and early-sixteenth-century decline in litigation reflected economic and demographic stagnation, so the gradual growth in litigation after 1530 and its spectacular take-off after 1550 were initiated by a new set of material circumstances. Between 1430 and 1520, the population of England had grown slowly, if at all. However, after 1520 a steady and quite significant increase in numbers began to take place. Between 1520 and 1580, population rose from about 2.4 to approximately 3.5 million, and by the middle of the seventeenth century the figure was closer to 5 million.[97] This change from a level to a growing population dramatically altered the general economic conditions which had prevailed in the fifteenth century. Since there were more mouths to feed, but little overall improvement in productivity, both agricultural profits and the price of land soared. In addition, these demographic pressures on prices were further compounded by repeated debasements of the coinage by English governments up to 1551, and afterwards by the influx into Europe of bullion from South American silver mines. Overall, there was a sevenfold increase in prices between 1500 and 1640, with particularly noticeable jumps between 1540 and 1560 and again between 1570 and 1600.[98] In the agricultural sector of the economy, the cumulative effect of these developments was that for those with enough land to feed themselves and still have some left over for the market, the sixteenth and early seventeenth centuries were a period of unprecedented prosperity. By the later sixteenth century, the number of men who could maintain the life-style of a country gentleman had increased significantly. Slightly lower down the social scale, the yeomen lived more modestly, but benefited as a class more than any other from the profits which accrued from the high prices which the products of their land could bring.[99] Men from both of these social groups had money to spend on relative luxuries such as new houses, tapestries, silver spoons, joined furniture, and feather beds, and they were major participants in the highly fluid Elizabethan land market.[100] Similarly in trade and industry, the sluggishness of the fifteenth century had by the middle of the sixteenth century given way to greater vitality. The export market for cloth, England's principal manufactured product, remained buoyant, and there were advances in the mining and metal industries.[101] In addition, although there was little or no increase in real wages, the growth in population combined with entrepreneurial initiatives gradually created a market for a number of cheap everyday consumables such as pans, pins, stockings, scissors, and caps.[102]

By the early seventeenth century, contemporary observers such as Sir Edward Coke and Sir John Davies were quick to point out the connections between the acceleration of economic activity and the increase in lawsuits. Davies, for example, made his point by analogy. When the citizens of Rome were little more than shepherds and

husbandmen, their laws were simple, but when they became masters
of the world, their laws became more complicated and disputes more
common. So, too, in England as the economy developed, more suits
naturally arose.[103]

There is little doubt that Davies' explanation of the increase in
litigation was essentially correct. The majority of litigants came from
precisely those social groups, the gentry, yeomanry, merchants, and
artisans who were prospering, and the plea rolls bulge with evidence
of their various business activities – suits for unpaid rent on land,
loans taken out by country gents from city scriveners, agreements to
secure possession or title, debts between chapmen in the provinces
and merchants in London, litigation involving men in the west
Midlands metal trades or coal miners from Leicestershire or the
north-east.[104] However, there were also a number of characteristics
within the economic and social structure of the period which helped
to generate a harvest of lawsuits which far outpaced the growth in
national population or wealth. Here the most important points are
that land ownership was not yet concentrated in the hands of a few,
and industrial activity was extremely decentralized. Until the later
seventeenth century, many smallholders participated in the agricultural economy, and, as one recent writer has put it, 'most manu-
facturing activity was still carried out by a multitude of small artisans
and craftsmen'.[105] Since so many people were involved as independent parties, even modest economic prosperity inevitably gave rise
to a large number of transactions, and each transaction was, of course,
a potential lawsuit. This was true of all types of business activity, but
it can be illustrated most clearly through an examination of
arrangements for the provision of credit.

Borrowing and lending were widespread amongst early modern
farmers and traders. Yeomen might borrow to pay for the purchase
of a new piece of land or flock of sheep. Merchants borrowed to pay
for stock; artisans used credit to obtain raw materials. The credit
chains involved in the cloth trade were very far-reaching indeed.[106]
However, whilst the use of borrowed money was common, there were
no centralized credit facilities such as banks and no credit guarantees
equivalent to the modern insurance policy which pays off a loan in
case of default.[107] Borrowed money was usually raised amongst
neighbours or through brokers who knew someone who had money
to lend.[108] Consequently, if large sums were involved, an individual
might find it necessary to borrow from a number of sources in order

to raise capital. Each of these loans would undoubtedly involve a penal bond, and so a default might well result in not one lawsuit, but several.[109] Furthermore, much to the distress of generations of English merchants, debts on bonds were not negotiable; they could not be used by a creditor to pay his own debts.[110] Thus, as the lawyer in the *Discourse upon Usury* put it, creditors had to be strict in enforcing the payment of bonds, because if the debtor broke his day, the creditor might well find himself unable to meet his own obligations.[111]

Inevitably, even though Tudor economic expansion was modest by any absolute standard, such arrangements led to more lawsuits. Yet explaining that there were more potential lawsuits after 1550 than there had been before does not explain why so many of them were coming into the courts in London. In Chapter 3 great stress was put on the importance of local jurisdictions within the sixteenth-century legal landscape. In theory, if legal business was growing, this should have been as manifest in manorial courts or borough courts as in the royal courts at Westminster. But in fact such local jurisdictions failed increasingly as the reign of Elizabeth progressed to absorb their share of the market. Therefore, the increase in litigation in courts such as Common Pleas, King's Bench, and Chancery resulted not only from economic and social change, but from a distinct centralization of the legal life of the realm, a shift from the provinces towards London.

One reflection of this was the relative growth between 1560 and 1640 in the amount of King's Bench and Common Pleas litigation which originated outside London,[112] but more direct evidence comes from the localities themselves. Although the great number and diversity of local jurisdictions make it dangerous to generalize about them, insofar as they have been studied it is clear that the local courts were the one part of the legal system in which the amount of civil litigation was declining rather than increasing. County courts, though not extinct, were very little used. By 1600, many manorial courts had clearly become useless as places for the resolution of civil disputes; more and more their primary function was simply the regulation of agricultural practices.[113] Some borough courts evidently continued to flourish,[114] but by the early seventeenth century it is common to find local jurisdictions of all sorts trying to restrict cases going to London by imposing penalties on tenants or freemen who took disputes about sums of less than 40s. to other tribunals.[115] Furthermore, contemporaries clearly identified the breakdown of

local justice as one of the major causes of the increase in litigation.[116]
A principal response of the central government to the influx of suits
was the passage of statutes which were intended to make it more
difficult to remove cases involving relatively small sums from the
localities. For example, an act of 1591 'to avoide trifling and frivolous
sutes in Law in her Majesties Courtes at *Westminster*' stipulated that
plaintiffs in personal actions worth less than £40 should receive no
more in compensation for their costs than was awarded by the court
in damages; a sister act of the same year prohibited suits from being
transferred from local courts once juries had been sworn.[117] Filazers
in the Common Pleas claimed at one point that the first of these
measures had produced some effect,[118] but in general the repeated
calls of Interregnum law reformers for the re-establishment of more
effective local justice is eloquent testimony to the extent to which it
had declined during the early seventeenth century.[119]

One obvious and important cause of the transferral of legal
business from the provinces to London was simply that sixteenth-
century inflation made virtually meaningless the medieval rule that
only suits involving more than 40s. should be allowed to come before
the central courts. In 1500, 40s. was still a significant amount of
money, but by 1600 when a wage labourer might earn as much as
4s. a week and oxen cost 50s. each, this was much less true.[120] Even
a modest yeoman or husbandman was likely at some time or another
to get involved in a transaction worth more than £2, and as soon as
this happened, he was perfectly entitled to take any litigation which
arose from that transaction to Westminster Hall. Indeed, although
cases entered in the record at 39s. 11d., but which almost certainly
represented larger sums, are not unknown,[121] if a man lived in a rural
area he had little choice but to go to Westminster for larger amounts,
because manorial courts were empowered only to hear suits up to
the value of 40s.[122] On the other hand, in towns, borough charters
frequently allowed local courts of pleas to hear cases well in excess
of 40s. (frequently as much as £40).[123] But these tribunals appear to
have been only marginally more successful in holding onto business
than those of manors, and so it would appear that there were a
number of other solvents quite apart from inflation which were eating
away at the authority of all types of communal jurisdiction.

First, in an economy where wool from Suffolk might be made into
cloth in Wiltshire, where coal from Newcastle came south by sea to
London, where cheese and dairy products from Warwickshire went

down-river to Bristol, the services of courts restricted to narrow geographical limits were bound to be less satisfactory in a large number of instances than those whose authority stretched throughout the realm. Such 'national' litigation made up a large proportion of the work of the common law courts in 1560, and it continued to do so right up to 1640. Second, those geographical areas, the so-called wood/pasture regions, which for a number of reasons saw the greatest development in the cloth, metal, and other rural industries during this period, were also areas where manorial structures were, and always had been, weak. Woodlanders had a reputation for lawlessness. More to the point, they lived in regions which supported large populations and, very often, a great deal of commercial activity, but which had no legal institutions to which disputes might be referred other than the royal courts in London.[124] The legal consequences of this combination of economic vitality within a jurisdictional vacuum is best briefly illustrated by the fact that ten out of eighteen common law attorneys active in early-seventeenth-century Warwickshire had located themselves along an eighteen-mile axis stretching between the towns of Coventry and Birmingham.[125] In other words, they had placed themselves strategically in the heart of the forest of Arden, an area of rising population in which thriving metal and tanning trades existed side by side with commercial agriculture, but where local jurisdictional ties were virtually non-existent.[126] Hence any legal business which might arise inevitably went to London.

Thirdly, even in those areas where manorial structures had traditionally been strong, there were now new obstacles in the way of their serving as effective agencies for resolving disputes. The dissolution of the monasteries after 1536 resulted in the fragmentation of estates which had formerly comprised about one-third of the land in England. On the whole, the monks appear to have administered their manors as effective juridical units, but when they were re-sold the lands were fragmented into hundreds of much smaller parcels.[127] For the most part, these were bought up piecemeal by prosperous gentry and yeomen who were gradually building up estates which might contain land having tenurial connections with a number of different manors.[128] Under these conditions, it was simply statistically less likely that any one dispute might involve two men who owed suit to the same court than had once been the case, and they would have had little alternative but to resort to the royal courts in London.

Fourth, although we know all too little about urban jurisdictions, it seems likely that town courts were undermined by two concurrent developments. On the one hand, the urban scene was transformed during the late-medieval and early modern period by the movement of much of England's industrial activity away from towns and into the countryside. Thus by the later sixteenth century, town jurisdictions were simply outside the nexus of much of the most important business activity in the realm.[129] On the other hand, the trends towards oligarchy and political paranoia which were so typical of early modern town governments did nothing to sustain the usefulness or quality of their legal institutions. In most towns, the administration of justice was dominated by the mayor, the recorder, and the town clerk, all of whom were answerable only to the town councillors and aldermen. As town governments became more restrictive in their memberships, two things frequently happened. The mass of townsmen who were excluded from the council often became deeply suspicious and critical of the oligarchs.[130] At the same time there is ample evidence that local court officials, all too free of any responsibility to the community, sometimes perverted the course of justice offered in their courts in the interests of themselves or their friends.[131] Given these conditions, a potential litigant might well prefer to take his chances in London than to submit to the evil he knew all too well at home. Although judges in the royal courts sometimes displayed favouritism, and although some clerical officials were hardly corruption-proof, courts such as King's Bench, Chancery, and Common Pleas did offer a country plaintiff the benefit of the king's writ, a long-established tradition of record keeping, and a relative anonymity which might at least reduce the number of enemies he would have to overcome in the pursuit of justice. All of these points were brought out in a debate during the 1614 Parliament on a bill for restricting the flow of suits on small debts into the royal courts in London in which several speakers spelled out their doubts about lesser tribunals. Local court procedures differed. All corporations north of the Trent awarded damages; those south of the Trent did not. Causes in urban small debt courts were often tried before mayors and bailiffs who were tradesmen without any experience of judgment or knowledge of law, and their decisions were liable to be partial. The king's subjects should not be deprived of the benefit of the law administered by the courts at Westminster.[132]

Finally, the greatest single weakness of all local jurisdictions was that their proceedings were subject ultimately to review by the

central courts. As is clear from the statutes which aimed to control
the abuse, there was little to prevent a defendant from transferring
a case from a town court to London in order to delay proceedings
or because he felt that he might get a better decision there.[133] Faced
with the prospect that it might never reach a conclusion, it was hardly
worth while for a plaintiff to launch his action in the lesser jurisdiction
in the first place.[134] Furthermore, it was as likely as not that his legal
advisors would in any case be encouraging him to go to London, for
the legal profession certainly did more to undermine than to support
the continued existence of vital local courts. Late-sixteenth-century
legal thought tended to emphasize the subordination of local customs,
jurisdictions, and rights to reason as interpreted by the judges or the
interests of the commonwealth.[135] The judges did little to stop the
influx of cases from local tribunals, and in many instances tried
actively to control and limit their powers. Legal writers such as John
Kitchin were unhappy about the unsystematic nature of local
jurisdictions, and members of the London profession were also
contemptuous of local officials.[136] Sir Matthew Hale thought that
litigation flowed towards Westminster because 'inferior courts were
so ill served, and Justice there so ill adminstered', that people could
hardly be blamed for seeking remedies elsewhere.[137] For Sir Edward
Coke, the desire to systematize and centralize lay at the heart of
attacks on conciliar jurisdictions in the north and Wales during the
first decade of the seventeenth century and formed the basis of a
number of decisions written up in *The Reports* which, according to
Lord Chancellor Ellesmere, dangerously diminished the authority of
local courts.[138]

Many attorneys and clerical officials may well have shared these
doubts about the nature and quality of provincial jurisdictions, but
in general their attitudes were more likely influenced simply by the
mundane consideration of whether or not they were permitted to
practise before a particular court. All local tribunals put quite tight
limits on the number of lawyers who were allowed to work in them.
Thus, particularly after the expansion of the Westminster profession
in the second half of the reign of Elizabeth,[139] any would-be litigant
seeking legal advice was much more likely to run into a practitioner
who was more interested in having him sue in London than in the
localities. The potential significance of this situation was epitomized
by the publication in 1627 of *The Attornies Almanacke*, a work which

consisted of nothing more than a list of writs for transferring cases from borough courts all over the country to the royal courts in Westminster Hall.[140]

V

To sum up, there were by the later sixteenth century a number of economic, social, and judicial factors which were creating more potential lawsuits and attracting those which did materialize away from the provinces towards London. Nevertheless, however important these circumstances were, the fact is that litigation would not have become so popular, or shifted in the direction it did, if it had not at the same time come within the reach of a wider proportion of the population. Throughout the middle ages, social critics harped on the costliness of English justice, and it is still a present-day historical commonplace that going to law in the sixteenth and seventeenth centuries was exorbitantly expensive.[141] Therefore, it cannot be emphasized too strongly that by 1560 litigation at common law was not prohibitively expensive, and that the cost of litigation actually declined steadily relative to prices over the next eighty years.[142] One of the reasons why this period was so litigious was simply that a desirable service was for a while quite within the financial reach of a large number of customers.

The total cost of a lawsuit was determined by the expense incurred in each of the procedural stages it went through before being decided upon. In King's Bench and Common Pleas, these can be divided into three: the initiation; the mesne process which got both parties into court; and the trial and decision at *nisi prius* in the country.[143] At each stage the procedures were determined by writs purchased from court officials. The cost of writs varied, but most of them could be bought for less than 5s. The money spent on these plus the expense of making pleadings and consulting barristers together with the fees of the attorney constituted the total cost of a suit. Naturally, these charges varied according to the length of time the suit took, the form of action involved, and the difficulty of getting the defendant to answer the summonses to appear. For these reasons, it is difficult to make estimates of the expense of hypothetical cases. Nevertheless, the effort is worth while, because such estimates give some idea of the cost of individual items, and they also provide benchmarks which can be compared to real costs as reflected in surviving bills of charges.

For example, on a suit for £100 in Common Pleas, the first action of the plaintiff's attorney would have been to take out an original writ from Chancery (the *precipe*), which allowed the Common Pleas to hear the case, and which also provided the initial summons for the defendant to answer. In cases over £40, the king took a fine, or tax, on the original writ, which for a £100 debt would come to 10s. The seal of the original plus the cost of processing it would add another 13d. to the cost, thus giving a total of 11s. 1d. for the initiation of the suit.[144] But there was no guarantee that the defendant would appear after the first summons. Hence, further process was required. If the defendant was a freeholder or had a considerable estate, his goods and chattels could be progressively distrained (taken into custody) by the sheriff until he answered. If he was poor, or the plaintiff wanted quicker action, the defendant could be arrested under warrant of writ of *capias*. Both of these groups of writs were obtained in the offices of the filazers of Common Pleas, and they cost in the early seventeenth century between 4d. and 6d. No matter whether the process used was distraint or arrest, the defendant could delay for some time, so three or four such writs might be necessary. So in order to force the defendant to appear, we should add another 18d. to our bill.[145]

Once the defendant was in court, there were fees for making pleadings and having them entered into the plea rolls. For drawing a declaration twenty sheets long, the prothonotaries were due, at the rate of the late 1620s, 19s. To enter it on the roll would cost £1 3s. 9d.[146] The case is now ready to go to *nisi prius*, and the costs thus far are £3 5s. 7d. *Nisi prius* was probably the most expensive part of any case. The fees for calling the jury, putting the record in at assizes, and the extra charges for the attorney amounted to about £2 2s., and another pound, or even two, might be necessary to pay for counsellors at law.[147] Assuming a decision was reached, another couple of shillings might be necessary to get it executed. Then the attorney would have to be paid for five terms' work at 3s. 4d. per term, which totals 17s. 1d. All in all the total cost of the case amounts to £7 2s. 8d., but this might be reduced by as much as a pound if the declaration, which was a formality, was cut down to ten sheets. On the other hand, other small expenses might have to be added if there were complications or delays, so, in order to allow for variations, we might say that a suit for £100 in Common Pleas would cost between six and eight pounds.

In the King's Bench the procedure was slightly different, but the costs of our hypothetical suit would be much the same. The first process in King's Bench was the writ of *latitat*, which cost 5s 1d., and on top of this a fine was due to the king of 5s. for a £100 debt, so that the total cost of starting the suit was about the same, although in the King's Bench the fine on the amount sought did not have to be paid until the issue was joined between the parties.[148] This was an advantage, because it meant that a man could initiate a suit, hoping to get the defendant to compromise before going to trial, for as little as 7s. or 10s.

Thus, from beginning to end, suits in debt for £100 cost between six and eight pounds. The cost of suits for more or less than this amount would depend primarily on the fine paid for the original writ. Since in our hypothetical suit, the fine on the original amounted to only one-fourteenth of the total cost of the suit, it is evident that suits for larger amounts were in a sense better value than suits for smaller amounts; on the other hand, the fine on the original diminished almost to insignificance where the amount sought was less than £40.[149] In actions other than debt – trespass, actions on the case, for example – common law costs were, if anything, less than those outlined in the hypothetical case.[150]

By comparison with that in King's Bench and Common Pleas, litigation was more expensive in courts such as Chancery, where the procedure was by bill and answer and where evidence was collected in written depositions taken in the country by commissioners appointed by the court to question witnesses.[151] Individual writs were not particularly costly; for example, the subpoena which initiated Chancery actions ran to no more than 2s. 6d., and the attachment of the defendant could be obtained for as little as 2s. 10d.[152] However, other features of Chancery procedure led to relatively high charges. Even to initiate a suit, the plaintiff had to pay for a bill to be drawn which would lay out his case against the defendant. This had to be done by a barrister or serjeant at law whose minimum fee was 10s.[153] Then the bill was engrossed and one or more copies made, a process which for a relatively short bill of twenty sheets would add another 10s. Therefore, the minimum cost for summonsing a defendant was something in the region of £3 2s. 4d. But, if the defendant was recalcitrant and the Chancery version of outlawry, a commission of rebellion, had to be issued in order to get him to appear, the figure rose to £4 6d.[154]

Once both parties had come into court, costs continued to mount. If the case advanced, commissioners were appointed to take evidence in the country. The basic charge for the commission itself was 7s. 10d., but this did not include any estimate of the charges for engrossing and making copies of the lengthy documents which contained the answers of witnesses.[155] But the real key to the expense of Chancery litigation were the fees which had to be laid out for legal advisors. Most litigants in Chancery needed a solicitor to handle the business for them as well as the services of someone in the six clerks' office to act as the attorney.[156] This meant that each term the case ran involved the payment of 3s. 4d. for an attorney from the six clerks' office plus a further 6s. 8d. for the solicitor.[157] In addition, barristers or serjeants were likely to be needed much more often than in common law cases. Counsel might be required to draw up further arguments on the original bill, the replications, and rejoinders. They were also called upon frequently to make motions in court, that is to raise particular points of law which might help to advance their client's cause.[158] Whenever a barrister appeared, the minimum charge was 10s. But by the early seventeenth century, these fees were beginning to rise,[159] and just after the Restoration, Roger North noted that whilst fees of one guinea (21s.) were the 'gage' of his practice, he often took five guineas for the 'better sort of causes' and two or three 'in ordinary ones'.[160] The extreme variability in the extent to which counsel might be employed and in the actual rates at which they were paid makes it difficult to estimate any total cost for Chancery suits, but they were certainly much more expensive both to maintain and to initiate than those at common law. We have it from no less an authority than James I's lord keeper, Bishop John Williams, that poor men praised the common law because they were 'not able to reach up unto the price of Equity'.[161]

That the range of costs at common law and in the Chancery corresponded to those estimated for hypothetical suits is confirmed by the bills of charges for litigation which have survived from the late sixteenth and early seventeenth centuries. Most miscellaneous bills are inadequate for finding the total costs of suits, because, usually, they contain information about only a single or, at best, two terms' work. However, what they do show is that charges for individual bits of procedure followed very closely the official rates which were laid down in the guidebooks for practitioners or in the presentments made to the royal commissions on fees.[162] Furthermore, this picture corresponds closely to that which emerges from a study of the account books of lawyers such as Christopher Mickleton of Durham or the Hitchin attorney George Draper, who carefully recorded the charges they made to clients for business conducted on their behalf.[163] For example, Draper's book contains the complete accounts for hundreds of cases dating from the late 1660s to the reign of William and Mary. Very few of the common law suits he handled cost much more than £5 and almost none more than £10. An action of ejectment for a local gentleman, Thomas Docwra, which went through to judgment was charged at £5 18s. 7d. Charges for suing fines (even on fairly valuable land) averaged about £5. A case for the widowed Lady Spencer for a debt of almost £200 in which the defendant was outlawed cost £2 7s. 10d. Simon Meriot of Badby, Northants. was charged £7 19s. for a Common Pleas case which was tried at assizes. Grace Oliver had to pay £8 12s. 10d. for a complete action of ejectment. John Fitzjohn's case, which ended at assizes, cost £8 9s. 7d., £1 11s. of which went to his counsellors at law. Draper's book also records many cases which were initiated, carried for two or three terms, and then terminated at a cost of between £1 and £3.[164] Presumably, in most of these instances, starting proceedings was enough to bring the defendant to some kind of settlement out of court.

On the other hand, although they were much less numerous than common law cases, Draper's accounts demonstrate that Chancery work was indeed more expensive than that in King's Bench and Common Pleas. Actions at equity frequently cost £10–£15 and sometimes ran to £20.[165] Charges in other prerogative and conciliar courts are much more difficult to verify either from surviving bills or from account books, but a series of bills which were presented in the Jacobean court of Wards so that the court could determine the amount of costs which should be awarded against the losing party provide useful indications about the level of expenditure which litigation in that tribunal might require. The lowest charge recorded in these sources was £4 10s., but the highest was £66, and a number of the others were in the region of £20–£40.[166]

Although the level of court fees was a crucial factor in determining whether or not an individual with a grievance could afford to go to law, another significant characteristic of the economics of litigation during this period was that attorneys evidently allowed their clients to undertake suits on credit. There is some evidence that court

officials in turn extended credit to the attorneys,[167] but the usual
method of conducting a case seems to have been for the practitioner
to make outlays for writs and other procedural necessities as the suit
ran its course through the courts.[168] Then at the end of each term
he would present a bill to his client. This might be accompanied by
a demand for immediate payment, but, on the other hand, it would
seem that the debt was often left to accumulate. George Draper's case
book illustrates this system well. Many of his accounts due from
clients were not paid off until several years after the case concerned
had been terminated, and, as we shall see in Chapter 11, other
attorneys often had large sums owing to them in the form of unpaid
fees.[169]

This system of suits on credit undoubtedly encouraged litigation,
particularly from the less wealthy. A man could start a suit without
having to pay immediately, and, if he thought he had a good cause,
he might hope not to have to spend anything until the issue had been
decided in his favour and his adversary had been taxed for costs.
However, this method of financing litigation was also a source of
misunderstanding, sharp practice, and loss which could affect attorneys and litigants alike. A client never knew for certain how much
he would have to pay until after writs and process had already been
purchased. Having commenced a suit, he might find himself surprised
by bills for large, perhaps even excessive or fabricated, expenditures
by attorneys.[170] The attempt to control abuses of this kind lay behind
the requirement of the statute 3 Jac. I c. 7 that attorneys present to
clients itemized, written accounts of the money they had spent on
a suit.[171] On the other hand, collecting the sums they spent for clients,
not to mention their own fees, could present difficulties for attorneys.
At worst the result would be a lawsuit, at best a badgering letter. In
1598, for example, William Booth of Witton wrote to Arthur
Gregory that he marvelled 'that a man of yo*ure* wisdome will soe
ove*r*shute hymself to send xx^{li} for a xxiii^{li} dett'. One hundred years
later, it was the prospect of being sued for charges which encouraged
Samuel Pointer to write to George Draper asking him to 'stope the
proceedings at Law. Pray send me the Charge and I will send the
money....'[172]

In general, these studies of legal costs suggest that going to law
in the late sixteenth and early seventeenth centuries was both easy
and relatively inexpensive. This is not to deny that a long Chancery
suit cost a lot of money or that some litigious landed gentlemen, like

Sir Thomas Pelham of Sussex, might spend as much as £100 a year on lawsuits.[173] Rather, the point is that £100 p.a. could satisfy a very heavy appetite for contention, and even large organizations such as urban corporations or All Souls' College, Oxford could meet their needs by making relatively modest expenditures of from £2 to £12 per legal term.[174] Nor, given the scale of their incomes and landed interests, is it at all clear that members of the peerage needed to lay out excessive amounts on litigation, or that it was very often the cause of the downfall of great families.[175] On the other hand, it is also true that for a wage labourer who earned a shilling or less for each day's work, sixteenth- and seventeenth-century royal justice was probably largely out of reach.[176] But, for those members of the population who were slightly better off – for example, a tradesman or husbandman who was worth £20–£50 a year – fees of £6–£8 (which could be paid in arrears) for the recovery of a debt of as much as £100 evidently did not prohibit recourse to law. Moreover, it must be remembered that actions which might result in out-of-court settlements could be commenced for even less. Indeed, our conclusions about the cost of litigation and the large numbers of litigants from less wealthy classes suggest that early modern courts were surprisingly accessible. It is true that contemporaries occasionally complained about high legal costs in the early seventeenth century,[177] but it was in the eighteenth and, especially, the nineteenth centuries that such complaints were accompanied by a movement of clients away from the courts.[178] Even in the twentieth century, seeking remedies for small debts is frequently prohibitive, perhaps more prohibitive than it was in Renaissance England.[179]

VI

Thus far, we have discussed the influx of suits into Westminster Hall between 1550 and 1640 with little regard for chronological divisions within the ninety years. However, as a look at Table 4.1 demonstrates, there were significant differences in the rate of increase between the late sixteenth and the early seventeenth century. Between 1580 and 1606, King's Bench and Commons Pleas business nearly doubled, but between 1606 and 1640 it rose by only 5587 cases, from 23,147 to 28,734. Procedural changes may account for some of this deceleration, but, as in the late fifteenth and early sixteenth centuries, economic and demographic circumstances were also important. In spite of the dislocation caused by harvest failures and high taxation in the 1590s, the early years of James I appear to have been relatively prosperous. But in the later 1610s, the Cockayne project disrupted the cloth trade, and from 1621 to 1625 this plus European war, bad harvests, and a severe outbreak of plague all contributed to a major economic depression.[180] Spot checks of the records of King's Bench show that in 1620–1, some 7544 cases in advanced stages were going through the court, only 905 more than 1606. In the plague year 1625, the number actually fell to some 4125.[181] It is unlikely that court business began to grow again to any very significant extent before the economy made a modest recovery in the mid-1630s.

At the same time, changes in contemporary opinion suggest that it was not just in the matter of numbers of cases that litigiousness may be said to have entered a new phase during the later 1590s and early decades of the seventeenth century. Before roughly 1590, most commentaries on and remedies suggested for the increase in litigation stressed the need to stem the flow of litigation into London by reinforcing local jurisdictions. Afterwards, although this strain of thought continued, two new preoccupations began to emerge – a concern about an increase in the amount of vexatious litigation and worry about what was known as the 'multiplicity of suits'.

The two could be, but were not necessarily, related. Vexatious litigation has been defined nicely 'as the exploitation of legal forms to express aggressive impulses unrelated to the ostensible grounds for action'.[182] The phenomenon was not new to the Elizabethan era. In an agricultural society where ambiguities about title or disputes about common rights could persist for years, even generations, long-standing animosity between neighbours inevitably led to instances where recourse to law was sought on the slightest chance of gain or merely to annoy an old rival.[183] What was new, however, was the extent to which late Elizabethan and early Stuart observers identified an increase in vexatious litigation with an increase in litigation generally. Religious thinkers thought that men were using the law simply to satisfy their covetousness. Social critics pointed to men who engaged in litigation simply as an aggressive pastime, pugnacious gents who seemed to take it for granted that they should spend money on suits at law just as they would spend it on flashy suits of clothes. The lawyer and recorder of London Sir Anthony Benn wondered how the American savages would 'marvayle at vs yf they should hear of vs ... that menn ... cann devoure one another w[i]thout blooding one another' by extortion, usury, and oppressing one another at law.[184]

If vexatious litigation was thought to be a product of human incivility, the potential for the multiplication of suits was built into the very fabric of a legal system which was composed of so many ill-defined and overlapping jurisdictions. Since there were so many courts on both the local and national level which were qualified to hear any one dispute, it was all too easy for any given litigant to try to improve his position by starting actions on the same issue in a number of different courts. Moreover, these possibilities were enlarged by the sixteenth- and seventeenth-century development of Chancery and Star Chamber as courts which could consider all kinds of extenuating circumstances (such as fraud, forgery, etc.) as a possible reason for blocking suits which could otherwise be pursued in a straightforward manner at common law, and by what seems to have been a general inability of the judges to arrive at consistent decisions in different cases about essentially the same kind of issue.

By 1600, the potential for multiplying actions had become a reality to such an extent that leading members of the legal profession such as Lord Chancellor Ellesmere and Sir Francis Bacon were forced to agree that it was no longer possible for litigants to be certain when, if ever, their causes had reached a final conclusion. In his proposals for law reform, Ellesmere listed it as a primary concern to

propound to the Judges how the Incertenty of Iudicature maye be reformed and howe the Infinite multiplicitye of suits maye be avoyded, with which the people are intollerablye reped, and put to excessive charge, as by verditte agaynst verditte, and by Iudgements, and by manifoulde sutes in severall Courtes for one and the selfe same cause.[185]

Likewise, Bacon saw the 'multiplicity of suits as the first consequence of the uncertainty of law which', he said, 'is the principal and most just challenge that is made to the laws of our nation at this time'.[186] Both men would have agreed that to some extent the increase in litigation was nothing more than an optical illusion created, not by more disputes, but by more suits on essentially the same dispute.[187]

There can be no doubting that both Bacon and Ellesmere knew what they were talking about. Barnes' research on the Star Chamber (with which both Bacon and Ellesmere were connected) shows that as much as 55 per cent of that court's business involved suits which were running simultaneously in more than one tribunal.[188] Beyond London, in the countryside, it is easy to find many examples of belligerent litigants. In Yorkshire, a bitter legal feud went on for years between the gentry families of Saville and Wentworth. In Devon, Thomas Roberts, a yeoman farmer, kept a memorandum book in which he carefully recorded the offences committed against him by his neighbours so that he would be supplied with plenty of ammunition if and when he decided to deliver his master blow and take them to court. A Welsh vicar, William Powell, launched twenty-six actions in seven courts in order to further a dispute with one of his parishioners.[189]

Nevertheless, in spite of the wealth of individual examples, neither vexation nor the multiplying of suits was all that significant statistically in comparison with the overall volume of litigation in the central courts. Neither contributed greatly to the most prodigious phases of the influx of suits. By 1600, when complaints about multiplicity were being heard most loudly, the growth in litigation was slowing down, not accelerating. Furthermore, even if, for the sake of argument, we accept that every one of the 300-odd Jacobean Star Chamber cases which were heard each year involved a simultaneous action in another court, they would still constitute little more than a statistical drop in a very large bucket of litigation, and we should also recall that Star Chamber litigants, and to a lesser extent those in Chancery, were usually richer men who could apparently afford to spend money at law. By far the most common types of lawsuits were the thousands of actions of debt in King's Bench and Common Pleas between men below the rank of gentleman, and the less common, but nonetheless significant, actions for trespass and on the case. Some of these suits, particularly those for trespass and case, could undoubtedly arise from petty animosities or pure vexation. The action of trespass could be a cover for aggression, and, amongst actions on the case, lawsuits for slander appear to have become so much of a mania that the judges were forced to narrow the definition of the offence in an effort to prevent even more from flooding in.[190] But it is important to note in this connection that the relative frequency of these types of case was actually declining over the period in comparison with actions of debt, and it is hard to see in actions of debt much evidence of either multiplication or vexation.[191] It is true that the tendency to take out conditional bonds to support other conditional bonds for loans could lead to chains of lawsuits. Equally, the great penalties exacted for defaults undoubtedly made creditors unwilling to relent if a debtor missed his day, and imprisonment for debt could leave the unlucky or the imprudent floundering in the despair and hopelessness which pervade so many squalid contemporary tales of life in the Fleet.[192] Under such circumstances, bitterness between creditor and debtor might easily emerge. Yet, since most debts arose from agreements previously entered into by both parties, and since in most instances the plaintiff was likely to get a fairly straightforward judgment, such cases can hardly be called vexatious, nor did they leave much scope for multiplication.

In conclusion, vexatious litigation and the multiplication of suits are best seen as a species of flotsam and jetsam which floated in on the flood tide of litigation which rushed into London from the country during the second half of the sixteenth century. On the one hand, they were long-standing problems which became much more acute under those very conditions which by the 1580s had made the central courts so frequently resorted to: the wealth of the gentry and yeomanry; the relative cheapness of legal processes; the decline of local institutions; the superabundance of legal advisors. At the same time they were also two of the deleterious effects which arose as a consequence of the inability of the court bureaucracies to adapt successfully to the expansion in business which they experienced. Both were part of a legal and social world where clerical officials competed for business and in which a lord chancellor of England was deprived of his office on a charge of taking bribes. This was the world in which Shylock exploited the conditions of the penal bond to the utmost and informers brought prosecutions for a stake in a share of the fines, in which the seedy and fraudulent characters of the Jacobean stage played cheap tricks with legal technicalities in hopes of a quick and easy profit.[193] In such an atmosphere it is hardly surprising that some litigants found vexatious litigation and the multiplication of suits easy and worthwhile games to play. They may have been a minority of all litigants, but their activities and the conditions which gave rise to them speak volumes about the legal scene during the first half of the seventeenth century.

6

THE INCREASE IN LITIGATION AND THE
LEGAL PROFESSION

I

Not surprisingly, the increase in central court litigation between 1550 and 1640 had a profound impact on the court bureaucracies and on the lawyers who worked within them. For a start, it contributed to a complete transformation in the size and shape of the legal profession. During the later sixteenth century, there was a dramatic rise in the number of practitioners qualified to work within the royal courts. Looking first at the upper branch, we find that admissions to the four inns of court increased steadily from around 50 per annum in the early sixteenth century to a high point of 300 in the later years of King James I, and between 1590 and 1639 as many as 2293 men were called to the bar and hence technically qualified to practise at Westminster.[1] Many of these men may not have become career lawyers, and there are no precise figures for the numbers practising at various dates during the course of the period, but W. R. Prest has calculated that in 1640 there was an active bar which numbered at least 400 people, a figure probably four times greater than that for the size of the upper branch in 1560.[2]

Within the lower branch of the profession, this picture of growth was even more startling. Between the 1590s and the 1620s, the number of underclerks in the offices of the six clerks in Chancery rose from about 60 to as many as 200, and there were similar increases, though on a smaller scale, in the size of the bureaucracies of Wards, Star Chamber, and Requests.[3] However, the increases in the size of the lower branch were most dramatic precisely amongst those groups of practitioners whose primary functions were to link litigants with the courts, the attorneys of the King's Bench and, especially, those of the Common Pleas. As Table 6.1 indicates, the numbers of such practitioners rose from about 250 in 1560 to some 1000 by 1606 and

Table 6.1. *Attorneys in King's Bench and Common Pleas, 1480–1640*

	King's Bench	Common Pleas	Total
1480	—	—	*c.* 180[a]
1560	20	*c.* 180	*c.* 200
1580	*c.* 100	313[b]	*c.* 415
1606	236	*c.* 800	*c.* 1050
1633	342[b]	*c.* 1388[b]	1730
1640	254	*c.* 1500	*c.* 1750
	(Prothonotaries' clerks)		

[a] J. H. Baker, 'The Attorneys and Officers of the Common Law in 1480', *Journal of Legal History*, 1 (1980), 185.
[b] *CSPD Charles I*, xxiv, p. 251.

Table 6.2. *Attorneys in Devonshire, Hertfordshire, and Warwickshire, 1560–1640*

	1560	1580	1606	1625–40
Devonshire	8–10	14	30	56
Hertfordshire	3	5	12	24
Warwickshire	?2	10	18	30
Total	*c.* 15	29	60	110
Norfolk	10–?15	—	36	—
Yorkshire	5–6	12	21	—

Sources: See n. 10, p. 291.

to approximately 1750 in 1640. These lawyers multiplied much faster than population increased over the period, for, whereas in 1560 there had been one attorney for every 20,000 people, in 1606 there was one for every 4000, and in 1640 one for every 2500 people in England. Moreover, since most of these practitioners actually lived in the country, they swelled the ranks of the provincial profession. Table 6.2 shows that there were twice as many attorneys in the counties of Devonshire, Hertfordshire, and Warwickshire in 1580 as there had been in 1560, and there was another fourfold increase in their numbers by 1640. Nor, according to contemporary comment, was this picture an untypical one. In 1608, for example, Lord Eure, the president of the Council in the Marches of Wales, wrote to the privy council to complain about increases in the number of practitioners in the English border counties, and claiming that there were now forty common law attorneys in Shropshire and Gloucestershire and fifty in Worcestershire.[4] Eure's figures may have been slightly exaggerated, but they illustrate an important general point. If attorneys attached to the central courts had been rare in 1560, by the mid seventeenth century they had become a common feature of provincial life.

To a large extent, this increase in the number of attorneys was accompanied by a decline of those semi-professional and amateur lawyers who were described in Chapter 3, and so there was also a significant change in the structure of the profession within the localities.

The most convincing evidence for this change comes from manorial court records, since the survival of series of rolls for individual manors makes it possible to chart accurately changes in stewards over a number of years. These show that by the turn of the sixteenth century, the semi-professionals and court holders active at the beginning of the period had given way to attorneys. For example, in Warwickshire, where there had been twenty-five stewards who were not attorneys in the late sixteenth century, there were only seven such men active during the three decades after 1610, and one of these, William Burgoyne, had been admitted to the Middle Temple in 1591, though he was never called to the bar.[5] Similarly, there is evidence of only five seventeenth-century stewards in Hertfordshire, and only one man in either county, Peter Wyke, who was steward of two Hertfordshire courts, appears likely to have been a genuine court holder.[6] By the time of the civil wars, court keeping was an important business for both common law attorneys and some barristers.

Yet, like most social changes, the transformation of the provincial profession did not occur overnight, nor, while overwhelming, was it complete. In Warwickshire and Hertfordshire by 1615, most local offices were in the hands of attorneys and barristers, and, apart from a handful of stewards, there is not much evidence that other kinds of practitioners were active. But, as we have seen already, in Devon purely provincial practitioners survived in some numbers well into the first half of the seventeenth century. In many places town courts still provided the venue for exclusively local practices, and this was true also of the palatine jurisdictions and the Council in the North. However, although these exceptions are important, there can be little doubt that the profession changed greatly between 1590 and 1640. In Warwickshire and Hertfordshire, and, if we can hazard a guess, in most of southern England, East Anglia, and the Midlands, the attorneys of the common law were by 1640 the largest group of legal practitioners. Over the eighty years between 1560 and 1640, the character of the provincial legal profession changed from one in which few men had connections with the royal courts in London to one in which by far the majority were linked to them. The only part of the country where this was unlikely to have been the case was in the counties of the Northern Assize Circuit, which sent few cases to London, and where the Council in the North provided an active jurisdiction in which local practitioners could pursue their trade.[7]

Several factors were involved in generating these changes in the size and orientation of the lower branch. First and foremost, there was the increase in litigation. Although the question of whether lawyers create lawsuits or lawsuits lawyers is a classic chicken-or-egg dilemma, in England it is clear that the lawsuits came first. Comparisons of the statistics for central court litigation with those for the size of the legal profession show that in the crucial period when litigation actually began to take off, the growth in the number of suits far outstripped the increase in the number of lawyers. Litigation grew by a factor of six between the late fifteenth century and 1580,[8] but the size of the profession no more than doubled, a fact which must be taken to imply that there was pressure from litigants looking for legal services rather than from lawyers chasing clients.

However, this demand from consumers did not remain unfulfilled for long. Those members of the gentry, yeoman, and merchant classes who were prospering in late-sixteenth-century economic conditions were anxious to find honourable and lucrative careers for their sons, and for many of them, the learned professions, particularly ones as potentially profitable as law, seemed to fit the bill. Hence, the sons of the more wealthy families amongst these social groups were sent in ever increasing numbers to the inns of court, and many of them became qualified to practise as barristers.[9] Slightly lower down the social scale, along the borderline between the gentry and yeomanry, or amongst the lesser urban artisans and merchants, fathers sought to find their sons an underclerkship in one of the offices of the courts or to obtain them a position as clerk to a country attorney who was enrolled in the Common Pleas and who could teach the youngster his trade.[10]

The impact of this enlarged pool of recruits into the profession can first be detected between 1580 and about 1600. In these years, litigation in the royal courts doubled, but so too did the size of the lower branch. Furthermore, in the next period, that between 1606 and 1640, the number of attorneys increased by another 70 per cent, but there was at this stage a distinct deceleration of the increase in litigation. In other words, by 1600 the increase in the size of the profession was beginning to outrun the increase in the number of suits, and the relationship between the two can be illustrated vividly by dividing the total number of suits in advanced stages in King's Bench and Common Pleas by the number of common law attorneys in practice at various dates. For 1580, the result comes to twenty-seven cases per man; for 1606 it is twenty-three, and for 1640 it drops to seventeen. What seems to have happened was that the attractiveness of a legal career, to which the increase in litigation had contributed so much, was by 1600 in fact a rather distorted reflection of the actual manpower needs of the legal system. As Nicholas Fuller told the House of Commons in 1610, as 'for lawyers, there is more increase of their numbers lately than of their wealth, save for some favorites, and some few wits among them'.[11]

In the most general terms, then, the London-based legal profession grew because the amount of litigation in the royal courts grew. However, there were several other factors which help to explain in particular why the rise in the number of practitioners connected with the central courts was accompanied by the decline of the court holders and other purely provincial men of law. We saw in Chapter 5 how the legal profession in London had little faith in and actually helped to undermine local jurisdictions. It will come as no surprise, therefore, to discover that there is considerable evidence from the middle of the reign of Elizabeth that the London profession was also hostile to the amateur court holders. The 1581 preface to the most authoritative contemporary guide for the keeping of manorial courts, John Kitchin's *Le Covrt Leet et Covrt Baron,*...stated no less than three times the importance of replacing stewards who were 'servantes à les seignours' and 'ignorant in la lay' by men with greater professional learning, more specifically by those members of the inns of court and chancery to whom the preface was addressed. Kitchin asked how those ignorant of the law could administer it properly and warned of the subversion of justice by the unlearned. At the same time, he praised the inns of chancery men, the professionals, as 'very expert in le common order de ceux courts'.[12]

Albeit more indirectly, the common law judges contributed to this attack on the semi-professionals and amateurs. None of the rules and orders which they issued during the period for the regulation of the profession was directed specifically at court holders, but many of them were intended to prohibit men who had not been admitted to the central courts from handling cases in them. Court orders of 1573, for instance, forbade any attorney of the Common Pleas to lend or rent his name to another person, a provision clearly aimed to stop men not enrolled in the court from handling cases there.[13] Rules of this kind prevented the purely provincial practitioners from taking part in what was becoming an ever growing influx of suits into Westminster Hall. Later in the reign of Elizabeth, the judges took up an increasingly hard line on the definition of solicitors, so that by 1600 the rules specified that only sworn attorneys, barristers, and personal servants were allowed to act in this capacity.[14] Again, this was a development which seriously limited the activities of the full- or part-time court keeper. He could continue to act as a steward or a local court attorney, but he was (in theory at least) cut off from taking cases to London.

Furthermore, at the very time when the London professionals were attacking the learning of the amateur court holders, their positions in the localities were also being threatened by new ideas about estate management which stressed to landlords the advantages of using men with legal training and experience to keep their courts and handle their legal affairs. An untrained or incompetent steward could make extremely costly mistakes, and it was in the interest of preventing the financial losses which might arise from the 'negligence or ignorance' of their servants that seventeenth-century 'experts' such as Thomas Clay recommended that landlords use only skilful, discreet, and honest officers. In addition to these moral qualities, Clay advised that men selected as stewards should have 'good knowledge and experience in the common lawes of this land, thereby to be able readily to know and distinguish of the authorities, privileges and jurisdictions of such Courts as are incident and belonging to any Manor'.[15] The best means of achieving these ends, he thought, was to appoint a man 'brought up at some of the Innes of Court or

Chauncerie, or who hath practised as a Solicitor, Attorney or Councellor at Law, whereby he hath gained good experience'.[16] Judging from the decline in the number of amateur court keepers active in seventeenth-century Devonshire, Hertfordshire, and Warwickshire, this advice appears to have won general acceptance amongst landlords.

Finally, the purely provincial profession declined simply because, for a man contemplating a legal career, a place on the rolls of a royal court such as King's Bench and Common Pleas offered many advantages which could not be obtained elsewhere. Common law attorneys could sue for fees and money laid out for suits, an important advantage in the difficult business of getting litigants to pay. They could practise as solicitors and thereby gain a share of the lucrative business handled by Star Chamber and Chancery, and in general they could make more money than a purely local practitioner. The usual attorney's fee in a royal court was 3s. 4d. as compared to 1s. in most local tribunals, and the differences in the charges for bits of procedural work were on a very similar scale.[17] In any case, as we have seen already, local court litigation was in decline by the early seventeenth century, and the business which did exist was monopolized by those local practitioners who were lucky enough to have gained one of the select places in a court such as the Exchequer at Chester or in one of the urban small debt courts.

II

The fact that the rise of the London-orientated lower branch was accompanied by the decline of the purely provincial practitioners makes it difficult to measure whether or not there were actually more men of law (defined in the broadest sense)[18] in 1640 than there had been in 1560. The increase in the number of barristers and the great proliferation of the common law attorneys certainly made an impact in the provinces, and the profile of the legal profession in English life and society seems to have been higher in the early seventeenth century than before. But, because it is impossible to arrive at any completely accurate estimate of the number of purely provincial practitioners who were active in, say, 1560 or 1580, any conclusions beyond these can never be more than subjective.

However, if the quantitative consequences of the growth of the common law profession are slightly ambiguous, the qualitative ones point distinctly to a significant alteration in the character of the lower branch. It was now much more centralized. Whereas many of the purely provincial practitioners had been semi-professionals or amateurs, by 1640 the common law attorneys were full-time career lawyers.[19] The court holders were largely free from any official supervision, but the attorneys and clerks who practised within the royal courts had at least to pay lip-service to standards of admission and professional behaviour which were laid down by parliament, the judges, and the lord chancellor. The inns of chancery in which most, though not all, of the practitioners were enrolled, and the courts themselves provided places of association and a professional self-image, and centralization meant also a profession which could in theory be subjected to more effective control.

Within the offices of courts such as Chancery or Wards new recruits to the bureaucratic underworld were of course taken immediately into the clerical families which were described in Chapter 2. The common law attorneys were a much larger and amorphous group which was composed of men who lived all over the country and only came up to London during term time, but they, too, enjoyed a sense of corporate identity both amongst themselves and with other branches of the profession. On admission, new practitioners in Common Pleas were sworn in by the prothonotary whose office they joined and were required to repeat the oath of attorney, which laid down the fundamental standards of professional ethics: 'You shall do no falsehood nor Consent to any to be done in ye Court and if you know of any to be done you shall give knowledge thereof to my L[or]d Chief Justice.... You shall delay noe man for luker nor malice.'[20] Orders published periodically by the judges set out rules for practice,[21] and on occasion there were group meetings at which professional matters were discussed. In 1567, for example, Chief Justice Dyer addressed the attorneys of the Common Pleas in order to remind them of their duties to queen and commonwealth, to exhort them to honest practice, and to instruct them not to commit the cardinal sins of erasing or changing the official records of the court.[22]

In this particular instance, moreover, Dyer appointed a jury of attorneys to investigate abuses within the court and amongst its practitioners.[23] Although virtually nothing is known of such juries in the early Tudor period, it seems that they had long been a familiar institution through which practitioners were able to exercise some degree of self-regulation over their profession. Both Dyer and later

Sir Edward Coke claimed that the jury was an ancient device, and Sayles has discovered the appointment of one in 1346 in order to investigate a case involving the erasure of plea rolls.[24] Certainly, throughout the latter sixteenth and early seventeenth centuries, the use of such juries was a regular feature of the Elizabethan and early Stuart commissions on fees. Apart from the names, there are few clues about how the individual jurors were selected, but an attempt was evidently made to choose senior men who were recognized as knowledgeable or known to have access to valuable documents.[25] What is quite clear is that practitioners from all over the country were included. For example, of the twenty-six men on a Common Pleas jury in 1628, at least eight, including Peter Noyes of Andover, John Tryer of Worcestershire, John Skinner of Hertfordshire, Robert Benson of Leeds, and Anthony Langston of Staffordshire, are known to have been provincial attorneys with well-established practices.[26] So, even though the profession was, except for term time, geographically dispersed, there were institutions through which all of the diverse elements could on occasion be brought together.

Equally important, these formal sources of unity were reinforced by more symbolic and personal ones. Every practitioner had to wear a black gown when he went to meals in the inns of court or chancery and when he appeared in court.[27] Ties of friendship, sometimes of marriage, were formed through the profession. Attorneys appointed fellow practitioners as overseers and executors of their wills.[28] Some clearly had acquaintances within the upper branch or amongst the court officials. For example, Robert Fletcher of Chesterfield bequeathed memorial rings to two serjeants at law,[29] and Alen Hendre, a successful Middlesex practitioner, left a clock to Prothonotary Richard Brownlow and rings to all of the judges of the Common Pleas.[30] Richard Cliff provided 20s. for a breakfast for the clerks within the offices of the Common Pleas prothonotaries.[31] The kinds of relationship which these gifts reflect had no doubt long been common amongst practitioners in the royal courts. The point is that by the later sixteenth century, this professional community reached much more extensively into the provinces. The obituary of the seventeenth-century London lawyer Richard Smyth contains the names of hundreds of fellow practitioners from all over the country whom he knew or knew of.[32] From the localities themselves, on the other hand, the extent to which attorneys identified with their vocation is perhaps best illustrated by funeral monuments. John

Skinner's epitaph in the Hitchin (Hertfordshire) parish church proclaims that he was 'a man of great learning and commended by all. He was deeply read in the Common Law, which he practised for a long time and he defended the causes of his clients with great industry and fidelity.'[33] That of James Mott of Norfolk reads more simply:

> He professed the lawe. Yet he embraced
> Peace and abhored bribes and faveors.[34]

III

Thus the increased size and cohesion of the lower branch are important aspects of its early modern history, but to concentrate on these alone would leave much of the story untold. The increase in litigation also put severe strains on the legal system, and these were felt amongst all the groups of practitioners which worked within it. At the upper levels, men such as Ellesmere, Coke, and Bacon struggled with the confusion of jurisdictions and the uncertainty apparently inherent in a system of judge-made law in an effort to find remedies for the 'multiplicity of suits'.[35] Within the lower branch, the issues were more mundane, but they were serious nevertheless, because the growth in legal business tended to exacerbate all of the centrifugal forces which were built into that 'network of private interests' which constituted the court bureaucracies.[36] The very success of the courts in attracting business to themselves intensified conflict amongst officials, made it difficult to control the profession, and ultimately helped to discredit royal justice in general.

The core of the problem was simple. Legal business was an Elizabethan boom industry and many people were anxious either to get a share of the trade or to maximize their profits once they got in. On the one hand, men swarmed into London planning to make their fortunes by studying for the bar. On the other, courtiers and profiteers began to set their sights on clerical offices which had been made increasingly valuable by the increasing number of lawsuits. Elizabethan and early Stuart governments starved of revenue and sources of patronage found it hard to resist cash offered in return for grants of offices held by the crown or to refuse to countenance the sale of those controlled by officials such as the common law judges or the master of the rolls.[37] In itself, the practice of selling offices was nothing new; the fact that an act of parliament forbidding the practice had been passed during the reign of Edward VI suggests that it was already an issue in the mid sixteenth century.[38] What was unique about the period between *c.* 1575 and 1640 was both the number of sales and the rapidly increasing amounts of money involved in each transaction.[39] Payments were made to courtiers, existing office holders, the crown, or any combination of the three. In addition to sales of existing posts, there was also pressure on the crown to lease its share of judicial profits or to erect completely new offices.[40] Some idea of the amounts of money involved can be gathered from the fact that Thomas Corie paid out £10,000 in 1638 for the office of chief prothonotary of Common Pleas. Earlier in the same decade, a seventh reversion to a relatively minor filazership in the same court went for £1000.[41]

Inevitably, as the costs of legal offices increased, so too did the efforts of the holders to see that their fields of operation were not being impinged upon by other officials and that they were recovering a return in fees which would compensate for the original outlays. From the latter part of the reign of Elizabeth right up to the outbreak of the civil wars, most of the major courts experienced bouts of internal dissension and dissatisfaction which were nearly always a consequence of competition for fees. For example, in the 1590s trouble erupted in Star Chamber as the clerk of the court, William Mill, engaged in an acrimonious dispute with its sworn attorneys over the conditions of their appointment and share in fees due for clerical work. The attorneys accused Mill of taking excessive fees. In one of his replies to the charges Mill, who was a second-generation Star Chamber man, explained how Lord Chancellor Sir Christopher Hatton had threatened to deprive him of his office unless he handed over £500, and then Hatton's successor, Lord Keeper Puckering, had also made demands. Given 'all their pinchinges', Mill wondered who could 'blame me of gynne if I have loked but to take my fees *and* those due with good moderacion'.[42]

The dispute in the Star Chamber was settled only after a great deal of private and semi-public mud-slinging, and after the appointment by Ellesmere of a commission to investigate the rival claims.[43] In other courts, although the particular issues differed slightly, similar kinds of tension can be discerned. During the 1590s, the six clerks in Chancery faced competition on more than one front. They were involved in a dispute with another set of officials, the examiners, about fees due for taking the written depositions which were used as evidence in Chancery, and at the same time they fought a long, and ultimately successful, rear-guard action against the newly erected office for keeping and filing bills in Chancery, which had been granted by the queen to a soldier named John Parker, probably through the patronage of his 'cousin', Lord Treasurer Buckhurst.[44]

Perhaps only because they are rather less well documented, disputes in King's Bench and Common Pleas appear to have been less severe than some of those in Chancery or Star Chamber, but there was, nevertheless, plenty for the denizens of the clerical underworlds in these courts to be worried about. Although they never seem likely to have achieved success, the filazers of King's Bench continued, during the first eighty years of the seventeenth century, to protest against the loss of business they had suffered as a result of the development of bill procedures and the clerical supremacy of the chief prothonotary.[45] In both courts, the judges had to fend off proposals to create new offices with the excuse that such moves were illegal and liable to injure one set of clerks or another. Even so, in spite of their best efforts over more than twenty years, James I finally granted a patent for the making of supersedeas in the Common Pleas, a development which apparently worried the court officials sufficiently for them to secure an undertaking from the king that he would not give away any more of their profits from fees.[46] In the late 1630s, a number of royal grants by letters patent of reversions to filazerships in the Common Pleas stimulated several of the filazers and clerks of the court to send a petition to the House of Lords in January 1642. It claimed that the posts had traditionally been at the disposal of the lord chief justice, that they could not be granted by letters patent, and that sales of offices 'at unreasonable and excessive prices', against the law and ancient custom, discouraged the 'able Clerks' within the court and was harmful to the commonwealth.[47]

In fact, at least up until the 1630s, the sale of offices does not appear either to have resulted in a drastic reduction of standards in the courts or to have seriously damaged the career prospects of members of the lower branch. Some posts, such as the chief clerkship of the King's Bench and that of *custos brevium* of the Common Pleas, were held by sinecurists who appointed deputies to do the work for them.[48] But most offices in the Common Pleas, including the expensive, lucrative and prestigious prothonotaryships, went regularly in the period before 1640 to men who had worked their way up from clerkships

or attorneyships. William Nelson, John Gulston, and Thomas Waller
are all known to have practised as attorneys. Both the long-serving
William Brownlow and Robert Moyle began their careers as clerks.[49]
Most of the early Stuart filazers had similar backgrounds, so the
petition of 1642 must not be taken at face value. Since the existing
filazers apparently had to surrender their rights in order to make good
the royal grants of reversions, they were certainly not as disinterested
as their rhetoric suggested. Nevertheless, they were clearly anxious
about the future, and the idea that the sale of offices might ultimately
result in injustice and inefficiency echoed the concern expressed in
parliament during the 1620s by men such as John Pym and Sir
Edward Coke.[50]

Furthermore, and quite apart from the sale of offices, it is in the
common law courts that we can see most clearly the problems created
simply by the sheer growth in the size of the lower branch. The
number of underclerks in offices such as those of the prothonotaries
of Common Pleas multiplied as business increased. This underworld
is too murky and obscure to penetrate with sufficient precision to put
a figure to the numbers involved or to specify exactly the conditions
of work, but what is clear is that when a litigant had business with,
for example, the chief prothonotary of Common Pleas, he was not
dealing with the individual office holder but with one of the sixty-odd
underclerks who worked in his office.[51] These underclerks did the
work, collected the fees due for it directly from the client, and then
paid some part of the 'take' to the head of the office.[52] The danger
inherent in the situation was that unless the master exercised
exceptionally tight control, his underclerks might well do serious
wrong to clients either through negligence or incompetence, or
simply by charging excessive fees, and, since the underclerks were
usually not sworn officers of their courts, it was often quite difficult
to exercise discipline over those guilty of unprofessional conduct.[53]

Even more significant in terms of the public debate it caused was
the spectacular increase in the supply of common law attorneys. Here
the difficulties centred on maintaining the standard of qualifications
required for entry into the profession and keeping numbers under
some kind of control. As we have seen, fifteenth-century statutory
regulations prescribed that the judges should establish control over
the admission of practitioners, who were supposed to be 'good' and
learned in their profession.[54] However, no specific procedures were
outlined, and what evidence there is indicates that by the mid

sixteenth century most of the responsibility for supervising the admission of attorneys had been delegated to the prothonotaries of the respective courts. In Common Pleas, for example, the prospective practitioner was supposed to choose which of the three prothonotaries' offices he wanted to join. Then, after he had handed over an admission fee, the prothonotary administered the oath of attorney, made a note on his remembrance roll that the new man had been sworn in, and sent off a certificate verifying the same to the clerk of the warrants, the official who, supposedly, kept a roll of all the attorneys qualified to work in the court. After admission, the rules of practice specified that the attorney should do business only with the office of the prothonotary who had sworn him, and not with that of either of the other two.[55]

Whether this process of admission involved any very thorough examination of the competence of candidates is not known. In the days before 1580, when the profession was still relatively small, it is most likely that the natural order of careers within the courts would have made rigorous testing seem unnecessary. Most new practitioners were trained up within the offices of the prothonotaries themselves or had served as clerks to other court officials or attorneys, so most of them would have been known personally to the prothonotaries who would eventually admit them. However, after 1580 and as numbers rose over the thousand mark, personal knowledge was less likely to have been an effective screen; but, apart from a judicial order of 1610 which required that new attorneys be sworn in open court,[56] there are few signs from the late Elizabethan or early Stuart years that new procedures were being introduced to handle the flood of new applicants. Even more to the point, since attorneys were the men who brought litigation into the courts, and since the prothonotaries competed with each other for the available business, the profitability of their offices was directly proportional to the number of attorneys they enrolled; therefore they were not always scrupulous about controlling admissions. This much was admitted in an indenture entered into by the three Common Pleas prothonotaries in 1594, a document which also makes plain that their resolve to exercise more care in the future was dependent on an agreement henceforth to share equally all the profits which accrued to the individual offices.[57]

It is unlikely that this deal, which broke down in 1618 did much to retard the growth in the number of attorneys.[58] The flood of new practitioners was apparently irresistible. As Chapter 7 demonstrates, questions about the number and qualifications of candidates remained real concerns of the public and politicians throughout the early seventeenth century. However, the increase in the size of this part of the profession also had some ironic repercussions for the prothonotaries themselves, because it created a very large group within the lower branch whose interests were not always identical with those of the court officials.

Attorneys occupied an ambiguous place within the legal bureaucracy. They were a part of it, but at the same time they earned their livings by representing the litigants who were its customers. The interests of these clients were usually best served by the quickest and cheapest possible resolution of disputes. Those of the clerical officials, on the other hand, involved maintaining or raising the level of their fees and insuring that none of the procedural steps for which they were paid was overlooked. The attorneys stood between the two, and on the whole their interests were bound to incline them in favour of the litigants. Practitioners in Common Pleas, for example, normally received no part of the fees they disbursed to court officials.[59] They saw no profit from newly erected offices or increased schedules of fees. The most effective way for an attorney to make more money was to make justice less expensive and faster so that more men would be willing to turn to it. For these reasons, the attorneys were at times vocal critics of early-seventeenth-century bureaucratic abuses, and they also helped to nurture a number of important innovations in court procedures.

On occasion the early Stuart royal commissions on fees provided an opportunity for practitioners to launch attacks on the prothonotaries and other court officials. For example, a deposition from ten common law attorneys in 1618 criticized the six clerks in Chancery for dividing the alphabet into thirds between them so that litigants whose surnames began with a certain letter were forced to go to a specified office. The attorneys claimed that this was an abuse, because 'whereas the sixe Clarkes and their Clark*es* before this devise were ready to doe their best for their Clyent and used all dilligence that they might gett a good Reporte, and so gayne more Clyent*es*', they now had no such incentive for efficiency.[60] In 1623, a jury of practitioners pointed out increased or newly exacted fees which were being taken by a number of Common Pleas officers including judges, prothonotaries, filazers, and exigenters.[61]

However, in spite of depositions such as these, the commissions

on fees were not very successful at bringing about reform. Their
purposes were mostly negative; at best they were intended to help
correct faults, not to introduce major changes in the way the courts
worked.[62] Nevertheless, one of the curious features of this period is
that, although administrative abuses abounded, some important
advances in procedural law were achieved, and in one or two
instances it is possible to see how tensions between attorneys and
court officials helped to bring them about.

This dynamic for innovation through conflict of interest operated
most vigorously in connection with the common law procedures for
initiating actions and for forcing defendants to appear to answer the
charges made by plaintiffs. By the mid sixteenth century, the King's
Bench had in the procedure by bill of Middlesex and *latitat* an
effective means of saving plaintiffs the cost of the original writ out
of Chancery and of speeding up somewhat the business of summoning
defendants. Although they were exaggerated, fears soon grew in the
Common Pleas that its traditional share of the legal market would,
as a result, be diverted into the King's Bench, and to some extent
this did happen. It is not surprising, therefore, that by the early
seventeenth century, Common Pleas practitioners had found a way
of gaining similar advantages for their court. The method adopted
was to sue out a *capias* on an action of trespass without taking out
an original writ in Chancery even when the true cause of action was
debt. Like those offered in the King's Bench, these new procedures
facilitated the arrest of defendants and enabled plaintiffs to commence
their actions without having to pay for the expensive original writs.
Consequently, by the later 1620s, the use of trespass writs where the
true cause of action was debt had become so popular that one of the
prothonotaries of the Common Pleas, probably Robert Moyle,
drew up a manifesto denouncing the practice.[63] The tract explains
in some detail how the new 'abuse' worked. The plaintiff's attorney
would sue out from one of the filazers of the Common Pleas a *capias*
which warranted the arrest of the defendant. On the delivery of this
writ in the country, the two opposing attorneys would attempt to
reach an agreement on the dispute without any further appeal to
judicial process. Only if this effort to reach a settlement in the
country failed would the case be brought to Westminster Hall, at
which time the plaintiff would make a new declaration 'on the
pretense of fyling a new original [writ] in debt'. According to
Moyle, the new procedures depended entirely on the 'invention'

and 'plots' of the attorneys who were acting 'without respect... to ancient order or rule of law'.[64] Furthermore, whilst one objective of the use of trespass writs was to save the costs on original writs, what is particularly interesting about Moyle's account is the claim that attorneys used mesne process associated with trespass precisely because it had the advantage of enabling litigants to reach agreements in the country without having to resort to the time-consuming business of bringing the action before the courts. Of course, this also explains his opposition to the device. The filazers of the Common Pleas, whom Moyle accused of conniving with the attorneys, handled the writs used in the new procedure, but the prothonotaries profited from a case only after both parties had come into court and were pleading the issue to be tried at assize. Moyle's worry was that the use of trespass was causing this to happen less often, and he collected statistics from the records of the courts to prove his point. The use of the new method had begun in Norfolk, Suffolk, Lincolnshire, and Yorkshire. Before its invention some time *c.* 1614, some 2400 actions of debt and 200 actions of trespass were sued out in each of these counties each year, but

Now since accons of trespass have increased in each of these Counties to ye number of 2,200 or 2,300 a year and *accons* of debt have decreased to 2 or 3 hundred in a year these Counties aforesaid are not onlie above halfe decaied in ye number of trialls in Court *and* Assizes but 3 p[ar]tes in 4 are decaied in all offices (but Philizers) as doth manifestly appeare by ye Records of this Court.[65]

Having declared his interest, Prothonotary Moyle then attempted to shore up his case against trespass procedures by reference to some general arguments which were fairly typical of those used by officers of the courts when their livelihoods were under threat. Attorneys addicted to the new procedures would forget how to draw original writs upon specialties, and so the ancient course of the court would be lost. Defendants arrested on trespass writs were unsure what complaint they were supposed to answer or how to brief their attorneys. Finally, he referred to the works of Sir Edward Coke in support of the contention that it was 'dangerous... for any Courte to give way to innovation w[i]th ye inconveniences th[a]t come by altering ye ancient rules and course of the common law....'[66] However, such sentiments had not always been characteristic of the prothonotaries. In the early 1590s, it had apparently been common for them to try to attract business by giving discounts on writs to certain favoured attorneys, and there is other evidence of procedural laxity in the later sixteenth century.[67] So a general lack of discipline within the clerical offices lies in the background to the evolution of the use of trespass where the true form of action was debt, and there is no doubting that Moyle's most deeply felt objection to it was the simple fact that it threatened to cut *his* income from fees rather than that of some other official. Nevertheless, his general opinions about the adverse effects of the new procedures were shared by the likes of Coke and Lord Chancellor Ellesmere, and the legal establishment in general seems to have been united against the innovation. In 1623 and again in 1627, the justices of the Common Pleas ordered that attorneys should not take out trespass where the true cause of action was debt on pain of a 20s. fine for the first offence and expulsion from the court on the second.[68]

The development of the trespass procedures is the best-documented example of a procedural innovation which was influenced by the attorneys, but it is not the only one. At least two others – changes in the process used for outlawing defendants who failed to answer summonses and alterations in practices having to do with the venue of actions – are known. In both cases diversions of the ancient course of the law by attorneys in the interests of clients were resisted by judges and clerical officials.[69]

However, while evidence such as the Moyle manuscript and the judges' orders enable us to identify areas in which attorneys helped to introduce procedural innovation, there is very little indication before 1640 of what the practitioners themselves actually thought about the process. Insights from the attorneys' point of view do not emerge until the Interregnum, when an unprecedented public debate about the legal system finally provided an opportunity for them to express their opinions openly. In late 1649, the Rump Parliament appointed a committee chaired by Sir Matthew Hale to investigate abuses in the legal system and to recommend reforms which would meet the demands of some of the radical critics of royal justice who had been raising their voices more and more loudly during the course of the civil wars.[70] As a response to the formation of the Hale Committee, a pamphlet appeared in 1650 which was entitled *Certaine Proposals of Divers Attorneys of the Court of Common Pleas, For the regulating the proceedings at Law*. According to information provided in the text itself, the work was the result of ten months' deliberation, and the measures it advocated had been approved by a general meeting of attorneys, which had been held at Staple Inn on 14 May 1650.[71]

Certaine Proposals was a resounding attack on the clerical officials of the Common Pleas. The attorneys praised the law of England, but criticized those officials who obstructed justice and took more care 'to catch the Fish for the benefit of the Officers, than for the dispatch or advance of the Client's business....'[72] They explained that in order to stop this abuse, practitioners had in the past contrived to alter procedures so that 'most of the gist will be ground without paying Toll at these unnecessary Milnes'.[73] And the bulk of their recommendations were either exactly along the lines of the device for using trespass where the true cause of action was debt or very much in the same spirit. Fines on original writs should be abolished. Distress as a means of forcing defendants to appear in court was a costly, 'prolix', and 'neglected' process which should be discontinued. Mesne process in suits to outlawry was unnecessary and caused delay. The method of trying titles by the action of ejectment should be improved. Debtors should not be allowed to defeat creditors by alienating property. The lands of imprisoned debtors should be sold after a year in order to satisfy creditors. According to the attorneys, all of these changes were aimed at shortening process and 'saving the greatest part of the charge of most suits' so that 'Lending, Trade and Commerce [can be] advanced: which is the end desire of the Proposers'.[74]

Various commentators have tried to evaluate *Certaine Proposals* within the context of the Interregnum movement for law reform. One conclusion is that, although the abolition of fines on original writs was a Leveller demand, the pamphlet generally represents the views of moderate reformers. Another is that the proposals were an attempt by the legal profession to 'anticipate radical demands by remedying glaring abuses'.[75] In fact, neither of these characterizations is absolutely correct. Insofar as the attorneys pledged their support for the existing legal system, their demands were indeed moderate, but, given what we now know about their role in legal innovation before the civil wars, their programme must be seen as the culmination of fifty years of pressure for change rather than as a response to the more immediate turmoil of the 1640s and 1650s. The civil war provided an opportunity to systematize and articulate views which had been smouldering for a long time, and the motives behind *Certaine Proposals* were quite simple. Attorneys had little interest in common with the clerks who ran the bureaucracy they used; they were more likely to sympathize with litigants who wanted cheaper and faster results. In pursuing these ends, they had always been resisted by clerical self-interest and by some of the leading lawyers, such as Coke and Ellesmere, who expressed real fears that alterations in the basic procedures of the common law would lead to abuses which these procedures were designed (in theory) to prevent.[76] And, as far as is known, *Certaine Proposals* received no more favourable a hearing from the Hale commission than the earlier contrivances had from the judges of the Common Pleas.[77] However after the Restoration many of the procedural innovations supported by the attorneys became regular features of the legal system. In particular, the key elements in the use of trespass where the true cause of action was debt – the failure to sue out an original writ and the use of *capias* as the leading process – came to be accepted as common practice. The development of such changes in the face of formal resistance from the judges led to the absurd and confusing legal fictions of the eighteenth century, but the attorneys must be seen among the leading agents in the devious transition of the medieval common law to the late-seventeenth and early-eighteenth-century world.[78] In many respects they were the only solvents in a legal system all too prone to become ossified in its own procedural and bureaucratic self-interest.

7

THE ATTITUDES OF LAYMEN AND ATTEMPTS
AT REFORM

I

Viewed from inside the lower branch, then, the late-sixteenth-century boom in legal business was something of a mixed blessing. The profession had become more centralized and it enjoyed plenty of work, but at the same time the traffic in legal offices and the growth in the numbers of practitioners created serious internal tensions. Even important changes in procedural law arose from internal conflicts rather than from the successful prosecution of agreed programmes of reform. If we turn now to consider public reactions to these same developments, we again find paradox and inconsistency. People were using the courts in ever increasing numbers. So, in one sense, the increase in central court litigation, and the increase in the number of lawyers who helped to make it possible, can be seen as a positive social good, as the spread of a valuable service to greater numbers of people. However, it is clear that most articulate men of the period did not see things in this way. To them, the increase in litigation was a disaster, and the lawyers who brought the cases into the courts a group of dishonest tricksters who were a cancer in the body of the commonwealth. Allegations that attorneys stirred up unnecessary suits were accompanied by accusations that court officials were corrupt and charged extortionate fees. Such views have greatly influenced the picture of the legal profession and the legal system which has come down in the writings of modern historians.[1] In the time of Elizabeth and the early Stuarts, they were the basis of calls for investigations into, reforms of, and stricter control over the lower branch.

The underlying cause of this hostility to lawyers and to lawsuits was closely connected with general ideas about the functions of law. In the sixteenth and seventeenth centuries, its role was quite comprehensive. Writers from Sir John Fortescue in the late fifteenth century to Sir Henry Finch in the early seventeenth thought that law was the means by which society was held together. Fortescue wrote that laws were the sinews which extended through the kingdom and held together the body of the people. Finch described law as a means of well ordering a civil society.[2] His contemporary William Fulbecke believed that without law, 'which I interpret to be an order established by authority, neither house, nor city, nor nation, nor mankind, nor nature, nor world can be'.[3] Lawyer historians, men like William Hakewell or John Doddridge, were well aware that law was no more than a human artefact which was subject to change as circumstances altered, and the idea that law functioned as a remedy or that increased wealth and trade made more suits inevitable did exist.[4] But at the level of highest theory and in the minds of laymen, law was more than a mere arbiter; it was a reflection of God's will about the way the world should be, a set of precepts which protected property and enabled men to tell right from wrong.

These notions about the functions of law implied that lawsuits were a potential breach of the social order, more the result of the ill will of men than a product of business dealings or personal accident. A 1576 parliamentary bill in favour of law reform mentioned the 'multitude of contentions which for lack of charity rise upon the smallest occasions between neighbours'. The Jesuit Robert Parsons thought that covetousness caused the multitude of suits.[5] Even the lawyers were ambivalent about the reasons for going to law. For example, Sir John Davies remarked that if only all men lived according to the law of nature, then there would be no need for suits.[6] Most commentators appear to have seen a mythical image of a society based on neighbourliness being undermined by the malicious propensity to go to law.[7]

Since lawsuits were seen as a social evil, it was only natural that in an age when their numbers were increasing rapidly, lawyers should have been discredited. The ideal lawyer should have been an agent of reconciliation; instead, the influx of suits reflected a legal profession which encouraged contention between neighbours. In particular, attorneys and solicitors were singled out as fomentors of suits. In the eyes of most writers, they were the principal villains in the painful drama at Westminster Hall which saw innocent clients detached from their money and inheritances by conniving pettyfoggers. In the 1590s, Bishop Overton told the privy council that inordinate numbers of attorneys in Staffordshire were 'breeding and nourishing strife and contention' at quarter sessions and assizes.[8] In 1608, Lord Eure explained to Ellesmere that law cases were being drawn away from the Council in the Marches of Wales and towards London by the large number of common law attorneys who were active in the English border shires.[9] Even Sir Edward Coke, who in general identified social and economic change as the cause of the increase in litigation, added the 'multitudes of attorneys' to his list.[10] No wonder, then, that there was wide agreement with the lesson which Robert Burton learned from Plato; it was a 'great sign of an intemprete and corrupt common wealth where lawyers and physicians did abound'.[11] In addition, economic thinking of the day for the most part held that lawyers, instead of adding to the nation's wealth, siphoned their incomes from those farmers, merchants, and tradesmen who did. For instance, the author of *Britannia Languens* thought that as men's estates crumbled, the lawyers made profits just '*as doubtless did some Bricklayers get Estates by the burning of the City*'.[12] All of these social and economic views of the profession were combined in the caricatures of lawyers, and especially of attorneys, which appeared on the Jacobean stage in plays such as Jonson's *Staple of the News* or Middleton's *Michaelmas Term*.[13]

Attitudes towards litigation and hence towards attorneys may also have contained political and class elements. By 1640 one in every eighty Englishmen was using the king's courts, and the use of these implied recognition of royal rule, often at the expense of the powerful magnate or lord of the manor. During the late sixteenth century, the common lawyers seriously undermined one aspect of seigniorial power by recognizing the right of copyholders to sue in the central courts. Most lawyers probably agreed at least in theory with Roger Wilbraham's assertion that 'it is every subjects natural birthright to enjoy the benefit of the princes law', and Coke claimed in public that if 'Justice [was] with held, only the poorer sort are those that smart for it', presumably because they would then be swamped by their more powerful neighbours.[14]

The point here is not that lawyers as a group can be seen as in any way especially committed to upholding the rights of the common sort of people. They are always found on both sides of a dispute. But the fact remains that the proliferation of practitioners made it easier for poor men to go to court. Despite perpetual complaints about increased fees, law in the early seventeenth century was not all that expensive, and the courts were open to a relatively large cross-section of society. In an age of rising prices, property rights, whether those of landlords or copyholders, became crucial, and enough examples of the struggles between landlords and tenants exist to make it clear that recourse to law was important for both sides.[15] In such circumstances men who were unlearned in the law could benefit from the increased availability of lawyers; more lawyers made the law a weapon which could be put into the hands of more men.

Several contemporary writers were quick to pick up these implications of the increase in litigation. In the 1570s, William Barlee, an obscure lawyer who was undertaking a *Concordance of All Written Lawes Concerning Lords of Mannours*, wrote to Lord Burghley that he feared that the judges might oppose his attempt to make manorial law known to both lords and tenants on the grounds that

Many suits have arisen in the Comens Courts, amongst subjects... since our Statute Lawes were published in the English tongue to the common sort of people. And for this only cause, some... would have the knowledge of our common laws obscurely hedd from the common sort of people, as they are now.

Against this position, Barlee argued that the same reasons had been put forward for the withholding of English scriptures from the populace, but had been defeated by natural reason and the express word of God. In conclusion he chastised 'Those lawyers who forgett, how by Just suits, wrongful dealings are quietly suppressed'.[16]

Barlee's mild support for the rights of the less wealthy to go to law was exceptional, and even he felt obliged to say that he was concerned that his work, which touched on the thorny question of the rights of copyholders, should not get into the hands of 'Rash headed fellows lest they vexe' lords of manors.[17] Much more typical was the quip by the satirist John Earle that countrymen were more likely to be loyal to their local attorney than to their landlord.[18] In a more serious vein, the lawyer Sir Anthony Benn claimed to believe that those men whom he called 'beggars' were primarily responsible for malicious and lengthy suits. He argued that it would be a great mistake to lower legal costs,

for the many headed multitude are all set vpon mallice or pleasure yf it weare as cheape to goe to law as to goe to the Alehouse what would become of the world... the vile people are as malitious as witches weare the Law low rated they would yse it familiarily as footeball or the Maypole.[19]

It is significant that the most vociferous attacks on the multiplicity of suits came from the legal and social establishment. Unfortunately, little is known about popular attitudes towards litigation before the civil wars. But the increase in the volume of litigation can be taken as a kind of vote through action, and it is worth remembering that Interregnum calls for law reform in general favoured making suits easier rather than more difficult to obtain. In this they differed fundamentally from some pre-war complaints.[20]

If one set of reasons for hostile attitudes towards attorneys and solicitors was based on the view that they stirred up suits, another, which was no less important, focused on the social origins and education of members of the lower branch. It was widely held that such practitioners were men of base birth and mean education. For example, Sir Anthony Benn appears to have shared the fairly common view that the men most likely to become attorneys were those who had been unsuccessful in their own trades or broken by their own intemperate litigiousness.[21] In addition, as a result of changes in attitudes towards education which occurred during the early sixteenth century, attorneyship came to be classified as a 'mechanical' occupation. This theme will be taken up in more detail in Chapter 8, but here it is enough to say that, since they were trained largely by apprenticeship, members of the lower branch were associated with other trades and manual crafts rather than with those men educated at the universities or those lawyers who learned their law at the inns of court. The latter were reckoned gentlemen and claimed to possess 'scientific' knowledge. The former, on the other hand, by virtue of their bonds of apprenticeship lost all claims to gentility and were 'mere pragmatics'. The distinction between scientific and mechanical occupations is found in Aristotle. In his works and in the later sixteenth and seventeenth centuries, it was heavily laden with social and political connotations. By definition mechanical men were unfit for government, and this disability was accentuated in sixteenth-century society, which differentiated between gentleman magistrates and the rest of the populace. Mechanical men were also reckoned to be irresponsible; not only were they unfit for government, they needed governing.[22]

II

The assumptions which lay behind contemporary attitudes towards the lower branch were not novel; at no time in English history have lawyers been the most popular of social groups.[23] Nor should criticism of them be taken entirely at face value. In many instances it reflects little more than the bookish tendency of Renaissance men to draw on classical examples mixed with a strong dose of social prejudice and a penchant for caricature. As far as we are able to tell, the increase in the size of the profession was as much a consequence as a cause of the increase in the number of suits, and when the seventeenth-century fortunes of the ordinary practitioner are examined in some detail, there are more signs of declining incomes than of successful attempts to stir up suits either by fair means or foul.[24] Although he was undoubtedly biased, it is worth considering the defence of the profession which was put forward by the distinguished Yorkshire attorney William West. He admitted that some practitioners could be faulted, but claimed that this should not be allowed to discredit the majority of them, who were honest men. In addition, West lamented the public inclination to

slander and condemne them all as covetious persons and disturbers of the common peace and quietnesse of all men by unnecessarie suits: where in verie trueth and the most part of the said Attornies being very peaceable, do oftentymes disswade their Clyents from the same so much as they can....[25]

Equally, it is a mistake to conclude from contemporary comment that the lower branch was either completely anarchic or of uniformly low standards. Many of the attorneys had a strong sense of vocation, were well educated in their trade, and were able to earn the respect of their friends and neighbours in the localities. Furthermore, there is ample evidence that the combination of statutory measures and judicial controls which had long existed to regulate the profession were indeed used. The numerous *Rules and Orders* passed down by the judges illustrate the attempts made by the judiciary to maintain guidelines for professional conduct.[26] There are also a number of references to attorneys and solicitors in the plea rolls and the published law reports. On the one hand, these show the judges implementing the law of slander against attacks on the professional competence of practitioners, and, on the other, debarring a Common Pleas attorney for failure to pay a £10 debt or making decisions relating to professional crimes such as maintenance, barratry, and embracery.[27] Similarly, one of the functions of the court of Star Chamber was the punishment of official fraud and malpractice. As officers of the courts, attorneys were liable to prosecution under this jurisdiction, and the Star Chamber records reveal a number of instances in which the court was used to test charges of abuse and corruption.[28]

However, having said this much, it is also true that there were problems enough within the legal system to put plenty of flesh on the skeleton of prejudice against lawyers which Elizabethan and early Stuart Englishmen inherited from the past. The size of the profession was growing rapidly, and, as it did, the ability or willingness of the prothonotaries and judges to maintain standards of admission apparently declined. At the same time, inflation and the traffic in offices put pressure on fees and contributed greatly to an atmosphere of quarrelsomeness and back-biting within the legal bureaucracy itself. These abuses in conjunction with the general conservative reaction against the new phenomenon of mass access to the courts lent colour to calls for reform, and since leading political figures from the Earl of Leicester to King James I shared public prejudices against the lower branch, the governments of both Elizabeth and the early Stuarts made some attempts to control the legal profession and to investigate bureaucratic abuses.[29] At one time or another, the crown, the council, the House of Commons, and the judges all tried to tackle these problems, even though, as we shall see, their efforts more often reflect the incomprehension which surrounded the increase in litigation, and the political weakness of the early Stuart state, than the effective realization of administrative reform.

Since contemporaries thought that litigation was a social evil, and since they assumed that multitudes of essentially irresponsible lawyers were one of the main causes of the increase, measures to control the number of common law attorneys began to be mooted at just about the same time as the increase in litigation first became widely perceived. In 1573 the judges of the Common Pleas proclaimed that in order to regulate the excessive numbers, any practitioners who disobeyed rules of the court or who had failed to attend the law terms within the previous two years were subject to being struck from the rolls. More generally, between 1580 and 1640, the size of the lower branch became a minor preoccupation of Parliament and the council. Plans for reform circulated within the government, and bills against excessive numbers appeared in parliament in 1580, 1589, 1601, 1604, 1610, 1625, and 1629.

In 1585, for example, Lord Treasurer Burghley received two proposals. The first, which was drawn up by the master of requests, Thomas Sackford, was endorsed as 'A Note for a Act touching the

Attorneys of the kinges Benche *and* Commen place'. Referring to fifteenth-century statutes limiting the number of attorneys in Norfolk and Suffolk, it pointed out that the 'superfluous nomber' of attorneys caused 'great discentions, disorder [and] sutes amongst the subjects for frivolous causes', and suggested that the judges should find out how many practitioners had been active between the years 1542 and 1585 so that the queen could take the matter into consideration.[30] The second scheme put to Burghley came from Francis Alford and was much more radical. Alford had recently been involved in a long and highly contentious series of lawsuits, and his primary concern was to reduce legal costs. To this end he suggested regulating both barristers and attorneys, the most interesting aspect of his plan being the idea that all lawyers should be restricted to practice in one court along lines modelled on the Parlement of Paris.[31]

No doubt because it threatened far too many vested interests to be politically viable, Alford's plan was ignored, and, interestingly, Burghley himself believed that 'this tyme for many respectes requirred an increase in the number of attorneys'.[32] Nevertheless, he made careful corrections on Sackford's note, and this draft bill may have been the basis for a measure to limit numbers which was introduced into parliament in 1589, but which did not become law.[33] Certainly there is little doubt that the council continued to take the problem seriously throughout the rest of the reign of Elizabeth. A commission appointed in 1594 for the reform of legal abuses was charged to consider complaints made against attorneys and other officers in the high courts of justice.[34] Equally important, with the appointment in 1596 of Thomas Egerton as lord keeper, the crown found a leading law officer who was genuinely concerned with law reform in general and with the need to regulate the lower branch in particular. His speech in the Parliament of 1601 in favour of a bill for avoiding 'trifling suits' contained a violent attack on 'Petty Foggers and Vipers of the Common Wealth... that [set] Dissention between man and man', and his 'Memorialles for Iudicature' (*c.* 1609) listed the limitation of the number of attorneys and solicitors to the 'most expert and honest' as one of the major reforms necessary for avoiding the 'Infinite multiplicytie of Sutes'.[35]

It is probable, though not provable, that Egerton was also responsible for the introduction into parliament of the bill which became the act 3 Jac. I c. 7, the only measure relating to attorneys and solicitors which found its way onto the statute book under Elizabeth and the early Stuarts.[36] In fact, this 'Act to reform Multitudes and Mis-demeanors of Attorneys and Solicitors at Law, and to avoid sundrie unnecessarie Suit*es* in Charges at Law' was not very original nor did it deal very extensively with problems relating to the number and qualifications of practitioners. Most of its provisions had been issued as court orders by the judges of King's Bench and Common Pleas in 1597, and its most novel features were concerned with the way attorneys presented their bills.[37] The main innovation was the requirement that practitioners should provide their clients with detailed bills of charges, including a 'Ticket' written out by serjeants and counsellors at law which stated how much money the attorney had disbursed to them in fees due for consultation or assistance on any given case. Bills of attorney, as prescribed by the statute, were certainly in use before its enactment, but their survival in very great numbers afterwards may be some testimony to its success. On the other hand, the surviving evidence suggests that the prescribed receipts from counsel were very rarely, if ever, used, either before or after the passage of the act.[38]

The parts of the statute which dealt with the size and qualifications of the profession were more conventional. The act proclaimed that in order to avoid 'the infinite numbers of sollicitors and Attorneys', no man was to be admitted as a practitioner who had not been 'brought up in one of the courts' or who 'was [not] otherwise well practised in Solliciting of Causes ... and have been found to be skillful and of honest Disposition'. The idea that practitioners should be trained in their court was new in terms of statutory requirements about qualifications, but it was no more than a statement of usual practice and, possibly, of rules which existed, at least in theory, within the courts themselves. Nor did the new act go significantly beyond the statute of Henry IV on the matter of how qualifications were supposed to be tested.[39]

All things considered, 3 Jac. I c. 7 looks suspiciously like a public relations exercise in which the government, or possibly the legal profession on its own, tried to convince its critics that something was being done about the lower branch. But if this was its purpose, then it was not very successful. The act set forth general terms for limiting future admissions, but it did nothing to cut the number of men currently in practice, and this was still the issue foremost in the minds of contemporaries. In 1610, both the king and members of parliament were again speaking vigorously about the need to stop the influx of litigation by reducing numbers, and the achievement of some measure of reform appears to have been seen by both sides as a government concession which would help to smooth the way for agreement on the major issue of the session, 'The Great Contract'.[40] However, in spite of this evident interest, the proposed legislation of 1610, like that introduced subsequently in 1625 and 1629, got nowhere.[41] In each of these cases the reason for failure was simply that during the 1610s and 1620s the political relationship between king and parliament went sour, with the result that very little legislation of any kind was passed.[42] There can be no question of interference from inside the profession; attorneys and solicitors were not well represented in parliament.[43] Nor can there be any doubt about the degree of agreement between the crown and MPs on the need for reform. Indeed, when we find Bacon adding an act for the limitation of the number of attorneys to a list of measures to relieve grievances in advance of the 1614 Parliament, or when the issue comes up repeatedly during the troubled Parliaments of the 1620s,[44] it is hard not to draw the conclusion that one of the reasons it is mentioned so often was that the need to limit attorneys, like the suppression of ale-houses or the punishment of sturdy beggars, had become a commonplace. The value of the idea lay entirely in the fact that its axiomatic truth was self-evident to privy councillors and backbenchers alike.

Given the failure to achieve any effective statutory reforms of the lower branch, by far the most important steps towards laying down regulations about the number and quality of practitioners in the early seventeenth century came from within the courts themselves. In the first place, although there was some disagreement about exactly what measures should be taken, the judiciary gradually developed a policy about who should be allowed to practise as a solicitor.

As we saw in Chapter 2, there were two kinds of solicitor – those who had no formal connections with any legal institution, and those who were clerical officials or attorneys, but who acted as solicitors in courts other than those to which they had been formally admitted. Needless to say, both types appear to have flourished during the great influx of suits into Westminster Hall, and, because solicitors were by definition men capable of dragging suits from one court to another, both types were seen as major contributors to the multiplicity of suits. This fear, along with the determination of the judges of the Common Pleas to stop business drifting away from their court, accounts for attempts to prevent the common law attorneys from acting as solicitors. In 1564, Justice Dyer ordered that no attorney of the Common Pleas should handle business outside of his own court, and during the course of the late sixteenth century several judicial decisions were given against the common law attorneys who attempted to sue for fees due to them for soliciting causes in other courts.[45] As late as 1602, the justices of both King's Bench and Common Pleas agreed with Lord Keeper Egerton that 'A clerk or attorney in one Court may not solicit a cause in another court.'[46]

Since they provided a definite sanction against the practice only if the collection of fees was at issue, these efforts to keep attorneys from acting as solicitors were probably not very effective. But, insofar as they may have inhibited the attorney-solicitor, they clearly had disastrous consequences. Litigants were not going to stop seeking remedies in Star Chamber or Chancery because of such measures. If the official attorneys were prohibited from helping them, then the other class of solicitors was inevitably going to arise to fulfil the necessary function. These were the practitioners over whom there was almost no regulation, and who gave rise to the most profound worries about qualifications and professional integrity. In the opinion of Egerton, they were 'caterpillars of the common weal', and William Hudson called them 'grasshoppers... [who] devour the whole land'.[47] Thus, in the 1590s, the unofficial solicitors were being harassed by attempts to prosecute them on charges of maintenance, but the law was unclear, and providing the practitioner was careful not to fee counsel he was able to ply his trade without much danger.[48]

By 1600, concern about solicitors seems to have reached a high point. In the Parliament of 1601, Egerton spoke about the need for reform,[49] and a bill was moved by a barrister of Lincoln's Inn, Heyward Townshend. However, there was at this date uncertainty about exactly what should be done. Speaking in favour of his bill, Townshend recommended that only four classes of men should be allowed to act as solicitors: barristers, attorneys, servants in livery, and kinsmen within four degrees of consanguinity.[50] In apparent contrast to Egerton and the judges, he was prepared to accept that attorneys be allowed to solicit. In any case, the 1601 bill foundered, and, remarkably, the statute 3 Jac. I c. 7 actually recognized the existence of solicitors without saying anything about how they should be defined or qualified.[51] Only in the course of the next two decades did some more or less clear consensus emerge about who should be allowed to act as a solicitor. Evidently fearing the worst of solicitors who were not attorneys, the judges reversed earlier decisions, and followed the guidelines advocated by Townshend in 1601. By the later 1620s, solicitors were officially recognized as long as they were attorneys, clerical officials, or men called to the bar at one of the inns of court.[52]

It is impossible to measure exactly the success of the attempt to eradicate the amateur solicitor. Some men are known to have used the mere fact of an admission to an inn of court as a justification for soliciting, and it may have been quite common for the activity to be undertaken by the clerks of established barristers, attorneys, or officials.[53] In both types of case, we see a reflection of the idea that soliciting was a function suitable for men learning the law, but, although such solicitors cannot be called amateurs, they would not seem to fall within the strict letter of the regulations.[54] On the other hand, evidence from Star Chamber cases shows that the judicial guidelines were recognized within the profession and amongst the public at large,[55] and after the first decade of the seventeenth century few men who could be described as amateur solicitors are found active in the countryside.[56] Furthermore, from the 1620s, attorneys began as a matter of course to describe themselves as both attorney and solicitor,[57] so that it is clear that soliciting had by that date been grafted onto the established profession. In general, the very increase in the number of recognized practitioners appears to have brought the problem of the untrained solicitors under control.

Similarly, although the effect on the number and quality of practitioners is far from certain, further attempts were made in the 1630s to tighten up the regulations about the qualifications required of the common law attorneys. In Hilary Term 1633, the judges finally produced specific rules about the standards of training they expected of men who desired admission to practise in King's Bench and Common Pleas.

> None hereafter shalbe admitted to be an Attorney of this Courte unless he hath served a Clarke or Attorney of this Courte by the space of six yeares att least or such as for their education and study in the lawe shalbe approved by the Justices of this Courte to be of good sufficiency and ev[er]y of them admitted of one of the Inns of Courts or Chancery.[58]

Here, for the first time, clerkship and membership of one of the legal inns were specified as prerequisites for all those who practised as attorneys. In terms of the usual course of careers in King's Bench and Common Pleas, these rules did not establish new standards. By 1633, the inns of chancery had long been the term-time residences of many practitioners, and clerkship had been for several centuries the traditional method of training. But the orders did make it theoretically possible to weed out the unqualified, and they were a reaffirmation of traditional standards in the face of the mighty increase in the numbers of practitioners who had entered the profession since the 1580s, and this, rather than the introduction of new ones, was what critics demanded. In addition, although the promulgation of these orders was undoubtedly stimulated partly by pressure from the privy council,[59] they were likely to have had the support of a large body of opinion within the lower branch itself. One copy of the order requiring six years of clerkship or study notes that 'it appeareth that many ignorant persons... have been admitted to be attorneys to the great discouragement of Many and sufficient numbers of the same',[60] a statement which conveys a sense of dissatisfaction amongst the practitioners themselves with the fact that too many untrained men, or perhaps just too many men, were now entering the profession.

Moreover, the next significant group of judicial orders concerning qualifications for practice in King's Bench and Common Pleas, those which were published in 1655, are notable both for a further tightening of control over admission and for the introduction of an unprecedented degree of self-regulation by the practitioners themselves. These stipulated a period of five years' practice in the courts as a common solicitor or as a clerk to an attorney, judge, barrister, or clerical official as the basic qualification for admission, but their real importance lies in three further points. The first was a requirement that some 'sufficient proof' of this service was to be produced before admission was granted. Second, a jury of attorneys, which was to be selected yearly, was delegated to examine and admit would-be practitioners, and, third, another jury (to be empanelled every three years) was to investigate incidents of malpractice and settle the course of proceedings in the courts.[61]

In theory these new orders were important landmarks in the history of the regulation of the lower branch, but it is not absolutely clear to what extent they became permanently established in practice. A 'Book of Attornies. Common Pleas', which begins in 1656, very likely represents an attempt to put on record the proof that newly admitted practitioners had served some kind of satisfactory term of apprenticeship. The 'Book' is divided into two parts. The first takes the form of a dated list of newly admitted attorneys which is divided according to county. Alongside the name of each new man appears that of an established practitioner who was, evidently, willing to sponsor him or to vouch that he had fulfilled the specified period of service. The second part of the book is an alphabetical list of attorneys admitted to practise between 1656 and 1761. Much more work is needed on the lower branch of the later seventeenth and early eighteenth centuries before any conclusions can be drawn about the completeness of this record, but it would appear to be reasonably full. For example, the numbers of men admitted from various counties in the reign of Charles II – sixteen from Warwickshire, one hundred from Norfolk, forty-one from Kent, forty-two from London – seem plausible for a period when the profession was growing relatively slowly. For the years after 1700, the county entries become patchy, but the alphabetical lists seem to have been continued with some diligence right up to the 1740s.[62] At the very least, the 'Book' provides sufficient evidence that attorneys were required to provide some kind of evidence about their training some seventy years before the passage of statutes to that effect during the reign of George II.[63] The juries of attorneys, on the other hand, were in 1655 already an old-established feature of the legal profession, but the quite wide powers which the judicial orders gave them over admission and procedure must be seen in the context of the Hale Commission on Law Reform and the special conditions which prevailed during the Interregnum, when the traditional authorities on such matters, the prothonotaries, were under attack.[64] As far as is known, these unique powers of self-regulation did not survive the Restoration of Charles II in 1660. Even so, the more important general point is that in the 1655 orders the judges combined stricter control over admission with self-regulation during a period when lawyers as a profession were subject to massive public criticism. This suggests that a strong feeling was known to exist within the lower branch in favour of limiting entry into the profession, and, on reflection, it is logical that this should have been the case. If the prothonotaries benefited by creating more attorneys who would bring more grist to the mill, the practitioners themselves can only have seen it to their advantage to limit the number of mouths litigious business might have to feed. This was, after all, the principle of self-interest which motivated every other group of officials within the legal system.

III

The attempts, both inside and outside the courts, to regulate the quality and number of attorneys and solicitors illustrate one set of problems created by the increase in litigation. Another, but not altogether dissimilar, perspective on the difficulties confronting the administration of justice in early modern England is provided by an examination of the royal commissions which were appointed from time to time to make inquiries into and correct abuses within the legal system. These inquisitorial committees are known collectively as the commissions on fees, and, since one of them was in operation in 1567, 1585, 1594, 1610, 1623, 1627–30, and for most of the 1630s, it is fair to say that they were a regular feature of the legal life of the period.[65] The Elizabethan and Jacobean commissions have left many fewer papers than those which sat in the time of Charles I, but the composition, methods of operation, and aims of all of them were very much the same. Before 1623, when some non-officials were appointed for the first time, the commissions were made up entirely of privy councillors and judges. Their basic method of gathering information was simply to invite individuals or groups of laymen to make complaints. But juries of attorneys were regularly appointed to make presentments about court fees, and court officials or any other practitioners could be called upon to give testimony.[66] The objectives of the commissions, which were laid down in the royal orders appointing them, were to investigate excessive fees, corruption, and other 'enormyties' committed against the king's subjects by attorneys, solicitors, and other officers in the high courts of justice.[67]

It is obvious that these aims of the commissions were to some degree both a response to expressions of public concern and relevant to some of the most unsatisfactory tendencies within the legal system. There are numerous stories of disgruntled litigants who complained that they had been ruined by astronomical legal bills. Charges of excessive fee taking and the need for measures to 'make certain' the fees of court officials appear frequently on the agenda of parliament,[68] and inflation and the traffic in offices did indeed put pressure on officials to raise their fees in order to maintain their incomes in real terms. Some groups, including the filazers of Common Pleas, occasionally petitioned for permission to increase fees, and some leading statesmen, including Bacon and Coke, accepted that fees should rise to keep pace with the cost of living.[69] But very little could be done in the way of making legitimate increases, because public opinion in general held that fees were sacrosanct. Witness, for example an action brought in the Star Chamber by citizens of Ipswich against town authorities who had tried to raise legal charges in the local small debt court or the antiquarian zeal with which some of Charles I's commissioners tried to insure that fees charged in the 1620s and 1630s were no higher than they had been in the mid fifteenth century.[70] So officials were inevitably strongly tempted to make their own increases. In 1576 the chief justice of the Common Pleas allowed some fees to be raised by as much as two to four times their previous levels. In 1621, parliament found increased fees in the Chancery and Exchequer. In 1627, and during the 1630s, the royal commissions flushed out abuses in the common law courts.[71] The chief prothonotary of the Common Pleas, Richard Brownlow, admitted that his office had increased the fees taken for drawing pleadings and for entering them on the rolls. In effect his increases doubled the charges for these stages in any lawsuit; if the hypothetical case discussed in Chapter 5 had been calculated at the old rate, it would have cost nearly a pound less.[72] A few other, less serious, increases were discovered in the offices of the filazers and the *custos brevium*, and the exigenters claimed that they had been forced to raise fees because they had lost business to the newly erected *supersedeas* office.[73] A couple of attorneys were reported for charging excessive fees in individual cases, but, on the whole, the commissions collected very little evidence against these practitioners, and, certainly, the basic attorney's fee of 3s. 4d. per term stayed the same for centuries.[74] In general, moreover, although there were abuses, the actual level of increases in official fees over the entire period did not altogether live up to the controversy they sometimes caused. The best general proof of this is the sheer magnitude of the expansion of court business during the later sixteenth century. People obviously did not find the cost of litigation so great that they turned away from the courts, and if the fees of court officials which are listed in *The Attourneys Academy* (1623) are compared with a compilation which dates from well before the reign of Elizabeth, possibly from the mid fifteenth century, such increases as there are appear relatively small in comparison with a change in the value of money of over 400 per cent.[75] Contemporary concern about fees actually appears to have been successful in restraining excessive rises in legal costs.

However, not all of the agitation about fees focused precisely on increases. For instance, some of the disquiet about the uncertainty of fees had little to do with court officials constantly changing their prices in an upward direction. It sprang instead from the fear of litigants (many of whom may have been inexperienced) that they were being charged too much, either directly by court officials, or, indirectly, by their attorneys and solicitors. This was a situation analagous to that of the person who goes into a café in a foreign country and is in constant fear of being cheated because he can barely understand the language and has no idea exactly what he should consider a fair price for a cup of coffee. Hence the repeated demands in the early seventeenth century that tables of fees be hung up in court offices[76] and the sensible provision of the statute 3 Jac. I c. 7, that attorneys and solicitors should provide their clients with itemized bills of costs. But the best solution of all was the complete exposition of court fees which Thomas Powell produced in *The Attourneys Academy*, a work which aimed to establish 'a certain course of compliance between the officers and ministers of our Lawes and their Clients', by enabling litigants to distinguish between those lawyers who tried to cheat them and those who did not.[77]

Other aspects of the fee problem had even less to do with charges to clients. As Bacon once pointed out, when contemporaries saw that court officials were making more money, they frequently complained about increased fees when what they were really noticing were the greater profits which accrued to officials and practitioners because of the increase in litigation.[78] At the same time, many of the most noisy parliamentary debates about fees had more to do with rivalries within the courts, or indeed within the king's government, than with the interests of litigants. In 1589, a bill about the cost of pleadings and process in the Exchequer was sponsored by one faction of Exchequer officials.[79] A lengthy debate in 1606 on a measure entitled 'what Fees shall be paid by the Plaintiff and Defendant for Copies out of Everie Court of Record' was in reality another round in the long-standing dispute between John Parker and the six clerks in Chancery.[80] In 1621, the search for increased fees in Chancery was closely related to the attack on Bacon by his political enemies Lionel Cranfield and Sir Edward Coke.[81]

Many of these same factors lay behind or reduced the effectiveness of the commissions on fees. They may well, at least in the reign of Elizabeth, have been appointed with real reforming intentions, but some of them seem to have been as closely associated with disputes within the legal system as with a desire to improve conditions for users. The 1594 commission came close on the heels of quarrels in Chancery and Star Chamber.[82] In the late 1590s, Egerton appointed a commission to resolve the dispute between the attorneys and clerk of the Star Chamber, and another, which he introduced in 1597 to settle fees and procedures in Chancery, was thwarted by mutual recrimination amongst the office holders themselves.[83] In 1610, despite pious statements about the damage done to litigants by rapacious attorneys, solicitors, and court officials, the only specific problems mentioned in the document establishing the commission were the question of the position of the attorneys in Star Chamber and the need to administer an oath to the attorneys of the King's Bench.[84] In any case, by 1610, but especially by 1621 when the Bacon affair gave rise to intense parliamentary investigation of fees, the commissions became a political concession which the crown used to soothe members of parliament increasingly sensitive about grievances of the subject.[85] At the same time, during the late 1620s and 1630s, the reforming purposes of the commissions were diluted by the government's discovery that they could be used to raise extra revenue. In the 1630s, officials who had increased fees were allowed to maintain their increases so long as they paid a fine or composition to the king in order to legitimize them.[86] Indeed, under the early Stuarts, the commissions on fees, like so much of the legal administration, became a political football which was used in a game where the interests of the players rather than meaningful reform was usually the goal. The filazers of the King's Bench could attack the chief prothonotary, the six clerks could attack the cursitors, the exigenters of Common Pleas could complain about the new *supersedeas* office, the attorneys could attack court officials generally,[87] and the crown could make concessions to public opinion and at the same time prop up its sagging finances. It is hardly surprising that the results were negligible.

The commissions on fees, like the concern about the increase in the number of attorneys, explain much about the plight of the legal system and the general unpopularity of lawyers and courts during the early seventeenth century. From one point of view, the increase in litigation and the centralization of justice were remarkable achievements, but neither the court bureaucracies nor the legal profession were all that well equipped to deal with them. Alarms about the excessive numbers and lack of training of practitioners, or about extortionate fee taking, were exaggerated, but there was enough truth in them to lend credence to traditional social prejudices and to exacerbate the unease which contemporaries felt about the increase in litigation itself. In addition, divisions within the legal profession contributed to the controversy, and so calls for reform were generated. Everybody, including the kings, acknowledged that the maintenance of the machinery of justice was one of the major responsibilities of government, and commissions were launched with the greatest expressions of good intentions. But, at the same time, nothing was done to stem the traffic in offices, and in many instances the judges and privy councillors who were appointed to investigate fees had a vested interest in seeing that they remained high in order to protect the value of offices at their disposal. Equally, the well-known convention of 'gift giving' made it difficult for such investigators to maintain relationships with the office holders which were completely impervious to the influence of friendship or pecuniary advantage. For example, in 1576, when the chief justice of Common Pleas allowed increases in his court, these were limited to those offices at his disposal to grant. The post of *custos brevium* was not amongst these, so the holder of that office, John Lennard, wrote to Sir William Cecil in hopes that the situation might be rectified. Lennard must have had high hopes of success. Cecil had sold him the office some ten years earlier and received an annuity of £240 in part payment. Moreover, Lennard and his Common Pleas colleague, the clerk of the juries, were willing to give Cecil 40 marks p.a. or 200 marks in cash if he managed to get privy seals or some other warrant from the queen to advance their fees. Similarly, it is little wonder that Richard Brownlow got away with increased fees in the early seventeenth century. In the year 1616–17 he disbursed £125 in cash and gifts to Judges Coke, Warburton, and Hobart.[88] Finally, whatever the human limitations involved in implementing a policy of controlling legal fees, by the 1630s the crown itself was using the commissions mainly to raise money. The legal system is a prime illustration of the dictum that 'the failure of the Stuart monarchy is partly the history of its failure to accomplish any reforms even where there was substantial agreement that something needed doing'.[89]

8

CLERKSHIP, THE INNS OF CHANCERY, AND LEGAL EDUCATION

I

The preceding chapter showed that one of the principal worries of contemporaries about the lower branch of the legal profession concerned standards of training. This one will explore in more detail the nature and quality of the training undergone by the mass of practitioners, the attorneys and solicitors, and at the same time consider their place in Renaissance England's version of law schools, the inns of court and inns of chancery in London.

Unlike that of their counterparts in most other European countries, the professional training of English lawyers had little to do with the universities. Medieval Oxford and Cambridge taught the canon law and the civil law, the laws of the church. But for several centuries before the accession of Elizabeth, men aiming to practise in the royal courts as counsellors or serjeants had learned the common law of the realm at the inns of court and chancery, which were located in Holborn, just down the river Thames from Westminster Hall. The inns offered learning exercises, readings, and moots, which enabled students to learn the elements of the law, and by the end of the sixteenth century, the call to the bar at one of the inns of court had become the accepted qualification which enabled a man to claim the right to audience before the courts and so enter the upper branch of the profession as a counsellor at law. Within the upper branch, in other words, membership of an inn became an essential prerequisite for becoming a lawyer.[1]

The relationship between practitioners in the lower branch and legal inns was never this straightforward. Since at least the late fourteenth century, the principal group of Chancery officials, the six clerks and their underclerks, had been segregated from the rest of the common lawyers, and in the early modern period the six clerks and the cursitors inhabited their own inns in Chancery Lane.[2] On the other hand, the rest of the clerical officials and the common law attorneys had long been associated with the inns of court and, especially, the inns of chancery. However, for such practitioners, membership of a legal inn was never a prerequisite for admission into an office or a qualification necessary for the right to practise, and the inns provided no formal teaching exercises which were designed specifically for men training to take up careers in the lower branch. For these reasons, the history of the relationship between the lower branch and the legal inns is best seen as the history of two more or less parallel developments which converge or diverge to a greater or lesser extent at different points in time.

As we saw in Chapters 2 and 7, statutes of Henry IV and James I, which were designed to control the entry into practice of attorneys, specified that practitioners should be diligent and learned in the law However, they did not say how these qualifications were supposed to be achieved. The judicial orders of 1632 were a little more precise in that they laid it down that no one was to be admitted to the courts as an attorney 'unless hee hath [served] a Clarke or Attorney of the courts or such as for their education and study in the lawe shalbe approved by the Justices of this Court'.[3] But, even by 1650, no single method of training was officially specified. Writing in 1658, the anonymous author of *The Practick Part of the Law* noted that attorneys were trained either by serving as clerks to older practitioners or by study at one of the inns of chancery.[4]

Although it is impossible to put a figure on it, there is little doubt that, of these two, clerkship was by far the most commonly used method. Since there were no hard-and-fast rules, one or two examples of men who became attorneys after time spent studying at the inns of chancery can certainly be found. But by comparison, the evidence for clerkship is overwhelming. The rules and orders of the King's Bench and Common Pleas, which begin in 1457, are filled with references to the clerks of attorneys.[5] In their letters practitioners frequently mention their servants or their 'men', words which were part of the language of apprenticeship. Clerkship to a country attorney was probably the most typical avenue into the profession, but there are examples of men who served as clerks to judges, serjeants at law, town clerks, and town court attorneys. In addition many were trained up as writing clerks in the offices of the prothonotaries, filazers, or other court functionaries. For instance, in 1580

George Needler, the third son of Simon Needler of Acton in Middlesex and aged about fourteen, became clerk to George Harrison of Gray's Inn, 'an antient attorney of Common Pleas and in varie good practise'. Needler served Harrison until the older man died six or seven years later; then he became a clerk for Robert Stanton, who himself had been Harrison's senior clerk. After three more years of service, Needler was admitted as an attorney of the Common Pleas. Similarly, Nicholas Allen was 'placed by his father' at the age of fourteen for six or seven years in the office of a successful Common Pleas attorney, Henry Burr.[6] John Rowe of Lewes, Sussex became a clerk to a local barrister in 1585. Rowe, who had been a precocious student of Latin and Greek at his local grammar school, began to practise in the 1590s, and was eventually elected principal of Clifford's Inn during the late 1630s. John Comber became a clerk in a prothonotary's office in 1552. He started work as an attorney in 1556 but continued to combine his own practice with service as a prothonotary's clerk until 1562. On the other hand, John Kele was a 'servant' for two or three years to an 'ancient' Common Pleas attorney before he became a clerk in Prothonotary Filmer's office in 1578.[7]

The examination of the wills of some attorneys who served as masters to clerks adds a few more pieces to the mosaic. In 1559, Thomas Hybbon gave his servant and 'prentice', John Manley, two sets of clothing and asked any of his friends who 'wolde sett forward learninge to favor and helpe him for surly he ys very apte thereunto and wanteth nothinge but exhibcon to maintayne hym in hit'.[8] In 1606, the King's Bench attorney William Astree of Staple Inn left £6 13s. 3d. to Richard Worley, his clerk and 'honest servant'. John Rosyer of Barnstaple gave John Seagar one of his books of entries and a copy of Rastell's abridgement of the statutes.[9] Richard Denton of Coventry, who died in 1593, left to his 'servant, Thomas Byrne, my Patten of the Registry shippe of the Archdeaconrye of Coventry w[i]th all fees and dewtys whatsoever thereto belonginge in as full and ample sort as the same is conveyed to me w[i]th all my bookes and wrytinges whatsoever because I will not have them dispersed abroade....'[10] Another Warwickshire attorney, Thomas Ashton, gave his servant, Randall English, many of the things that the younger man would need to establish his own practice. Ashton passed on his gown, chest, desk, and law books in London, along with the essential means of transport for termly trips between home and

London, a horse, bridle, and saddle. So, too, Hugh Willington gave to Henry Tadlow, who Willington presumed had 'well profitted in abilitie and learninge since he came to me and by my service all [his] law book*es* both imprinted and written....' In his turn Tadlow trained up yet another Warwickshire practitioner, Edmund Palmer.[11] However, relationships between master and clerk were evidently not always so good as these benefactions might suggest. In July 1632, Richard Cromwell was hanged for poisoning his master, Joseph Lane, an attorney of Fetter Lane in London.[12]

All of the instances cited above suggest that the training of attorneys was very much like that of other occupations for which apprenticeship was the principal means of entry. The choice of the profession was made for the future practitioner by his parents. The clerk then served for a period of approximately six or seven years, the traditional period of apprenticeship which was legally recognized in the Elizabethan Statute of Artificers (1562/3). During this time, he lived with his master, was part of his family, and acted as both law clerk and menial servant. For instance, in addition to reading Littleton and West's *Presidents*, Serjeant John Hoskyns' law clerk, William Taylor, was supposed to rise at five every morning, wait on table, keep an eye on the stable and horses, brush clothing, cut wood, do the garden, teach the children to read and write, and 'yf any stranger com, to attend your mistress in a reverent posture of body and readiness to serve'.[13] Moreover, the benefactions made in the wills of practitioner-masters resemble the traditional gifts of tools or clothing which were sometimes bestowed on apprentices in other trades after they had completed their training.[14] Finally, although evidence about the cost of becoming a clerk is frustratingly rare, it is likely that the master received a sum of money in return for a guarantee to teach his clerk the business of the profession. In 1625, Edward Osborne, a bencher of the Inner Temple, requested that his executors sell plate in order to pay for his son's training with 'some expert attorney', and in 1652, another barrister, Godfrey Copley, left £80 to a practitioner of the King's Bench who was supposed to 'bring up' his son in the profession.[15] By the early eighteenth century, when the evidence is much fuller, attorneys quite commonly took apprenticeship premiums of as much as £200 or above, amounts which compare very favourably with those demanded for entry into the most prosperous businesses or trades.[16]

There is therefore every reason to believe that the clerkship undertaken by attorneys in the late sixteenth and early seventeenth centuries was an apprenticeship in the strict sense; that is, the product of a formal legal agreement between master and parents which guaranteed that the clerk would be taught his trade in return for a cash premium and service. However, this point is impossible to prove because records of the details of indentures do not survive before the early eighteenth century.[17] The absence of such documents does not necessarily mean that practitioners were not trained through formal apprenticeship; the indentures themselves are exceedingly rare for every early modern occupation. But it does call attention to the fact that the training of members of the lower branch was uncontrolled by organizations such as livery companies or guilds whose archives preserve notes of formal apprenticeship for most other trades.

This lack of control over clerkship in the legal profession is at first sight surprising. On the other hand, guild supervision of apprenticeship was introduced in the middle ages by tradesmen who had no other means of overseeing the number and qualifications of men entering their occupations. In the case of the lower branch, such supervision had from the very earliest times been delegated by the crown to the courts; apparently, this means of control had made others seem unnecessary. Nevertheless, the informality surrounding the training of the lower branch is one characteristic which set it apart from other early modern occupations. It is also ironic that formal regulations requiring the registration of indentures relating to apprentice attorneys were not created until the second quarter of the eighteenth century, by which time the formal supervision of apprenticeship in other trades was beginning to decline.[18] The statute 2 Geo. II c. 23 (1728) stipulated for the first time that only attorneys who had been bound apprentices by contracts in writing should be sworn to practise in the courts, and a continuation act passed in 1749 finally required that affidavits relating to the contracts between attorneys and their clerks should be filed in the Westminster courts. Although concern for the quality of legal training played some part in the passage of these acts, the provisions about clerkship also owed a great deal to what must have been unexpected consequences of the stamp acts. In the early eighteenth century, every attorney who was sworn to practise in the courts had to pay £6 for a stamp. In order to avoid this fee, a number of practitioners entered the profession by having themselves made entering clerks in the offices of the prothonotaries of the two common law courts. Men who entered the profession in this way were subject neither to the educational requirements already established, the oath of attorney, nor the £6 duty. Thus a major aim of the two acts was to insure that this form of tax evasion was extirpated.[19]

Returning to the late sixteenth and early seventeenth centuries, the remaining significant point about training by clerkship is that the inns of court and inns of chancery played no direct role in the process. In fact, most practitioners joined a legal inn only after they had already finished their apprenticeships and were about to begin practice on their own. For example, George Needler, John Rowe, and Nicholas Allen all joined an inn only after they had completed their training, and none of their masters was associated with the inn which his clerk eventually joined.[20] More generally, of the forty-five men admitted into Barnard's Inn between 1634 and 1640 who are known to have become practitioners, the overwhelming majority were already in practice or just beginning to practise in the year of their admission.[21]

Nevertheless, although prospective practitioners were not members of the inns during their years as clerks, most of them probably did have some contact with the inns during this period of training. Clerks to attorneys, barristers, court officials, or judges accompanied their masters on their termly trips to London, and if the master was a member, they stayed at the inns of court and chancery while they were there. Thus, all of the inns contained thriving clerical sub-cultures. For example, at Lincoln's Inn a rule of 1517 prescribed that benchers should be allowed to keep two clerks in commons, and another of 1528 stated that barristers should be allowed only one. During the second half of the sixteenth century, only clerks who could read Latin, and who could write or intended to learn to write it, were allowed to dine in the clerk's mess in commons.[22] At meals in the Inner Temple, clerks occupied the so-called 'Yeoman's Table', which was separated by the hall screen from the tables of students and benchers of the society. At the Middle Temple, they were accommodated in their own building called the Clerk's House.[23]

The presence of clerks at the inns of court and chancery provides the final element in our picture of the usual course of training for an early modern practitioner. After he had learned to read and write at a local school, he was apprenticed to a legal practitioner, usually but by no means always a local attorney, at about the age of fourteen. The clerk was present with his master at the inns of court or inns of chancery during his time in service, but, although he may have profited to some extent from the general intellectual environment of the inns, the learning exercises provided no systematic part of his training; indeed, like his master, he was probably not even in London when the most important of them took place in the vacations between legal terms.[24] Only after he had served out his apprenticeship in the clerical underworld did the young practitioner move on to become a member of an inn, usually an inn of chancery.

A good individual example of the last stages of this general pattern is provided by the accounts of a Bedfordshire practitioner called Giles Blofield. His background is obscure, but when Blofield came up to London to join Barnard's Inn in Michaelmas Term 1564, he had already completed his legal training, and his accounts are very much those of a man starting out in the world. His admission to Barnard's Inn cost 10s., and his expenses for meals there came to two or three shillings weekly. Blofield's largest single outlay of the term was £1 2s. 2d., given for the black gown which members of the inns were required to wear at meals in commons. In fact, a large part of the £9 6s. 11d. he spent in London went into clothes. But there were also some professional expenses. Of these the most costly was £1 11s. paid to William Holland of Southwark for a 'flee bitten nagge', a necessity for a lawyer who needed transport to and from London and for visiting clients in the country. He also spent 2s. for nine quires of paper and 4d. for a box 'to put wrygthing*es* in'.[25]

Blofield's accounts break off after Trinity Term 1565, but, judging from his costs for the first three terms, he could have finished his first year at the inns of chancery for just under £20.[26] It is worth comparing this outlay with the expenses incurred by students at the inns of court. Prest has written that 'the accepted minimum cost of maintaining a student at the inns was about £40 a year' in the late Elizabethan and early Stuart perid.[27] If some allowance for the 70 per cent price increase between 1559 and 1602 is made, the £20 Blofield spent in 1564–5 might well be expected to increase to something over £30 by 1600. But, since Blofield spent a good deal on clothing which appears to have been not absolutely necessary, a less prosperous man could conceivably have lived for perhaps half as much. Nevertheless, it is obvious that the aspiring practitioner who joined an inn of chancery could not hope to begin a career without some financial support from parents, relations, or friends.

However, Blofield, like other attorneys, had an advantage which could help to overcome personal or paternal impecuniosity. During his first term in London, he was able to earn £1 13s. 7d. from legal work. Some of this income came from his own casework; the accounts show that he was handling a series of suits for a Mr Hardyng during his first few terms at Barnard's Inn, but some additional income appears to have come from clerical work for other attorneys. Blofield notes similar sources of income in Easter Term 1565, but after this date his account book turns into a record of his case load. His work for one man in 1564–5 in fact turns into a practice of five cases in Easter Term 1566. By May 1569, some sixteen clients owed him, by his own reckoning, £39 9s. 7d.[28] Although a load of six or ten cases per term was small by comparison with those of better-established attorneys, Blofield's practice was in reasonably good condition. He had successfully launched his career.

II

By 1600, then, although they had not, strictly speaking, been trained in them, it was the usual practice for members of the lower branch to take chambers at one of the legal inns. However, before going on to consider the communal life within the societies, we must first establish how this relationship between the inns and the lower branch had come about. In the early seventeenth century, the close connections between the inns of chancery and practitioners were of relatively recent date. In 1500, the functions of the inns of chancery and the place of the lower branch within legal inns generally was quite different from what they were to become one hundred years later.

The four so-called greater houses of court – Gray's Inn, Lincoln's Inn, the Inner Temple, and the Middle Temple – still have important places both in the legal life of the realm and in the architectural landscape of the legal district of London. The fate of the 'lesser houses', the inns of chancery, has been less fortunate. In the year 1600, eight of these inns – Clifford's Inn, Clement's Inn, Barnard's Inn, Lyon's Inn, New Inn, Thavies Inn, Furnival's Inn, and Staple Inn – occupied sites in Holborn, Fleet Street, and Chancery Lane. But, unlike the inns of court, none of the inns of chancery has survived into the twentieth century. Thavies Inn, the smallest of the societies, was dissolved in the late eighteenth century. The others were disbanded and largely demolished during the reign of Queen Victoria.[29] Partly because of this discontinuance, and partly as a result of bomb damage to the archives of the inns of court during the Second World War, the records of the inns of chancery are extremely scanty. Therefore, even at the best of times, a reconstruction of their memberships, functions, and daily life inevitably contains many gaps.[30]

Like that of the inns of court, the early history of the inns of chancery is obscure. All that is certain about the crucial fifteenth century, when most of the inns came into existence, is that their constitutions, locations, and functions were all in a state of continuous flux. The best hypothesis about their origins is that both types of inn began essentially as the households of prominent lawyers who housed and trained up their clerks within them. Eventually, as the profession grew, the role of individuals became less significant, and groups of lawyers took it upon themselves to hire a house and employ a cook so that they could have a reliable and congenial place to eat, work, and sleep while they were in London for the law terms. At this stage, such legal education as there was would have been in the form of clerks working for and learning from the older practitioners.[31] But, either gradually or, possibly, suddenly, at the order of the chancellor and the judges, the inns emerged during the course of the fifteenth century as organized societies where teaching was carried out by means of formal learning exercises. Thus by 1450, the inns had become law schools, but their role as such was never specified by any set of statutes or royal charter of incorporation. Furthermore, the educational function had been grafted onto societies which had been, and continued to serve as, the term-time residences and places of business of practising lawyers.

The only contemporary account of the fifteenth-century legal inns was written by Chief Justice Sir John Fortescue in the 1460s or 1470s. Fortescue's general picture was one of academies where the common lawyers learned their craft, but he also stressed that the inns of court and the inns of chancery were frequently resorted to by the sons of knights, gentry, and magnates who came to London, not to study the law in any detail, but to learn the manners and the courtly accomplishments which 'men brought up in the king's household are accustomed to practise'.[32] More particularly, he depicted the inns of chancery as subordinate to the inns of court and as places where young men learned 'the originals and something of the elements of the law, who becoming proficient therein as they mature, are absorbed into the greater houses of the academy, which are called the inns of court'.[33]

The reasons for the division of the societies into greater and lesser houses is something of a mystery, but the surviving evidence about the fifteenth-century inns of chancery for the most part verifies Fortescue's account. Non-professional gentry students or residents did make up a significant proportion of the memberships.[34] At the same time, like the inns of court, the inns of chancery exercised discipline and organized learning exercises. Both types of inn contained the ranks of inner and outer barrister, the former being junior and the latter senior students.[35] As early as 1407, the majority of the members of Furnival's Inn 'continued' on at the inn at the end of the Lent Term for several weeks, presumably so that they could participate in the learning exercises which were held in the vacations between law terms. In the reign of Henry VI, the records of the house mention moots, readings, the study of writs, and the putting of pleadings.[36] At Clement's Inn, 'the youngest of the First Mess of every Table at Meals' was supposed to read a writ out of the *Natura Brevium* on every working day both in term and in vacation.[37] At Clifford's Inn, writs were examined and the 'declaration of the opening of a court baron' was discussed before meals. Other exercises included mooting and the making of 'reports'.[38]

The one puzzling and disappointing feature of Fortescue's description is that he says nothing about attorneys and clerical officials. As far as we can tell, at this stage and indeed for the rest of the period up to 1550, the presence of the lower branch in the inns was a fact, but it was not a matter to which anyone attached a great deal of significance. Biographical studies of practitioners active in the late fifteenth century indicate that some, possibly the majority of, clerical officials and common law attorneys were members of legal inns.[39] But they showed no clear proclivity for membership of inns of chancery rather than inns of court, and it is clear that the educational activities of the houses were not directed towards them.[40] The only reference which alludes to the issue in any way, a statute of Clement's Inn, specifically excuses such practitioners from the learning exercises.[41] Furthermore, prior to 1550, attorneys and clerks probably constituted only a tiny proportion of all the members of any particular inn. Lists of members of Furnival's Inn, Clifford's Inn, and New Inn in 1553, which contain some 160 names, mention only a handful of practitioners, a fact which is not entirely surprising when it is recalled that the total capacity of the legal inns was something in the region of 1400, whilst the number of practitioners was not more than 300.[42] Nor were attorneys and clerks invariably prominent as leading members of the houses. John Hatton, the principal of Clifford's Inn in the 1550s, was a Lincolnshire attorney, but a list of the principal and ancients of Furnival's Inn in 1551 contains no known practitioners, and a number of the men on it apparently migrated soon afterwards to the parent house, Lincoln's Inn.[43] To sum up, attorneys and clerical officials were members of the late-medieval and early Tudor inns of chancery, but they were also members of the inns of court, and the inns of chancery appear to have been dominated in terms of numbers by young law students and gentry residents rather than by established legal practitioners.

The particularly close relationship between the lower branch and the inns of chancery, which was characteristic of the reign of Elizabeth and the early Stuarts, emerged only during the second third of the sixteenth century, and was a consequence of the increase in the size of the profession and of the further development of the inns of court as 'nurseries' for the education of the sons of the aristocracy and gentry.

The image of the inns as a 'third university of England', which had first been introduced by Fortescue, was cultivated by writers on the inns of court for two hundred years after his death. His idea that the inns were academies where the aristocracy and gentry received both a smattering of law and training in the courtly arts was easily compatible with those of early Tudor humanists such as Sir Thomas Elyot, who proposed that some legal training should crown the education of those men destined to become governors of the realm.[44] In the early 1540s, in fact, Henry VIII raised the possibility of making out of the inns a school specifically designed for young aristocrats by adding the study of foreign languages and the courtly arts to the legal curriculum. Elyot, the educational theorist, was a close associate of Thomas Denton, one of the three men charged with drawing up the project.[45] Nothing came of this particular proposal, but there is no question that by 1550 study at the inns of court was well established as a conventional part of the upbringing of the English gentleman.[46]

However, the lower branch, particularly the attorneys and solicitors, did not fit very well into this vision of the Renaissance inns of court. Trained mainly by apprenticeship, and of a social status inferior to that of most entrants, they conformed to neither the academic nor the social aspirations of the inns.[47] It is likely that these factors had always made their connections with the inns somewhat tenuous, but, beginning in 1556, the judges and benchers passed a series of orders designed to exclude attorneys and solicitors from the inns of court. Until the early seventeenth century, these orders contained provisos which mitigated their force, and even as late as 1650 there were still a few attorneys resident in the greater houses; but during the course of the late sixteenth century, it was made clear that such practitioners were unwelcome.[48] The principal reasons for the development of this policy were the claim that attorneys failed to participate in the learning exercises and a growing awareness of the supposed social exclusiveness of the houses and of the distinctions between the two branches of the profession. Both of the latter points are well illustrated by an exclusion order of 1614, which declared that the purpose of the inns was the education of the nobility and gentry of the realm, and which went on to state that 'there ought always to be observed a difference betwene a Councelar at Law which is the principal person next to Sergeants *and* Judges in the administracon of Justice *and attorneys* and *solicitors* w[hi]ch are but ministeriall persons *and* of an inferior nature....'[49] As the academic and social pretensions of the inns of court grew, so the attorneys and solicitors were made to feel more and more uncomfortable as members of them.

Excluded from the 'greater' houses but growing in numbers, it was perhaps inevitable that the lower branch should become entrenched at the inns of chancery. By 1585, when a detailed survey of Barnard's Inn and Staple Inn provides good information about the composition of the houses, active practitioners made up at least three-quarters of the membership, and of the ninety-nine men who were admitted to Barnard's Inn between 1634 and 1640, at least forty-eight are certain to have been common law attorneys.[50] In addition, by 1600 all of the lesser houses contained a large number of clerical officials, and their governing bodies were dominated by practitioners.

The growing domination of the inns of chancery by the lower branch was accompanied by significant alterations in the functions and activities of the inns as institutions. Gradually during the course of the reign of Elizabeth, most of the attributes which had characterized the inns as first stages in the careers of men who were going on to the inns of court withered or died away completely. Between 1573 and the mid-1580s, a large number of 'barristers' from the inns of chancery migrated to the inns of court, where many of them were subsequently called to the bar. Thereafter, ranks of membership below the governing bodies of principals and ancients disappeared from the inns of chancery.[51] By 1585, when we have fairly reliable information about Barnard's Inn and Staple Inn, it is clear that relatively few men stayed on for the learning vacations, and that many of these were bachelor attorneys or resident gents rather than young law students.[52] Sir Edward Coke, who went up to Clifford's Inn in 1571, remembered the inns of chancery as schools for students bound for the inns of court, but by the time he wrote (in early seventeenth century) this was very rarely the case.[53] For example, the number of entrants to Gray's Inn who came from an inn of chancery sank from 124 in the years 1586–91 to 47 between 1596 and 1600.[54] After the turn of the century, only a few members of the inns of chancery trickled into the inns of court, and sometimes these were attorneys migrating from the lesser to the greater houses.[55] The learning exercises survived until the Restoration in 1660, but they were clearly in decline during the early seventeenth century. Some readings failed because barristers from the inns of court did not show up in order to give them, but on other occasions there was clearly a lack of interest from within the lesser houses themselves. In 1628, for instance, members of Furnival's Inn stayed away from a reading because the reader neglected to distribute the customary gratuity.[56]

One reason for this transformation of the inns of chancery was simply that the active practitioners were taking over places which might otherwise have been used by students. In the Jacobean period, Barnard's Inn and Clement's Inn passed ordinances aimed at insuring that at least one or two chambers were kept aside for students in spite of the demand from attorneys and solicitors.[57] But, equally, it seems likely that the educational role of the inns was already beginning to fade in the early sixteenth century. The years from around 1530 to 1558 were a time of crisis for the lesser houses. Student numbers declined and financial troubles set in. In the fifteenth century, the treasury of Furnival's Inn had enjoyed a surplus of £200; in the 1540s the house was unable to pay its rent.[58] Partly because of these economic difficulties and partly as a result of government policy, the early sixteenth century saw the submission of the inns of chancery to the four inns of court. By 1550, the greater houses had bought up the sites of most of the lesser inns, and, although the inns of chancery were still nominally independent societies, ultimate responsibility for each of them had been delegated by the lord chancellor to one of the four inns of court.[59] Each of the lesser inns was said to 'belong' to one of the inns of court, and the dominance of the latter was solidified under Elizabeth and the early Stuarts in order to facilitate control over religious dissent and to insure internal order.[60]

Much more damaging, however, was the failure of student numbers to pick up again during the great increase in demand for higher education which took place during the second half of the sixteenth century.[61] In the 1560s, the inns of chancery rather desperately petitioned the inns of court not to admit men who had not first spent some time at one of the lesser societies. The inns of court responded by creating a special admission fee for students from the inns of chancery, but this did little in the long run to preserve their role as institutions for students aiming to move on eventually to the senior houses.[62] The inns of chancery evidently lacked the social cachet to attract large numbers of gentry members who were flooding into the inns of court. At the same time, the advent of printed legal texts and the increasing tendency for aspiring lawyers to come to the inns with university backgrounds made the preliminary sojourn at an inn of chancery seem unnecessary.[63] After a long courtship, the marriage between the lower branch and the inns of chancery was a matter of convenience for two misfits from the 'educational revolution'.

III

On the whole, the association between the lower branch and the inns of chancery was a happy one, but, as was the case with the education of practitioners, it must be seen in a context of informal connections and tradition rather than as a consequence of any rules of professional practice.

To begin with, not all members of the lower branch joined a legal inn. A survey carried out in 1585 indicates that the inns of chancery then accommodated about 750 men.[64] On the basis of a fairly complete picture of the memberships of Barnard's Inn and Staple Inn, it appears that about 255 of these places were taken by non-professionals and that of the remaining 525, about three-quarters, or 390, were occupied by clerical officials and common law attorneys.[65] Allowing further for the probability that the inns of court may still have housed at least another 50–100 practitioners, it is reasonable to estimate that nearly all of the 450–500 members of the lower branch active in the middle of the reign of Elizabeth joined one of the houses.[66] And this is verified by a list in the State Papers which almost invariably gives the inns as the term-time residence of 76 clerical officials and leading attorneys of the Common Pleas.[67]

Up to 1615 or 1620, the size of the lower branch was growing, and so, too, were the inns of chancery. Staple Inn and Furnival's Inn built new halls in the late 1580s, and new chambers are known to have been erected at Staple Inn, Barnard's Inn, and Clement's Inn.[68] Since the number of students was declining, it seems likely that there was plenty of room for practitioners and that up to 1620 or thereabouts most of them joined. However, after 1620 there was probably a decline in the proportion of practitioners who enrolled in an inn of chancery. By 1632, there were at least 1400 common law attorneys alone. If, as was the case at Clement's Inn, the total capacity of the inns of chancery between the 1580s and 1640 doubled to something in the region of 1500 places, then all of the practitioners could conceivably have been accommodated.[69] But the admissions register of Barnard's Inn, which covers the years from 1620 to 1660, suggests that the number of entrants each year in fact remained static throughout this period when the size of the lower branch was still increasing. Furthermore, only about half of those admitted to Barnard's Inn during the 1620s and 1630s can be proved to have been active practitioners.[70] There seems, therefore, to have been a movement of practitioners away from the inns, and this is confirmed by the judicial orders of 1632 (and repeated in 1654), which commanded that all attorneys and solicitors were to join an inn of court or inn of chancery. Since in the recent past it had been the usual course for such practitioners to join a legal inn, these orders can hardly have been intended as an innovation; instead, they were an attempt to maintain the *status quo* in the face of changing habits.[71]

The reasons for this drift away from the inns lay in the tension which existed between the country and the London sides of the practices of attorneys. In the late seventeenth and the eighteenth centuries, country work grew so dominant that attorneys rarely came to London.[72] In the early seventeenth century, most practitioners still travelled to Westminster for the law terms, but by the 1620s the influx of litigation had reached its peak, and, as the importance of country practices grew, some men began to spend less time in the capital. In the 1620s, for example, Clement's Inn was forced to require members to pay commons for the entire term even if they came up to London only for a week.[73] If some attorneys who were members of the inns of chancery made little use of them, it appears that other practitioners may have felt that membership of an inn was hardly a necessity if they were only going to be in London for short periods of time. Under these circumstances, the public houses of Holborn were a perfectly satisfactory alternative.[74]

At the same time, just as not all attorneys chose to join an inn, admission to an inn of chancery was not necessarily conditional on any claim either to legal expertise or a desire to learn the law. As the figures just quoted suggest, one-third, perhaps one-half, of those admitted to the inns did not, so far as is known, undertake legal careers. Some of these men, like the Harris brothers of Milton in Cambridgeshire, were minor gentleman farmers who were sent up to London to finish off their educations.[75] They were the descendants of Fortescue's gentleman students who came to the inns to learn the courtly arts rather than to study the law. They also had numerous counterparts in the inns of court, but the inns of chancery men were generally of lower social origins, and the lesser houses had nothing like the reputation of the inns of court as centres of wit, literature, and courtly accomplishment.[76] Other non-legal members pursued more serious interests. Henry Tamworth, a member of Barnard's Inn, who died in 1605, was a London scrivener. Richard Willet, an ancient of Staple Inn, who built chambers and contributed to the decoration of the new hall, had connections with the Clothworkers' Company of London, and George Roberts, who was specially admitted to Barnard's Inn in 1623, was a neighbourhood draper.[77] Finally, a number of the non-professional members – William Cobb of Felmersham in Bedfordshire, Stephen Pecke, jun., of Bedford, or John Rowley, jun., of Hertfordshire, for example – were the sons of successful practitioners. Sometimes such men were admitted with the clear intention that they should follow in their father's footsteps, but, just as often, the second-generation connection with an inn seems simply to have been designed to maintain the family tradition, perhaps to maintain contact with London, rather than to launch another legal career.[78]

In those instances where a son followed his father into a particular inn, the reason for his choice of society and for his successful admission was obviously the parental connection. However, in most other cases, too, there was probably some kind of pre-existing link between the inn and the new member. As far as is known, the inns had no established regulations or procedures concerning admissions, but for a man wishing to join an inn, particularly if he intended to embark on private practice, the quality of the available accommodation and the personal and professional characteristics of potential chamber mates were important considerations.[79] As a result of the system by which chambers were held, these questions were more likely to be resolved through negotiation with existing members than by any corporate decision taken by the governing bodies of the societies. Leases on chambers usually ran for a term of ninety-nine years, and the holder of such a lease could choose to pass it on to whomsoever he liked so long as the new man paid the nominal fee required for admission to the inn.[80] Those members of the societies who erected sets of chambers at their own expense had even greater powers of selection. No one could be admitted into the new rooms without the permission of the builder, and, equally, those to whom he chose to lease were assured of an admission into the inn.[81]

These conditions, and the desire for familiar companions, tended to foster family and personal connections within the inns. Thus, for example, the Gaddesden family of Hitchin in Hertfordshire had an association with Barnard's Inn which lasted from the middle of the reign of Elizabeth right up to the time of the civil wars. Thomas Gaddesden was a termer at the inn in 1585, and three other members of the family, including a town clerk of Hertford, were admitted in the early seventeenth century. In addition, another Gaddesden was schoolmaster of Hitchin school, and so very probably taught yet another Hitchin man, the attorney Robert Papworth, who entered Barnard's Inn during the same period. These men, along with John Rowley, jun., who has already been mentioned, and John Gulston of Wigell, the son of a Common Pleas prothonotary, account for five of the six admissions from Hertfordshire that are recorded at Barnard's Inn during the early seventeenth century.[82]

Another, slightly different, set of connections linked the town of Cambridge with Barnard's Inn. John Wickstead, a town alderman and Common Pleas attorney, was principal of the inn during the 1620s, and Christopher Rose, another local practitioner, was a senior member. Rose's son was admitted to Barnard's Inn in 1640, and another Cambridge man called Clarke was admitted 'at the instance' of Wickstead in 1623.[83] Furthermore, the Harrison brothers, John and Peter, who joined the inn in the late 1620s were the sons of North Harrison, who was town clerk of Cambridge and so an associate of Wickstead's in local government. Altogether, Wickstead and Rose can be associated with at least four of the nine Cambridge men who joined Barnard's Inn between 1620 and 1640, and the number would no doubt be higher if more biographical details were known.[84] More generally, ties such as these contributed to the strong regional bias which was characteristic of all those inns of chancery where any evidence survives about the make-up of the memberships. Clement's Inn was inhabited mainly by men from the west Midlands.[85] Lyon's Inn was the term-time home for many practitioners from Somerset, Devon, and Cornwall.[86] Barnard's Inn drew a high proportion of its members from East Anglia. For example, of 238 entrants to the inn between 1622 and 1639, 21 per cent were from Suffolk, 10 per cent from Cambridgeshire, 6 per cent from Essex, and 7 per cent from Norfolk. Thirteen per cent of the entrants came from London, and these along with those from East Anglia (including Bedfordshire, Hertfordshire, and Huntingdon) account for 64 per cent of all admissions where the geographical origins of the new members are known.[87]

Once they had joined an inn, members, whether practitioners or not, were obliged to obey the rules of the house, which were legislated and enforced by the governing bodies. In general the administration of the inns of chancery was slightly more democratic than that of the inns of court, which were controlled absolutely by the oligarchic benchers.[88] At the lesser inns, the company was divided into three estates, the members, the ancients, and a principal. The ancients were a self-recruiting group of twelve to fifteen senior members who, along with the principal, decided on and enforced the internal regulations of the house.[89] In addition, in some of the inns the ancients had the sole power of electing new principals, but in others the entire membership had a voice in the election of the principal or was at least given a chance to select one from two or three candidates put forward by the ancients.

Although the nature of the sources makes it difficult to produce exhaustive studies, it is clear that by the later sixteenth century the governing bodies of most of the houses were composed very largely of practitioners from the lower branch. Four of the six rulers of Staple Inn in 1596, including the principal, Thomas Frere, were attorneys. All four of the principals of Thavies Inn during the late 1620s and 1630 were practitioners, and so too were at least six of the eight governors of Furnival's Inn in 1608.[90] The majority of the seventeenth-century principals of Clement's Inn were common law attorneys, but at this house, which was located near the Six Clerks Inn in Chancery Lane, there was also a strong contingent of Chancery clerks and underclerks.[91]

Detailed biographical research would tell a good deal more about these men, but from the plea rolls and other miscellaneous information available for some of them, it is possible to produce a very general collective portrait. Most were country attorneys, who, like John Rowe of Sussex, had been a member for many years before becoming first an ancient and then principal of Clifford's Inn. The system of appointing ancients was based on seniority, so it is not surprising that most of them (and the principals) were men with successful, though by no means overwhelmingly large, practices. The principal of Thavies Inn in 1633, Peter Noyes, was town clerk of Andover, and he had already had a flourishing Common Pleas practice thirty years before, in 1606. Henry Plombe, a successful Norfolk attorney, was an ancient of Furnival's Inn in 1608. Jerome Alexander, another of the ancients of Furnival's Inn, was a practitioner in the King's Bench.[92] Of the nine seventeenth-century principals of Clement's Inn, five were men from the west Midlands. This regional solidarity among the rulers must reflect the way in which associations formed in the country found their way into the inns at London. Two of these men, Rowland Fryth and Anthony Langston, had prosperous practices. The other two, Thomas Holbeache and James Prescott, can safely be described as among the leading practitioners in their home county, Warwickshire. Holbeache was a member of a prodigious legal dynasty. He had a large, but by no means enormous, practice. One of his relations, Ambrose Holbeache, became an ancient of the inn in the 1640s, and yet another Thomas Holbeache was a principal of the house for many years during the early eighteenth century. Prescott, principal in 1649, was another successful lawyer. He was undersheriff of Warwickshire several times in the 1650s. In 1649 he was probably near the apex of his career, for when he died in 1661 he passed on a thriving practice to his son.[93]

The senior members of the inns took meals on high table and were due respect from their juniors, but it is unlikely that they exercised any authority over the professional activities of those members of their houses who practised law. This was left largely to the judges and prothonotaries of the courts. Therefore, the governing bodies of the inns were concerned mainly with the regulation of life within the societies, accounts received for admissions and commons, and money spent for food and the wages of domestic staff. The surviving statutes of the inns, such as those of Clifford's Inn and Clement's Inn, which date mainly from the days when the houses were filled with students, contain a number of regulations concerning the behaviour of members, mainly prohibitions against beards, staying out late at night, bringing women into the inns, gaming, and bad manners at meals in commons.[94] In the absence of any complete sets of minutes of the governing bodies of the inns, it is difficult to say precisely whether such rules were enforced consistently during the Elizabethan and early Stuart periods when the majority of members were grown men and professional colleagues, but interesting glimpses of the relationship between individual members and the governors are provided by two incidents from Barnard's Inn.

The first of these occurred in 1615, when John Wilkinson, a practitioner member, was reported to

have been with a lewd woman in bed about midnight, whereupon his chamber door was broken open and he and the said queene ... were found together in bed, to the great dishonor of God and scandal of the Society, if the same should not be made an example according to the rules of the House, whereupon he was fined 20s. and expelled the society.[95]

However, Wilkinson refused to accept this decision without protest and proceeded to sue the ancients and principal for making the intrusion.[96] The outcome of this dispute is not known, but a later incident from the 1630s shows that the governors of the inns could uphold their authority. In this one, a King's Bench clerk, Thomas Marsh, was accused of various unspecified 'misdemeanours and insolences' which seem to have amounted to a disregard for the power of the governors. He was expelled from the society unless he agreed to conform to the rules of the house, and on one occasion during the course of a six-year-long dispute the governors locked him out of his chamber. This brought an action of trespass from Marsh and a demand for £500 damages, but the principal of Barnard's Inn petitioned the judges of the King's Bench, and Marsh was imprisoned in the Marshalsea until he had signed a formal apology.[97]

Similarly, there were from time to time conflicts between the principals and ancients and the rest of the memberships. At New Inn in 1609 and at Clifford's Inn in 1615, the principal's handling of the accounts aroused the suspicion of junior members.[98] The selection of principals was another source of tension, and in at least two of the societies, Furnival's Inn and Clifford's Inn, the principal could be deposed if the members joined together with the ancients against him. In 1567, for example, the benchers of Lincoln's Inn had to intervene in an incident caused by an attempt by members of Furnival's Inn to drive their principal from office on a charge of misgovernment, which was probably connected with his accounts.[99] Trouble erupted at Staple Inn when the principal tried to dismiss the butler, and there was another flare-up at Furnival's Inn in 1600 when the ancients and outgoing principal were accused of fixing the election of a new principal in favour of the candidate of the old one.[100] In each of these disputes, most of the members of the inns concerned appear to have become involved. Members of Furnival's Inn were accused of 'labouring voices' for the election in 1600. The companions of Staple Inn used the incident about the butler to vent other grievances, and the ancients complained of the 'great hart *and* stomach that the unruly youthes of our house by the incident have taken against their governours....'[101] In many respects, these disagreements are reminiscent of the conflicts between oligarchies and outsiders which occurred in towns during this same period.[102] In both the inns and in towns, friction arose because of the disproportionate power wielded by a small minority which was, in every respect apart from its hold on authority, little different from the majority over which it ruled. In the inns as in towns, particular incidents most likely involved factional alignments or clashes of personality which are in the case of the inns hidden from view. Also as in towns, most of the disputes at the inns appear ultimately to have been resolved in favour of the authorities.

Nevertheless, even though their educational role had atrophied, even though their association with the lower branch was ill defined and transitory, and even though there were tensions between the governors and junior members, the inns of chancery did have a sense of community which transcended all of these shortcomings, and which contributed to the collective identity of their lawyer members. At Barnard's Inn, there were informal initiation parties for new entrants.[103] In all of the houses, chamber-fellows frequently became close friends, and some members asked brethren and servants of the inns to participate in their funerals.[104] There was also a sense of pride in the houses. In 1608, for example, the ancients of Furnival's Inn reminded the benchers of Lincoln's Inn that 'there hath proceeded from O[u]r society most Honourable Counsellors of Estate and

Pillers in the Kingdom'.[105] It was not unusual for members to donate
money to the societies or to buy pieces of commemorative silver. One
practitioner, Alan Hendre, even went so far as to chastise his fellow
members of Thavies Inn for having too little interest in making
improvements to the place.[106] Although the intellectual life of the
inns of chancery was hardly sparkling, there was at Staple Inn a circle
of early-seventeenth-century senior members whose interests
stretched well beyond the confines of the law. One member of the
group, Henry Farmer, was principal of the inn in 1609 and a man
who believed that it was not 'amiss for him that shalbe a common
Lawyer, to have some knowledge also in other liberal sciences'. In
addition to lawbooks, Farmer's will mentions books on medicine and
several works on divinity, including Calvin's *Institutes*, a synopsis of
papism, and *The Practice of Christianity*, by Richard Rogers. The
library of another member of the circle, Richard Barton, contained
works on physic and astronomy, a Chaucer, maps, and a number of
dictionaries.[107]

Admittedly, and not surprisingly, bachelors who lived at the inns
more or less full time were the members who maintained the closest
ties with the societies.[108] For the vast majority of entrants, country
attorneys who came up to London for the law terms, the inns of
chancery were first and foremost a convenient place to stay and work,
but some of these men, too, became active members and principals.[109]
At the very least, the inns were places which threw together
practitioners at the heart of the legal world. Dinner in commons,
once, and at times perhaps still, the scene of learning exercises, was
doubtless dominated by legal gossip. When members of the lesser
houses accompanied the ceremonial processions from Holborn to
Westminster Hall which marked the creation of judges and serjeants
at law, they participated in events which clearly distinguished the
entire body of the legal profession from the rest of English society.[110]
Indeed, the survival of the inns of chancery in this period of
transition is testimony to the strength of tradition which had long
been established at the legal inns and within the lower branch. The
disputes at the houses and the resistance of some members to their
discipline are signs of the strains and impending breakdown which
changes in the profession were creating. But the willingness of the
majority of members to submit to the rules of the houses and to the
authority of the ancients and principals demonstrates the attraction
which membership of guild-like communities still held for a group
of men who were otherwise highly mobile and independent.

IV

Having established that most lawyers within the lower branch were trained by clerkship, and having discussed their place within the inns of chancery, we can now attempt an assessment of the nature and quality of the legal training which this career pattern enabled practitioners to achieve. This is an important subject for two reasons. First, it tells us a good deal about the nature of the common law as practised within the lower branch. More important, since attorneys and solicitors were very often the first points of contact between litigants and the courts, some estimate of what they knew provides insights into the quality of the legal services which clients were able to procure.

In his *A Preparative to Pleading... [Being] A Work Intended for the Instruction and Help of Young Clerks of the Common Pleas*, which was published in 1675, the prothonotary and former Common Pleas attorney, George Townesend,[111] set out his views on who clerks should be and what they should learn. Townesend thought that a potential clerk should be a 'good *Latin-Scholar* (and a little *Greek* may do him good)... of an able and healthy Body to endure Cold and sitting at his Writing, and his Estate in present or future hope not to be so large as to lessen his industry'. Six years of clerkship was best; five the absolute minimum. The first skill a clerk need acquire was the ability to write in a neat 'clerk-like' hand. Having mastered this task, he should then begin to make up his precedent books. These were best if written on good paper and bound in vellum, and one volume should be devoted to each of the major forms of action: case, trespass, slander, promises, nuisances, etc.[112] The precedents were the mainstay of the attorney's learning, but Townesend, like the anonymous author of *The Practick Part of the Law*, thought that 'the office of an Attorney requires much knowledge both of the Theorique and Practice parts of the law', so the clerk's master should allow him time for deeper reading. Even after he was admitted to practise, the young man should, if possible, continue his study.[113] The books recommended for this advanced work include *The Terms of the Law*, Cowell's *Interpreter*, Finch's *Law*, Littleton, *Doctor and Student*, Coke's *Institutes*, and the more popular reports. The attorney who followed such a course could certainly claim to be well learned in the law. The question is how many men were as well prepared as these ideal clerks of a post-Restoration writer.

Books, both in manuscript and in print, provide the main clues about the legal knowledge of attorneys. Books, mainly books of precedents, are mentioned often in wills and inventories. Dying practitioners were frequently concerned that their compilations of precedents did not go to waste. A caricature of an attorney which dates from the time of Charles I depicts books labelled 'West's Presidents', 'Lawyers Light', 'Proclamations', and 'The Attourneys Academy'.[114]

The last of these works, which was published in 1623, is the book most commonly associated with the lower branch. However, in conception and to a large extent in execution, *The Attourneys Academy* could not have been an original work by its reputed author, Thomas Powell. A number of quite similar works, which date from as early as the 1580s, have been found amongst the papers of attorneys.[115] A manuscript in the Inner Temple library entitled 'The Perfect Instruction of an Atturney in the Common Place... with all Rules, Orders, Actions, writt*es*...', which has much the same form and content as the published *Academy*, was compiled in 1592 by Richard Robinson.[116] This tract is perhaps the most likely source of the printed version, but the large number of surviving manuscripts indicates that works of this kind were a common means of passing on the basic knowledge of the profession from late in the reign of Elizabeth, and probably long before.

In either printed or manuscript form, manuals like *The Attourneys Academy* were very useful tools for young practitioners. They explained the general course of procedure in the major courts, how to start an action, where to go for writs, and what fees needed to be laid out. A typical passage on how to commence a suit reads: 'First you are to understand of what nature the Action which you would sue must be. If it be for Debt upon a Bond, you must take special care that your Original dow agree with the Bond....'[117] However, although it contained essential information, the *Academy*, or works like it, could not alone have produced a very satisfactory practitioner. It defines few terms, and though it explains how to start an action, it gives no guidance about how the attorney, given a complaint from a client, might decide whether or not he could offer a remedy at law. Indeed, in the hands of the unscrupulous, self-styled solicitors so often decried by contemporaries, the *Academy* contained just enough information to make the law a costly and confusing weapon, and in the third edition Thomas Powell himself wrote that the work was intended more for the illumination of laymen than for professionals.[118] During the legal publishing spree of the 1650s, better works of this kind were produced, but, as the author of one of them put it, a real knowledge of the more theoretical aspects of the law had to be learnt 'out of the body of the Law, and cannot be expected to be ascertained in one small tract'.[119] Fortunately, several good examples of the working libraries of attorneys survive, so that it is possible to see in some detail how works like *The Attourneys Academy* were supplemented by deeper reading.

In each of these cases, the basis of the attorney's art was his precedent book. Precedents covered several categories of legal learning. In the books of John Clifford of Frampton (fl. *c.* 1640–80), for example, there are precedents for drawing leases, and conditions to perform covenants, jointures, bargains and sales, along with examples, copied from the plea rolls, of how to plead in cases of dower, formedon, debt for rent in arrears, trespass of cattle on corn, and actions on the case for carrying tobacco.[120] Clifford, who had a manuscript copy of 'The Office of an Atturney...', collected information on how to sue out fines and recoveries and how to take interrogatories in Chancery cases.[121]

The precedents served two functions. On the one hand, they provided fairly mechanical examples of legal instruments, leases, wills, and so on, which the practitioner could easily adapt to particular circumstances providing these were not unduly complicated. The same was true of precedents for pleading as well, but as the lawyer gathered examples of how to plead a certain action (say, actions on the case for words) he also collected information which could serve as a guide which might help him to tell a client whether or not he could expect help from the law. Moreover, although Clifford made his collection in manuscript books of his own, there were from the mid sixteenth century printed compendiums which could serve as sources. In 1541, for example, John Tysdale printed *The Tenours and Forme of Indentures, Obligations, Quitances, Bylles of Payment, Letters of Sale and Letters of Exchange*, which included forms for everything from the sale of wool to how to make a will. There were also useful published books on pleading and more basic matters such as the definition of legal terms.[122]

Precedent books were useful, and during the course of collecting his precedents, the young clerk or attorney could no doubt learn a great deal about the law. However, an even more studious practitioner might advance his studies by beginning a commonplace book. This device, which was characteristic of the learning of barristers, consisted of alphabetical headings of various legal topics under which the student entered precedents of pleadings and also extracts from the law reports on cases in which new circumstances produced arguments in court and new decisions by the judges. Under the heading of actions on the case for slander, for example, the lawyer would write out definitions and note the most important recent decisions of the court about the conditions under which the action succeeded or failed. For most lawyers, the commonplace book was probably the most sophisticated means of organizing legal knowledge.

John Clifford of Frampton began a commonplace book in the same thick volume he used for his precedents and 'The Office of an Atturney'. However, he did not finish it, nor is his collection of precedents particularly impressive.[123] It is tempting to judge his diligence by the fact that at some stage he turned his precedent book into a register of the cases he was handling for clients. But since he was a son-in-law of the legal author William Sheppard, Clifford, like others of his generation, may well have used printed books to supplement his knowledge.[124]

John Clifford was a moderately successful country attorney. Another sort of practitioner is represented by the manuscripts of Elias Ashmole, the antiquary and astrologer, who began his working life as an attorney and solicitor. Ashmole was of course an exceptional man, but his short legal career illustrates that of a man who practised law without formal training either as a clerk or as a student at one of the inns of court or chancery. The son of parents who were respectable but of modest means, Ashmole owed what prospects he had in life to his friendship with Justinian Paget, a son of James Paget, a puisne baron of the Exchequer.[125] As a young man, Elias went to London with the Pagets and spent some time there sharing their interests in music and, possibly, the law. This connection was also no doubt helpful when Ashmole set about his career of soliciting causes in Chancery in 1638. As far as is known, he had no special training before or after this date, but in 1640 he was taken into the household of Lord Keeper Finch, where he was probably allowed to develop his studies as best he could. Admitted an attorney of Common Pleas in 1641,[126] Ashmole's legal manuscripts include a few items of antiquarian interest (addresses to new serjeants at law; a book of reports on exchequer cases), but the mainstays of his study as an attorney were a precedent book, some notes about the courts by Coke, which he copied from a Finch manuscript, and the predictable 'Instruction for an Attorney'.[127] This last work, though very much like other examples of the genre, is particularly interesting because it demonstrates how an intelligent man might go about making a quick study of the work of an attorney. The emphasis in Ashmole's notes was on finding out what actions applied to which circumstances rather than on the course of procedure in various offices or fees charged. He made lists of offences for which trespass lay, and noticed that an action of detinue could be brought for anything 'you have bought and cannot have'. For ejectments, rents, covenants, and debts upon specialities, the practitioner was reminded of the bare necessities, i.e. 'gett the writing w[i]th the Circumstances of Tyme and place and the breach of Covenant and note of soe much money as is vnpaid at the tyme of the Eiectment'.[128]

Ashmole might have been able to render reasonably good advice to a client, and he was doubtless capable of following a suit competently. However, other attorneys, quite possibly any who went through systematic apprenticeship, were certainly more learned than he. For example, in his *Symbolaeographia*, a popular and useful work, which went through several seventeenth-century editions, the attorney William West provided not only an encyclopedic list of precedents for judicial and extra-judicial instruments, but prefaced his examples by theoretical discussions of them which frequently drew on civilian and continental scholarship.[129] The most prodigious library of an attorney that has yet come to light belonged to the Durham attorney and member of Clifford's Inn, Christopher Mickleton. Mickleton owned precedent books and the instruction manuals for attorneys, but in addition he took notes on readings at Clifford's Inn during the 1620s. Instead of having a mere commonplace book, he collected treatises on pleading, matrimonial law, wills, ancient statutes, and the course of practice in Star Chamber. He owned an English–Hebrew grammar and started a tradition of collecting historical documents which was passed on to his son, and which has resulted in one of the most impressive local antiquarian collections in England.[130] If he read and understood everything he owned, Mickleton must have been a very good lawyer.

In general, attorneys were a fairly bookish group of men, and, although the details of their working libraries have not survived, there is some evidence about the wider intellectual interests of a number of individual practitioners. One of the principal tasks of an attorney engaged in litigation was the responsibility for searching out and organizing evidence for trials. Disputes about titles to land often involved the study of local genealogy, and service as town clerks or manorial stewards gave practitioners an interest in local customs and history. Thus a number of early-seventeenth-century attorneys became notable antiquarians. For example, James Prescott of Warwickshire was an associate of both Sir Simon Archer and Sir William Dugdale. John Rowe of Sussex and Thomas Jekyll of Essex are reckoned amongst the earliest historians of their counties. Henry Trussel of Winchester wrote a history of England from Edward III to Henry VII as well as a work on the antiquities of his town. Henry Menship is the earliest historian of Great Yarmouth. Anthony Bradshaw collected precedents from a number of different sources to produce a usable reference work on the customs of the royal honour of Tilbury, where he was steward. Three generations of Exeter town clerks, the Izackes, were responsible for collecting historical notes on their city.[131] An important aspect of more celebrated works such as Dugdale's *Warwickshire* and Burton's *Leicestershire* is their concern with the descent of land, precisely the kind of question which many a local practitioner must have had to ask himself. From the point of view of utility, local history rather than the history of the common law was more likely to have been of interest to a provincial practitioner, and this is a subject to which some of them made significant contributions.

From these wider interests of particular men, it may be justifiable to infer some professional competence. Any generalization about the quality of the lower branch as a whole is of course more difficult to make. A fair guess would be that the average country practitioner knew more than Ashmole and less than Christopher Mickleton. He could draw extra-judicial instruments, sue out a fine, follow a case through all of its procedural stages, and probably be expected in most instances to give a sensible opinion on whether or not the complaints of clients were likely to find remedies in the courts. He might also know a good deal about the history of his locality.

Finally, it is of interest to set this evaluation of the training of practitioners against contemporary attitudes towards their learning. The popular satirical image of the attorney was that of the pompous ignoramus. In his *Micro-cosmographie*, the bishop and Oxford don John Earle depicted the attorney as a man with only a smattering of learning which he used badly while trying to make as much money as possible.[132] Though less vituperative, the views of some writers on the legal profession were hardly more favourable. Sir George Buc, for example, wrote that the accomplishments of barristers and attorneys were different and unequal.[133] The fellowships of both Lincoln's Inn and the Middle Temple claimed that the presence of attorneys and solicitors was a disgrace to the honour and glory of the societies.[134]

In part these notions were based on distinctions between the learning of attorneys and that of barristers which were not without foundation, but more than anything else they were simply the product of prejudices against training by apprenticeship. As Richard Robinson wrote in 1592, the law consisted of two parts, practice and judgment. The former was the preserve of attorneys; the latter, that of barristers.[135] However, although such distinctions between the scientific learning of the barristers and the 'mechanical' learning of attorneys were real enough, they had neither clear definition nor very much importance before the middle of the sixteenth century when attorneys were excluded from the inns of court and the call to the bar became the necessary qualification for practice before the central courts. Furthermore, the crucial development which exacerbated these differences was the association, by Fortescue, Tudor humanists like Sir Thomas Elyot, and later writers such as Buc and Sir William Dugdale, of the inns of court with the academic training of the nobility and gentry of the realm. This association was part of a web of social and educational ideas which simultaneously raised the status of legal education offered by the inns and disparaged the training by apprenticeship which was characteristic of the lower branch.

For writers like Elyot, the ideal man of law was modelled on the 'prudente' of classical Rome. Presumably from their own experiences, but certainly from classical authors, Renaissance social theorists developed a strong dislike for lawyers and lawsuits.[136] Since litigation was a social evil, the ideal lawyer became the man who could avoid it, who was rich enough not to have to worry about fees, and who could combine his leisure and learning in the service of the commonwealth or jurisprudence. Most commentators evidently agreed with Quintilian that the perfect lawyer was 'no hack advocate, no hireling Pleader, nor yet, to use a harsher term, a serviceable attorney... But rather a man... uniquely perfect in every detail and utterly noble alike in thought and speech'.[137] At the same time, humanist writers also stressed the value of general legal studies as a desirable background for gentlemen who would subsequently serve the state as magistrates; and the gentry did flood into the legal inns during the course of the reign of Elizabeth.[138] Hence there was a concern to maintain the purity of blood of the entrants. For example, a set of proposals for parliamentary legislation in 1559 explained that no person should be allowed to study laws 'except he be immediately descended from a nobleman or gentleman, for they are the entries to rule and government....'[139]

Attorneys and solicitors did not benefit from the emergence of this association among law, gentility, and the exercise of magistracy. By contrast with students of the inns of court or universities who were supposedly undertaking liberal studies which would prepare them to govern, members of the lower branch entered their profession through apprenticeship, a form of vocational training which was identified with mere 'mechanical men', artisans and tradesmen. There was nothing inherently deficient about this method of training lawyers. Before 1400 it had probably been the means by which all members of the profession acquired their skills. In the later seventeenth century, Roger North warned young barristers not to concentrate exclusively on theory, but to look also at more practical aspects of legal learning if they hoped to become good lawyers.[140] Indeed, it is not clear how far the learning exercises at the inns of court ever contributed to the education of barristers. Barnes has argued recently that most barristers probably learned their trade through the informal and practical exercise of watching established lawyers work in court. He speculates further that a large number of them may have been trained within the clerical offices.[141]

However, whatever its merits or the extent of its use, sixteenth-century educational theories did not regard apprenticeship as an appropriate means for the training of gentlemen. In the later middle ages even the sons of the nobility and gentry had been prepared for their future roles in life by service in magnate households or at the royal court. But humanist writers who urged the ruling élite to exchange their martial and chivalric values for those of the Latin grammar and devotional tract also contributed to the abandonment of service in favour of the school and the university.[142] At the same time they emphasized the Aristotelian distinction between the liberal education fit for governors and the training through apprenticeship which was characteristic of 'mechanical' trades. Elyot believed that apprenticeship destroyed good minds.[143] Some contemporaries subscribed to the view that it derogated from gentility; many others took it for granted that mechanical men were not fit to become magistrates.[144] Thus practitioners in the lower branch were vilified, not because of the insufficiency of their learning – to accept such a view is merely to accept contemporary sneers – but because they had the wrong kind of education. Theirs is a good example of the way in which educational changes during the Renaissance began to erect social and cultural barriers between different groups of men.

9

PRIVATE PRACTICE

I

Thus far in this study, most of the questions which have been examined focus on changes in the size and shape of the legal profession and on the relationship between various groups of practitioners and the courts and the legal inns of London. However, in order to consider the wider role of lawyers in English society, both as providers of legal services and as participants in public life, we must turn away from London and look once again to the provinces, for it is only in the local setting that we can place the particular profile of the lower branch against the background of a more general picture of early modern social and political life.

The most important single development in the relationship between the lower branch and English society was, of course, simply the enormous increase in the number of practitioners which occurred between 1560 and 1640. But, quite apart from this, there are two other general features of the early modern profession which are worth observing before we go on to look in more detail at the private practices and public careers of practitioners.

First, by the early seventeenth century the lawyers who figured most prominently on the local scene were the attorneys of the Common Pleas. The principal reason for this was simply that they were more numerous than any other group. In Warwickshire in 1606, for example, the only King's Bench attorney of note was John Harborne of Middlesex, a man who owed his connections with the west Midlands to his marriage to a daughter of the prominent Warwick barrister Rowley Ward.[1] In Devonshire, there were at least eighty-six Common Pleas attorneys active during the course of the first half of the seventeenth century as compared to some fourteen or fifteen men from the King's Bench. Some of the King's Bench men, Thomas Shapcott of Exeter and Gilbert Eveleigh of Totnes, for instance, were active members of their local communities,[2] but, on the whole, the work of practitioners in King's Bench, like that of the six clerks in Chancery and their underclerks, or like that of attorneys in the court of Wards or Requests, tended to some extent to draw them away from the countryside towards London. In all of these courts the numbers of practitioners were limited, and the men who acted as attorneys were also deeply involved with clerical work. The consequences of these factors can be well illustrated by consideration of the case loads and life-styles of the King's Bench attorneys. Studies of the geographical origins of cases handled by individual practitioners in 1606 show that the overwhelming majority of them (about 90 per cent) drew between 50 and 70 per cent of their business either from a single county, adjacent counties, or a single assize circuit.[3] Thus, one part of the work of a King's Bench attorney was locally based. But, equally important, a second, though smaller, part consisted of cases from all over the country which must have been brought up to him in London by other practitioners, and this dual basis of their practices – one part local attorney, one part clerical official in London – was reflected in their residential habits. They frequently owned houses in London in addition to property in the country, usually in their place of birth.[4] They had important professional and personal connections with specific places in the country, but the nature of their work attracted them towards London, and hence drew them more outside the world of local affairs than were their contemporaries in the Common Pleas, the men who were the true 'general practitioners' of the lower branch.

However, just as some groups of practitioners moved away from the country towards London, even amongst those who continued to be based in the provinces there was a marked shift in residential preferences which resulted in a movement away from rural areas and towards provincial towns. Of the practitioners active in the three counties Devon, Hertfordshire, and Warwickshire between 1560 and 1600, only a handful lived in towns, and these were concentrated in the largest places. At least three Common Pleas men, Hugh Willington, Richard Denton, and Thomas Tyllesley, worked in Coventry during the late sixteenth century, and there were four attorneys in Exeter at the same time – Philip Biggleston, Walter Borrell, John Trosse, and George Izacke.[5] No doubt the same was true of other major urban centres such as Bristol, Norwich, and York,[6] but the majority of late-sixteenth-century practitioners lived in the country and, as far as we can tell, frequently had agricultural interests.[7] However, with the turn of the sixteenth century, this picture begins to change. The place of residence of ninety-nine members of the three-county sample who were active in the early seventeenth century are known, and sixty-seven of these (68 per cent) lived in towns.[8]

Several different kinds of variable appear to have determined the concentration of attorneys in any particular place. The largest and most important towns naturally tended to attract the largest numbers of practitioners. Exeter had at least ten early-seventeenth-century attorneys, and four more lived within six miles of the city.[9] There is evidence of only one attorney, Henry Tadlow, in Coventry during this period, but several practitioners lived in villages not more than three miles away, and we have already noted a concentration of ten attorneys along the fifteen-mile axis between Coventry and Birmingham.[10]

However, attorneys were not confined to the largest towns and their neighbouring countrysides. Most of the prosperous towns in Hertfordshire and Devonshire – Hemel Hempsted, Totnes, Tiverton, for example – had one or two attorneys, and in an important market town such as Hitchin there might be two or three. Furthermore, towns which were of some administrative importance appear to have attracted unusually large numbers of practitioners. The seven or eight attorneys who lived in seventeenth-century Warwick (pop. *c*. 3000) reflect its status as the county town and venue for meetings of assizes rather than any great economic prosperity.[11] The same was true of Stafford, another west Midland town whose economy was not strong, but where the prospect of regular legal work at assizes attracted attorneys.[12] Similarly, the four attorneys of Barnstaple may be connected with the fact that the Devon assizes met there as well as in Exeter. Even at Exeter itself, the large contingent of attorneys was doubtless a consequence of its administrative as well as its economic importance. Thus it appears that attorneys were to be found in most early-seventeenth-century towns of any importance, but that they were most heavily concentrated in the largest of them, and also in towns such as Warwick which served as the administrative centres of their localities.

Although there were exceptions, the majority of attorneys appear to have been born in the countryside; therefore those who lived in towns must have made a choice to migrate to them. The most important factor governing this choice may well have been whether or not they inherited much land in the country. This can be illustrated if we turn for a moment from those practitioners who lived in towns to those who stayed on in the country. The only significant pattern which emerges from a look at the geographical distribution of rural attorneys is that there were concentrations of them around places like Coventry or Exeter. Apart from this, their main common characteristic was that they all had family ties, usually ties of inheritance, in the places where they lived. In Warwickshire, notable examples are the Knights of Barrells, William Clarke of Tysoe, and Josias Bull of Coleshill; in Hertfordshire, Edward Hyde of Great Hadham, James Willymot of Kelshall, and John Rowley of Barkway.[13] All of these men inherited land in the country. The exact financial status of the four attorneys – Thomas Hawes (fl. 1560), George Averell (fl. 1600), Thomas Jackson (fl. 1600), and George Palmer (fl. 1600)[14] – who lived near Solihull is unknown, but these families, which were related by marriage, had long been resident in the vicinity. In any case, the proximity of Solihull to Birmingham meant that they could both live in the country and enjoy the benefits of town practices. Much the same was true of Simon Blythe of Allesley and the Holbeaches of Meredin, though in this case the nearest town was Coventry.[15]

If an attorney had strong ties in the country, he stayed there; if he did not have such ties, he was likely to work in a town. As the profession expanded during the course of the early seventeenth century, there was probably a slight decline in the social status of men who entered it, so that more of them came to it without land of their own. Under such circumstances, towns were a natural place to settle. But to describe the migration into towns solely in these terms would be misleading. Towns evidently had their own attractions no matter what the economic circumstances of individual practitioners. In the early seventeenth century at least three attorneys, John Halford, Edmund Rawlins, and Thomas Shapcott, are known to have left modest inheritances to settle in Warwick, Stratford, and Exeter respectively.[16] Even in the sixteenth century, two country attorneys, Thomas Hore of Chudleigh and Thomas Ashton of Sheldon,[17] kept rooms in the major cities of their region, and many others may have shared this practice. Finally, as we have seen, a number of practitioners who did not reside in towns lived near them.

In the case of important trading centres such as Exeter, Coventry, and Birmingham or important market towns like Hitchin, Tiverton, and Barnstaple, the attraction was no doubt the prospect of clients created by active economies. But the lure of an urban economy does not seem to have been of singular importance, for a 'declining' town such as Warwick attracted the largest single concentration of attorneys in its county simply because it was an assize town, a known place for the conduct of legal business. In this respect the attraction of towns for lawyers was part of the evolution of some lesser market towns from centres of production into centres of consumption. Lawyers were one of the many services which towns offered and which, increasingly as the seventeenth century progressed, people came to expect of them. Moreover, for members of a rapidly expanding profession, in which competition for business was increasingly keen, living in the pastoral isolation of a country village was a luxury which few could afford. Large numbers of attorneys settled in towns during the seventeenth century because towns were the best available shop windows for the various services they were anxious to display. Before 1600, with the exception of those who lived in the largest towns, attorneys must be seen in the context of rural society, but after that date any account of them must portray a sizeable part of the profession in terms of London and provincial town life. Like the apothecaries and physicians, they had become typical features in the urban landscape.

II

Having followed practitioners back to the country and placed them within their rural and urban settings, we can now stop to look more closely at their activities there. These fall roughly into two categories – the practice of their profession and their involvement in public life.

For the typical country attorney, the first prerequisite for establishing a successful private practice was finding clients who would pay him to do legal work for them. Family connections might be helpful for this purpose. For example, Elias Ashmole spent the early part of his practice as a solicitor working for friends and relations, and attorneys from large Devon clans such as the Prideauxs, the Calmadys, and the Rolles could doubtless have been kept fairly busy with family work. But the migration of attorneys into towns would seem to suggest that few men could live exclusively on work acquired through kinship networks. The period of apprenticeship, during which an aspiring practitioner learned his trade, was probably more important in helping to launch careers. Clerks had the opportunity to meet people who might become clients, and some of them, like Henry Tadlow and Randall English of Warwickshire, were lucky enough to inherit already established practices from their masters.[18]

These elements of continuity were a particular advantage to attorneys who followed their fathers into the profession. In most of these cases, the father appears to have been relatively successful, so his son was able to start his practice in a strong position. The Skinners of Hitchin provide an interesting example of such a family practice. Its founder, John Skinner (1570–1660), came from Norfolk to Hitchin around the turn of the sixteenth century. Until his death, he shared his practice with his two sons, John junior (1596–1669) and Ralph (1606–97), who then carried it on afterwards. Ralph Skinner, who died heirless, was the last of the male line of this long-living family, but John junior's daughter married Sir Thomas Byde, a rich London brewer, who settled at Ware Park in Hertfordshire.[19] The wealth and local influence of the Skinner family make them exceptional, but there were a number of other instances – Yardley of Warwick, Knight of Barrelis, Rosyer of Barnstaple – in which sons inherited the prosperous practices of their fathers, and there were still others – Prescott of Warwick, Booth of Witton, Rawlins of Stratford, Willymot of Kelshall – in which sons who became barristers benefited from local reputations established by their fathers.

However, inherited practices were relatively rare. Eleven of two hundred attorneys in the three-county sample were the sons of older practitioners, and it was also probably fairly common for two generations of the same family to work as attorneys in the King's Bench,[20] but most practitioners were not so lucky as these. Some of them might have found clients amongst family or friends or have made contacts during the course of clerkships. Others like John Skinner senior and William Booth senior of Witton were successful even though they had migrated from other counties to their eventual homes.[21] How did such men find their clients?

Contemporaries alleged that attorneys hung around on market days encouraging countrymen to sue, often on insecure grounds, and it does indeed seem likely that practitioners congregated at local markets and at the major assemblies of the county communities which occurred at meetings of the assizes or quarter sessions.[22] No doubt because of this element of mobility in private practice, a considerable amount of legal business was conducted at inns and ale-houses. Such places were frequently the settings for petty sessions, assizes, and town council meetings, and countrymen congregated in them when they came to town to attend markets or on other business.[23] So the ale-house was a likely place to find clients, and it is probably for these reasons that at least three attorneys, John Rosyer of Barnstaple, Richard Cliffe of London, and Jonathan Waller of Ashwell in Hertfordshire owned inns, and that several other practitioners who lived in the country made it a point to keep rooms at an inn in nearby towns.[24]

Nevertheless, legal business did not always gravitate towards the potentially dangerous mixture of beer and parchment. The administrative centre of most practices was usually a room at home which was furnished with a few pieces of joined furniture, lawbooks, paper, a couple of chests for documents, and in the case of prosperous practitioners a clerk or two.[25] The earliest surviving casebook of an active attorney, that of George Draper of Hitchin, which runs from 1669 into the 1680s, shows that his clients came mostly from the immediate vicinity of Hitchin and neighbouring market towns, and that there were frequently kinship ties between them.[26] No comparable evidence about the nature of local practices survives from before 1640, but an examination of the case loads of individual Common Pleas attorneys as they appear in the plea rolls suggests that most practices had a distinctive local orientation.[27] In small-scale communities local reputation and the recommendations of family or friends must frequently have been responsible for bringing together lawyer and client.

If business was recruited in the country, it was there, too, that the arrangements were made which led the attorney to manipulate the ponderous machinery of writs and procedure which constituted a lawsuit. Correspondence suggests that some clients simply ordered an attorney to begin an action by taking out a writ,[28] but in most instances some kind of consultation about the feasibility of the case and its cost must have taken place. Once the case was under way, the attorney was responsible for directing it through the courts, and, as letters between litigants and their lawyers show, there was very often some discussion about what procedures should be taken when.[29] However, in addition to manipulating writs, attorneys also had to oversee their delivery and execution. Judicial orders of the King's Bench and Common Pleas, dated Michaelmas 1573, specified that sheriffs should appoint deputies who were attorneys in order to facilitate the carrying of writs and other procedural documents back and forth between London and the country.[30] But, in spite of these provisions, it is clear that attorneys themselves frequently carried writs from London into the country and attended to their execution. Getting a sheriff to make the execution after a writ had been delivered could be a problem. For example, John Stampe, the seventeenth-century attorney of Corpus Christi College, Oxford was constantly badgering the high sheriff of Kent to carry out writs against Sir Michael Sands, an opponent of the College.[31] Although attorneys and sheriffs are usually seen as allies in conspiracy against litigants, the attorney could find himself thwarted in an attempt to get an execution carried out by a disagreeable sheriff or his deputy. A late Elizabethan Star Chamber bill describes how an attorney who was attempting to get a *capias ultigatum* executed against a citizen of the city of Lincoln was abused, thrown in jail, and then denied a room in the town by the local sheriff, who was a friend of the man against whom the writ had been directed.[32]

Once the defendant had answered the summons of the plaintiff, pleadings were exchanged. Then, if there was a failure to reach an out-of-court settlement, common law actions had to be prepared for trial at *nisi prius* in the country. Here, the most important jobs of the attorney were the selection of jurors, the preparation and presentation of evidence, and the briefing of counsel. Lists of jurors were returned by sheriffs to Westminster, and the attorneys were responsible for making exceptions to them until a satisfactory panel had been installed.[33] The search for evidence was an essential part of every practitioner's work whether he was employed by individuals, institutions, or urban corporations. It might involve checking the records of the courts for past decisions or ransacking the archives of a gentry family in order to find a deed.[34] Once a case reached trial, the attorney presented his evidence to the jury, and these documentary facts along with a statement of the details of the case constituted the briefs which were prepared for counsel.[35] After the trial was over, the attorney returned the *postea* with the decision of the jury at assizes to the clerks in Westminster so that it could be entered into the plea rolls.[36]

In the localities, of course, not all of a lawyer's contentious business would have involved cases at issue in royal courts such as King's Bench and Common Pleas. Some practitioners worked in town courts, and there were also occasional appearances in other local jurisdictions such as hundred and county courts.[37] Moreover, by the early seventeenth century, if not before, quarter sessions had become one of the more important venues for the work of both attorneys and barristers. In Warwickshire, for example, attorneys frequently appeared before justices of the peace to represent towns or parishes in disputes about the disposition of vagrants or the assessment of rates.[38] In addition, it was apparently quite common for attorneys to act for individuals accused at quarter sessions of minor criminal offences. By the early seventeenth century, defendants to felonies such as murder, rape, and major theft were usually tried by the royal justices at assize, and, according to law, they were not allowed to use a lawyer to present their case. By contrast those charged with misdemeanours such as petty theft and minor breaches of the peace were still dealt with by the justices of the peace, and by law they were permitted legal advisors.[39] In general, evidence about the extent of the use of lawyers in these circumstances is scanty, but in his study of Essex quarter sessions records, Quintrell found that representation was common in cases involving misdemeanours, and a similar picture emerges for Lancashire from a Star Chamber dispute of 1615.[40] In this case, a Common Pleas attorney, William Brere, claimed that he had been sworn before the justices of assize 'for and concerning all pleas of the crown', and that the judges had always allowed attorneys to put in pleas and to advise clients in cases depending before justices of the peace. He alleged that in the past, 'for the ease and better and more speedy understanding of the cause' by the magistrates, attorneys had been allowed to open the cause 'in a few word*es* w[hi]ch otherwise would not be so easily conveyed and understood by and from the relacion *and* dealing of poor Ignorant Countrey people'.[41]

Brere is clearly saying that defendants regularly took advice on points of law and used lawyers to present their cases at quarter sessions, and, given the informal relationship between the types of offence tried at sessions as opposed to assizes, his evidence must lead to the suspicion that a countryman might at least have been able to consult with a practitioner even if he were accused of a serious crime to be tried at assize. What is absolutely certain is that this sphere of practice was sufficiently important to the lawyers to cause demarcation disputes between barristers and attorneys over it. The basic question at issue in the Lancashire case involved the extent of the right of attorneys, as opposed to barristers, to appear before JPs. More light is shed on the struggle between the two branches at this level by an order made by the Hampshire justices of the peace in 1633 which laid it down that attorneys were no longer permitted to appear at sessions. The reasons given were that 'Counsellors at Lawe whoe usually here attend ... are but seldome ymployed by reason that Attornies and others under the Degree of Barresters are suffered to make motions and to plead in causes ... to the distresse of the said Councellors and whereby other inconveniencies have haponed which ought not to be.'[42] Since barristers were more nearly the social equals of the gentry magistrates who sat on commissions of the peace than were the attorneys, orders such as these are more likely to have been the product of social prejudice than of any deep concern about professional qualifications. In either case, they were eventually successful in excluding attorneys from the right of audience at quarter sessions, and so deprived poorer members of local communities of relatively cheap legal services.[43]

As this particular conflict demonstrates, before 1640 the division of labour between barristers and attorneys in the country was still largely ill defined, and this extended to dealings with clients who were involved in civil litigation in the royal courts. There was in this period no rule that barristers could be consulted only through a member of the lower branch. Nevertheless, it is possible to trace developments which contributed to its evolution. From around 1550, it seems likely that attorneys and solicitors were increasingly the lawyers most commonly consulted by litigants in the first instance, and that barristers were called in only when necessary.[44] By the 1630s, newly appointed serjeants at law were reminded by Lord Keeper Finch not to be overindulgent in their efforts to get attorneys to bring them work, and after the Restoration Roger North described a legal profession in which attorneys dominated contacts with clients.[45] Nevertheless, there were exceptions. Large landowners continued to consult directly with counsellors throughout the period, and less-esteemed litigants sometimes did so as well.[46] But, in fairly simple common law cases, such as actions concerning debts on bonds, for example, the attorney was probably the only lawyer who would be involved before a case went to trial at *nisi prius*. When George Draper charged four or five shillings for 'counsel', this was evidently due to himself, whereas he charged fees for named barristers only when they were retained at assizes.[47] Procedure at common law did not necessarily require the services of members of the upper branch, and attorneys could also handle the more straightforward pleadings. On the other hand, causes in Star Chamber and Chancery required barristers to draw up bills and to make pre-trial motions. Moreover, common law cases of greater complexity, and certainly those which involved questions of law, required more learned opinion. Thus both John Frogmer, the Littletons' steward in Worcestershire, and John Stampe, the attorney of Corpus Christi College, Oxford, refer frequently to consultations with barristers, usually barristers selected by themselves rather than by their clients.[48] Finally, barristers were absolutely necessary at trials where they 'said what they could' for their client after the attorney, having selected the jury, had presented his evidence.[49] However, barristers were expensive, and it is likely that this is why clients found it advantageous to avoid using them whenever possible. George Draper constantly records fees of £1 to pleaders at assize,[50] and it was with the thought of this expense in mind that George Palmer wrote to Edward Ferrers in 1650 that he could save costs by not retaining a barrister in a case because his opponent had said he would confess the action at *nisi prius*.[51]

Although the complexity of English law, on the procedural no less than the substantive side, meant that, just as in the middle ages, the lawyers of this period held the fortunes of their clients firmly in their hands, practitioners appear to have treated litigants, at least the richer of them, with considerable deference. The King's Bench man John Stampe went out of his way to thank Corpus Christi for retaining him, protested that his fee was too high, and pledged his best efforts in their causes.[52] Litigants were usually kept well informed by letter about the progress of their causes, but more urgent communications might be conveyed by using clerks as messenger boys, and practitioners themselves sometimes made 'house calls' on more important clients.[53] Procedural steps were usually recommended as possible courses of action rather than insisted upon. Thus in 1604 the King's Bench attorney Ralph Featherstone wrote to William Carensew, his client in Cornwall, 'to signifie vnto you for your better satisfaction the procedings of your Cause this term', and on another occasion sent down the declaration in the case so that Carensew could better understand 'the whole proceeding'.[54] In a society in which much information travelled by word of mouth and much depended on patronage or reputation, the need to maintain the good will of clients must have been as important an element in the regulation of the profession as any institutional restraints.

Gossip about the abilities of a local attorney may, therefore, have helped people in need of legal assistance to make wise choices of lawyers. Nor should we automatically dismiss even the poorer members of the populace as being completely ignorant of the ways of the law, since the ubiquity of local jurisdictions, particularly the biannual manorial courts, meant that the average man was probably in court more often than he is today. But, if we can too easily exaggerate the vulnerability of men to lawyers, sharp practice by these 'experts' did inevitably occur. Since the costs of litigation were so often laid out by attorneys in advance of payment by clients, they were inevitably open to the charge that they were maintaining the suit in return for a share of the amounts recovered if they won the case, and there is no reason to doubt that this did sometimes happen.[55] In 1604, for instance, John Bishe of Worth in Sussex was taken before the Star Chamber and charged with maintenance, stirring up suits, and taking money for compounding and ending causes. According to a report of the case, he was so notorious that 'all men condemned him for a most dangerouse *and* turbulent person to lyve in a countrye', and local people 'for the most parte stoode in awe and Feare of him *and* durst scarce delyver any evidence ag[ain]st him'.[56]

In other cases of malpractice, attorneys and solicitors simply took advantage of the ignorance of their victims, and frequently it was the manipulation of writs, particularly those which warranted the taking away of a man's property through distraint, which terrorized the unwary. For example, in a petition to the Stuart commissioners on fees, Dorothy Croydon, who said that she could neither read nor write, alleged that the Common Pleas attorney, Henry Harvey of Bridgwater, Somerset, had charged her excessively for a suit in Star Chamber, and then brought an action at common law against her for £94 on an account for the suit which included expenses for the attorney, his father, and his brother while they were in London.[57] In another petition a Devonshire man called Mahoon described how he was unable to pay the principal and costs he owed after losing a suit against him for a £4 debt. Mahoon's opponent's attorney, John Hiddsley, promised to stop the execution against him if Mahoon would enter into a bond with him (Hiddsley) for the principal and costs, so Mahoon gave Hiddsley a bond for £11 10s. Hiddsley, it was alleged, gave his client only £5 of this money, and continually extorted more from Mahoon. The affair ended with Mahoon facing another execution, this time for £23 'under colour of the bond'.[58]

Yet another example of the kinds of malpractice uncovered by the commissions on fees involved a case in the Stannary Court of Chagford in Devon. In this one a local attorney named Squire simply threatened a fictitious execution against one Poke who had already settled a £40 debt in a case in which Squire had served as the attorney for Poke's opponent. Poke, 'being terrified' by the message about the execution, ran out of the 'country' and had not been heard from since.[59]

It is difficult to go beyond these examples to a more general evaluation of the level of corruption in the profession. Evidence drawn from the commissions of fees or from the Star Chamber archives tells only about the black sheep (although it is worth pointing out that depositions from ordinary people which were taken by the sub-commissions of Devon and Surrey suggest that the ecclesiastical courts and their personnel, rather than the common lawyers, were the main targets of popular complaints).[60] Certainly the fact that they were so often delivered by practitioners rather than by public authorities made writs a particularly dangerous weapon in the hands of the unscrupulous, and the danger was compounded by other kinds of procedural informality. In 1606, for example, a Devon practitioner claimed that it was quite common for attorneys to break the seals on *latitats* to 'check for mistakes' before the writs were given to the sheriff so that he could draw up warrants for arrest. Furthermore, 'for manie years' the sheriff's officers had issued the warrants themselves with blank spaces into which the attorney could insert the names of the parties concerned. It is little wonder that some practitioners, such as Lewis Lashbrooke of Somerset, made a name for themselves as forgers and hardly surprising that ordinary men and women should have been suspicious of legal process.[61] Similarly, juries were notoriously corrupt during this period, and attorneys were well placed to make attempts on their integrity.[62]

On the other hand, the oath of attorney did provide a set of rules for practice, and, more important, the means existed for enforcing breaches of them.[63] Finally, if there is evidence of sharp practices by some members of the profession, there is also some which sheds a more favourable light on their activities. For example, in 1599 John Pennyfather wrote from London to Arthur Gregory in Warwickshire that he dare not proceed in a case 'vntill I can find a sure ground to work on'. In 1633 John Wicksteed of Bagington, near Coventry, told John Gregory that he would arbitrate in a dispute between

Gregory and Simon Chambers only on two conditions: that the two men entered into bonds to abide by the decision and that the other arbitrator was 'no Rangler'.[64]

III

Today, work outside of courts (for example, conveyancing) constitutes the bread and butter of a solicitor's business.[65] In the sixteenth and seventeenth centuries the relative importance of contentious versus non-contentious work is much more difficult to assess. Contemporary descriptions of the activities of attorneys always emphasize their role as conductors of lawsuits. Evidence of this kind, along with the enormous volume of central court litigation, may suggest that if contentious work was not the primary source of income for most practitioners, then it was probably a more important part of their business than it has since become. However, it would be a mistake to carry even this cautious conclusion too far. It is easy to identify the contentious work of practitioners because it appears in court records. By contrast, out-of-court work is difficult to detect in the sixteenth and early seventeenth centuries because of the dearth of the kinds of working papers, such as day and letter books, which survive for periods after 1660 and which contribute enormously to any complete picture of professional activity. Nevertheless, even the meagre evidence which is available suggests that early modern practitioners offered a wide range of non-litigious services that included acting as trustees for friends and clients, drawing legal instruments, and the provision of rural credit. Whatever its exact proportions, out-of-court work was certainly a significant feature of an attorney's practice, and it is quite possible that what can be learnt about it is only a modest reflection of what actually went on.[66]

One important sphere of such non-litigious work was the making of wills, deeds, and other written legal instruments. Some idea of the nature of this activity can be gleaned from printed and manuscript guides on the subject. Several formulary manuals giving examples of how to prepare legal writings were published in the second half of the sixteenth century.[67] Then, in 1590, the attorney William West published his authoritative *Symbolaeographia*, a book which aimed to raise the quality of English legal writing to the heights it had supposedly reached under the Greeks and Romans. West specifically identified the first edition of his work with the men who had traditionally handled such work, the scriveners and the notaries,[68] but the fact that he was himself an attorney does appear to be indicative of the extent to which legal writing was drifting into the hands of his fellow practitioners. In the 1620s the judges held in an action of slander that the making of writings was not necessarily a function of attorneys, but they were not forbidden to do it. In any case, by the early seventeenth century, provincial scriveners were beginning to disappear as a distinct occupational group on the local scene,[69] and it is clear that country attorneys were regularly drawing up deeds, wills, and other writings. A number of attorneys' precedent books from this period include large sections devoted to examples of how to draw up trusts, bargains and sales, mortgages, marriage settlements, and other instruments associated both with the personal affairs of individuals and the finer details of local administration.[70] Although they seem to have been exceptional, some mid-seventeenth-century practitioners, like Richard Dowdeswell of Gloucestershire and Ambrose Holbeache of Warwickshire, actually made their reputations as conveyancers.[71] Thus when Roger North complained after the Restoration that conveyancing, like so much else in legal practice, had been taken over by attorneys, he was almost certainly commenting on a development which was already well advanced rather than one which was just beginning.[72] Furthermore, although there is little direct evidence, when a local practitioner wrote up an instrument such as a will, marriage agreement, or bargain and sale, he must have been called upon to counsel his clients on the steps they were about to take. If this assumption is correct, then legal writing may well have promoted the role of the country attorney as a general advisor to his clients on a wide range of issues which were not directly concerned with lawsuits.

By comparison with legal writing, money lending is one of the better-documented non-contentious activities of early modern practitioners. Since they were frequently in London and had a wide circle of county acquaintances, attorneys were well placed to fix loans. Robert Abbott, an attorney of the Common Pleas and a scrivener of London, was involved full time in a kind of banking business.[73] He kept money on account for about twenty-five clients, some Londoners and some countrymen, and he made payments out of these sums to their creditors. Abbott made loans out of his own funds (at 8 per cent on small debts in the late 1650s) of anywhere from £10 to £20, but he also fixed loans for larger amounts, usually by finding a lender who was willing to invest some excess cash.[74] For country attorneys, lending was not such a full-time activity, but the richer ones like James Prescott of Warwick or Thomas Gregory of Coventry probably made small loans fairly frequently;[75] more important, they served as brokers who could either lend a client's money or help him to borrow some.[76] Returns on loans may not have been great; the attorney would take fees for drawing up the necessary bonds, and interest on small short-term loans. But if the loan was guaranteed by a mortgage on property, he might be in a position to augment his own estate. A glimpse of how such a deal might have worked is contained in a deed dated 1606 between Thomas Vilvaine of Keene in Devonshire, yeoman, and John Trosse, an attorney of Exeter. In this document Vilvaine grants twenty acres of land to Trosse, but a final clause declared the grant void if Vilvaine paid £200 to Nicholas Wadham of Somerset before Michaelmas 1611, which payment had been guaranteed by Trosse and two other men.[77] This may well have been a case in which Trosse arranged the loan and guaranteed that the lender would not lose his money. Trosse laid out no cash unless Vilvaine defaulted, but in that case he would also acquire some real property. This is a scenario for the archetypal drama in which the lawyer does little and ends up with the land. However, there is no hard evidence that it was performed very often. Stone has argued that in spite of the fact that decisions in Chancery during the early seventeenth century were making them a more attractive form of collateral, mortgages were not very frequently used before 1650.[78] Furthermore, although they are very far from a complete source for all property transactions conducted in the county during the period, the Devonshire enrolled deeds contain only one or two items which suggest deals like the one involving Trosse.[79] Indeed, there is little evidence either here or elsewhere that practitioners were able to entangle clients sufficiently to wrest their lands away from them. Most unpaid loans probably ended as actions for debt at common law. In these the defendant's real property was protected by law;[80] if he was lucky, the plaintiff got back his principal and the costs of the suit.

Another, and perhaps the most important, non-litigious activity of country lawyers was their employment by lords of manors as stewards of manorial courts. As we have seen, the jurisdiction of courts baron over civil pleas was probably somewhat in decline by the beginning of the seventeenth century, but manorial courts remained an important venue for the regulation of agricultural practices within local communities, and they still played an important role in recording transactions relating to the inheritance or alienation of copyhold land. At the same time, in many parts of the country, courts leet continued to function effectively in the administration of justice relating to petty crimes, minor breaches of the peace, and the enforcement of statutes for the protection of consumers against sharp practices by local bakers, butchers, and ale makers.[81]

Appointed at the discretion of the lords of manors, and serving in the dual role of magistrate and secretary, the steward was at one and the same time a central figure in the functioning of the manorial courts and, very often, a major legal advisor to the lord. Yet in spite of the thousands of manorial court rolls which survive from the early modern period, it is much easier to state the prescribed functions of stewards than to detail how they carried out their duties in practice. Little evidence of individual initiative emerges from behind the rigid formality of the records they kept, and in general the subject of estate management has received much less attention than it deserves.[82] However, as Chapter 6 demonstrates, around the turn of the sixteenth century there does appear to have been a significant change in the qualifications of the men who became manorial stewards. The local, semi-professional, or amateur court holders began to disappear, and they were replaced by men such as the common law attorneys or barristers of the inns of court, men who had connections with the legal institutions of London.

Some of the consequences of this change are worth exploring. In the first place, quite unlike the amateur court holders, many of the 'professional' stewards of the early seventeenth century appear to have held courts for more than one landlord. This can only have meant that their interests in the lord's business were defined more by fees and a professional–client relationship than by the older ties of personal loyalty and dependence which had often been character- istic of the court holders.[83] Second, although manuals indicating the bare outlines of the duties to be performed by stewards and the basic forms they were to follow in compiling court rolls had long been in existence, the reign of Elizabeth saw the London legal profession taking a new, and quite intense, interest in manorial jurisdictions and in the nature of the customary law they administered.[84] Writers such as Kitchin, Coke, and Calthrope tried to impose a systematic order on the great variety, not to say chaos, of practices and customs which constituted the reality of manorial activity.[85] They provided the jurisdiction with a theoretical underpinning which linked manorial courts into the royal system of law and government, and they tried to create from the confusion of customary land tenures a branch of the land law which could be made sense of when, as was increasingly the case, disputes between landlords and their customary tenants were brought from the local manor into the central courts at London.[86] John Kitchin, who, it will be remembered, was a strong advocate of the replacement of amateur stewards by men with professional legal training, stressed that royal justice had been ordained so that peace could be maintained throughout the realm, and he emphasized the need for the law to be administered well at all jurisdictional levels.[87] Sir Edward Coke and Charles Calthrope, on the other hand, devoted themselves specifically to the question of what qualities were required of manorial customs and tenures if they were to be upheld by the judges of the common law.[88]

As stewards connected with the central courts in London replaced the amateur court holders, so the ways of thinking exemplified by these writings percolated more freely throughout the provinces. For example, a late-sixteenth-century manuscript formulary on the keeping of manorial courts found amongst the papers of the Warwickshire lawyer Arthur Gregory shows how many of Kitchin's views were taken over into a working guide for country practitioners. The work contains lengthy speeches which were intended to accompany the charges delivered to the juries of courts leet and courts baron at the commencement of their proceedings. Such speeches are not included in Kitchin, but many of the principles enunciated in Gregory's manuscript are precisely the same as those put forward in the printed text. The address to the court baron includes a short history of the institution based on an interpretation of feudalism, and concludes by noting that 'although they are kept by prescription *and* custome, yet doubtless they originally began by ye kings graunt of them who is ye fountaine of Justice *and* can erect *and* make Courts of Justice at his pleasure'.[89] The charge for courts leet was longer and placed even more emphasis on royal authority. Leets were introduced by the crown to save people the expense of having to go to the royal courts in London. It was requisite and consonant with reason and the scriptures 'that there be a head *and* a ruler to gouern and rule the people and to keepe them in obeydyence'. In England that ruler was the queen, and she should be given the obedience of her subjects. Finally, the leet was exhorted not to fail to make presentments because 'if any thing be owte of tune, and not consonant w[i]th his fellowes, yt must be wrested *and* brought into tune'.[90]

The outlook contained in these speeches brought a new emphasis on law, order, and the authority of the crown into the isolated and particular world of the manor. Similarly, the scores of manorial surveys and compilations of customs which date from the late sixteenth and early seventeenth centuries are a reflection on the local level of the concern shown by writers such as Kitchin and Calthrope with bringing custom into line with the national common law of the realm. As we have seen already, many country practitioners became experts in local history, but this was not mere antiquarianism.[91] It often had an important point, which was to transform informal, and often unwritten, customary practices into clearly articulated and carefully recorded customary laws which could be verified, if need be, by reference to the king's courts in London. For example, Anthony Bradshaw of Duffield, a Common Pleas attorney and under steward of the royal Honour of Tutbury, consulted the common law abridgements and the statutes of the realm as well as local custumals in order to prepare works on the laws of the Honour which were 'drawn into a mixt agreeable to custome *and* the course of Common Law'. The object of the exercise was partly to achieve 'the better *and* more upright *and* easy performance of my dutie in that place *and* the better understanding *and* advocating of my sonnes and clerks'. But, as the title of one of his works, 'A Lanterne for Copyholders', suggests, Bradshaw was also attempting to help the tenants of the manor achieve some certainty about the nature and extent of their rights.[92] A not dissimilar motivation lay behind a manorial survey which was drawn up in the 1560s or 1570s by the steward of the Percy estates in Northumberland, George Clarkson. According to M. E. James, what is striking about Clarkson is his emphasis on law-abidingness and the role of the royal courts as the ultimate authority for deciding between the claims of lord and tenant. For Clarkson, 'the rule of custom and commonwealth involved the penetration of the common law way of thinking into remote northern countrysides, and the conferment... of rights on those whose posture had previously been solely one of submission'.[93]

However, if there was a tendency amongst the new breed of professional stewards to emphasize the rule of law and to attempt to solidify the fluid customary claims of landlord and tenant into rights which could be maintained at common law, this should not be taken to imply too radical a change in the attitudes of stewards towards the interests of the lords they served. If common law attorneys like James Willymott of Hertfordshire, who kept courts for more than one person, may have had a more coolly balanced attitude towards the justice of their lords' cases, they were nevertheless employed by the lord and their job was to keep a careful eye on his interests.[94] Thus, for example, John Frogmer, an attorney of Worcester and Staple Inn, and steward of some of Gilbert Littleton's estates in Staffordshire, considered, amongst other business, what action to take against two copyholders who refused to pay their entry fines and against another who was digging coal on his land against the wishes of the lord.[95] Similarly, John Farthing, Lord Petre's steward, wrote to his master in 1633 about the lands of a tenant who had been convicted of murder. Farthing was unsure of the exact extent of Petre's lawful claim to the lands and goods of the felon, but he had stopped the sheriff of Devonshire from taking any action on the property until Petre's rights had been determined.[96] Stewards may not always have been as diligent as these. Cliffe tells of a family in Yorkshire who were ruined during the last years of the sixteenth century by the management of a fraudulent and incompetent attorney.[97] But on the whole the advent of the better-trained and more responsible stewards must have benefited landlords.[98] John Frogmer's appearance on the scene coincided with the introduction of more business-like management on the Littleton estates.[99] In Warwickshire, leading gentry families such as the Throckmortons, Lucys, Farrers, and Archers could call on the services of the most prominent members of the lower branch and may therefore have monopolized the best legal advice available in the county, although it should be added that the prosperity of the men who worked for them no doubt depended to a large extent on the patronage of these well-connected and politically important families.[100]

A crucial question, but one which is difficult to answer definitively, is how far did the improved legal administration of estates enable landlords and lords of manors to take advantage of their tenants? Francis North scourged those stewards who extorted excessive fines from the courts they kept,[101] and two stewards in Surrey were presented to the commissions on fees for overcharging for copies of court rolls.[102] Campbell concluded that the poorer yeoman probably found going to law in defence of his rights a difficult proposition, and Cliffe agrees that in Yorkshire landlords used lawsuits to break copyholds.[103] On the other hand, if the turn of the sixteenth century saw the proliferation of professional stewards, the entire period from 1560 to 1640 was one in which the growth in the number of lawyers connected with London rapidly outpaced that of the population as a whole, and litigation was relatively cheap. Thus, although the poor were undoubtedly disadvantaged in the courts, royal justice was probably more accessible than it had ever been before, and Kerridge has shown that, once in court, neither common law nor equity was prejudiced against tenants, even customary tenants.[104] In addition, tenants, particularly those of manors, could find ways to defend themselves. Where customary rights were at stake, it is likely that unions of tenants suing in a joint action against their landlord were fairly common.[105] In many cases, attorneys themselves may have been amongst them, since they were more likely to be freehold, copyhold, or leasehold tenants than lords of manors. In Norfolk in 1609, for example, an attorney named Heyward was among a group of rebellious tenants of Sampson Leonard, lord of the manor of Horsford.[106] Patrician social commentators certainly expressed alarm about the way in which the expansion of the legal profession enabled tenants to trouble their lords with lawsuits,[107] and the epitaph of a ninety-five-year-old farmer, John Gladwin, which was inscribed in 1615 on his tomb in Harlow, Essex suggests that on some occasions this concern could be justified. Gladwin

> with longe and tedious suites in lawe
> with ye lord of ye mannor of Harlowe
> did prove the custome for the
> copieholds to ye great benefit of
> posteritie for ever.[108]

The reality, of course, was that country practitioners were always to be found working for each of the parties in a suit. The main consequence of their proliferation was that litigation became easier, and insofar as this was the case, they may well have helped small-holders to protect their interests against the more immediate pressures they faced from landlords as a result of the sixteenth-century increase in the profits which could be made from agricultural land. On the other hand, ultimately lawyers cannot be said to have had much impact on fundamental economic relationships. The decline of the small farmer in England had more to do with price fluctuations, bad harvests, and the nature of inheritance customs than with the common law or its practitioners.[109] Nevertheless, the legal profession did contribute to a significant change in the quality of seventeenth-century life. There were now more lawsuits, and common law attitudes towards society and government penetrated more deeply into the countryside than ever before.

10

PUBLIC OFFICE AND POLITICS

I

The participation of well-known common laywers such as Sir Edward Coke, John Selden, Francis Bacon, and William Noy in some of the more important political debates of the early seventeenth century is a familiar feature of early Stuart history. In the case of these eminent barristers, it is usually possible to find out something about their political attitudes and activities either by looking at the speeches they made in parliament or by reading their published works.[1] By comparison, the public careers of members of the lower branch are much more obscure. Very few of them sat in parliament, and, although some practitioners wrote books, the instances in which the thought and action of individuals can be analysed in conjunction are extremely rare.[2] Consequently, a study of the political role of the lower branch must take us away from national politics to the county and the town, and any conclusions about the characteristic impact of this group of lawyers must perforce be drawn somewhat obliquely.

Even in the provinces, most practitioners lacked the wealth and social cachet necessary to lay claim to important positions such as a place on the commissions of the peace or the office of sheriff.[3] But there were a number of local administrative offices which could provide a means of entry into public life. By the early seventeenth century, country attorneys frequently filled a long list of posts such as that of undersheriff, coroner, feodary for the court of Wards, clerk of the peace, clerk of assize, and, perhaps most frequently, town clerk. Just as attorneys were responsible mainly for the procedural rather than the substantive side of ordinary litigation, so, too, most of these local offices involved attention to administrative detail rather than political decision making. As clerks of the peace, they handled paperwork whilst the justices actually decided on the substantive issues. Much the same could be said of clerks of assize, those men who accompanied the judges on their perambulations of the shires and set agendas or drew up judicial process.[4] Undersheriffs were appointed by members of the gentry who did not care to carry out in person all of the onerous administrative chores which were associated with the office of sheriff. Therefore, the value of these posts must be measured mainly in terms of the potential financial gain that they might bring to their holders. Yet men who possessed local offices were also in a position to influence events and make decisions by virtue of their control of administrative machinery. For example, since they constituted the only permament officials of the commissions of the peace, clerks of the peace were able to set agendas, and they may have been able to control information which came before the justices.[5] At the same time, the increasing involvement of practitioners in local government created a pool of middle-rank administrators who brought both clerical expertise and a shared common law perspective to the provinces.

A source of patronage and the ability to make outlays of money were the main prerequisites for obtaining most of the offices which were normally held by members of the lower branch. For example, prior to 1548 clerks of the peace had been granted their offices by letters patent issued by the crown, but after that date the right to make the appointment was placed in the hands of the *custos rotulorum*, the senior member of the commission of the peace in each county.[6] In general this meant that the clerk was likely to be appointed either because he had connections with the *custos* or because he was able to buy the office. The Staffordshire clerks of the 1580s were clients of the Earl of Essex. In the 1590s, the Devonshire clerkship was reportedly sold for £300.[7] By the early seventeenth century, the practice of selling the office evidently put some informal limits on the freedom of a newly appointed *custos* to install the clerk of his choice. A dispute arose in Hertfordshire in 1619 when a clerk who had paid at a 'dear rate' for his office, but who had 'enjoyed it' only for a few years, was in danger of being ousted as a result of a change of *custos*.[8] A series of similar situations occurred in Yorkshire as clerks of the peace tried to weather the storms created by the struggle between Sir Thomas Wentworth and Sir Henry Savile over the *custosship*.[9] In all such cases which have thus far come to light, the rights of the *custos* were ultimately upheld, but there is some evidence that towards the second quarter of the seventeenth century clerks were beginning to enjoy long tenures in office. In Somerset, for example, the office was passed down through the hands of the Wykes family for well over thirty years, as Edward Wykes succeeded his father in the post. Furthermore, the Wykeses survived at least one discoverable change in the *custosship*, for it is known that Sir Robert Philips held the office in 1614 and that Sir James Ley had taken his place by 1619.[10] Similarly, after undergoing several changes in the early part of the seventeenth century, the Warwickshire office was held from 1628 to 1649 by William Gibbons,[11] and in Lancashire the Rigby family provided clerks of the peace for the first two-thirds of the seventeenth century.[12] Of these cases, the exact conditions under which the office was held are known only for the Rigbys, who had got life tenure plus the rights of reversion from the crown in return for their original purchase of the office during the 1590s.[13] We simply cannot say whether or not the long tenures of the clerks in Somerset and Warwickshire are accountable to the tendency for offices which had been paid for to be considered the rights of the holder (as was nearly the case in Hertfordshire) or whether the need for a competent and experienced administrative assistant for the commissions of the peace was beginning to outweigh considerations of patronage. It would probably not be wrong to expect that both factors were important.

After the clerkship of the peace, the other important county post which was held frequently during this period by a member of the lower branch was that of undersheriff. As their title suggests, undersheriffs served as assistants to those members of the gentry who were appointed annually by the crown to serve as sheriffs of their shires, and to a very large extent the value of the office was directly proportionate to the amount of authority the sheriff was willing to delegate to them.

In the middle ages, sheriffs had been the king's chief administrative officers in the shires. By the middle of the sixteenth century, they had lost much of their previous judicial and military power, but the office continued to be one through which considerable influence could be exercised. Sheriffs were responsible for carrying out the decisions of JPs, and they were the receivers of directives to the magistrates from the privy council. Since they were charged with executing writs, selecting jury panels, and feeding and entertaining the justices of assize, their office was also crucial for the effective processing of the civil litigation which was heard by the royal courts at Westminster. The nature of these duties demanded a great deal of attention to detail, the supervision of a large number of deputies and bailiffs, and, finally, the prospect of facing a difficult and notoriously costly accounting with the exchequer at the end of the term of office.[14]

For all of these reasons, the sheriffalty appears to have been regarded by its potential holders with a good deal of ambivalence. Sir William Wentworth, for example, warned his son to go to considerable cost to avoid the office, because 'By the sheriffwik of Yorkshire there comes great losse and danger', and in Somerset and Gloucestershire attitudes appear to have been much the same. On the other hand, in Elizabethan Norfolk members of the gentry frequently thought that they could use the office to further their factional or political causes, and so they sought it.[15]

However, regardless of whether or not they wanted the office, sheriffs needed a staff to help them carry out their duties. It was in this connection that an undersheriff was appointed as a deputy who could handle the writs and procedural paperwork and at the same time supervise the hundredal bailiffs who dealt with the execution of them. These were the tasks which attorneys, as supposed experts in procedural law, were perfectly suited to perform; hence a large number of them were selected for the office. Moreover, for a local practitioner, the undersheriffship was potentially profitable. Fees were collected for the delivery of writs, and the office put a practitioner in control of the local end of the administration of justice, obviously an advantageous position for a man in the business of litigation, even though, according to statute, undersheriffs were not supposed to practise as attorneys during the year in which they were in office.[16] At the same time, this power over procedure, and the opportunities it afforded for extortion and corruption, earned a notoriously bad name for the integrity of undersheriffs.[17]

The means by which undersheriffs obtained their offices varied considerably from place to place, but much depended on whether the sheriff wanted to exercise close control or whether he was content to leave his duties to someone else. Sir William Wentworth advised his son that if he selected a reliable friend or servant as his undersheriff, 'all the monie levyed will com to your own hands', and it would be easier to keep an eye out for his own interests.[18] This is exactly the pattern of appointments which Smith has found in Norfolk when sheriffs were seeking to gain financial or political advantage. But, when the sheriff was less concerned with the office, the undersheriffship might be sold or simply conferred on a reliable man.[19] Again Wentworth's advice seems to coincide with normal practice; in these circumstances he recommended that his son have a deed of covenant prepared which set out in detail the arrangements made between himself and the man he chose as undersheriff. The selection was to be made from amongst men known to the sheriff, or on the basis of advice given to him by others. For example, Sir William himself faced endless trouble as the result of appointing a nominee of his enemy, the Earl of Shrewsbury, and in 1618 the prominent barrister William Noy recommended his 'honest' cousin James Boynton for the post of undersheriff of Cornwall.[20]

Although very few of them survive, the indentures between sheriffs and their deputies, the form of which is given in Dalton's *Officium Vicecomitum*, are informative about the terms on which undersheriffs held their posts.[21] In 1647, for example, Francis Eades completed an agreement with Grevil Verney, the sheriff of Warwickshire. Under the terms, Eades, who was barred from acting as an attorney during his term, got the profits of the position and was bound to the sheriff for £120 to be paid if Eades failed to make a satisfactory settlement with the exchequer. Nor did he have absolute control over the office. Verney stipulated that the undersheriff should not open letters from the Council, nor was he to return any juries or to dispose of distrained property without consulting the sheriff.[22] Another agreement, between James Prescott of Warwick and Edward Peyto, the sheriff in 1654, lays down similar conditions for the execution of the duties of undersheriff, but Prescott appears to have been allowed a good deal more independence of action, since neither the appointment of jurors nor the disposal of distrained goods is mentioned in the agreement. Furthermore, Prescott was empowered to replace bailiffs and other sheriff's officers who refused to enter into bonds for the satisfactory performance of their duties or who 'misdemeaned themselves' in the execution of their places.[23]

Eades and Prescott were among the most substantial of the Warwickshire practitioners. Sheriffs who became associated with them were probably safe from financial disaster which might rebound on them if an undersheriff proved unable to meet the exchequer account. As the size of the lower branch grew during the course of the early seventeenth century, more such worthy practitioners were available than ever before, but whether this made the selection of a reliable man as undersheriff more likely is hard to tell. There is no evidence that the reputation of the office improved, or that those who occupied it were dependent on anything more than patronage or chance in coming to fill it.

County offices such as the clerkship of the peace and the under-sheriffship gave country practitioners access to significant sources of power, patronage, and financial gain. The clerk of the peace had the opportunity to influence events because he was an expert among amateurs, and he controlled the details of administration. The patronage he exercised may have been restricted largely to the attorneys who served him as underclerks or who worked before the JPs, but it was there nevertheless. Much the same was true of the office of undersheriff.

However, clerkships of the peace and, to a lesser extent, under-sheriffships were offices held by relatively few members of what had become by the early seventeenth century a large legal profession even when it is considered in the county context. For example, only a handful of men occupied the early-seventeenth-century Warwick-shire clerkship of the peace, and in Somerset the office was dominated by one family during the course of the entire period. In general more men were able to become undersheriffs, but, according to T. E. Hartley's lists, in a number of counties the post appears to have been dominated by relatively few. Seventeen different people were undersheriffs of Staffordshire during the first twenty-five years of the seventeenth century, but in Cambridgeshire, Essex, Hertfordshire, and Kent it was monopolized by small groups of from six to a dozen men, and not all of these were full-fledged attorneys.[24] Thus many attorneys never held any county office, nor were offices the only means through which a practitioner could gain professional success. Many of the most prosperous county practitioners never held them.

In fact, towns provide a more promising venue than the county community for the study of the public careers of members of the lower branch, because in towns practitioners carried a good deal of weight both as officials and as prosperous local citizens. By the mid sixteenth century most incorporated towns relied for advice and administrative assistance on two classes of legal official, the recorder and the town clerk. Urban charters frequently specified that recorders be learned in the law of the realm, and, as a rule, barristers were appointed to fill this office whose major function was to give counsel to the city fathers and to act as justices at the urban equivalent of quarter sessions.[25] Recorders ranked high among town governors, and their advice was crucial to towns involved in important legal disputes, as in Coventry's conflict with the crown over city property or as at Exeter when the city was threatened with a suit by the Bishop of Exeter.[26] Recorders were also frequently elected members of parliament by the towns which employed them. However, recorderships were part-time posts which often paid more in prestige than in fees, and the extent to which recorders were actively involved in the day-to-day running of town affairs varied considerably. In larger towns the office might go to a well-known barrister who was appointed for the influence he could wield for the town in the capital rather than for his participation in town life. This was true in early-seventeenth-century Exeter, and also at Coventry, whose governors had to send the town clerk to Stoke Poges to consult with their recorder, Sir Edward Coke.[27] Smaller towns might appoint lesser men, but this was no assurance that the recorder would be on the spot. Some early-seventeenth-century towns in fact had trouble getting their recorders to attend diligently to their duties.[28]

The more mundane details of administration and the responsibility for giving advice to the town magistrates fell, therefore, on the shoulders of the town clerks, men who were frequently, but not always, local attorneys.[29] In the 1580s the great antiquarian of Exeter, John Vowell alias Hooker, set out at some length the qualifications of the town clerk of Exeter, a description which sums up in sixteenth-century terms the nature of the office in most towns. First of all, the clerk was to be 'alwais learned and of good experience and knowledge in the lawes, vsages, customes, and orders of the citie',

For what thinges so ever are donne or to be donne yn this Cittie either yn Civill causses w[i]thyn the ordynarie courtes, or by the course of the common Lawes to be decyded, or yn matters of pollycies for the common welth of the magistrates to be exqueted; or yn matters of counsel, by the order of the xxiiii of the common counsel to be ordered and determyned ...he is to regyster sett downe and recorde the same....[30]

The clerk was supposed to be able to tell the magistrates all the things they needed to know about town customs, for, although the clerk was 'neither master nor quarter master of the ship[,] he is the man who sets the compass needle and tells the captain how and in what order he is to keep his course and to make his way'. Moreover, the clerk should attend the auditing of town accounts and engross them in parchment. He was responsible for charging the night watches, attending at the weighing of bread, and in general upholding the laws and liberties of his town.[31] In addition to these comments of Hooker's, we can add that the town clerk kept the records of the city courts, acted as clerk of the peace, and in some towns such as late-sixteenth-century Warwick acted as magistrate as well.[32] The general qualities Hooker expected to find in such an officer were true religion, sound conversation, and fidelity to the city and its magistrates.[33]

In towns such as Exeter, which had been incorporated during the middle ages, the office of town clerk was an old one, 'even as old as the oldest'. According to Hooker, in earlier times the clerk had been chosen from amongst a number of men, frequently stewards and bailiffs of the town 'who were alwaies learned and of good experience and knowledge in the lawes, vsages, customes and orders of the city, but in the end for sundrie reasons and considerations, this office was [later] altogether cast vpon one man' for the most part of his life.[34] However, many of the towns in our sample, Barnstaple, Hertford, St Albans, Warwick, and Stratford, for example, were amongst the large number of places given charters between 1540 and 1558,[35] and some other of the west country towns, Bideford, Southmolton, Tiverton, Torrington, and Okehampton, gained charters only during the reigns of Elizabeth and James I.[36] In all of these places, the advent of town clerks was a direct consequence of a town having been granted corporate status.

Royal charters of incorporation conferred the right to select town officials, keep courts with both civil and criminal jurisdictions, regulate markets, and own land.[37] For both old and new incorporations, the administration of town lands, many of which came into their hands as a result of the Reformation, was the biggest single cause of both legal entanglements and political disputes.[38] Although town clerks were not for the most part specifically mentioned in town charters until the early seventeenth century, they were an inevitable consequence of these developments in urban government. As a result of them towns had special need of a single man to keep records, remind magistrates of the laws and customs of the town, and organize lawsuits.

In at least two of the towns in the sample, Warwick and Stratford, the earliest town clerks appear to have been men with no formal legal training. In Stratford, the first holder of the office was a tradesman and burgess.[39] In Warwick, John Fisher, the son of a client of the

Duke of Northumberland, and perhaps a man of affairs rather than a professional lawyer, was town clerk during the 1570s, 80s, and 90s.[40] Before the rapid growth of the legal profession during the course of the late sixteenth century, it is likely that many smaller and medium sized towns employed men with similar backgrounds as their clerks.

By 1640, however, in many of these same places the town clerkship was held by attorneys connected with the central courts, some of whom, like John Rosyer senior of Barnstaple and Edward Rainsford of Warwick, were only moderately successful practitioners, and some of whom, like Peter Noyes of Andover, appear to have had large common law practices.[41] In other incorporated towns of the early seventeenth century, but particularly in larger places such as Coventry, Exeter, and Ipswich, the town clerks practised as neither attorneys nor barristers. Humphrey Burton, the early-seventeenth-century town clerk of Coventry, had been a clerk of Thomas Bannester, his predecessor in the office, and when Burton retired his son Simon in turn replaced him.[42] In Exeter, too, the office was dominated during the seventeenth century by one family, the Izackes. Samuel Izacke was the son of a late-sixteenth-century Exeter attorney, and he became town clerk in the early 1620s after an education at Oxford. His son, Richard, then followed him into office and held it well into the late seventeenth century.[43] There is no evidence that any of these men had personal legal practices.

The substantial profits from fees, favourable leases of corporation lands, and fairly high stipends,[44] which larger towns could afford to pay their town clerks, no doubt explain why the Burtons and Izackes held onto the office for more than one generation. They also explain to some extent why these men evidently did not engage in private practice. But equally important in determining the nature of the town clerks in these towns were rules against the town clerk leaving his post for more than one night or from acting in the central courts at Westminster. The administrative duties of a town clerk were great, and, as Hooker pointed out, one of the main requirements of him was that he should have an extensive knowledge of the laws and customs of his town.[45] Consequently, loyalty and devotion to the urban magistracy were evidently considered more important in such an officer than general training in the common law. In this respect, Humphrey Burton, who was trained up specifically for his job, was an ideal town clerk, and the city of Coventry paid him a salary of £30 p.a. on condition that he did not take up any outside employment.[46]

Ipswich pursued a similar policy, and Bacon's *Annalls* of the town provide excellent evidence of the efforts of the corporation to ensure that its town clerk was not distracted by other interests such as practice at Westminster.[47] Smaller towns were less able to demand the single-minded devotion of their town clerks, since, as we have seen, many medium sized and smaller towns employed attorneys. For instance, when Gilbert Eveleigh was appointed town clerk of Totnes in 1634, the city fathers stipulated that he give up his practice in the King's Bench, but Eveleigh's patron, the Earl of Bedford, was able to intercede with them so that Eveleigh was allowed to continue his work as an attorney.[48]

The methods by which town clerks were appointed and selected varied enormously from place to place. In some towns royal charters stipulated particular individuals; in others, the high steward or recorder was permitted to make the choice. Most frequently, however, the clerks were elected by the ruling oligarchies of the towns they served.[49] No matter which of these methods was involved, the appointment and dismissal of town clerks was often an occasion for magnate patrons to exert their influence and for the play of faction within town government.[50]

As far as outside influence is concerned, there is probably a distinction to be drawn between the larger and the smaller towns. There is little evidence of such pressure in such places as Coventry or Exeter. But in medium and smaller towns such as Totnes or Warwick (where Lord Brooke exercised considerable influence), local oligarchs may well have taken the views of the powerful into consideration before making an appointment. On the other hand, in the selection of town clerks, as in so many other aspects of their affairs, towns, while anxious to court patrons, frequently had more than one suitor to choose from, and so they rarely had a candidate forced upon them.[51] Equally, while the attempts of outsiders to influence the appointment of town clerks were no doubt sometimes part of a more general effort to gain a say in urban politics, they were very often nothing more than a consequence of the simple desire to exercise patronage. For instance, in 1600, the recorder of Chester, Richard Birkenhead, accepted £80 from Peter Starkey as part payment for the office of town clerk, which, as it turned out, was not even Birkenhead's to grant.[52] In the 1620s, Charles I and the Earl of Suffolk acted on behalf of the son of the late town clerk of Cambridge, Henry Slegg, when the corporation decided to appoint North

Harrison to the post instead of Slegg's son, Roger. The younger Slegg had been a servant of King Charles when he was Prince of Wales. Moreover, he claimed that he had been trained up for twenty years in the office of town clerk by his father. Thanks to this outside intervention, Cambridge displaced Harrison in favour of Slegg, but then Harrison sued Slegg successfully, and managed in 1630 to get himself reappointed as town clerk and to secure the reversion to the office for his son. What we see here, therefore, is the rivalry between two families who had invested a great deal of time and effort in cultivating this particular post in local government, and who were using outside influences simply to maintain their grip on it.[53]

In general, despite the influence of patrons and the disruptions caused by some elections, it was unusual for towns to lose control over their clerks. By the mid seventeenth century there were so many resident practitioners available for the position that it was difficult for patrons to intrude outsiders. More important, once in office a number of factors worked to tie the interests of town clerks in with those of the city authorities. Until the later seventeenth century, they were not usually made members of the corporations they served, but they shared nevertheless in the profits of local government, and they were often the recipients of favourable leases on town property. Finally, at least in terms of internal urban politics, these officers quickly became associated with the policies of the oligarchs.[54]

Town clerks were significant figures in local government, but, like the clerks of the peace or the undersheriffs, they were essentially the servants of other men who held the real magisterial power. However, in contrast to their role on the shire level, in some towns local practitioners also came to enjoy an influence quite apart from the offices they held simply because they were important residents and so became members of the governing bodies of the corporations. By 1640, as many as 50 per cent of the members of the lower branch lived in towns, and most of these men owned urban property.[55] In fact, in some 'declining' towns such as Warwick and Stratford, the wealth of individual practitioners made them leading members of their communities. As a result of their strong economic position, local attorneys in these towns were absorbed early into places of importance in urban government. Three practitioners, John Corbyson (1621), Richard Booth (1637), and Richard Yardley (1621), served as principal bailiffs of Warwick during the first half of the seventeenth century,[56] and Edmund Rawlins was a member of the Stratford-upon-Avon corporation in 1642.[57]

The presence of lawyers in urban governments was not unprecedented before 1600, and there are indications from several other places, such as Wells and Cambridge, that they had begun to make considerable inroads after the turn of the sixteenth century.[58] Nevertheless, the extent of their invasion at Warwick may have been unique, even for a town of its type. For example, at Stafford, a place in a many respects similar to Warwick, attorneys began to have a real influence in town affairs only during the second part of the seventeenth century. But once in government, they made their presence felt. Over the course of the seventeenth century, five attorneys and one town clerk were made members of the corporation, compared with seven mercers and seven ironmongers, the two most numerous groups in the town's government.[59] Furthermore, two rich late-seventeenth-century attorneys, Willaim Green and Humphrey Parry, held the office of mayor more times than any other man.[60] As in Warwick, it can by no means be said that attorneys had taken over the town government, but they had become in a century very important members of it.

Although no conclusion can be absolutely certain without extensive studies of other, similar, towns, the rise of local lawyers in the governments of Warwick and Stafford was probably typical of 'declining' towns which were also the centres for the legal administration of their shires or for the general distribution of services. County towns which were the location for meetings of assizes and quarter sessions inevitably attracted large numbers of resident lawyers. If, as was the case in Warwick and Stafford, these characteristics were combined with a decline in traditional industries and a change in their economies towards the provision of services, then the legal practitioners were likely to emerge as figures of considerable local consequence.[61] Thus we might hypothesize that in medium sized and smaller towns, which specialized in service trades rather than in wholesale merchandising or industry, we will find first that the attorneys become well-established citizens – sometimes inside, sometimes outside – of the urban corporation during the first part of the seventeenth century, and that by the end of the century, at the latest, they are likely to have become prominent members of the ruling élite.

However, in other types of towns, the picture was entirely different. During the early seventeenth century, there were a fairly large number of practitioners living in the two largest towns in the sample, Coventry (three) and, particularly, Exeter (ten), and, according to John Hooker, it was not unknown for lawyers to serve in the municipal government of Exeter.[62] But in both of these cities, although local attorneys can be seen serving the towns in their numerous lawsuits, they do not appear to have been made members of the corporations. In Exeter, not one of the early-seventeenth-century burgesses was an attorney, and much the same was the case in the other major cities of the realm, London, Bristol, Norwich, and Newcastle upon Tyne.[63] In towns with strong economies and rich merchants, local legal practitioners were neither wealthy enough nor important enough to break into well-established oligarchies.

The evidence for the smaller towns of both Hertfordshire and Devonshire is not very good, but by and large these towns were more prosperous during the late sixteenth and early seventeenth centuries than either Warwick or Stafford.[64] Hence the attorneys who lived in them were not particularly economically conspicuous, and, if the town had no very great administrative importance, they were not likely to be very numerous either. In most of the Hertfordshire towns, practitioners made little impression on early-seventeenth-century town politics. There were some rich practitioners in the county – James Willymott of Kelshall, William Houlker of King's Langley – but they did not live in towns. Those who did were men of only moderate means, and they had no role in town government.[65] The one important exception to this generalization was Hitchin, but Hitchin was a unique type. A prosperous market town which was part of a royal manor, Hitchin was administered during almost the entire first sixty years of the seventeenth century by the Common Pleas attorney John Skinner, who acted as deputy for the crown's steward there, the Earl of Salisbury.[66] No doubt partly as a result of this position of considerable power, Skinner was, by the measure of the 1662 hearth tax, second in wealth only to Ralph Radcliffe, Esq. (fourteen hearths to ten), and was virtual ruler of the town.[67]

Although there are some significant variations on the theme, the situation in Devonshire was much the same as in Hertfordshire. With the notable exceptions of Exeter and of Barnstaple, where there were at least four early-seventeenth-century practitioners, the members of the lower branch were spread fairly evenly amongst the numerous incorporated boroughs of the county.[68] There were a couple of attorneys in Tiverton, a couple in Totnes, a couple in Plympton, one, possibly two, in Okehampton, and a couple in Ashburton.[69] Thus, while the Devon county profession was large, its members rarely appear in force in any one of the smaller towns, which were in any case experiencing the most prosperous period in their long histories during the early seventeenth century. The attorneys frequently served them as town clerks but were rarely members of the corporations. Only after 1660, when some of these places began their decline into the notorious rotten boroughs of the early nineteenth century, would the lower branch begin to make any significant impact.[70]

II

If we turn now to the political attitudes and ways of thinking which members of the lower branch brought to the offices they held or to their activities in town politics, the only course available is to begin by drawing inferences. One of the reasons for the interest which historians have traditionally taken in questions about the role of lawyers in politics is the assumption, more often taken for granted than proven, that legal practitioners bring from their professional backgrounds to their public careers a particular set of ideas and ways of thinking which might be shown to affect their political actions or influence those of others.[71] In the case of the lower branch, there are some reasons for taking this assumption seriously, but at the same time there are others which dictate caution.

The common law tradition did contain works of undoubted political importance. Sir John Fortescue's *De Laudibus Legum Angliae*, which was written in the 1470s and first printed in 1545, made great claims for the role of law in the English polity and staked a claim for the place of parliament in its system of government.[72] By contrast, such specific and detailed statements about the nature of the English constitution were relatively rare in the legal writings of the late sixteenth and early seventeenth centuries. But a number of authors put forward a distinct view of the origins of political society, and the problems of political obligation which were raised by the Reformation caused both lawyers and the state to reiterate in ever louder voices that the rule of law and obedience to established authority (the crown) were vital components of political stability.[73] This tradition, as summed up by, for example, William Lambarde, postulated a change in men's affairs from a time when the family was both the only and a sufficient source of authority to one in which, for the sake of protecting the weak from the strong, governments or civil societies had been founded.[74] Moreover, according to Lambarde and any number of other commentators, within this framework of civil society it was the law which helped men to distinguish between right and wrong, protected their goods, and generally prevented the dissolution of the community into chaos and anarchy.[75]

For most of the standard writers of the Elizabethan period, the requirement to obey the law was given much more prominence than any attempt to define its nature or discover its origins. However, in the works of Sir John Davies and Sir Edward Coke, there came a new emphasis on the ancient and unchanging nature of the English common law, and during the course of the early seventeenth century, arguments based on the idea of a timeless ancient constitution began to appear in the disputes between the early Stuarts and their parliaments. This occurred first during the debate over impositions raised by James I in 1610 and, most spectacularly, in 1628, when the House of Commons eventually passed the 'Petition of Right' in protest against irregular crown financial measures and the use of martial law.[76]

Nevertheless, given that all of this is true, it is much easier to sketch out a general outline of a common law ideology than to show how it may have motivated individual practitioners, particularly those in the lower branch. Attorneys, chancery clerks, and solicitors were trained mostly by apprenticeship; this could only mean that the standards of legal knowledge which individuals attained varied enormously. Some of them may have read works such as those by Fortescue, Lambarde, Davies, and Coke, but there is no reason to assume that all of them did. Practice in the office of a six clerk in Chancery required a knowledge of the procedures of the court of Chancery, not a familiarity with *De Laudibus*. Similarly, the training for and practice of their profession taught common law attorneys to think in terms of what was actionable and what was not, and of the appropriateness of a writ (a procedural move) in any given circumstance. In other words, they were more likely to be interested in the *Register of Writs* and Littleton on the land law than in works of jurisprudence. This practical learning was reflected in the books they collected, and the ability to think in these ways was also a measure of their professional competence. The 'common law mind', at the level of the upper as well as that of the lower branch, always put more emphasis on practical, concrete knowledge of details than on a mastery of political philosophy. Then, as today, a legal career was a business activity in which most of the participants plodded along working on conveyancing, taking out writs, and chasing up clients. It did not necessarily provide the skills, the time, or the inclination to delve into deeper matters.

Yet, by the same token, it is difficult not to detect a certain resonance between the general litigiousness of early modern English society and the fact that some of the leading constitutional disputes of the age – those over impositions and extra-parliamentary financial exactions – found their way into law courts (Bate's Case, the Five Knights Case, Ship Money). If lawsuits could be used to protect private property against other citizens, why should they not be used to protect it against the encroachments of the crown?[77] Equally, the argument that the relations among king, parliament, and people were founded on immutable custom could not but have been familiar to lawyers, landlords, and tenants who regularly ran their affairs according to the same principle.[78] And when, as in 1628, leading lawyers such as Coke and Selden stood up in the House of Commons and claimed that the common law should decide such matters, this can hardly have been ignored in the inns of chancery or amongst a legal profession which, as it happens, was at that point much more centralized than it has ever been since. On the other hand, so long as the matter is being discussed at this level of generalization, it must also be pointed out that the lower branch and the likes of Sir Edward Coke may not always have been at one over the unalterability of the common law. As Chapter 6 indicates, Coke, the judges, and the clerical officials stood against the procedural innovations which were being carried out effectively by practitioners in the Common Pleas. Indeed, there is a real irony in the fact that one of the main planks of William Hakewill's argument in the impositions debate depended on illustrating the certainty of law by reference to an analogy with the immemorial use of the original writ out of chancery to initiate litigation just at the time when it was being systematically by-passed in everyday legal practice.[79]

More importantly, beyond the suggestion that they may have had a vested interest in, and perhaps even an ideological commitment to, promoting the rule of law, there is little evidence that the lower branch made any very important or characteristic contribution to politics on the county level or to the relationship between the royal government in London and the shires. They served as administrators in posts such as that of clerk of the peace, but, unlike the barristers, they were not members of the commissions themselves. Despite the increase in the number of lawyers, power and political initiative in the counties remained firmly in the hands of the gentry.[80]

In towns, on the other hand, practitioners had a higher profile both as important officials and, in some cases, as members of the corporations. In towns, too, there are some clear signs of what can only be called professional self-assertiveness. Quarrels between town clerks, local attorneys, and the oligarchies they served are an interesting and recurring motif in the relationship between towns and the profession. At one time or another, such disputes are known to have occurred in Shrewsbury, Bodmin, Stafford, Southampton, Great Yarmouth, High Wycombe, Weymouth, Winchester, and Warwick.[81] In most instances, the exact causes of these outbreaks are obscure, but what seems often to have lain at the heart of the matter was an offence against the professional standards of a practitioner who also had a strong and dynamic personality, or, alternatively, a reluctance by townsmen to take heed of legal advice which conflicted with their own ideas about the nature of their affairs. For example, in 1584 articles were presented by the borough of Weymouth and Melcombe Regis against the former town clerk, John Keate, who had evidently called the mayor a 'dolt' and had tried to indict the mayor and aldermen at Dorchester assizes. In 1607, an attorney in the Southampton mayor's court threw his papers down in the midst of a trial, claimed that the mayor was always prejudiced against his clients, and pledged that he cared 'not if I never pledd at barr hedd again whilst he is maior'.[82] An outburst against the town governors and an attack on the competence of its members of parliament cost Henry Manship his place as the town clerk of Great Yarmouth, and the town clerk of Stafford, Thomas Blackerne, was bustled bodily out of an assembly meeting in 1603 when he told the city fathers that, as a result of the queen's death, only the town coroner was qualified by law to take responsibility for its government.[83] In what may have been a typical occurrence, John Trussel, attorney, official, and sometime mayor of Winchester, found himself criticized on all sides when he tried to explain, according to the town charter and the law, the respective roles which the mayor, bailiffs, and freemen were supposed to play in the town's affairs.[84]

At the same time, although excessive scrupulousness about legal niceties may sometimes have got practitioners into trouble, the very nature of early modern town politics also made legal expertise an extremely valuable commodity. In towns, lawsuits rather than the

discussion of principles were the usual medium of political disputa-
tion. The exact issues varied from place to place, but the main
reasons why borough 'politics in the seventeenth century were...to
a great extent a record of litigation' can be easily summarized. First,
both the institutional nature and the extent of the powers of town
governments were established in charters which were granted by the
crown, and which had to be renewed with the accession of each new
monarch. Second, from at least the end of the fifteenth century most
town governments had become increasingly oligarchical. They
usually consisted of a group of councillors or aldermen who had the
right to control recruitment into their ranks and to elect leading
officials such as mayors, recorders, and members of parliament.
Third, the corporation was responsible for expenditure of public
funds and for the administration of town lands.[85] One consequence
of these aspects of urban government was that the legal niceties of
charters had to be carefully negotiated, often at very great cost, when
a new monarch came to the throne.[86] Another was that corporations
used lawsuits in order to maintain their rights, while at the same time
the best way for townsmen outside the government to assert their
influence was for them to sue the rulers of a corporation either for
breaches of a charter or for maladministration of town revenue. The
full legal history of such disputes has never been written, but it is
clear that royal courts, especially the court of Chancery, were willing
to hear such cases, and, as a result, faction fighting in towns between
oligarchs and outsiders or amongst the oligarchs themselves was
frequently turned into lawsuits. As Styles has suggested in the case
of Warwick, since there were few political restraints on the power
of oligarchies, legal ones based on the charters of incorporation were
often resorted to.[87]

Not surprisingly, evidence about the activities of attorneys in
urban government is found most often in conjunction with this
legalistic side of town affairs. Humphrey Burton, the town clerk of
Coventry, was praised by the city fathers for his efforts in obtaining
a new town charter and for organizing a reference book containing
evidence about town lands and customs. In Totnes, another town
clerk, Gilbert Eveleigh, compiled a rental of town property, which
included histories of the various lands concerned. In Ipswich and a
number of other towns, local attorneys were frequently engaged to
search for records supporting corporation rights or to conduct
lawsuits in London on behalf of the town.[88]

On the other hand, in some early-seventeenth-century towns, members of the lower branch were active assistants in and fomentors of confrontations between the ruling élite and outsiders. In Lincoln, the Common Pleas attorney Richard Smith advised men displaced from their offices as a result of faction fights to go to law in order to recover them. Edward Rainsford, the town clerk of Warwick, recorded that four local attorneys, 'men of prowed and vnquiet sperits', had stirred up trouble, including a suit in Chancery, for the corporation over the handling of town revenues.[89] In Ludlow, another local attorney, Philip Bradford, led a popular protest, again including a lawsuit, against the magistrates which was based on grievances similar to those in Warwick. In addition, Bradford was accused of breeding disobedience in the 'meaner sort' by advocating the overthrow of the old government and bringing 'all in common'.[90]

The protest led by Bradford appears to have been a typical attempt by outsiders to gain some say in the election of town governors and to see that town properties were not administered solely for the benefit of the ruling oligarchs. The motives of the Warwick attorneys may have been more mixed. Rainsford claimed that they acted with the favour, if not the positive encouragement, of Sir Thomas Leigh, a local gentleman who was annoyed at not having been elected to the recordership of Warwick. If this version of the story is true, then the rebellious attorneys should be seen little differently from those practitioners described by John Smith of Nibley, who led groups of riotous folk in pursuit of the aims of their employers.[91] Nevertheless, both of these examples suggest that, in theory, attorneys were natural poles around which local discontent might take shape. They knew something about the law and could easily explain what steps might be taken against corporation governors. If, as in Warwick, a town was torn by one of these classic late-sixteenth- and early-seventeenth-century clashes between oligarchs and commons, and attorneys were among those excluded from power, it is not surprising that they should be found leading the fray.

However, activity against urban political establishments was by no means particularly characteristic of members of the lower branch. To cite Warwick again as an example, for every attorney who opposed the corporation in 1618 there was one who served or supported it, and some of them were clearly connected with the group which opposed Sir Thomas Leigh.[92] Although they sometimes quarrelled with their fellow townsmen, the two most articulate urban practitioners, John Trussel of Winchester and Henry Manship of Great Yarmouth, are notable for their civic pride and for their ultimate support for established authority.[93] Like so many other town clerks, they were deeply interested in the history of their towns. Also, insofar as they discuss law, the strain of thought they drew upon most heavily was that which laid stress on the need for order and obedience. According to Trussel, ' All Communitie is confusion yf by Order yt bee not kept in unity, ffor Order...is the hyht of Decency, the bewtye of Nature, the M[as]ter of Artes, the Neste of amitie, and the onely lief of Traffick and Commerce.'[94] In the works of both men, the writer referred to most directly was not a common lawyer, but the Oxford Aristotelian John Case, whose *Sphaera Civitatis* was a bulwark of conventional Elizabethan political thought.[95]

Indeed, it may well be a mistake to see provincial practitioners as particularly active political animals. If some members of the lower branch were involved in local politics, many others in both town and country held no office, and were therefore outside the ambit of political life, much farther outside it than many a local gentleman, artisan, or tradesman. There is certainly some evidence of political indifference amongst practitioners. For example, a town clerk of Stratford, Thomas Greene, took pains to remain neutral in a dispute between his town and a local encloser, William Coombes. Another Warwickshire practitioner's views on a tithe dispute consisted of a desire that the two opposing groups of rioters annihilate themselves.[96]

Indifference (or simple prudence) also seems to have been the most prevalent reaction of the lower branch to that acid test of seventeenth-century political life, the civil wars of 1642–60. On the face of it, there were some general factors which one might expect to have inclined practitioners towards the parliamentary side. For example, in the provinces disruptions within the ruling élite sometimes opened up local government to members of the lesser gentry and other outsiders, like the attorneys, who had hitherto enjoyed only a limited role in county affairs.[97] However, in reality, no clear-cut general trends are detectable in the political allegiance of practitioners. A few members of the lower branch made significant contributions to the cause of parliament. For instance, Daniel Noddel, who had acted as a solicitor for fenmen opposed to drainage schemes in the Isle of Axeholme in the 1630s, became a military and political leader in Lincolnshire in the 1640s and 1650s and had friends amongst the Levellers. The regicide Thomas Harrison had once served as a clerk to the Hertfordshire attorney Thomas Houlker.[98] But there were also royalist practitioners. Several sympathizers of Charles I were dismissed from town clerkships in the 1640s, and at least fifteen attorneys were fined by parliament for supporting the royalist cause.[99] Yet, in spite of these individual examples, what is most striking given the magnitude of the conflict is the relatively small number of men who are known to have become involved on either side. The fact that only 15 out of some 1500 practitioners were fined for supporting the king speaks for itself. More surprisingly, searches of the memberships of parliamentary county committees in Devonshire, Hertfordshire, and Warwickshire reveal the names of no more than one or two practitioners.[100] In Warwickshire, for example, the only man known to have become deeply involved in the wars was Thomas Halford, who served as a captain in the parliamentary army and, later, as a county committeeman. But Halford's allegiance is perhaps most easily explained by reference to the fact that he was the steward of the leader of the parliamentary cause in the county, Lord Brooke.[101] Provincial practitioners were not rich men. Many of them lived solely off the fees earned through their practices. Whatever their political views may have been, the need to continue to work, and the desire for peace and prosperity which would enable men to continue to use the law, may well have been strong incentives towards neutrality.[102]

In conclusion, the political impact of the increased number of late-sixteenth- and early-seventeenth-century legal practitioners is difficult to define precisely. On the shire level, they provided a large pool of technical expertise. In towns, the participation of practitioners in public life was important to the urban corporations for whom they worked and also in some cases provided a means by which the lawyers could become involved in local politics. To some extent there was nothing new about this; medieval incorporated towns had always needed the services of lawyers.[103] Even so, the large number of charters issued between the Reformation and the Civil War created a new market for legal experts, and the proliferation of practitioners combined with changes in some urban economies enabled provincial attorneys to achieve a say in local government which was unprecedented. In the absence of much research on late-medieval and early Tudor town politics, it is hard to say whether the litigiousness so typical of their affairs during the reigns of Elizabeth and the early Stuarts was a new development. Certainly, some towns are known to have experienced internal strife before attorneys came on the scene.[104] The increased availability of legal talent contributed to the tendency to litigate, but the conditions that gave rise to the disputes which ended up in the courts – the tension between oligarchies and outsiders – are best seen as a part of the internal dynamics of urban history which had little to do with the legal profession.[105] The nature of town politics changed very little as a result of the increase in the number of practitioners resident in them after 1600.

More generally, it is sometimes argued that the spread of the common lawyers helped to break down local particularism by linking the provinces with the common law of the realm and with the ways of thinking of the capital.[106] In some respects this is undoubtedly true. Attorneys travelled regularly back and forth from London; they did bring a wide cross-section of the population into contact with the royal courts. However, the real difficulty for the historian lies in trying to identify the nature and significance of the values they carried with them. The extent of their theoretical knowledge should not be exaggerated, and in any case the common law tradition put as much stress on the importance of obedience to established authority as on fundamental rights and liberties. Equally, for most attorneys the local element in their professional lives figured at least as heavily as the London one. Practitioners who sought local office were completely dependent on the good will of patrons and local élites. Undersheriffs were frequently accused of using their offices for factional ends. Some town clerks helped to reform local borough courts and to put town government on a more secure legal footing,[107] but others are known to have become deeply involved in the personal and group rivalries which were characteristic of urban politics, and allegations that they used their offices to further personal quarrels were not unusual. For example, William Harvey of Bridgwater was accused of mishandling business in the borough court there, and the town clerk of Shrewsbury in the 1630s was largely responsible for hindering governmental reform by blocking the town's efforts to secure a new charter.[108] The legal bureaucracies of commissions of the peace or of towns often had their own particular way of doing things.[109] Indeed, with the decline of the practice of appointing clerks of the peace by letters patent in the mid sixteenth century, the crown in effect lost direct control over an office which was a linch-pin in local administration,[110] and as the bureaucracies and work of both the commissions of the peace and of towns grew larger during the next century, so the number of practitioners who became involved in local matters actually increased. In the end, there may have been nothing inherently contradictory about the growth of a 'county community' mentality, which emphasized local practices and customs, and the growth of a legal profession which brought the localities into closer contact with London.

11

FEES AND INCOMES

I

Throughout English history, the law, along with marriage, the church, and diligent management, has been reckoned by both contemporaries and historians as one of the principal means by which men of humble origins could hope to raise themselves into the national or at least the local élite. In this chapter, therefore, we will explore the economic prospects of members of the lower branch. The principal variables that must be considered are the differing levels of income of different groups within the profession, changes over time, and the relative importance of patrimony versus the fruits of professional practice in determining the success which individuals could achieve.

As we have seen in previous chapters, the lower branch was in fact composed of a range of practitioners which stretched from the officials of the courts at Westminster to the country attorney who worked in a village in one of the more remote parts of the realm. Consequently, the prospects offered by a legal career were extremely diverse. The office holders were at the apex of the profession in terms of wealth, and, given the Elizabethan boom in litigation, it is certain that legal offices were steadily gaining in value throughout the period. For example, an assessment of members of the legal profession for a 'loan' to Queen Elizabeth in 1589 was largely disdainful of the wealth of the twenty-four cursitors in Chancery, but by the time of Charles I each of these places was said to be worth some £300 p.a.[1] Similarly, Jones has summed up the position of their colleagues, the six clerks, with the comment that in the Elizabethan period most of the holders of these offices rode horses, whilst by the early seventeenth century their successors travelled in great style by carriage.[2] Certainly, there is no doubt that by the 1630s the six clerks were making a lot

of money. Estimates put the annual value of each of their offices at
between £800 and £1600 p.a., and fee income at this level very often
propelled their owners into the market for large landed estates. For
instance, after six years as a six clerk in the 1630s, Richard Colchester
was able to achieve a surplus of income over expenditure of between
£2000 and £3000 p.a. He died in 1643 owning land in four counties,
was able to leave 1000 marks for his daughter's marriage portion, and
had firmly established a place for his family in the landed gentry.[3]

However, in the legal bureaucracy, as in the gentry or the merchant
communities, there were many gradations of income. Some offices
were a great deal more profitable than others. A place as a six clerk
in Chancery was one of the richest. At the other end of the scale we
might take as an example the post of messenger in the court of
Exchequer, an office held in the 1640s by John Harris of St Clement
Dane's, London. A schedule of his money and goods in 1647 came
to £305 13s. 4d. Of this total, some £24 was in silver, another £10 was
due in salary, and a further £45 in unspecified debts was owing for
'Exchequer process'. The rest of his assets were livestock, summer
and winter corn (£40), and farming tools. Harris' will gives the
impression of a man who was doing reasonably well, but his estate
was nowhere near as great as that of Richard Colchester, and was
probably not much larger than those of his two brothers who were
yeoman farmers in his native Shropshire.[4]

In fact, most clerical offices led to prospects somewhere between
these two examples. Charles I's commission on fees divided up the
one hundred underclerks of the six clerks in Chancery into three
different categories. Forty earned £100 p.a. from fees; twenty roughly
£50 p.a., and another forty no more than £30 p.a.[5] Thus in one single
office there were incomes which mirrored those in agricultural
society of men whose life-styles ranged from the wealthy yeoman or
minor gentleman to the humble husbandman. Details gleaned from
a selection of wills suggest that many of the seventeenth-century six
clerks' clerks lived in or near London. If they were successful, or
enjoyed some inheritance, they also maintained a small amount of
landed property, but there is little evidence of men who were making
great leaps upwards into the landed gentry. For example, the estate
of John Somers of St Margaret's, near Rochester in Kent, consisted
largely of a lease of twenty-one acres of land from the dean and
chapter of Rochester, and two of his sons were apprenticed into
trades. Thomas Naylor of St Dunstan's in the West, London, was

able to leave his wife a sum of £800 in accordance with their marriage agreement, and each of his four children received a legacy of £200. Edward Procktor, also of St Dunstan's in the West, inherited land in his native Nottinghamshire which was of sufficient annual value to maintain his eldest son first at Cambridge and then at one of the inns of court. In addition, Procktor had accumulated other properties, presumably with the aid of his legal income, and he seems to have anticipated that these plus the inheritance would be enough for his son and heir to live on. However, there were distinct limits on the value of this estate. Procktor's second son inherited little, and the family plan dictated that he be placed in some 'honest calling or profession'.[6]

In courts such as Star Chamber or Wards, where the work was monopolized by relatively few men, incomes were generally a great deal higher than those enjoyed by the six clerks' clerks. In the 1630s, the clerkship of Star Chamber was worth £1600 p.a., and the co-clerkship of the Wards about £1500.[7] On the basis of the latter income, one of the coholders, Richard Chamberlain, who obtained his place in 1617, was able to build up a substantial landed estate. Originally from Oxfordshire, Chamberlain invested his profits in property around Nuneaton in Warwickshire, and established his family amongst the gentry there, even though he was not as wealthy as men within the first rank of the county élite.[8] On a more modest level, the career of Edward Latymer, a sworn attorney in the court of Wards, provides a quite typical example of the prospects of a middle-ranking practitioner in the early seventeenth century. Latymer began his work in the Wards in the 1590s as a deputy to the receiver-general at a salary of £40 p.a. Then, in 1601, he secured one of the sworn attorneyships in the court and continued to practise in that capacity until 1620. During these years his profits from office were in the region of £150–£200 p.a., and on the strength of them he was able to build up a tidy landed estate. During term time, he lived in Fleet Street, but he also owned a country house just outside London, bought ninety-six acres in Fulham for £1600, and held leases on land in Hammersmith. By the end of his life his income from land was worth £200 p.a. in addition to what he earned from court fees, and his total estate was valued at £10,000.[9]

Of course, it was the busiest of courts, King's Bench and Common Pleas, which offered the most potential to a young man aiming to make his fortune through a clerical career. Worth something between

£4000 and £6000 p.a., the chief clerkship of the King's Bench was probably the most valuable of all legal offices, and after 1617, when the Ropers finally gave it up, it even attracted the attention of the royal favourites, Somerset and Buckingham. Not all common law offices were quite so profitable. In the 1620s posts in the Common Pleas such as that of clerk of the warrants or clerk of the fines were reckoned to bring in as much as £1000 p.a., whilst lesser offices such as those of the clerk of the errors or exigenters ranged in value from £200 to £400 p.a.[10] In the 1630s, there was a flourishing market in reversions for places as filazers, but the value of these offices in fact depended on the amount of business which they handled. Sir James Pitt's filazership for London was worth £1000 p.a., but all of the others were rated at no more than £250 p.a., and some probably brought in no more than £120.[11] As we shall see, incomes at this lower level were not very much greater than those enjoyed by the more successful country attorneys, and the life-styles of some of the lesser filazers also lead to the same conclusions. Robert Harrison, filazer for Sussex in the 1580s and 1590s, built himself a new 'mansion' house in Colchester, and was able to leave his two daughters reasonably handsome legacies of £500 each. However, he expected that both of his sons would become apprentices in trade, and his circle of acquaintances was drawn entirely from the urban élite. John Farwell of Somerset seems to have been a richer man. He had a manor house at Charlton Holbrook and bought land from the gentry. He left £400 in marriage portions to each of his daughters and styled himself as an esquire. Yet Farwell evidently anticipated that his son would not be able to live from the profits of his broad acres alone, for he went to 'extra-ordinary expense' to have him trained up as an utter barrister.[12]

By comparison with these comfortable, but modest, estates, those which could be accumulated by the greatest of Common Pleas office holders, the *custos brevium* and the prothonotaries, were truly monumental. The three prothonotaries declared their fee income in the late 1620s at between £2500 and £3000 p.a., and the *custos brevium* admitted to making as much as £5000 p.a.[13] Two well-documented biographies, that of John Lennard of Sevenoaks in Kent, *custos brevium* during the reign of Elizabeth, and that of Richard Brownlow, chief prothonotary for forty-seven years from 1591, show both the use to which such profits from legal work could be put and the way in which men reached the top within the clerical underworld. John

Lennard came to his legal career neither empty-handed nor lacking useful connections. He enjoyed an inheritance of lands and a house at Halsted in Kent, and after he had 'attayned the Latin tongue' his father was able to place him in the office of his uncle, prothonotary of the Common Pleas, Weston. From this point on, his career was marked by a series of successful moves. Lennard 'profited' so greatly under his uncle's guidance that in 1536, at the age of twenty-five, he was made prothonotary of the nine shires in Wales. Then, in 1543, he became second prothonotary in Common Pleas, and at about the same time was appointed a justice of the peace in Kent. Queen Mary granted him a lordship worth £1000, and in 1562 he acquired his greatest prize, the office of *custos brevium*, by buying it from William Cecil, the future Lord Burghley. Already in the 1550s and 1560s, this plum must have been growing rapidly in value. In 1547 Cecil had calculated that the fees were worth £284 p.a., but a deed amongst the Lennard papers indicates that the purchase price in 1562 included an annuity to Cecil of no less than £240, a fact which must mean that the profits at this stage were already very much greater than they had been a mere fifteen years earlier. Enjoying a legal income on this scale, Lennard was able to continue to build up his landed estate, and he also appears to have been an active JP. When he died in 1590, he left a landed income of at least £2500 p.a., and was able to provide marriage portions of £1000 to each of his two daughters. Lennard was every bit as wealthy as the richest country gentleman.[14]

The social origins of Richard Brownlow are a good deal more obscure than those of John Lennard, but they are more likely to have been urban and professional than rural and agricultural. Brownlow was born in 1552 in St Andrew's, Holborn, which suggests that his father may have been a member of some branch of the legal profession. Virtually nothing is known of Richard's early career. He very probably began as a clerk in one of the offices of the Common Pleas, and he may have received some help from Sir Gilbert Gerrard, master of the rolls, to whom he was distantly related by marriage. In any case, by 1589 he had secured a moderately profitable place as an exigenter in Common Pleas, and he ran the office out of chambers at Clement's Inn. Brownlow's great step forward came in 1591 when he secured the office of chief prothonotary, perhaps with the help of Gerrard, but certainly in return for a capital sum of money which was greater than anything he might possibly have inherited. Thereafter he enjoyed a long, distinguished, and extremely profitable career. By the late 1590s, he was purchasing his first parcels of land in Lincolnshire, and in the 1610s he bought Belton in reversion from an impoverished knight, Sir Henry Pelham, for £4100. By 1617 his income from rents was £2400, and this in addition to his legal fees must have produced a total disposable income of nearly £6000 p.a. He kept houses in London as well as in county Lincoln. His sons were educated at Oxford and the Inner Temple and his daughters married into the gentry. When he died in 1638, he left land worth at least £5100 p.a.[15]

The biographies of Lennard and Brownlow bring out a number of elements which were common to most of those who were able to achieve success on the clerical side of the lower branch. Some kind of family link was undoubtedly helpful in distinguishing those who were able to progress upwards from the hundreds of young men who came to London to seek their fortunes in the clerical maze. Such a connection insured a better starting point and must have been essential in securing grants of the more profitable offices once they became available.[16] Indeed, in this respect connections may have been more important than inherited wealth. Very few of the men who made their way in the legal world at any level could have come to it penniless; some are known to have had modest patrimonies. As in the case of Brownlow and Lennard, fees earned in the earlier stages of a career may have been helpful in raising capital sums, but once an office had been secured, it seems most likely that the capital necessary to pay for it could be borrowed.[17] Of all the elements required for a climb to the top, skill and hard work are the most difficult to measure with any degree of accuracy. All we can say for sure is that most early modern legal office holders began their careers as lowly clerks, or, as was the case with some filazers and prothonotaries, as practising attorneys.[18] In addition, even those who came from relatively affluent backgrounds often displayed the values of aggressive, self-made men. Richard Brownlow concluded his quarterly accounts with the combative, if pious, invocation ' Dominus dat incrementum et mirabilia sunt opera ejus...ipse enim exaltavit me de stercore supra inimicos meos, eripiens me de manibus eorum, et collocans me inter divites hujus mundi'.[19]

John Lennard's will contains the precept to his children that they should be careful to keep a watchful eye on their servants and children so that they should not fall away from the fear of God and into a 'loose and dissolute life'. His autobiography indulges in an openly self-congratulatory evaluation of his own achievements.

All ages and states well ordered have ever had in greate regard those men who by their painful and vertuous courses have been the Authors of their owne advancement. Wherefore his [Lennard's] wealth *and* reputation obtayned not by base *and* manual trade but by service of witt and learning will be adiudged by ye equal minded as proper rewards of his vertue *and* memorialls of his wisdome: howsoever the envious, whose only grace consisteth in disgracing others, may labour to detract him.[20]

II

In 1617, Richard Brownlow spent over £50 on clothes, including 11 guineas on a single silk gown. When he rode to Belton for a short visit in April of the same year, even his horse was lavishly decorated with £3 11s. 4d. worth of 'lace and stuff'. A friend of Sir Edward Coke, the owner of a vast landed estate, Brownlow was a prince in the world of clerks and attorneys;[21] there is no better example of the full potential of upward social mobility which a successful legal career could offer. However, the fact is that the office holders, not to mention the prothonotaries, were the élite of the lower branch and their numbers were limited. The real core, and from the point of view of social history the much more numerically significant part, of the profession was composed of the attorneys of King's Bench and Common Pleas. It is to their rather less spectacular prospects that we must now turn.

Systematic evidence about the incomes of attorneys is not very plentiful. No account books survive, and even the reports of the early Stuart commissions on fees provide little indication of the kinds of annual income which an ordinary country practice was likely to produce. Consequently, a picture of the wealth of these practitioners must be built up on the basis of a number of different measurements. The logical starting point is a consideration of the kinds of income which they received in return for legal services.

The only fee to which an attorney was officially entitled for handling a suit at common law (as opposed to fees taken for the drawing of instruments such as writs and pleadings, etc.) was the ancient one of 3s. 4d. per term for each case handled.[22] The potential value of this fee to the individual practitioner is illustrated by Table 11.1, which sets out the average number of cases which each attorney of the King's Bench and Common Pleas might have handled in selected years between 1560 and 1640. These figures were calculated by dividing the total numbers of cases in advanced stages in each year studied by the number of attorneys practising in the court during that

Table 11.1. *Average numbers of cases per attorney per year in King's Bench and Common Pleas, 1560–1640*[a]

	King's Bench	Common Pleas
1560	78 (£52 p.a.)	64 (£42 13s. 4d. p.a.)
1580	76 (£50 13s. 4d. p.a.)	60 (£40 p.a.)
1606	58 (£38 13s. 4d. p.a.)	42 (£28 p.a.)
1640	50 (£33 6s. 8d. p.a.)	34 (£22 13s. 4d. p.a.)

[a] Figures for the numbers of cases in the courts and for the number of practitioners can be found above, pp. 51 and 113.

year; then, since each case in advanced stages involved two attorneys, this figure has been multiplied by two. The figures are crude at best, but, if each attorney is allowed his fee of 3s. 4d. per case for each of the four terms in the legal year, we can speculate that in 1606 the average King's Bench attorney earned £38 13s. 4d., and the average Common Pleas man £28 p.a.

Of course, there is no reason to expect that cases should have been equally distributed amongst all of the practitioners in a profession where skill, connections, or the geographical location of a practice might give one man an advantage over another, Consequently, simple averages, although useful, might be misleading, and there is another approach to the analysis of individual case loads which can give them better definition. From the King's Bench roll of warrants for Hilary Term 1606, it has been possible to learn how many cases each of 183 individual attorneys handled in that term. Table 11.2 displays these results.[23] Because fifty-three attorneys who acted exclusively for defendants are not included in these figures, and because the number of new cases for any one man might vary considerably from term to term, the numbers of cases in the table cannot be taken as an absolute guide to the number of cases any attorney might handle in any one year. What they do show is how widely the sizes of individual practices varied. Therefore, they provide some important qualifications to the average case load of fifty-eight per King's Bench attorney in 1606, and by extrapolation to the averages for both courts in all the years covered by Table 11.1. In Hilary Term 1606, 62 per cent, or almost two-thirds, of the attorneys handled between one and ten new cases. That might mean that in a single year they acted for between four and forty plaintiffs, and, when possible services for

Table 11.2. *Numbers of new cases in which each of 183 King's Bench attorneys acted for a plaintiff, Hilary Term, 3 Jac. I*

Number of cases	Number of attorneys in each grouping	Percentage of attorneys with a certain case load
1–10	113	61.7
11–20	42	22.9
21–30	16	8.7
31–40	9	4.9
Over 40	3 (104, 43, 63)	1.6
Total	183	99.8

defendants have been alllowed for, those with between seven and ten cases in Hilary Term might expect to handle just about the average number of new cases each year. On the other hand, those with between one and five cases in this term probably handled well below the average number of cases. Thus a majority of the attorneys in the court could expect to be at or below the £40 p.a. level, with a few slightly above and some certainly well below. Another smaller group of 23 per cent were perhaps twenty or thirty cases above the average, and yet another 15 per cent well above the average.

The large numbers of attorneys active in Common Pleas make exact tabulations of their case loads extremely laborious, but the impression gained by looking through the rolls of warrants of that court is much the same as that given by Table 11.2. The majority of attorneys handled between one and ten new cases each term, but there were a few men – for example, Ralph Bovey of London – who might have acted for plaintiffs in as many as eighty new cases each term. In both courts the differences in the sizes of practices were enormous. Some attorneys handled fewer than ten new cases in a year, others as many as 200 or 250.[24] On the basis of elementary calculations using the 3s. 4d. attorney's fee, this suggests a range of earnings from £6 to well over £100 per annum. As we shall see, this wide spectrum of possible earnings from legal work was matched by the greatly different fortunes of individual practitioners.

Although calculations based on the 3s. 4d. fee and the size of case loads give some idea of basic incomes, they can be taken as no more than minimum estimates of the earning power of attorneys. This is not because the 3s. 4d. fee was inflated by dishonest practitioners or because of special or extraordinary charges. The surviving fee books of George Draper of Hitchin and John Clifford of Frampton, as well as numerous miscellaneous legal bills of the period, make it evident that this basic charge was rarely exceeded.[25] Nor did attorneys in the sixteenth and seventeenth centuries charge their clients for expenses incurred on the way to London or for staying there while they were attending to a case. There is some evidence that these charges were taken by men acting as solicitors (and hence by attorneys when they were handling cases in jurisdictions like Chancery or Star Chamber), and since in the 1820s it was considered appropriate for attorneys to charge for travel, such fees may have been adopted by all members of the lower branch some time in the eighteenth century.[26] But in the period before 1640, expenses for travel never appear on bills for common law cases.

Nevertheless, there were a number of other fees which practitioners took for legal work, and which supplemented the basic termly charge of 3s. 4d. In general, these can be divided into four categories: first, those fees for the drawing up of procedural documents such as writs which were an integral part of common law litigation and which the attorneys took or shared with the prothonotaries, filazers, and other court officials; second, those taken by attorneys for giving advice and handling business at assizes; third, those taken in jurisdictions other than King's Bench and Common Pleas; fourth, charges for writing up non-judicial instruments such as conveyances, deeds, bonds, marriage agreements, wills, and so on.

The fees which attorneys could take for writing out documents which were directly related to common law litigation constitute a complicated subject, but the most important factor in determining how great a share an attorney took in the costs of mesne process or pleading was his relationship to the clerical officers of the courts.[27] Thus, the King's Bench attorneys, who were normally members of the clerical staff of the chief prothonotary, shared greatly in the profits reaped from litigation. Every stage of every suit put money in their pockets. For example, mesne process in the King's Bench was based on the *latitat*. This cost the litigant 4s. 1d., and this sum was divided between the prothonotary (22d.), the judges (4d.), the attorney (20d.), and the seal office.[28] Other steps in litigation, such as the entry of actions in the plea rolls, could bring in for the attorney as much as 2s. or 3s. per entry, and the attorney-clerks also received fees for drawing pleas.[29]

The additional income from clerical work involved in litigation must certainly have enabled the average King's Bench attorney to earn a good deal more than the £38 p.a. calculated solely on the 3s. 4d. fee. But exactly how much a place as an attorney-clerk was worth is difficult to say. Given the huge number of procedural variations involved in any single case, hypothetical calculations seem likely to be of little help. A roughly similar group of legal functionaries, the 120 clerks of the three prothonotaries of Common Pleas, were said to have earned £100 p.a. in the early seventeenth century.[30] After due consideration has been given to the differences in the sizes of the practices of individual King's Bench attorneys and allowances made for slight differences between the two groups, £100 p.a. would seem close to a reasonable estimate of the income of a prosperous King's Bench attorney, and it is one which is verified by the surviving evidence about the estates of individuals. None of the King's Bench men who were active in the early seventeenth century, and about whom something can be discovered, were as wealthy as the holders of the most lucrative legal offices, but their surviving wills leave no doubt that the most successful of these men enjoyed a very solid affluence. John Harborne, who was probably the richest of them, had an interest in the manor of Knowle in Warwickshire and a number of houses in St Clement's Churchyard, London. His two daughters were granted annuities of £40 each until they were married, where-upon they received the very handsome portions of £1000. Even Harborne's son, Edward, could expect a legacy of £2000 when he finished his apprenticeship.[31] Amongst many of the King's Bench attorneys, investments in parcels of land in the country were very frequently combined with the ownership of houses in London. The two Devonshire men Ambrose Mudford and William Crosse both owned considerable amounts of property in east Devon and just across the border in Somerset. But, in addition, Crosse had land 'in Essex, as well as his house and lots of groune in Orchard Street' in the parish of St Margaret in Westminster. Mudford had even more extensive London holdings which included his own house in Milford Lane, St Clement Dane's, and leases for at least nine messuages in Gravel Lane, Covent Garden.[32] John Whitacres of Colchester had property in Essex, which was in the occupation of at least thirty other people, plus lands, tenements, and houses in the City of London which he had bought in conjunction with another Essex practitioner, John Eldred. The £50 p.a. in annuities which he granted as benefactions to his law clerk and his cousins must have constituted only a fraction of his total landed wealth. Thomas Bland of Tunbridge Wells owned property in London worth £500–£600 (capital value) and was able to leave a legacy of £450 to his daughter, Elizabeth. William Langhorn owned a farm in Steventon in Bedfordshire and kept £500 in a 'bagge' for his daughter's marriage portion. John Hill of Bromyard owned lands in Herefordshire, Gloucestershire, and Shropshire. He expected his fees due from law charges to be worth at least £200 in cash.[33] In general, as we have seen in other parts of this study, the King's Bench practitioners maintained a very profitable and remarkably close-knit enclave in the legal establishment. Sons frequently followed fathers into practice, families inter-married, individuals borrowed money from each other and witnessed each other's wills. With their emphasis on the London property market, even their investments adhered to a similar pattern.

Because of the organization of their court, Common Pleas attorneys were on the whole entitled to a much more restricted range of fees than those in King's Bench. In the Common Pleas, although some men certainly acted in both capacities, the functions of the attorneys and of the prothonotaries' clerks were in theory kept separate. In any case, at just over one hundred, the number of prothonotaries' clerks was by the early seventeenth century only a small fraction of the total number of attorneys.[34] Consequently, it would seem that the ordinary attorney was entitled to little or nothing for clerical work such as copying out writs or for making entries on the plea rolls. However, they did take fees for drafting the pleas and declarations which were subsequently entered on the rolls by the prothonotaries' clerks. The exact fees for this service, which involved some skill, are unclear, but they were probably much the same as those charged in the King's Bench for similar work; in other words, in the range of a shilling or two for the initial cost of each piece plus an additional charge of about 4d. for every sheet after the first. These fees were not negligible, but there is no reason to think that they change the order of magnitude of the average incomes of the Common Pleas practitioners as set out in Table 11.1.

In most common law actions, an attorney's earnings would have been confined mainly to the termly attorney's fee and to whatever extra he might be entitled to for drawing writs. However, if a case ended up going to trial at *nisi prius*, he was paid quite handsomely. Attorneys were allowed 15s. for taking the record of a case to the trial, and an additional 15s. for directing it there.[35] Yet another occasional source of fees were the extra charges for counsel or advice which appear to have been made in some instances. Although it frequently must have been an important aspect of an attorney's work, printed and manuscript schedules of fees say nothing about what he might demand for advising clients, and this may suggest that such fees were technically illegal. Nevertheless, legal bills of costs sometimes mention '*consilio*', and George Draper's case book shows that in a small number of cases (perhaps 10 of 170) he took something in the region of 6s. or 7s. for giving counsel. In a few others, he charged as little as 2s. and as much as £1 for 'his pains' or for 'extraordinary work'.

Thus far, only those fees due for litigation conducted in King's Bench and Common Pleas have been considered, but most attorneys also did some work in other jurisdictions; that is, either in courts in London such as Chancery, Star Chamber, or Wards, or in local hundred, county, or municipal courts. In the equity and prerogative courts at Westminster, their take was probably limited to the termly 6s. 8d. solicitor's fee. This may have been augmented slightly by charges made for writing out copies of bills, interrogatories, or the answers of witnesses, but attorneys do not appear to have profited in any other way from work connected with procedure.[36] Although they varied somewhat from place to place, fees in local courts were a good deal lower than those at Westminster. But for the practitioners who worked in them, this disadvantage was balanced by two other factors. The number of attorneys allowed to work in municipal or hundred courts was usually limited, and they were permitted to take fees for a wide range of services. In 1638, for example, attorneys in the Plymouth town court claimed that they took 12d. for drawing declarations and answering replications and that they were due 12d. for suing out each of several different kinds of writs. If no counsellor was retained at the time of the trial, they took 3s. 4d.; if counsel was retained they charged 2s.[37]

The value to the average practitioner of fees taken in courts other than King's Bench and Common Pleas can be estimated in only the most general way. Equity and prerogative court litigation was fairly lucrative, but the volume of such work was small in comparison with business conducted in the common law courts. Similarly, though many municipal and perhaps some hundred and county courts were still active in the early seventeenth century, none of them handled very many cases, Moreover, in many of the more profitable of such jurisdictions, practice as a local attorney precluded a practice in King's Bench and Common Pleas. Even where it did not, the profits from such work were likely to have been measured in shillings rather than pounds.

On the more general question of how much fees taken for litigation in all jurisdictions were likely to bring a seventeenth-century attorney, the only satisfactory evidence is the account book of George Draper of Hitchin. During the year 1669–70, Draper handled about 170 cases in the common law courts at Westminster, in Chancery, and in the Hertfordshire county courts. His accounts show that he laid out approximately £479 for writs and other procedural necessities connected with these suits. Out of this total, the fees which he might have expected to take as his own profit amounted to £108, or roughly a quarter of the cost of litigation he conducted, and, on the basis of this and the evidence provided by bills of legal costs, it seems safe to conclude'that common law attorneys (who were not also entering clerks in their courts) could expect to keep between one-third and one-quarter of the fees involved in any suit. It is also interesting that Draper's case book lends some support to the calculations about earnings, based on the number of cases a Common Pleas practitioner handled, which are set out in Table 11.1. Draper's practice was well above the average in size, and his income from fees was just about in line with what would be expected for a man with about 170 cases in a year.

However, as Chapter 10 showed, attorneys earned money from non-contentious as well as from contentious work, so any attempt to elucidate their sources of income must take into account business outside of the courts. As their frequent, if random, survival in local record offices indicates, conveyances, bargains and sale, and bonds given for loans or for sums due were the common currency of business transactions during the early modern period, but there is little evidence about how often they were drawn up by professionals or what charges were made for the service. Books of court fees such as Powell's *Attourneys Academy* say nothing about charges for legal instruments, and it is unlikely that standard rates for such work were ever established. This probably means that charges for instruments, unlike court fees, rose to some extent to keep pace with inflation. In any case, they were evidently always quite costly to the client. In the mid sixteenth century, Thomas Gregory of Coventry noted that he was owed £2 14s. 4d. for helping to draw up deeds.[38] Although George Draper's case book records only those instruments which he drew as part of litigation, and although the date of the book (1669) may mean that his charges are misleadingly high in the context of the period 1560–1640, it nevertheless adds to the impression that fees earned for drawing instruments must have been an important source of income. Draper's charges for such documents were based on the value of the lands or goods involved and on the legal complexities encountered. In general they varied between the 13s. 4d. he charged Richard Benson of Islington for a mortgage and a lease and the £1 paid by G. Nedes of Stevenage for an indenture on a fine for land worth about £5 p.a.[39] These fees were large compared with those taken for suits. Indeed, the drawing of instruments may well have been as lucrative as litigation, which involved set fees, travel to London, and the extension of credit to clients.

Even after computing fees due from litigation and for making extra-judicial documents, we have still not produced an exhaustive catalogue of the income which attorneys might earn from their legal work. For those who were fortunate enough to hold them, offices in town and county government or in the service of individuals added substantially to income. The most lucrative of local offices were clerkships of the peace or assize. In the mid seventeenth century, for example, Thomas Shapcott of Exeter reckoned the clerkship of the peace of Devon to be worth £100 per annum.[40] Cockburn estimates that assistant clerkships of assize (offices frequently held by attorneys) might have earned their holders as much as £20 at each assize.[41] Town clerkships or positions as attorneys for a town could supplement income, though, as we have seen, the office of town clerk often made exlusive demands on its holder.[42] The value of these offices varied considerably from place to place and at different dates as compensation was made for inflation. In the 1580s Northampton paid its town attorney the very generous allowance of £3 p.a.;[43] more typical at this date was the 20s. given to Thomas Goddard of Southampton in 1573–4.[44] In the early years of the seventeenth century, Hugh Willington, a Common Pleas attorney, was granted a retainer of £4 p.a. to serve the city of Coventry in its legal causes.[45]

Though their true value is difficult to evaluate, town clerkships were probably quite lucrative, though certainly less so than clerkships of the peace or assize. Stratford-upon-Avon gave its clerk £10 p.a. in 1627,[46] a figure which is probably typical for small towns. In 1637

Coventry granted Humphrey Burton the large sum of £30 p.a. 'for his good services', an unusually high salary.[47] However, neither of these figures provides any idea of how much could be earned in fees taken, or on advantageous leases to town property such as Burton and doubtless many other town clerks enjoyed.[48]

Evidence about the regular fees and retainers earned by attorneys employed privately by members of the gentry is patchy, but enough exists to suggest that they could be significant and that some practitioners established fairly formal relationships with regular clients. In November 1588, Thomas Green of Knapton in Norfolk noted annuities of 10s. or 20s. p.a. which were due to him from six local gentlemen.[49] At about the same date Arthur Gregory of Warwickshire received 20s. yearly for keeping the courts of small manors; in addition he had the very large annuity of £40 from the Earl of Huntingdon as a retainer for his legal services.[50] Two seventeenth-century practitioners, James Prescott of Warwick and William Knight of Barrells, regularly kept courts for the more modest, but nevertheless substantial, Warwickshire landowners, the Lucys, Ferrers, and Throckmortons. Prescott's 'friend' Sir Thomas Lucy left him £40 in his will.[51] Knight had an annuity of £12 p.a. out of the Ferrers' manor of Baddesley Clinton (in 1631), and doubtless he earned more by keeping courts and providing other services for the Throckmortons.[52]

III

Keeping in mind the various sources of income available to them, and using the three-county sample of attorneys from Devonshire, Hertfordshire, and Warwickshire as the basis for the discussion, we can now attempt to assess the value of the profession to its practitioners. In order to do this, it is necessary first of all to establish how much land and/or money an attorney might have had when he started his practice. Thus we must begin by discussing patrimony or the social origins of attorneys.

Good evidence about the social origins and inherited wealth of practitioners is thin. The social status of fathers can be determined only in exceptional cases, and even if statistics about the status of fathers could be compiled, they would in most cases tell very little about how much the young man who set out on a legal career actually had in his pocket. On the other hand, although it is not perfect, evidence is in many respects abundant. About one-third of the men in the three-county sample are very well documented, and either a will or a pedigree exists for another third. Thus there is enough to produce an impressionistic picture of the origins of attorneys, but not enough for a quantitative one. For this reason, it is best to start by drawing some inferences from what the evidence does not say and then to use what is known in order to focus the picture more clearly.

It is easy to say what the fathers of attorneys were not. None of them appear on the commissions of the peace for their counties. This is a less than perfect measure of social status, but the commissions can be relied upon to include some of the esquires and gentlemen of more than parish note in a county. Next, with only a few exceptions from the late sixteenth century, no father was able to pass on to his attorney son the unit of lands (though undefined) and jurisdictional rights known as manors.[53] Finally, it must be a fair assumption that attorneys came from families who planned a legal career for one of their sons, but who could not afford to send him to the inns of court where he could have trained to become a barrister. On the other hand, if Spufford is right in arguing that even elementary education (and more than a rudimentary education was required of future attorneys) was restricted to the sons of farmers of greater than average wealth,[54] this gives some kind of minimum lower limit for the wealth of parents. This can be further defined by the fact that, as we saw in Chapter 8, in 1600 it might have cost a family between £30 and £80 to finance the training of an attorney. So some patrimony must have been available.

If we turn now to what is known about the social origins of attorneys, these speculations seem to be confirmed. Most appear to have arisen from the lesser gentry and yeomanry, but there were a few who were the sons of townsmen. As Table 11.3 demonstrates, in those cases where anything at all is known of the family backgrounds of attorneys, the majority sprang from families which had been living in their region for at least one generation.

Given the large number of unknowns in the table, it might be a mistake to jump to the conclusion that 87 per cent of all country attorneys came from families with their roots firmly established in a particular area, but at the very least we can safely conclude that as many as 40 per cent of them did so, Hence it is likely that at least a large core of practitioners within any area were likely to be known by name and family in their localities. In Devonshire, where the

Table 11.3. *Families of attorneys who had been in their county for*
at least one generation

	Old families	New families	Number in the sample	% known
Devon	45	1	113	41
Warwickshire	21	8	55	53
Hertfordshire	14	3	45[a]	38
Total	80 (87%)	12	213	43

[a] This figure includes some Essex attorneys.

Sources : The sources used in this table and in much of the rest of the chapter include wills, genealogies, and various works of local history, for example, J. L. Vivian, *Devon Pedigrees* (Exeter, 1898); *The Visitation of the County of Warwick in 1619*, ed. J. Featherston (Harleian Soc., xii, 1877); *The Visitation of the County of Warwick in 1682 and 1683*, ed. W. H. Rylands (Harleian Soc., lxii, 1911); *The Visitations of Hertfordshire in 1572 and 1634*, ed. W. C. Metcalfe (Harleian Soc., xxii, 1886).

pastoral economy carried out in a region with a plentiful supply of land provided livings for well over 400 gentry families,[55] 9 of the 113 attorneys in the county could trace their ancestors in the pedigrees prepared by the heralds. Even more significantly, 13 more were members of cadet branches of families which are mentioned in the *Visitations*, and a number of the others – Newte, Prince, Risdon, Sloleigh, Shapcott, for example – lacked pedigrees but nevertheless had deep roots in the county.[56] Although the attorneys of Warwickshire and Hertfordshire were less closely connected with armigerous families as defined by the heralds (probably because there were fewer such families in these counties) than those in Devon, they too sprang from the yeomanry and lesser gentry. Examples abound. Thomas Hawes of Solihull, who was active early in the reign of Elizabeth, could trace his ancestors in Hemlingford hundred back five generations.[57] George Averell, who practised during the same period, and who was also from Solihull, was a descendant of a local family which had produced churchwardens in this small town from at least early in the reign of Henry VIII.[58] The father of Thomas Smallbroke, an early-seventeenth-century Birmingham attorney, had been a trustee of the King Edward VI School there at its foundation.[59] Simon Blythe of Allesley was a member of a parish gentry family

Table 11.4. *Family status of attorneys in the three-county sample*

	Sons and heirs	Younger sons	Total
Devonshire	7 (3)[a]	11 (2)	18
Hertfordshire	7 (1)	5	12
Warwickshire	14 (3)	8 (2)	22
Total	28 (7)	24 (4)	52

[a] The numbers in brackets refer to men who were the sons of attorneys.
Sources: As Table 11.3.

which had connections with Sir William Dugdale. Even among those men about whom little is known, there are many whose surnames are familiar in the areas where they practised.

However, patrimony was dependent only in part on the status of fathers. As Thomas Wilson makes clear,[60] a man's fortunes as he stepped out into the world, particularly if he came from a family of modest means, depended very much on whether or not he was an eldest or younger son. As the wills of attorneys themselves illustrate, it was ordinary practice in the seventeenth century to give the bulk of an estate to the eldest son, and, if there was a little left over, to try and provide for the younger sons by giving them a cash legacy of perhaps £100 or so, often with the stipulation that it be used to bring up the child in a trade or a profession.

Table 11.4 sets out some figures for the sibling status of some of the attorneys in the three-county sample. These statistics demand careful appraisal, since the number of attorneys for which the relevant information is available amount to only 25 per cent of the sample, but the results seem credible. Since the fathers of attorneys were men of only modest means, it is not surprising that the number of eldest sons who entered the profession is about equal to the number of younger sons. If fathers were rich enough, only the younger sons had to take up trades; on the other hand, less wealthy families must have encouraged their eldest sons to supplement the family fortune by entering a profession which was not inordinately expensive to learn, but which retained or conferred nominal gentility.

A look at the specific areas under consideration adds some colour to this general picture. In Devon, a number of younger sons from families of established gentility – Copleston, Upton, Cottle, Rolle,

Prideaux – became attorneys. Fewer, but a still not insignificant group of practitioners, were the first sons of families of similar status (Fry of Yerty, Rattenbury of Okehampton, Shapcott of Shapcott), but in general younger sons outnumber eldest ones. In Warwickshire and Hertfordshire, this pattern was inverted. John Skinner of Hitchin was a younger son of Richard Skinner, registrar of the diocese of Norwich, who was said to have had twenty-one children.[61] Richard Masters of Warwickshire was a younger son of the personal physician of Queen Elizabeth,[62] and William Baldwin the fourth son of a Coventry merchant.[63] These men were born into business and professional families, but in these counties, too, the younger sons of minor gentry also took up the profession. Examples include James Willymott of Kelshall in Hertfordshire and William Frith of Staffordshire, who settled down to practise just across the Warwickshire border in Merevale.[64] But in Hertfordshire, and particularly in Warwickshire, where the evidence about sibling precedence is reasonably good, it was evidently common for first sons, who we can be certain inherited something, to become attorneys.

Thus, in spite of the small statistical sample, and taking regional variations into consideration, it seems that eldest sons were as likely as younger sons to enter the profession. Furthermore, this conclusion is reinforced by the fact that more is known about richer than about poorer families. Poorer families were presumably less able to provide heirs with income sufficient to prevent them having to take up a trade or a profession; hence it can probably be assumed that if poorer families were better represented in Table 11.4 the tally of eldest sons would be correspondingly higher. Another reasonably safe assumption is that some of the eldest sons, but not all of them, had a source of income other than work as attorneys, and that the younger sons came to the profession with relatively little. Consequently, the relative importance of patrimony versus fees as sources of income for practitioners was likely to vary greatly from individual to individual.

It is obvious that inheritances had no standard value. The evidence about how much attorneys received from their parents is insufficient to yield anything as conclusive as an average for the sample groups, but enough individual examples exist to produce a series of types. For instance, Thomas Shapcott of Knowstone parish in north-eastern Devon inherited his family's lands, which were worth about £45 p.a.[65] This is the largest inheritance which has come to light, although William Knight of Warwickshire inherited the manor of

Barrells (value unknown) from his father.[66] Two other Warwickshire attorneys also inherited land, but chose nevertheless to practise law. Edmund Rawlins was the son and heir of Thomas Rawlins of Marston Secca, and inherited a tenement and three yardlands of arable, pasture, and meadow in the parish where he was born.[67] John Halford, on the other hand, was the fifth son of a family from Walton in Leicestershire, where he had lands out of which he expected his own first son, Nathanial, to pay £200 to his second son, John.[68] Rawlins' three yardlands almost certainly provided an income well above subsistence level, and judging from the £200 legacy he expected them to provide, Halford's Leicestershire lands must have been of considerable value. But both Halford and Rawlins evidently decided to move into towns and follow careers as attorneys.

All four of these men were well enough endowed to have lived without becoming lawyers. For others, inheritance offered less easy prospects. John Harding of Shrewsbury inherited an estate worth only £6 p.a.,[69] and Robert Benson of Leeds one worth £10 p.a.[70] Others like Richard Booth of Witton, a younger son, no doubt entered the profession with a legacy of only £100 or so.[71] Whether those who were forced to practise outnumbered those who had the choice of living off inheritances is difficult to say, but, given the large number of men about whose ancestors we know nothing, it is probable that it is easier to overestimate than to underestimate the inheritances of practitioners.

With this picture of the patrimony of members of the lower branch in mind, it becomes easier to assess the importance of legal careers and hence of fees in their economic fortunes. For men like Richard Williams of Chichester, who came to the profession with only meagre estates, fees were their basic means of support. During the Interregnum, Williams told the parliamentary committee of compounding that his only income was what 'by lawful waies he shall gaine by his profession'.[72] But even for Thomas Shapcott of Exeter, who had inherited lands worth £45 p.a., fees were an important source of income. When he compounded with the commissioners, Shapcott noted that he had had an income of £100 p.a. as Devon clerk of the peace. In addition, the commissioners alleged that his debt books as an attorney in the King's Bench showed that he was owed about £500 in fees.[73] As in the case of George Draper's accounts, some of this amount, indeed probably a large part of it, represented money Shapcott had put out for clients, but it still suggests a legal income which might compare well with the £200 p.a. which he could expect from a landed estate built up over the course of a number of years in practice.

Other kinds of evidence confirm that fees were an important source of income for attorneys. It can be shown that members of the lower branch continued in practice during most of their working lives. Moreover, although the point needs to be explored in more detail, the wealth of attorneys can be linked to the size of their practices in King's Bench and Common Pleas. For example, Ralph Bovey handled nearly ninety cases in one term in 1606. He died a very rich man in 1633, and his son eventually became a baronet and MP for Berkshire in 1660.[74] The family had connections which stretched from Warwickshire to Hertfordshire and Cambridgeshire. Bovey, a member of the Inner Temple, was predominantly a London practitioner, but for provincial attorneys, also, sucess in London business is a likely measure of their financial fortunes. John Skinner senior of Hitchin had a consistently heavy case load during his long years of practice during the first half of the seventeenth century. It was his practice which in the late 1660s promised to earn George Draper, his successor, more than £100 a year from litigation alone. So, too, in Warwickshire, the large late-sixteenth-century practice of William Booth enabled him to establish his family at Witton, and that of Henry Tadlow of Coventry to disperse £1120 in cash legacies to his heirs.[75] Because of the value of fees, it is not surprising to find that many practitioners took care to see that money owed to them from legal work was collected after their deaths. For example, Tadlow's clerk, Edmund Palmer, was given £5 for helping Tadlow's heirs to sort out the debts due to them from their father's clients.[76]

The limited evidence remaining about the income individuals received from fees, mainly their own statements about debts owing to them, reflects the variation in the sizes of practices which Table 11.2 illustrates. In his will, Thomas Ashton of Sheldon in Warwickshire calculated that he was owed £15 2s. 8d. from case work.[77] Thomas Barrington of Chester and William Milton of Devon claimed that they had £100 coming to them, a figure which perhaps represents practices of moderate size.[78] On the other hand, the £600 claimed by Christopher Potter and the £500 of Thomas Shapcott must represent large practices like that of George Draper of Hitchin, which might be worth as much as £100 p.a.[79]

IV

Thus far, we have seen that the fortunes of attorneys were affected by two sets of variables – on the one hand their patrimony and on the other the fees which they earned from practice in the courts, as manorial stewards or local officials, and from conveyancing.

Fees were a useful source of income. Some idea of the value to a practitioner of £50 p.a. earned in fees can be illustrated by the fact that land producing an equivalent annual income would have cost at least £1000 to purchase. Thus a parent could hope to give a child considerable earning power by spending at most perhaps £100 for his apprenticeship and initial expenses. Obviously, this was one of the main reasons for the popularity of legal careers. However, income from fees was simply income; unlike rents from land, fees had no capital value, and they must have provided very little in the way of collateral for loans. Purchasing land, which in the seventeenth century usually sold for twenty times the annual value, required large sums of cash. Hence income from fees, at least at the levels at which they were earned by attorneys, could not be turned quickly into large holdings of land. It is of interest that a mere handful of the attorneys in the three-county sample purchased manors.[80] The surviving evidence about the sizes of estates, the royalist composition papers and wills, suggests that most landed estates were pieced together by slow accumulation. Deeds in the Hertfordshire Record Office record small purchases in the Hitchin area by John Skinner over a period of thirty years.[81] The diarist Walter Powell of Monmouthshire, who was twenty-two years old in 1604, records his first land purchases, for sums of £87 and £50, in the early 1620s.[82] The papers of the committee for compounding give the same impression of small, slowly accumulated parcels of land. Perhaps typical was William Broadhurst of Leek in Staffordshire. He was a man who claimed a large practice with £400 in debts owing to him. His landed estate was worth £43 16s. p.a. and was composed of his wife's inheritance (£16 p.a.), a house in Leek (£2 p.a.), and two other pieces of land worth £2 and £22 respectively.[83] Another attorney, Richard Higdon of Sherbourne, Dorset, purchased a lease for ninety-nine years for one hundred acres of pasture, which was worth £100 p.a. But in order to do so he was obliged to borrow £600.[84] This debt was unusually large, but most attorneys, like members of the gentry in early Stuart England, very frequently owed sums of money in excess of £100.[85]

The best, indeed the only precise, evidence about the total size of the estates of attorneys in the early modern period is contained in the papers of the parliamentary committee for compounding. These documents, which were compiled in the late 1640s, are concerned with the property of men who were fined by parliament for their adherence to the royalist cause. They provide itemized accounts of annual income from land, list the value of moveable property, and give details of debts owing to and by the compounders. As these accounts were compiled by the delinquents themselves for the purpose of paying a penal tax, there is reason to suspect that the composition papers tend to undervalue estates, even though there were severe penalties for deliberate falsification.[86] Moreover, it cannot be claimed that the fifteen attorneys who were forced to compound constitute a random sample of practitioners, and in fact the regions most widely represented are the north, the Welsh borders, and the south-west. On the other hand, as Stone argues, the composition papers are probably a more accurate estimation of wealth than most taxation documents of the period,[87] and thus far no one has successfully shown that there is any correlation between wealth and the side any particular individual was likely to take in the war between the king and parliament. Thus it seems safe to use these estimates of the value of estates as a quantitative signpost of the wealth which attorneys of the early to mid seventeenth century were likely to be able to accumulate, one which lends some precision to the less uniform evidence of wills, pedigrees, or deeds.

The average yearly income from land of the fifteen attorneys[88] mentioned in the composition papers is £59 p.a. (mean value £46 16s.). Four were worth less than £20 p.a., six between £20 and £60, and four more could expect over £100 p.a. The poorest attorney in the group was John Harding of Shrewsbury. He had an estate consisting of a tenement divided into two dwellings worth a yearly rent of £6 total. He also claimed a personal estate of £30 in goods, chattels, and debts. Evidently he himself owed no money.[89] The richest attorney was Thomas Shapcott of Exeter, a King's Bench attorney and former clerk of the peace of Devon. Shapcott, who inherited property worth £45 p.a., reported an annual income from land of £145, £110 of which came from rents due from the tything-gard of Ashburton, which was granted to him for two lives from the dean and chapter of Exeter at a rent of £40 p.a. Shapcott valued his personal estate in pewter, brass, plate, books, and bedding at about £40.[90]

Table 11.5. *The wealth of attorneys based mainly on the evidence of wills*

	Number	Percentage of sample
0–£20 p.a.	6	11
£20–£60 p.a.	28	53
Over £60 p.a., perhaps as much as £100	19	36
Total	53	100

As far as can be judged from wills, both the range of wealth and the distribution of practitioners along it, as revealed by the composition papers, provide a reasonably accurate picture of the landed wealth of attorneys during the course of the period. Wills are not a satisfactory source from which to attempt calculations of gross income. Although they frequently give details of land holdings, and even of that property destined for first sons, valuations of parcels of land are rare, and the possibility that additional property was transferred to children by other documents always exists. Nevertheless, in spite of these problems, but with them kept firmly in mind, Table 11.5 has been compiled.

In general, the table tends to confirm the ranges of wealth of practitioners which emerged from the composition papers, but two further provisos about the use of wills have to be made before it can be interpreted accurately. First, wills which provide enough information to permit an estimate of wealth survive for only about 25 per cent of the attorneys in the three-county sample. Second, these wills which are drawn mainly from the registers of the Prerogative Court of Canterbury, are likely to be biased towards the more wealthy members of the profession. The fact that a will does not survive for an individual does not necessarily mean that he was poor, but corroborative evidence frequently suggests that this may have been the case. Both of these factors strongly suggest that, at a conservative estimate, by far the majority of the profession (perhaps two-thirds) accumulated or inherited land worth not more than £50 p.a. during the course of their lives.

V

The evidence from the composition papers and Table 11.5 are attempts to look at the wealth of attorneys across the entire period from 1560 to 1640 without taking into consideration any possible chronological changes. However, these eighty years witnessed a number of important economic developments which greatly affected the fortunes of attorneys. Between 1560 and 1640, the prices of agricultural products nearly doubled. About 75 per cent of the increase occurred during the second half of the sixteenth century, and was a manifestation of the 'price revolution'[91] in England which began, largely as a result of population growth, around 1500. Yet over the entire period, the attorney's fee remained at its medieval rate of 3s. 4d. per case per term. Sayles has noted that, in the thirteenth or fourteenth century, this fee constituted a considerable source of income for practitioners,[92] but even by 1550 its effective buying power would have been cut by two-thirds, and as the inflation proceeded its value continued to decline.[93] To some extent the devaluation of this fee could have been, and no doubt was, offset by increases in fees for services such as conveyancing and by the expropriation by attorneys of clerical work formerly undertaken by the officers of the court. But, as we saw in Chapter 7, increases in legal fees failed in general to keep pace with inflation. Thus it is quite probable that total earnings per case declined in real terms between the accession of Elizabeth and the outbreak of the civil war.

Of course, there was at the same time a vast increase in the amount of litigation, but from the point of view of individual earning power this must be considered in conjunction with the growth in the size of the profession. Table 11.1 clearly demonstrates that the average case loads of Common Pleas attorneys steadily declined between 1560 and 1640. In 1606 the average practitioner handled perhaps only two-thirds as many cases as his counterpart in 1580, and case loads drop even further, if less dramatically, during the first half of the seventeenth century.

Table 11.1 is the product of abstract calculations. As we shall see, individual examples lend some colour and variation to the bland picture presented there. But the main point is that, for the profession as a whole, evidence about the individuals in the three-county sample tends to confirm that the double effect of inflation and the decline in the number of cases handled by each man made practice as an attorney more lucrative before 1600 than it was after that date.

The plea rolls of King's Bench and Common Pleas suggest that in 1560 twelve attorneys of the central courts were active in the three counties in our sample, seven in Devon, three in Hertfordshire, and two in Warwickshire. Five of the Devon men, Hore, Copleston, Calmady, Luscombe, and Prideaux, were from well-established families who, at one time or another, registered pedigrees with the heralds. The attorneys in Hertfordshire and Warwickshire were descended from the yeomanry and lesser gentry of their counties; all of their families had been in the area for at least one generation. One of the Devonians, Robert Prideaux of Ashburton (his ancestral home), lived in a town, Thomas Hore of Chudleigh kept rooms in Exeter, and several others had rooms in London, but in general these attorneys lived in the country (the Devonians lived in the arable band running along the south coast), accumulated considerable blocks of land there, and took what was apparently a considerable interest in farming. For eleven of the twelve attorneys, some kind of evidence survives about their estates, and it suggests without doubt that every one of them was a man of considerable landed wealth, the majority being worth well over £60 p.a. at the least. Two, Thomas Hanchett of Uphall in Hertfordshire and Anthony Copleston of Axminster in Devon, used the style 'esquire'. An assessment of 1593 suggests that Hanchett's son was one of the richest men in Hertfordshire.[94] He was probably an exception amongst the attorneys; most of the others had landed wealth which corresponded to that of the lower or middle ranks of the landed gentry. For example, the inventory of Thomas Hawes of Solihull (d. 1574), which values his goods at £123 12s. 8d.,[94] implies that he was considerably richer than the largest of the peasant farmers in the forest of Arden who have been studied by Skipp.[96] Nearly half of Hawes' personal estate, £60, consisted of livestock, and he gave a ewe sheep to each of his grandchildren. This suggests that for Hawes, as for Thomas Hore of Chudleigh, whose will also mentions sheep,[97] and for Thomas Gregory of Coventry (active in the 1540s and 1550s), farming was an important activity.[98] But the attorneys active in the 1560s were also quite clearly professional lawyers as well. For example, two of the Hertfordshire attorneys, Hanchett and Bricket, kept chambers in London.[99]

The careers of the Devon practitioners in particular, and those of the other early Elizabethan practitioners in general, seem to follow a pattern similar to that of John Furse of Moreshead in Devon (d. 1549), whose life was chronicled by his greatgrandchild, Robert Furse (d. 1593).[100] John Furse, who came from an old Devon family of modest means, attended an inn of court, was sworn an attorney, and by holding various local offices such as the undersheriffship of Devon and various manorial stewardships, added considerably to the family fortunes. At the time of his first marriage, Furse had little, but when his first wife died, he could count four hundred bullocks and 'grette store of money'.[101] By virtue of his education and profession, Furse was reckoned as learned and wise, and, according to his biographer, he 'kept a bountefull howse. No many yn the cunterye of his abyllytye did the lyke but spissyally at Crysemas for then he hade his lords of mysserule [and] hys mynstereles.'[102] In provincial counties such as Devon and Warwickshire, before the 'matriculation revolution' at the universities and the inns of court made the English gentry more highly educated (at least on paper) than at any time before or again until the early twentieth century, the learning of the attorneys, which later came under such savage attack,[103] evidently made them men of note in the parish if not necessarily in a county context. They owned books, and their association with the inns of court and chancery (where, incidentally, John Furse could have learned to keep Christmas revels) put them into contact with the latest social conventions. These men were not great lords, nor were they even among the upper ranks of the gentry. But in the microcosm of parochial society, they could evidently display convincingly many of the attributes of the Renaissance gentleman.

What is certain is that these attorneys were able to live in comfort and to pass on enough landed wealth to ensure a place in the gentry for their sons. Thomas Hawes lived in a hall house with eight rooms and a number of outbuildings.[104] He and John Kettel of King's Langley had a large number of those sixteenth-century luxuries, feather beds, as well as joined furniture and wall hangings.[105] Thomas Hawes' son, William, built a large new house in Solihull called Hillfield Hall, and his son purchased the manor of Solihull in the early seventeenth century. Thomas Hanchett's son was chosen for the Hertfordshire commission of the peace, at this date a fairly reliable, if not absolute, sign of social recognition. The careers of the sons and daughters of other attorneys active early in the reign of Elizabeth are more obscure. The pedigrees of Calmady, Luscombe, Prideaux, and Copleston suggest that their heirs probably lived on the estate accumulated by their fathers.[106] Most of their children married locally. The careers of younger sons are also largely unknown, except for those of Ralph Kettell, second son of John of King's Langley, who went to Oxford and became president of Trinity College,[107] and Thomas Prideaux, who, like his father, Robert of Ashburton, became an attorney.[108]

If we move outside the sample of men from Devon, Hertfordshire, and Warwickshire to a more general consideration of the practitioners active in 1560, this picture remains much the same. Thomas Green of Knapton in Norfolk is known to have had lands worth £163 p.a.[109] His Norfolk colleagues Thomas Barsham and Thomas Payne were probably less wealthy, but they owned numerous small parcels of land and had agricultural interests.[110] Christopher Crow of Bilney left legacies worth £600. William Bygott of Starston owned a manor.[111] Moving north, Robert Fletcher of Chesterfield left his corn, sheep, and agricultural implements to his son and charged him to be 'good and loving to my tenantes'.[112] John Stokes of the city of Gloucester owned a farm called the White Barn and a number of leases of land. His legacies included sheep, oxen, and horses as well as the law books which he kept in his chambers in London.[113]

So the most striking thing about the attorneys of the 1560s is that a very large proportion of them were highly successful. By the 1580s there are signs that this was no longer always the case. The size of the profession had by then grown significantly, and this growth was evidently not accompanied by equally great worldly success for all practitioners. With the possible exception of Marc Cottel of North Tawton in Devonshire, none of the attorneys in the three-county sample who were active in 1580 were able to acquire the kind of wealth which has been described for those of 1560. Thomas Jackson of Solihull and his sons were figures of considerably less note than Jackson's father-in-law, Thomas Hawes, had been.[114] Two Coventry attorneys, Richard Denton and Thomas Tyllesley,[115] were men of very moderate means, almost certainly worth less than £20 p.a. apart from fees. Even a man like William Booth of Witton (d. 1610), who had a flourishing practice, had to be satisfied with leaving his four younger sons only 100 marks each after they had finished their apprenticeships. He gave each of his three daughters £100, and left his son and heir, William, a considerable but unknown estate in land, but he also clearly anticipated that William would have to earn money, since he educated him to become a barrister.[116] The Booths were a successful family, but it can hardly be said that they established themselves firmly in the landed gentry within one generation. William Booth the younger eventually bought the manor of Witton, but his son, another William, also became a barrister,[117] though it is unclear whether this was the result of financial need or what might have by then become a family tradition.

It is tempting, even on the basis of this meagre evidence, to see the late sixteenth century as a time of relative economic hardship for the lower branch of the legal profession. In addition to the general factors such as inflation and greater competition for clients, the depression of the 1590s might have further weakened their prospects.

However, it is only with the start of the seventeenth century that changes in the fortunes of the profession become clear. By this time, probably as a result of overcrowding, many men failed to amass a significant estate. It is for this period after 1600 that the evidence of the composition papers and the figures in Table 11.5 about the distribution of wealth in the profession are most helpful. As we have seen, these show that for the attorneys about whom something is known, the possible range of individual wealth varied widely indeed. Moreover, virtually nothing is known about the fortunes of another 60 per cent of the profession, and we have concluded that most of these men must be relegated to that group who were worth less than £50 p.a., perhaps worth less than £20 p.a. Some practitioners were very successful, but a great many more were not.

Another great change in the fortunes of attorneys after 1600 is that there was a notable shift of their interests towards the accumulation of urban property. As Chapter 9 demonstrates, in the sixteenth century most attorneys lived in the country, but in the seventeenth century almost two-thirds of those in the three-county sample whose place of habitation is known resided in towns. Perhaps surprisingly, purchases of land appear to have followed residential choices. If an attorney lived and worked in a town, he was likely to build his estate there. Urban attorneys were not the archetypal townsmen who spent their money on rural real estate. Instead, they were for the most part men from the country who moved into towns and bought land there.

Evidence of the economic interests of attorneys in the towns where they lived is abundant, and this interest seems usually to have manifested itself in land rather than in industry or trade. It is probable that poorer attorneys were more likely to live in towns than any other members of the profession, and their interest in urban property was usually quite straightforward. They owned a house in the town where they lived and little else. Thus William Foster owned a small and sparsely furnished house in Warwick.[118] The total value of the landed estate of John Harding was a house in Shrewsbury, and William Martin of York evidently owned no land at all.[119]

Urban attorneys of middling wealth, men like John Yardly and Edward Rainsford of Warwick, for example, were likely to have more than one piece of town property and in some cases some land in the countryside as well. Yardly owned his house in Churchgate Street, Warwick, along with at least two other parcels of land in the town.[120] Rainsford, who lived in a house owned by another Warwick attorney, James Prescott, considered urban property to be an excellent investment. In his will Rainsford mentions that he plans to leave his eldest son Nunnery Close and Fluries Meadow in Warwick, property (rent, £9 p.a.) which he thought could be sold at the unusually high rate of twenty-six years' purchase, because 'Closes of that Convenientecy so neare to the town [can] hardlie... be obteyned for any reasonable or ordinarie sum*m*ee of money....'[121] On the other hand, John Rosyer junior of Barnstaple, a second-generation attorney, owned considerable property in Chillehamholt, which was about ten miles from the town, as well as his house in Corkstreet, Barnstaple, which was known as the Ship Tavern.[122]

Richer men had more complicated landed interests. This was particularly true of the King's Bench attorneys, many of whom had, as we have already seen, interests in London. As far as is known, none of the Common Pleas attorneys in the three-county sample owned London houses, but the most prosperous of the town dwellers combined considerable interests in both urban and rural property. For example, James Prescott of Warwick mentions seven parcels of town land in his will not including his own dwelling house in Jury Street.[123] But he also had important country holdings including six yardlands (about 180 acres) in Solihull and land in Pillerton (about ten miles from Warwick) worth at least £40 p.a. Similarly, John Skinner of Hitchin owned houses in Hitchin, Luton, Stevenage, and villages in north Hertfordshire which were occupied by at least forty different people. But he too had other, rural, lands including the manor of Westbury.[124]

Those attorneys who did not live in towns do not appear to have invested heavily in town lands, but apart from this there were no great differences in the wealth of town-dwelling as opposed to country attorneys. The most prosperous members of the profession – Prescott of Warwick, Skinner of Hitchin, Willymott of Kelshall, Shapcott of

Exeter – include representatives of both groups. In general, however, the more prosperous country attorneys tended to be men who inherited large parcels of land there – for example, Knight of Barrells or Cottel of North Tawton – and since men with lesser inheritances like Edmund Rawlins of Stratford moved into towns, we might conclude that these landowners were less completely dependent on practice than the townsmen. Otherwise distinctions about the wealth of the two groups are difficult to make. And beyond this, generalities about the economic fortunes of attorneys in the period after 1600 have to be generously laced with caveats. Perhaps two-thirds or more of the profession lived in towns and the majority of these probably made their main investments there, but another third continued to live in the country. A number of practitioners obviously made a lot of money, accumulating estates worth at least £100 p.a.; on the other hand, a larger number failed to amass more than one-fifth as much as this.

For the more successful of the early-seventeenth-century country attorneys, there can be no doubt but that their profession brought them both prosperity and a comfortable life-style. They were able to accumulate land; they employed servants; many of them lived in hall houses with well-furnished parlours and comfortable bedchambers. Some decorated their rooms with wainscotting which kept out damp and draughts; others had painted wall hangings. Silver spoons and serving dishes feature regularly in wills, and one man, Henry Tadlow of Coventry, even had a set of Venetian glasses. Many were able to enjoy joined furniture such as the walnut desk which John Yardly kept in his office in Warwick.[125] Amongst the very richest, such as Lewes Atterbury of Haughton in Northamptonshire, Henry Skarburgh of Norfolk, and Alexander Rolle of Tavistock in Devon, daughters might be endowed with £400 or more as a marriage portion.[126] Even the much less successful practitioners were hardly destitute. They could provide legacies worth a few pounds for their relations, and, perhaps, a marriage portion of £40.[127]

Nevertheless, one of the most important features of the economic life of the attorneys in the early seventeenth century was that some men were noticeably more successful than others. Apart from luck, the most obvious sources of these differences were differences in skill, differences in patrimony, and different degrees of success in obtaining either patrons or offices. Of all of these, it is most difficult to assess the importance of an attorney's professional ability in his worldly success. Contemporaries certainly recognized that some attorneys were more skilful than others. References to the ability of one man or the incompetence of another are fairly common,[128] but it is impossible to connect these comments with the particular fortunes of individuals. On the other hand, it is clear that some men who lacked all of the other ingredients of success did well, and the reason why may have been that they were more skilful.

As this chapter should already have demonstrated, patrimony was an obvious advantage to those who were lucky enough to enjoy it, if only because it made them less dependent on legal fees. But some successful men, Skinner of Hitchin, Prescott, Booth senior, and Tadlow of Warwickshire, for example, had extremely lucrative careers even though they did not inherit land. In the seventeenth century, moreover, when a fairly large number of attorneys' sons began to follow their fathers into the profession, the inheritance of a well-developed practice was certainly as important a factor in developing the family fortunes as any inheritence of land for which evidence survives.

Office was perhaps a more obvious boon to the local practitioner. In some cases such as that of the Somerset attorney Robert Chute, a minor office such as a deputy clerkship of the peace could be valuable simply because it made him known in his county and enhanced his reputation.[129] In others, office could provide the road to great riches. For example, according to the papers of the committee for compounding, Robert Benson of Leeds was worth only £40 p.a. in the 1640s but from 1662 to 1673 he was the clerk of assize for the Northern Circuit, and died worth £1500 p.a. His son went on to become an MP and chancellor of the excequer, and he was made a peer in 1713.[130] Similarly, one of the important elements in the fortunes of the Rigby family during the seventeenth century was the clerkship of the peace of Lancashire, which was reckoned to be worth £200 in the 1660s.[131] Clerkships of the peace and town clerkships were frequently in the hands of powerful local magnates, and clerkships of the peace appear to have been offices which had to be bought.[132] Many practitioners of modest means held town clerkships, but clerkships of the peace may well have been available only to those attorneys who could afford to buy them and who had the patronage of the *custos rotulorum*.

There is no doubt about the value of the major local offices, but their importance for the prosperity of individuals can be overstressed.

Thomas Hunt held the Warwickshire clerkship of the peace for several years during the early seventeenth century without becoming a man of notable wealth,[133] and certainly the majority of the most successful practitioners in the three-county sample are not known to have held local offices of the first rank or, indeed, even town clerkships. However, lesser offices, particularly manorial steward-ships, do seem to have been positions shared by most of the successful practitioners. In both Warwickshire and Hertfordshire, leading attorneys – Prescott, Eades, Willymott, Rowley – all had steward-ships from leading county families.[134] Stewardships put practitioners into contact with potential clients among the copyholders and freeholders of manors, and also gave them access to both the legal business and patronage of important families within the local com-munity. Unfortunately, the means by which attorneys came to acquire stewardships are not very clear. In some cases, it is probable that family connections were a major factor. For example, William Knight of Barrells was a close neighbour of the Throckmortons, whose manors he presided over. But in other cases, such as those of James Prescott and Francis Eades, who were both town attorneys and men without local roots, reputation might have been the most important factor in bringing them to the attention of their employers.

If, for whatever reasons, the fortunes of attorneys varied more greatly after 1600 than they had done in the early or mid sixteenth century, we would expect that those of their sons did so as well. Once again, evidence is completely lacking for the families of the majority of practitioners, who presumably found themselves among the less wealthy. We can only speculate about what course the lives of their sons might take, but it seems unlikely that they entered the gentry. An apprenticeship in some kind of trade was probably the most lucrative path which even the eldest sons of lesser practitioners could hope to follow.

More is known about the careers of the sons of better-off attorneys, and these provide some patterns as well as some reflections on the poorer men. In a few cases, mostly in those in which attorneys themselves had inherited significant amounts of land – Hide of Great Hadham and Bull of Kingshurst Hall in Warwickshire, for example – it is probable that the eldest sons of the practitioners inherited enough property to allow them to live the lives of country gentlemen. However, what is most striking about even the the most successful of the attorneys in the post-1600 sample is that there is little evidence that this was very often true of the majority. A notable group of attorneys, both urban and rural, were followed into practice by their sons, who either went to the bar or simply continued in their fathers' footsteps as local attorneys (eight sons followed their fathers into the profession). Amongst the latter was John Knight, the son of William Knight, who owned considerable land in west Warwickshire, and among the less wealthy practitioners John Rosyer junior, son of John Rosyer of Barnstaple. Few of the sons of attorneys in our sample went to the inns of court, but the noticeable exceptions were the heirs of successful practitioners;[135] for example, James, son of James Prescott of Warwick, and Thomas, son of Edmund Rawlins of Stratford, who left a considerable estate. Similarly, the admissions registers of the universities show that few attorneys sent their sons to them, but here too the few exceptions occur amongst those practitioners who can be placed in the middle or upper categories of wealth. Nathanial Halford, a younger son of John Halford of Warwick, took his BA at Oxford in 1677, though it is unknown whether or not he became a priest. William Dowdeswell, the son of Roger Dowdeswell, a prosperous Gloucestershire attorney, took a BCL from Pembroke College, Oxford in 1631 and went on to become vicar of Turley and eventually a canon of Worcester.[136]

There is a good deal of circumstantial evidence that many attorneys may have considered apprenticeships in trades, preferably in London, as the best means of establishing their sons with a steady income. For example, Henry Tadlow of Coventry willed that all of his sons be put out as apprentices,[137] and the grandson and heir of another prosperous Warwickshire attorney, Richard Booth of Bishop's Tachebroke, was about to finish his apprenticeship when his grandfather died.[138] Not surprisingly, it is clear that the younger sons of attorneys were likely to have to work for their livings. The example of one family, that of Josias Bull of Kingshurst, who died in 1671, can serve to illustrate the possibilities open to the younger sons of a successful Midlands attorney in the third quarter of the seventeenth century. Three of his eight younger sons were in trades in London (an ironmonger, a packer, a milliner), and two others were in the overseas trade (one in the East and one in the West Indies). The other son, about whom something is known, was a schoolmaster at the local school in Coleshill.[139] Bull's sons were probably lucky. Apprenticeships in London led to the possibility of very good incomes, but they were relatively expensive to obtain.[140] A number of other attorneys procured similar advantages for their sons, but these were members of the élite of the lower branch rather than the majority who have left little trace either at the universities, at the inns of court, or in their own communities. For their sons, a bright prospect would have been the chance to take up an apprenticeship in a local town or perhaps careers as modest farmers. If their profession entitled attorneys to use the style 'gentleman', it appears that in only a minority of cases did the estate they accumulated enable their sons to continue to enjoy the status so earned. Most attorneys sprang from the middling ranks of English society, the yeomanry, the lesser gentry, and the urban tradesmen, and the majority of them remained within that same broad, prosperous, but too often ignored, social grouping.

12

CONCLUSION

In concluding this study of the lower branch of the legal profession, two related problems need to be addressed. First, the place of the early modern practitioners within the wider context of the history of the professions in general must be established. Second, the various pieces presented in earlier chapters must be brought together into a more concise picture of the role of these lawyers in late-sixteenth- and early-seventeenth-century society.

Amongst social theorists and modern historians, it is a common-place that, since the Industrial Revolution, the professions have come to occupy a uniquely important place in the social and political life of modern capitalist society. Some have gone so far as to welcome this development as heralding new occupational structures and new class interests. Others are more doubtful about the benefits of the process of 'professionalization'. But few would question that the emphasis on specialized training, self-regulation, and sense of voc-ation which are characteristic of professional men have greatly influenced modern attitudes towards work and social structure. As Talcott Parsons has put it, the importance of the professions in the twentieth century is unique in history.[1]

In the most general sense, this comment is no doubt true enough. The decline of the landed interest and of traditional vocational structures associated with craft guilds, coupled with the emergence of groups such as engineers and scientists who are associated with modern technology, has indeed given professionals an important role. However, from the point of view of the historian, this twentieth-century familiarity with professions has had the effect of severely distorting our perspectives on their development. Since it is taken for granted that professions are a modern phenomenon, their history before the development of industrial capitalism tends to be ignored, or, insofar as they have been considered, early modern professions such as those of doctor and lawyer are assumed to have been small and closely tied to the most important status groups of the 'pre-industrial' world, the aristocracy and gentry.[2]

It is, of course, at precisely this point that some of the more elementary observations to be drawn from this study become relevant. There were important differences between the lower branch of the early seventeenth century and the lower branch of nineteenth-century industrial England, and some of these will be considered shortly. But, by any set of commonsense criteria, including most of those established by sociologists, the early modern practitioners constituted a profession. They were a distinct occupational group with a specialized training and skill, and the vast majority of practitioners devoted their entire working lives to the job. They provided a service in return for fees which were given on a case-by-case basis. The oath of attorney and the orders of the judges set rules for practice. The courts and the inns of chancery were sources of a group identity which turned into a sense of vocation that was frequently recorded in wills and funeral epigraphs. More important, by the mid seventeenth century this profession was large, very highly centralized (London-oriented), and by no means exclusively dependent on the aristocracy and gentry for its clientele. In 1640, the number of common law attorneys alone was sufficiently numerous for there to be one for every 2500 of the population at large. It is true that further growth over the next ninety years reduced this ratio to one in 1500 by the 1720s, but the supreme importance of the period from 1560 to 1640 with respect to numbers is amply illustrated by the fact that the ratio of central court practitioners (that is, excluding purely provincial lawyers) to population at the accession of Queen Elizabeth was one in 20,000, whilst in 1913 it was one in 2100.[3] In order of magnitude, the eighty years before the civil war witnessed a change in the relationship between the lower branch and English society far greater than anything which would come afterwards.[4] Furthermore, we know from the studies of the social status of litigants that about 70 per cent of those who used the services of these lawyers were yeomen, husbandmen, artisans, and merchants, and it is by no means certain that clients of the later Stuart, Georgian, or Victorian eras were of any more diverse social origins. In other words, it would seem that an agricultural and 'pre-industrial' society such as that of Elizabethan and early Stuart England was just as capable as industrial and advanced capitalist societies of supporting a large legal profession which offered a wide range of services to large numbers of people.

The significance of the sixteenth- and early-seventeenth-century growth and consolidation of the lower branch was twofold. On the one hand, the decline of the purely provincial practitioners and their replacement by a large number of lawyers connected with the central courts witnessed the crystallization of a national profession which reached out into every corner of the land. In addition, the rise of a large and centralized profession came about largely in conjunction with a dramatic centralization in many other aspects of the legal life of the realm. Thus the early modern profession was closely involved with an important stage in the development of a society which was deeply imbued with the importance of the idea of the rule of law. In turn, this reverence for law was a characteristic of English culture which would insure a special place for the legal profession in subsequent generations. If we combine these developments with other less important ones such as the emergence of stricter divisions between the upper and lower branches, then, even allowing for our ignorance of developments before 1500, the period from 1550 to 1640 clearly marked a major watershed in the history of the legal profession.[5]

However, at the same time as we can discuss the continuities between the lower branch of the early modern period and that of later eras, it is also instructive to highlight the differences between them. For instance, by contrast with the increase in numbers, the centralization of the Tudor and early Stuart professions on the central courts in London appears to have been both unique and relatively short-lived. By the mid eighteenth century, the lower branch had become decentralized, much more oriented towards the provinces than towards London.[6] In the absence of detailed research, the exact chronology of the break-up of the London-based profession and the reasons for its decline are difficult to chart precisely, but, as we have seen in connection with the inns of chancery, the tensions between London work and country work were already apparent in the early seventeenth century. By the late seventeenth and early eighteenth centuries, these evidently became more severe. Local, non-litigious practice – estate work, conveyancing, and so forth – apparently grew to such proportions that it surpassed the profits which could be gained by taking cases to London. The comparative advantages of membership in the offices of the central courts thereby declined, and local practitioners adopted the system of using London attorneys as agents in central court litigation.[7] A consequence of these changes was that voluntary and independent regional law societies became the principal instruments through which the profession was organized.

The Society of Gentlemen Practitioners in London was founded in the 1720s and the first of the provincial law societies, that of Bristol, in 1770.[8] However, these regional societies never included all members of the profession. Only in the nineteenth century, after the provincial societies had amalgamated, and the resulting Law Society had negotiated with government for control over the entire lower branch, was the profession again subject to as much centralized supervision as it had been in the time of Elizabeth and the early Stuarts.[9]

Since the late nineteenth century, responsibility for the training, admission, and regulation of practitioners within the lower branch has been delegated by act of parliament to the Law Society (the professional organization of the solicitors), and in general these qualities of control over admission and self-regulation of practice are considered the hall-marks of a modern profession.[10] To a very limited extent, some of these characteristics also existed in the early modern period. The prothonotaries, who were supposed to examine the qualifications of new attorneys, were members of the legal profession. Juries of attorneys from time to time investigated incidents of malpractice. And in the 1650s, it seems to have been recognized that the best way to maintain standards and control the numbers of practitioners would be to put the power of regulating admission into the hands of established members of the profession who were sensitive to the problems caused by excessive numbers.[11]

Nevertheless, the fact remains that no major shift of power towards the profession at large occurred during the seventeenth century. The crown continued to delegate its ultimate responsibility for controlling the lower branch through a hierarchy of officials – the lord chancellor, the judges, and the clerical officials – and at the same time it was acutely aware that the council or king in parliament could and should intervene in professional affairs. Indeed, by comparison many other early modern occupational groups were much more free to regulate their own affairs than either the attorneys or even the barristers before the end of the reign of Elizabeth. The scriveners, the apothecaries, the barber surgeons, and any other livery company of London exercised more autonomy of control over entry into practice than the lawyers; that is, they examined qualifications and kept registers of practitioners. The only other occupations subject to quite so much 'state' control as the lawyers were two other classical professions – the clergy and the schoolmasters (both licensed by bishops).[12]

The 'system' of control which was maintained over the lower

branch did contain a number of inherent problems, and many historians have mentioned some of these – lack of formal qualifying examinations, insufficient control over numbers – in the course of depicting the profession as largely undisciplined and anarchic. However, this interpretation, which is heavily influenced by the socially biased comments of contemporaries, ignores the degree of centralization which existed in the early-seventeenth-century profession, and the study of the careers of practitioners in their local environments would seem to make it debatable whether a system of regulation through the courts with provision for the punishment of malpractice in a tribunal such as Star Chamber was in fact any less capable of producing a responsible profession than one based on a professional organization which puts such matters into the hands of the practitioners themselves. Moreover, even some of the failures of early modern regulation such as the inability to limit effectively the number of practitioners may not have been all that disadvantageous to society at large, since they apparently made it relatively easy for large numbers of men to have access to legal advice and the courts. But the more important point is that whatever view one takes of the effectiveness of early modern regulation, the state took responsibility for administering it. Thus one of the most important questions about the evolution of the legal profession up to the twentieth century is not how did lawyers come to have regulation imposed on them, but, rather, how was it that by the end of the nineteenth century so much autonomy had been achieved?

In the case of the barristers, an important episode in this story occurred under the Tudors and Stuarts. During the middle ages, the apprentices and serjeants, although never so strictly controlled as the attorneys, were subject to a similar regime of regulation by royal ordinance, judicial authority, and statute.[13] This did not change significantly until the 1590s, when for the first time the call to the rank of utter barrister at an inn of court came to be recognized as the only qualification for practice in the courts at Westminster.[14] This was the result of decisions taken in the privy council and by the judges, and the inns of court continued to be nominally under the supervision of the bench; but the change marked a shift of direct control over the bar from the judges to the benchers, the oligarchic group of practitioners who ran the inns of court. From this date, therefore, the barristers can be said to have gained considerable powers of supervision over their own professional affairs.

This increased autonomy of the upper branch was partly a

response to the growth in the number of barristers which was occasioned by the increase in litigation after 1550 and partly a consequence of institutional changes which led to a decline in the serjeants' monopoly over pleading.[15] But more important than either of these developments were changes in Tudor educational ideals and in the self-image of the profession. During the course of the sixteenth century, the inns of court became associated even more closely with the education of the aristocracy and gentry than they had been before, the law became an important element in the composition of the new ideal of the lay magistrate, and the lawyers themselves developed a new image modelled on the *prudentes* of classical Rome which fitted in well with both.[16] Unlike the attorneys, the barristers claimed that they practised a liberal and scientific profession, one fit, unlike the mechanical work of the attorneys, for men who were the rulers rather than the ruled. Thus the reason why more effective controls over the upper branch were never instituted is that the idea of the *prudentes*, and the association of barristers with academies which had become nurseries of the aristocracy and gentry, made it appear largely unnecessary. As late as the 1930s, this notion left the barristers one of the most inadequately trained and regulated occupations in England.[17] Nevertheless, many parts of this Renaissance ideal of a profession – payment by honoraria, autonomy, and liberal learning – are the essence of what professionalism is supposed to mean today.

The image of the lower branch did not improve as a result of these changes in the status of the upper; it got worse. As the liberal and magisterial qualities of the barristers were emphasized, so in theory at least the mean and mechanical nature of the occupation of attorney or solicitor was thrown into bold relief. At the same time, although members of the lower branch shared the barristers' pride in their vocation as lawyers, in the early modern period being a lawyer without any other attribute of status was not necessarily a mark of distinction. As we saw in Chapter 6, many contemporaries were suspicious of the social consequences of the increase in litigation and of the lawyers who helped to make it possible. Attorneys and solicitors were seen as primary causes of the worst characteristics of this new phenomenon and so there was pressure for more rather than less control over their activities. Self-regulation for the lower branch came in the nineteenth century only after strenuous efforts to improve the public image of the profession.[18]

In connection with this last point, it is also worth observing that one other major difference between the profession of the nineteenth and twentieth centuries and that of the early modern period was that, in the reigns of Elizabeth and the early Stuarts, practitioners were neither particularly distinctive nor could they claim much social cachet simply because they were 'professional men'. The attorneys and clerical officials had a number of 'professional' characteristics, but one of the most significant things about these traits was that they were not unique to doctors, lawyers, or clergymen. Just as other trades which were organized into guilds had institutions which supervised training and regulated admissions, so, too, many of them had a sense of group identity, standards of practice, ceremonies, and rituals which were very much like those of the lawyers.[19]

Nor, as far as we can tell, did professionals display any particularly characteristic ways of looking at their prospects or their place in the world. For example, the notion of a career, which is commonly associated with modern professions, had no exact analogue in the early modern period; the word was then associated mainly with horse racing.[20] The idea that men went into the law in order to make money or become gentlemen was a sixteenth- and seventeenth-century cliché. But it is also important to keep in mind that attorneys and clerks, like men in many other occupations, were put into training for their profession at an early age. Boys 'bredd' or 'trained up' in their profession through apprenticeship in fact had little choice about their 'course of life'. The avowed reasons for becoming a lawyer rarely express ambition for riches or earthly glory, and attitudes towards work seem generally to coincide with those of clerical writers like William Perkins, who stressed the importance of service and commitment to one's calling.[21] For instance, Richard Booth of Bishop's Tachbrooke in Warwickshire hoped that his children would be trained for 'some fitting and expedient Trade and ymployments which they may by God's blessing make the better provision of livelyhood for themselves hereafter'. Christopher Crow of Norfolk asked that his children 'be instructed and trayned up in suche services and Trades and course of life as Theye may hereafter live in this commonwealth as the servants of God and dutifull subiec*tes* of the prince'.[22] Indeed, despite the bad image of the profession which usually emerges from contemporary literature, it is hard to read the wills of practitioners and not come away with the impression that they cared for their families, rarely failed to leave at least something for the poor, and sometimes expressed more than mere conventional piety. Many attorneys thanked God for the worldly estate he had seen fit to lend or bestow upon them.[23] Although it is impossible to give any meaningful percentages, some clearly held very strong religious beliefs of the kind which can be labelled 'puritan'. Francis Hardpenny valued his books of divinity. John Rattenbury owned a Bible, a book of resolution, and 'the perfect pattern of man's imperfection'. Thomas Ashton asked for a funeral sermon which would ignore his worldly achievements and concentrate on the 'sureness of death'. Peter Blackaller of Colyton hoped that God,

> as he hath hetherunto most favourably in mercy delt w[i]th me so it would please him to give me grace through his holy Spirit to leade my life while I remayne in this miserable world accordinge to his holy precept*es*... and that after this life I may be a partaker of his heavenly kingdom, of those unspeakable ioyes w[hi]ch he hath prepared for his elect children....[24]

These views, including the range of religious commitment, were quite conventional in the early seventeenth century. It is difficult to detect much of a difference between them and similar ideals which were laid down for and sometimes followed by men in other occupations and by members of the landed gentry. Most writers on work seemed to agree that some kind of worthwhile activity or service to the commonwealth was required of every member of society from the lowest born to the wealthiest peer. Not even the landed gentry of this period saw itself simply as a leisured class, and, of course, 'puritans' existed at all social levels.[25]

No doubt because there were so many similarities in institutions and attitudes between occupations such as that of draper or apothecary and the classical professions, the very meaning of the word 'profession' was a good deal more general in the early modern period than it was later to become. In the nineteenth century, a profession could be defined as the kind of work which dealt primarily with 'men as men' as distinguished from trades which provided for the 'external wants of men'. In the twentieth century, professions are typified by the forms of occupational organization and other characteristics which are usually associated with doctors and lawyers, and the word 'professional' also implies a claim to special social status.

In the late sixteenth and early seventeenth centuries, distinctions between professions and other occupations do not seem to have been drawn in this way. A profession in the broadest sense was thought of simply as the way a man earned his living. Most writers on the subject appear to have assumed that, except in the case of wage labourers, most occupations contained the main prerequisites of professional status, special kinds of skills. In his *Treatise on Vocations*, William Perkins referred to the profession of a shepherd.[26] In a discussion of the application of the law of slander, the Elizabethan judge Sir Henry Hobart held that every public profession required two things, 'science and fidelity, and when a man who hath a public profession is scandalized in either of those an action' for slander lies.[27] Hobart was ruling on a case which involved an attorney, but actions for slander based on the same criteria were allowed for carriers, tradesmen, and merchants as well as for justices of the peace, barristers, and bishops. Another commentator on the same subject, William Sheppard, found it easy to associate practice as an attorney with a trade.[28] Professions, trades, vocations were more or less interchangeable terms, and all implied little more than a way a man earned his living. The sixteenth century did see a growing, and perhaps novel, distinction between mechanical and academic learnings. For example, Perkins wrote that the callings of lawyer, schoolmaster, physician, and minister, all of which required academic learning, occupied the first place among vocations.[29] But this was a ranking of callings and certainly not an attempt to define the 'professions'. According to such a view, attorneyship might or might not have been amongst the most noble vocations, but it was certainly a profession.

However, the distinction between academic and mechanical learning did have one other consequence which was of considerable importance. Clergymen, doctors, barristers (who used the style 'esquire'), and attorneys were allowed to use the styles of gentility. For example, in most contemporary documents, including wills, attorneys are styled, not according to their vocation, but as gentlemen ('gent.').

The technical reason for the association of these callings with gentility lies in the nature of their work, in the way men who entered them were educated, and in the notion of service. The history of gentility as opposed to the history of the landed gentry has never been written, but it is clear that as the concept of gentility began to take shape in the late fifteenth and early sixteenth centuries[30] it combined a revulsion against manual labour with an advocacy of the importance of education as a means of serving the commonwealth. In many respects the 'liberal' professions, especially lawyers, epitomized this ideal. They worked with their heads, not with their hands; they were trained at academies which catered for the aristocracy and gentry; they served the state.[31] As we saw in Chapter 8, the 'mechanical education' of attorneys posed a threat to their claim to gentility, but the threat was not fatal. Their status as officers in the king's courts and their association with the 'third university' through the inns of chancery evidently continued to justify the use by them of the style 'gent.'. Even as late as the 1620s, every man admitted to Barnard's Inn, whether or not he was a lawyer, was automatically styled as a gentleman without any reference being made to his social origins.[32]

The use of the styles of gentility by attorneys and by similar social groups has always led historians to classify them as members of the gentry and to conclude that a legal practice was a reasonably secure means of achieving upward social mobility. In fact, however, no serious attempt has ever been made to see how far the wealth and life-styles of such men justify these assumptions.

Chapter 11 provides some raw materials which can be used to answer this question with respect to practitioners in the lower branch. There we saw that common law attorneys active in the reign of Elizabeth maintained an active interest in agriculture and were able to accumulate, and pass on to their heirs, estates which can with some certainty be said to have gained them a modest place in the landed gentry. But, after 1600, prospects within the profession became much more variable. Clerical officials such as the prothonotaries of Common Pleas continued to grow richer, and for perhaps one-fifth of the ordinary Common Pleas practitioners in the three-county sample, fees plus accumulated landed income may have come to as much as or more than £100 p.a. Incomes at this level compare reasonably well with the £100 p.a. which Aylmer has reckoned to be the average income in the 1630s for men who used the style of gentleman,[33] and an even more precise picture of the place of some of these richer attorneys in their local communities can be drawn from a study of their valuations in the hearth tax returns for 1662.

This tax was based on the number of fire-hearths contained in individual dwellings, and both Styles and the Stones have found some correlation between the tax assessments and the wealth of individuals. Richer men tended to live in warmer houses; consequently, Styles is able to estimate that in Kineton hundred in Warwickshire the average rural gentleman was assessed at five hearths and the average urban gentleman at six.[34] No seventeenth-century tax assessment is a fool-proof guide to the wealth of individuals, and in particular the late date of the hearth tax means that the returns cannot be used comprehensively as a measure of the standing of the early-seventeenth-century attorneys who have been the subject of this study. But they do provide a few valuable signposts.

First, the returns confirm that even wealthy attorneys rarely, if ever, reached the top ranks of county society. The Stones have calculated that the Hertfordshire élite of the late seventeenth century consisted of men who were assessed at twenty or more hearths,[35] but no attorney in either the Hertfordshire or Warwickshire returns was rated at more than twelve. On the other hand, several of the richer practitioners in both counties were rated at ten or twelve hearths, and an assessment in this range certainly put them well above Styles' averages for both urban and county gentlemen. In the borough of Warwick, for example, James Prescott's house in Jury Street was rated at twelve hearths. Similarly, the house of another of the most prosperous attorneys in our sample, John Skinner of Hitchin, had ten hearths. A dozen or so men in Warwick were taxed at a rate equal to or greater than Prescott, but in small towns like Warwick and Hitchin an assessment of twelve hearths suggests that a man was among the local élite. However, none of the other urban attorneys were as well off as these two. Francis Eades, a prosperous Warwick practitioner, was assessed at seven hearths and John Halford at six. Neither of these was an exceptionally high rating.[36]

If we turn from the most prosperous of the urban attorneys to their counterparts in the country, the hearth tax returns show that a wealthy attorney might very often have been the leading figure in the limited world of his home parish. Two successful Hertfordshire attorneys, James Willymott of Kelshall and Jonathan Waller of Ashwell, were assessed at twelve hearths in 1662.[37] They lived in the largest houses in their parishes, and their hearth tax rating may suggest that they were the equals of many an esquire. None of the rural attorneys of Warwickshire were assessed so highly as these two. Even so, those with moderately successful practices were often the most highly rated men in their immediate neighbourhoods. This was true of Richard Booth of Bishop's Tachbrooke (seven), Francis Leving of Baddesley Ensor (seven), and Josias Bull of Coleshill (seven).[38]

Nevertheless, if these studies show that some attorneys could amass wealth equal to that of the gentry, Chapter 11 also demonstrates that for perhaps two-thirds of all Common Pleas practitioners in the early seventeenth century, annual income from land and fees probably did not exceed £60 p.a. These men were not poor. Hugh North of Hertford (two fire hearths) is the lowest-rated attorney whose name has survived in the hearth tax returns, and some of them, like Richard Yardley of Warwick, who was rated at six hearths, even built rather fine houses.[39] But the important point is that the incomes of these men hardly compare with those of Aylmer's average landed gentleman. In fact, they are much closer to Grassby's estimates of the wealth of merchants in provincial towns.[40]

That the wealth of the majority of the early-seventeenth-century practitioners was more nearly comparable to that of merchants than to that of the landed gentry is not surprising. For, as Chapter 10 shows, the early Stuart period saw the migration of many practitioners, including the richest of them, into towns. Nor was their use of the style 'gentleman' in any way distinguished or unusual in an urban context. During this period, it was regularly adopted by many wealthy townsmen, in particular by those who held public office as mayors or town councilmen. Thus in terms of their incomes, their place of residence, and their occupation, the majority of attorneys had more in common with townsmen than with members of the gentry, and this would also seem to be borne out by what is known of their life-styles and acquaintances.

Some practitioners, like James Prescott of Warwick or John Skinner of Hitchin, had friends among the gentry, and, of course, even in the seventeenth century there were still a fairly large number of attorneys who made their homes in the country.[41] All the same, as far as we can tell from wills and literary evidence, practitioners appear to have identified more with the legal profession than with any of the attributes of the landed gentry. Similarly, circles of friends were drawn most often from amongst fellow practitioners or townsmen. In Warwickshire, there were a number of marriages between the families of local attorneys. Richard Booth married a daughter of Amillion Holbeache. The barrister Rowley Ward married James Prescott's daughter, and Prescott himself was related to the Rainsfords of Warwick. The Palmers and the Averells of Solihull intermarried. Amongst practitioners who lived in towns, close associations with townsmen in other occupations seem to have been the rule rather than the exception. For example, the executor of Alexander Rolle of Tavistock, the scion of a well-known country family, was an ironmonger.[42] A merchant, a dyer, and a brewer of Coventry served as overseers of the will of Hugh Willington, and Henry Tadlow, also of Coventry, appointed two apothecaries in the same capacity.[43]

In general, then, both the material circumstances and life-styles of most of the seventeenth-century practitioners diverged significantly from those of the classic landed gentry. This means that we must tread very carefully as we approach the question of whether a practice in the lower branch was an avenue for upward social mobility. Some time ago Stone argued that the period between 1560 and 1640 was one of 'unprecedented individual mobility', and one in which the professions were probably improving their economic position.[44] However, the fortunes of the majority of practitioners within the lower branch appear in fact to have been rather more complicated than this hypothesis might suggest. Early in the reign of Elizabeth, the profession does seem to have been a modest pathway to gentility, but after 1600 this course was blocked by several obstacles. The status of the lower branch seems to have declined in the eyes of contemporaries as a result of the sixteenth-century changes in attitudes about education. More important, though some men became quite rich as a result of their practice after 1600, most of them became associated with the urban or pseudo-gentry rather than with the country gentry. Since most members of the lower branch sprang from the borderline between the yeomanry and lesser gentry, or from the more prosperous townsmen, a legal career did not in the vast majority of cases significantly broaden their social horizons so much as provide an opportunity to stay within the same broad, middle rank of English society into which they were born.

In this respect the lower branch differed little, either in the origins of its recruits or in the prospects it offered, from a number of other prosperous occupations ranging from that of wholesale merchants involved in the overseas trade to small-town retailers, apothecaries, and barber-surgeons. Relative to the other possibilities available, neither the status it conferred nor the economic rewards it promised made a practice as a country attorney, as opposed to one of the better positions in the legal bureaucracy, an outstandingly desirable career. Its main advantage was that for a relatively small initial outlay for training, a reasonable income could be procured, and the title of 'gent.' could be added to one's name. But, although more risky and probably more expensive to enter, a successful career in business or trade could with luck bring much greater rewards, every bit as much social status, and a good deal more political influence. Judging from Grassby's recent studies of seventeenth-century businessmen, there is no reason to assume that parents, even gentry parents, found law a more attractive destination than trade for their sons.[45] In fact, many country attorneys appear to have thought that the procurement of a London apprenticeship for their children was likely to provide a step up in the world. Moreover, when it is compared with other occupations, the increase in the size of the lower branch during the early modern period (insofar as it is not simply an optical illusion), and even its centralization, seem much less unique than might at first sight appear. Recruitment from the same social groups that supplied attorneys during the late Elizabethan and early Stuart years also swelled the ranks of those provincial and, especially, those London guilds which offered entrance into the most lucrative business occupations. Furthermore, the scale of this movement was in fact much more dramatic than that experienced in the legal professions. At the turn of the sixteenth century some four to five thousand new apprentices came to London each year, and the numbers continued to grow right up until at least the middle of the seventeenth century. The significance of the increase in the size of the lower branch of the legal profession connected with London is not that it provided new avenues of rapid upward social mobility. Rather, the lower branch was one of a number of possibilities open to the sons of men from the middling ranks of society in both town and country which contributed to an enlargement of that sector of the population which earned its living from trade and services rather than directly from the land.[46]

Finally, these changes in the economic fortunes of members of the lower branch were accompanied by an apparent increase in their participation in various aspects of local government, especially in towns. Chapter 10 shows that it is difficult to detect evidence of any strong ideological, class, or group interests in this participation. On the other hand, one of the most constant themes in this book has been the extent to which the proliferation of the common law profession helped to facilitate, even to accelerate, the tendency for all groups in society to settle both their public and their professional disputes through litigation in the royal courts. This is certainly the most tangible development of the early modern period with which the lower branch can be directly associated, and it is in itself of considerable significance. English government and administration had always been legalistic, but the spread of the common law and its practitioners undoubtedly did much to emphasize further the rule of law and in particular the supremacy of the law which was administered from Westminster Hall. It may well be for this reason that the common law appears to have reached a high point of political importance during the early seventeenth century and why so much attention was paid to legalistic arguments in the early Stuart House of Commons. But what is most interesting about the increase in litigation is that most articulate laymen, including the king's councillors, appear to have seen it as a sinister development. Particularly amongst those writing from a patrician point of view, mass access to the courts implied a breakdown of traditional values based on deference, social custom, and neighbourliness. Hence attorneys and solicitors were attacked because it was believed that a growth in their numbers made it easier for tenants to vex their landlords, urban commons to attack their oligarchic rulers, and men to take disputes out of local jurisdictions and into the anonymous world of King's Bench and Common Pleas. At best, lawyers were men who lived off the misfortunes or un-Christian animosities of others. At worst, they were a threat to the established social order.[47] Indeed, in the later seventeenth century, the latter attitude was sometimes incorporated into contemporary interpretations of the English civil war. For instance, an anonymous post-Restoration proponent of stricter control over attorneys launched a vicious attack on their dangerous social and political behaviour: 'They are bold Impudent fellowes that will scarce allow any privilledges, noe not to the very best of his Ma[jes]ties subiect*es*....' Furthermore, one of them had been 'somewhat Instruementall in drawing up of that unparaleled Treacherous Indightment against o[u]r Late most gratious Soue*r*aigne Charles the first the holly martyr'.[48] In a similar vein, the Duke of Newcastle explained to Charles II how the number of lawyers had grown since the Reformation, and how they had 'been no smale meanes to formente *and* continue this late *and* unfortunate Rebellion'.[49]

In terms of the actions of individuals, accusations such as these greatly exaggerate the political radicalism, even the political activity, of members of the lower branch. Nor is it easy to see how the purely professional interests of practitioners might have led to any clear-cut group attitudes towards the authority of the monarch versus potentially rival claims by parliament. Professional amplification of the ideal of the rule of law put as much stress on the necessity for obedience to the king as on the liberties of the subject. The general opprobrium which attorneys and solicitors suffered in the early seventeenth century was so widespread that calls for stricter control over the profession provided a rare area of agreement between James I, Charles I, members of the upper branch, and gentry MPs. This suggests that the lower branch might have found much to oppose in the existing regime, but their enemies were not confined to any one political camp and they had virtually no allies. Moreover, despite much bluster, such reforms as were achieved were fairly trivial, and by the 1630s at the latest, some measure of increased regulation of the profession was probably welcomed by many of the practitioners themselves. By contrast, the traffic in legal offices under the early Stuarts did create anxiety within the lower branch, and conflict between attorneys and court officials over fees and procedures was a constant theme from the reign of James I through to the Interregnum. Some of these tensions may have been translated into hostility to the crown in 1640 or 1642, but there is little evidence on the point, and for most individuals such professional concerns would inevitably have been weighed in the balance against religious convictions and interests and associations formed in the localities. In the later 1640s and early 1650s, some practitioners clearly saw in the abolition of the monarchy and general calls for law reform an opportunity to attack the vested interests of office holders. Furthermore, many of their proposals for change which aimed to facilitate and simplify legal procedures in the interests of business and trade were not dissimilar in spirit from the more sweeping programmes advocated by radical reformers such as the Levellers, yet attorneys and solicitors were by no means spared from the general criticisms of the learned professions which were so characteristic of such groups.[50]

Nevertheless, the Duke of Newcastle's reflections do suggest the more general observation that the increase in the number of common lawyers represented and contributed to the evolution of a society in which it was possible for people to argue in terms of general principles which had in theory to be applied to all men. As Newcastle put it, wrangling at law had taught the subjects how to wrangle about everything, 'even the Kinges Prerogative'.[51] At the very least, the many thousands of cases of debt which made up the bulk of court business in the late sixteenth and early seventeenth centuries reveal a society in which contractual relationships were existing alongside or replacing older ones which were based on tenures, custom, and status. This was an aspect of the increase in central court litigation upon which contemporaries commented, and it signifies an important change in English culture. Equally, the large number of non-gentry litigants who used the royal courts, and, indeed, the existence of a group of men like the practitioners of the lower branch, are reminders of the social and economic importance of the middling sort of people between the gentry on the one hand and the wage labourers on the other.

Some historians, like some contemporaries, assert that the intrusion of the common law into the provinces undermined traditional neighbourly relations and was used by local élites as a means of exerting control over their inferiors.[52] Yet, however true this may be in relation to the application of the criminal law and to aspects of local life having to do with the regulation of ale-houses or the godly reformation of manners, it is equally relevant to point out that, although they may have smacked of post-lapsarian individualism and impersonality, the increased availability of lawyers and the royal courts also offered compensatory benefits which could accrue equally to all ranks of society. By the early seventeenth century, smallholders could protect their rights to copyhold land in the king's courts, and a man accused at quarter sessions could, if he wished, call on a lawyer to present his case to the local squires sitting on the magisterial bench. In addition, large numbers of people evidently thought that London law could provide a means of escaping the petty tyrannies of neighbourhood control or biased local officials. Witness, for example, the case of William and Margaret Cripple, two new arrivals in Burton upon Trent, who managed to establish dubious sexual reputations for themselves, but who gained a successful out-of-court settlement by bringing a Star Chamber prosecution against fellow townspeople who had treated them to a particularly nasty rendition of 'rough music'. In the 1620s, a group of inhabitants from Weardale in county Durham petitioned the House of Commons asking that they be allowed to try a case concerning their tenant rights in any court in the realm rather than within the palatine jurisdiction of the Bishop of Durham, who was also their landlord; the advice of local lawyers who helped them to use the royal courts at Westminster was of considerable aid in achieving these aims.[53] For better or worse, the increase in the number of lawyers and the number of lawsuits in the central courts constituted an important process of social integration, and it seems most likely to have been one which was embraced by the middle and lower orders of society rather than one which was imposed on them from above.

So by 1640 the influence of the royal courts in London and their agents, the common lawyers, permeated widely throughout the realm. But it is also the case that this development brought problems in its wake. The stream of justice did not always flow evenly or equitably. During the early seventeenth century, the courts and the legal professions were sorely tested by the increase in litigation and the need to accommodate the common law to modern conditions, and none of them emerged completely successfully. The failure to accomplish any reform before 1640 left the entire legal system vulnerable to the massive criticisms which were launched against it during the civil wars and Interregnum.[54] Greater access to the courts and the law created expectations amongst all ranks of society that justice should be administered fairly and effectively, but the sheer weight of the increase in litigation on traditional bureaucratic and professional structures made these expectations difficult to fulfil.

APPENDIX: ANALYSIS OF THE SOCIAL STATUS OF LITIGANTS IN KING'S BENCH AND COMMON PLEAS, 1560–1640

Percentages are given in round brackets.

A. 1560

	King's Bench			Common Pleas			
	Plaint.	Defend.	Total	Plaint.	Defend.	Unclear who sues whom	Total
Peers	—	—	—	1 (0.1)	2 (0.2)	3 (1)	6 (0.2)
Knights	2 (3)	2 (2)	4 (3)	19 (3)	14 (1)	11 (2)	44 (2)
Esquires	6 (6)	9 (11)	15 (9)	67 (11)	51 (5)	33 (6)	151 (7)
Gentlemen	8 (12)	11 (13)	19 (12)	87 (14)	169 (18)	74 (15)	330 (16)
Total gent. and above	16 (21)	22 (26)	38 (24)	174 (28)	236 (24)	121 (24)	531 (25)
Yeomen	2 (3)	—	2 (1)	10 (2)	201 (21)	58 (11)	269 (13)
Husbandmen	—	5 (6)	5 (3)	6 (1)	208 (22)	35 (7)	249 (12)
Commercial/artisan	3 (4)	3 (4)	6 (4)	84 (14)[a]	145 (15)	68 (13)	297 (14)
Miscellaneous	—	2 (3)	2 (1)	3 (0.4)	113 (12)	20 (4)	136 (7)
Clergy	2 (3)	—	2 (1)	14 (2)	14 (1)	10 (2)	38 (2)
Attorneys/lawyers	1 (1)	—	1 (0.6)	2 (0.3)	—	3 (1)	5 (0.2)
Widows	5 (6)	4 (5)	9 (6)	54 (9)	34 (4)	45 (9)	133 (6)
Below gent. unspecified	49 (63)	46 (56)	95 (59)	260 (43)	8 (0.8)	149 (29)	417 (20)
Total below gent.	62 (79)	60 (74)	122 (76)	433 (72)	723 (76)	388 (76)	1544 (75)
Grand total	78 (100)	82 (100)	160 (100)	607 (100)	959 (100)	509 (100)	2075 (100)

[a] Includes 57 members of London livery companies.

Sources: PRO KB 27/1194 (Easter, 2 Eliz.); CP 40/1187 (Easter, 2 Eliz.).

B. 1606

	King's Bench			Common Pleas		
	Plaint.	Defend.	Total	Plaint.	Defend.	Total
Peers	8 (0.4)	—	8 (0.2)	10 (1)	7 (0.3)	17 (0.5)
Knights	71 (4)	37 (2)	108 (3)	59 (4)	65 (3.3)	124 (4)
Esquires	87 (5)	54 (3)	141 (4)	95 (7)	118 (6)	213 (6)
Gentlemen	311 (16)	239 (12)	550 (14)	211 (15)	460 (24)	671 (20)
(Sheriffs)	2 (0.1)	—	2 (0.1)	20 (1)	—	20 (0.6)
Total gent. and above	479 (25)	330 (17)	809 (21)	395 (28)	650 (34)	1045 (31)
Yeomen	16 (1)	253 (13)	269 (7)	—	522 (27)	522 (16)
Husbandmen	—	60 (3)	60 (1.5)	—	133 (7)	133 (4)
Commercial/artisan	39 (2)	119 (6)	158 (4)	4 (0.3)	328 (17)	332 (10)
Miscellaneous	16 (1)	49 (3)	65 (1)	3 (0.2)	139 (7)	142 (4)
Clergy	22 (1)	48 (2)	70 (2)	13 (1)	48 (2)	61 (2)
Attorneys	3 (0.2)	17 (1)	20 (0.5)	2 (0.1)	34 (2)	36 (1)
Widows	41 (2)	33 (2)	74 (2)	58 (4)	28 (1)	86 (3)
Below gent. unspecified	1316 (68)	1043 (53)	2359 (61)	936 (66)	47 (3)	983 (29)
Total below gent.	1453 (75)	1622 (83)	3075 (79)	1016 (72)	1279 (66)	2295 (69)
Grand total	1932 (100)	1952 (100)	3884 (100)	1411 (100)	1929 (100)	3340 (100)

Sources: PRO KB 27/1395 (Hilary, 3 Jac. I); CP 40/1735 (Easter, 3 Jac. I).

C. 1640

	King's Bench			Common Pleas		
	Plaint.	Defend.	Total	Plaint.	Defend.	Total
Peers	3 (0.5)	1 (0.1)	4 (0.3)	3 (0.3)	—	3 (0.1)
Knights	12 (2)	12 (2)	24 (2)	28 (2)	43 (3)	71 (3)
Esquires	44 (7)	49 (7)	93 (7)	84 (8)	176 (12)	260 (10)
Gentlemen	82 (13)	104 (15)	186 (14)	156 (15)	342 (24)	498 (20)
Total gent. and above	141 (23)	166 (25)	307 (23)	271 (25)	561 (39)	832 (33)
Yeomen	—	108 (16)	108 (8)	—	314 (22)	314 (13)
Husbandmen	—	16 (2)	16 (1)	—	88 (6)	88 (4)
Commercial/artisan	22 (3)	142 (21)	164 (13)	5 (0.5)	255 (18)	260 (10)
Miscellaneous	4 (0.6)	20 (3)	24 (2)	2 (0.2)	92 (6)	94 (4)
Clergy	8 (1)	12 (2)	20 (2)	15 (1)	43 (3)	58 (2)
Attorneys	2 (0.3)	21 (3)	23 (2)	7 (0.7)	37 (3)	44 (2)
Widows	27 (4)	17 (3)	44 (3)	60 (6)	23 (2)	83 (3)
Below gent. unspecified	433 (68)	169 (25)	602 (46)	706 (66)	13 (1)	719 (29)
Total below gent.	496 (77)	505 (75)	1001 (77)	795 (75)	865 (61)	1660 (67)
Grand total	637 (100)	671 (100)	1308 (100)	1066 (100)	1426 (100)	2492 (100)

Sources: PRO KB 27/1649 (Easter, 15 Chas. I); CP 40/2476 (Easter, 15 Chas. I).

NOTES

1. INTRODUCTION

1 Earlier books on the lower branch include E. B. V. Christian, *A Short History of Solicitors* (1896), and his *Leaves of the Lower Branch: The Attorney in Life and Letters* (1909); R. Robson, *The Attorney in Eighteenth Century England* (Cambridge, 1959); M. Birks, *Gentlemen of the Law* (1960). Important new work on early modern legal history has appeared within the last fifteen years. See, for example, W. J. Jones, *The Elizabethan Court of Chancery* (Oxford, 1967); W. R. Prest, *The Inns of Court under Elizabeth I and the Early Stuarts* (1972); J. S. Cockburn, *A History of English Assizes 1558–1714* (Cambridge, 1972); J. A. Guy, *The Cardinal's Court: The Impact of Thomas Wolsey in Star Chamber* (Hassocks, 1977); M. Blatcher, *The Court of King's Bench, 1450–1550: A Study in Self-Help* (1978); and J. H. Baker, *Spelman's Reports* (Selden Soc., xciv, 1978). E. W. Ives, *The Common Lawyers of Pre-Reformation England* (Cambridge, 1983), was published as this book was in an advanced stage of preparation, and so I have been able to make only limited references to it.

2 PRO CP 40 and KB 27. The 'Rolls of Warrants' are bound at the end of the plea roll for each legal term.

3 C. Holmes, *The Eastern Association in the English Civil War* (Cambridge, 1974), pp. 7–8.

4 J. Thirsk, 'The Farming Regions of England', in *The Agrarian History of England and Wales*, vol. iv, ed. J. Thirsk (Cambridge, 1967), pp. 50–2.

5 L. Stone and J. C. F. Stone, 'Country Houses and their Owners in Hertfordshire, 1540–1879', in *The Dimensions of Quantitative Research in History*, ed. W. O. Aydelotte *et. al.* (1972), p. 59.

6 Thirsk, 'The Farming Regions', p. 73.

7 W. G. Hoskins, 'The Estates of the Caroline Gentry', in Hoskins and H. P. R. Finberg, *Devonshire Studies* (1952), p. 84.

8 R. Schofield, 'The Geographical Distribution of Wealth in England, 1339–1649', *Economic History Review*, 2nd ser., 18 (1965), 504.

9 Thirsk, 'The Farming Regions', p. 92.

10 V. H. T. Skipp, 'Economic and Social Change in the Forest of Arden, 1530–1649', *Agricultural History Review*, 18 (1970), 107.

11 *Victoria Co. History of Warwickshire*, ii (1908), p. 172.
12 *The Visitation of the County of Warwick in 1619*, ed. J. Featherston (Harleian Soc., xii, 1877). A. Everitt, *The Community of Kent and the Great Rebellion* (Leicester, 1973), pp. 33 n. 3, 34.
13 C. Phythian-Adams, *The Desolation of a City : Coventry and the Urban Crisis of the Later Middle Ages* (Cambridge, 1979).
14 P. Clark and P. Slack, *English Towns in Transition* (Oxford, 1976), p. 83.
15 *Victoria Co. History of Warwickshire*, viii (1969), pp. 504–11. P. Borsay, 'The English Urban Renaissance: The Development of Provincial Urban Culture, c. 1680–c. 1760', *Social History*, 5 (1977), pp. 581–605. For the town's own assessment of its economic position in the 1630s see *CSPD : Charles I*, cccxli, p. 42.
16 Phythian-Adams, *Desolation of a City*, p. 25. Clark and Slack, *English Towns*, p. 38.
17 R. L. Hine, *The History of Hitchin* (2 vols., 1927–9), i, 51. Clark and Slack, *English Towns*, p. 38.
18 W. G. Hoskins, *Devon and its People* (1968), p. 88.
19 J. Roberts, 'Reflections on Elizabethan Barnstaple Politics and Society', *Trans. Devon Assoc.*, 103 (1971), 137–47. Hoskins and Finberg, *Devonshire Studies*, p. 230.

2. LAWYERS AND THE ROYAL COURTS IN LONDON DURING THE REIGN OF ELIZABETH

1 The best short introduction to the history of the profession can be found in J. H. Baker, *An Introduction to English Legal History*, 2nd edn (1979), ch. 10. See also F. Pollock and F. W. Maitland, *The History of English Law*, 2nd edn by S. F. C. Milsom (2 vols., Cambridge, 1968), i, pp. 216–17; A. Pulling, *The Order of the Coif* (1884), pp. 10–11, 106ff; and R. C. Palmer, 'The Origins of the Legal Profession in England', *Irish Jurist*, 11 (1976), 126–46.
2 Baker, *An Introduction*, ch. 10.
3 J. H. Baker, 'The English Legal Profession, 1450–1550', in *Lawyers in Early Modern Europe and America*, ed. W. R. Prest (1981), pp. 27–31.
4 Baker, *An Introduction*, ch. 10.
5 *Ibid.*
6 S. F. C. Milsom, *The Historical Foundations of the Common Law* (1969), pp. 22–6.
7 For more on the jurisdictions see above, pp. 66–74, 84–93.
8 Baker, *An Introduction*, chs. 3, 6–7. J. A. Guy, *The Cardinal's Court* (1977). H. E. Bell, *An Introduction to the History and Records of the Court of Wards and Liveries* (Cambridge, 1953), p. 16. W. J. Jones, *The Elizabethan Court of Chancery* (Oxford, 1967), p. 9. For a description of the layout of the courts in Westminster Hall see I. M. Cooper, 'Westminster Hall', *Journal of the British Archaeo-*

logical Assoc., 3rd ser., 1 (1937), 168–228, and Plate X in A. Nicholl, ed., *Shakespeare in his Own Age* (Cambridge, 1964).

9   Richard Robinson, 'A Briefe Collection of the Queenes Majesties Most High and Most Honourable Courts of Recordes', ed. R. L. Rickard, *Camden Miscellany*, 3rd ser., 20 (1953), pp. 18–20. Lincoln's Inn Library, Miscellaneous MS 586, 'Robert Moyle's Practice of the Courts', fol. 7.

10 Robinson, 'A Briefe Collection', pp. 15–18. PRO E 215/11/849, fols. 11–18.

11 Jones, *Chancery*, pp. 119–34, 143–7, 161–2. Robinson, 'A Briefe Collection', pp. 11–15.

12 G. E. Aylmer, *The King's Servants: The Civil Service of Charles I 1625–1642*, 2nd edn (1974), p. 477. W. H. Bryson, *The Equity Side of the Exchequer* (Cambridge, 1975), pp. 34–77.

13 Robinson, 'A Briefe Collection', pp. 21–4. T. G. Barnes, 'Due Process and Slow Process in the Late Elizabethan – Early Stuart Star Chamber, Part II', *American Journal of Legal History*, 6 (1962), 340–3.

14 Robinson, 'A Briefe Collection', pp. 24, 29. I. S. Leadam, ed., *Select Cases in the Court of Requests, A.D. 1497–1569* (Selden Soc., xii, 1898), pp. lxxiv–xcix. Bell, *Court of Wards*, pp. 26–9. There were, of course, other officials in the court of Wards who were connected with revenue rather than litigation.

15 See the discussion in Aylmer, *King's Servants*, p. 455.

16 M. Hastings, *The Court of Common Pleas in Fifteenth Century England* (Ithaca, N.Y., 1947), pp. 107–8. For King's Bench see M. Blatcher, *The Court of King's Bench, 1450–1550: A Study in Self-Help* (1978), pp. 40–4.

17 Jones, *Chancery*, pp. 9, 156–62. J. S. Wilson, 'The Administrative Work of the Lord Chancellor in the Early Seventeenth Century' (London Univ. unpub. Ph.D. thesis, 1927), pp. 2–15.

18 Bell, *Wards*, p. 16. Barnes, 'Due Process and Slow Process', p. 342.

19 Aylmer, *King's Servants*, pp. 106–7.

20 Barnes, 'Due Process and Slow Process', p. 342. Hunt. Lib. EL. MS 2677. Bell, *Wards*, pp. 26–8, 33. *Dictionary of National Biography, sub.* Roper, William. Another example is the Fanshawe family, who held the office of king's remembrancer in the Exchequer from 1565 to 1716. Bryson, *Equity Side of the Exchequer*, p. 67. Long tenures of office were rarer in Common Pleas and Chancery.

21 Wilson, 'Administrative Work of the Lord Chancellor', p. 31.

22 Some interesting examples of this in the Common Pleas are revealed in *Hele* v. *Coke*, a Star Chamber case of 1604. PRO STAC 8/9/4. Also see above pp. 127–31.

23 M. Blatcher, 'Touching the Writ of Latitat: An Act of No Great Moment', in *Elizabethan Government and Society*, ed. S. T. Bindoff, J. Hurstfield, and C. H. Williams (1961), pp. 181–211, and the same author's *The Court of King's Bench*, pp. 119–35; J. H. Baker, *The Reports of Sir John Spelman* (Selden Soc., xciv, 1978), pp. 55ff. For

the lament of the filazers see John Trye, *Jus Filizarii : or, the Filacer's Office in the Court of King's Bench* (1684).

24 Robinson, 'A Briefe Collection', pp. 18, 15–16. PRO SP 12/224, fol. 154. STAC 8/93/08.

25 Bell, *Wards*, p. 172.

26 Jones, *Chancery*, p. 159. J. Conway Davies, *Catalogue of Manuscripts in the Honourable Society of the Inner Temple* (3 vols., 1972), i. p. 145.

27 Trye, *Jus Filizarii*, pp. 104–5.

28 Jones, *Chancery*, pp. 119–21, 158. Hunt. Lib. EL. MS 2914 lists the names of fifty-four clerks of the six clerks who were sworn in November 1596. Wilson, 'Administrative Work of the Lord Chancellor', p. 9.

29 Bell, *Wards*, p. 31. PRO WARDS 10/16 lists sixteen underclerks of the Wards in the 1590s. In the 1620s, the three prothonotaries of the Common Pleas were said to have had 120 underclerks among them. PRO E 215/629. There are no known comparable lists for the late sixteenth century.

30 Pollock and Maitland, *History of English Law*, i, pp. 211ff. H. Cohen, *History of the English Bar and Attornatus to 1450* (1929). G. O. Sayles, *Select Cases in the Court of King's Bench under Edward I* (Selden Soc., xlv, 1936), pp. xci–xcvii. Warrants of attorney are also filed in the plea rolls of the Exchequer of pleas, PRO E 13.

31 T. Powell, *The Attourneys Academy* (1623). Bodl. MS Rawlinson C. 65, 'Instructions for an Attorney', fols. 4–7.

32 F. W. Maitland, *The Forms of Action at Common Law* (edn 1976), Lecture I. Also see above, pp. 66–71.

33 Baker, *An Introduction*, ch. 5.

34 Milsom, *Historical Foundations*, p. 33.

35 A. Harding, *A Social History of English Law* (1966), p. 74.

36 Baker, *An Introduction*, ch. 5.

37 Brit. Lib. Hargrave MS 491, fol. 4. This reader mentioned the following statutes: 20 Hen. III c. 10 (Merton); 27 Edw. I; 3 Edw. I c. 29; 10 Hen. IV c. 4; 19 Hen. VI c. 9.

38 Pollock and Maitland, *History of English Law*, i, p. 216.

39 A. Luders, T. E. Tomlins, J. Raithby, *et al.*, *Statutes of the Realm* (11 vols., 1810–28), ii. 4 Hen. IV c. 18.

40 For numbers at various dates under Elizabeth and the early Stuarts see Table 6.1 above. A parliamentary bill of 1455 claimed that traditionally no more than six or eight attorneys from the counties of Norfolk and Suffolk came to the king's courts, and proposed to limit the number henceforth to six in Norfolk, six in Suffolk, and two for the city of Norwich. However, the bill did not become law although it was sometimes referred to in later debates. Baker, 'The English Legal Profession, 1450–1550', p. 25.

41 M. Blatcher, 'The Workings of the Court of King's Bench in the Fifteenth Century' (London Univ. unpub. Ph.D. thesis, 1935), p. 168. Baker, 'The English Legal Profession, 1450–1550', p. 24, comes to similar conclusions.

42 For example, comparisons have been made of PRO CP 40/1187 and KB 27/1194.

43 PRO SP 12/96, p. 238.

44 PRO KB 27/1395, 'Roll of Warrants of Attorney'. Men styled as clerks of William Roper, the prothonotary, include Thomas Webb, Richard Worley, Simon Harborne, H. Turner, William Symmonds. Four men, William Cox (m. 51), William Dandy (m. 54), John Whitehead (m. 72), and Robert Gilbert (m. 73), were called attorneys of the King's Bench. William Dandy (m. 74) was a servant of one of the judges of the King's Bench. Common Pleas attorneys are almost always described as such in the plea rolls. See, for example, PRO CP 40/1735, 'Roll of Warrants of Attorney', m. 1.

45 Docket roll used was PRO IND 1356. Plea roll consulted was PRO KB 27/1395.

46 PRO E 215/11/849, fol. 9. In return for 11s. 13d. paid to the chief prothonotary for each full 'rowle on both sides' that they wrote up in the plea rolls, the clerks were able to share in the fees due for making procedural writs and drawing pleas.

47 PRO E 215/11/849; Bodl. Bankes MS 24, fol. 9. For the numbers of King's Bench clerks and attorneys see Table 6.1.

48 Compare, for example, the names of practitioners in the rolls of warrants of PRO CP 40/1753, 1757, 1763, 1796 with those in PRO KB 27/1395 and PRO IND 1355–6.

49 Sir George Cooke, *Rules, Orders and Notices in the Courts of King's Bench and Common Pleas* (1747) (no pagination), Common Pleas, Michaelmas 1564.

50 In either case the attorney would be due his 3s. 4d. fee, but in Common Pleas a Common Pleas attorney was much more likely to collect additional fees for clerical work.

51 Cooke, *Rules and Orders*, King's Bench, Easter 1615. PRO SP 14/90, item 25, 'King James to the Chief Baron and other barons of the Exchequer'.

52 J. B. Post, 'King's Bench Clerks in the Reign of Richard II', *Bull. Institute of Historical Research*, 47, no. 116 (1974), 150–1. Baker, 'The English Legal Profession, 1450–1550', p. 24.

53 PRO E 215/756.

54 For the number of attorneys see above p. 113. PRO E 215/629.

55 Jones, *Chancery*, pp. 9, 119–21.

56 Robinson, 'A Briefe Collection', pp. 29, 24, 22, 32. A fourth attorney emerged in the Star Chamber during the 1590s. Barnes, 'Due Process and Slow Process', p. 342. A third and then a fourth attorney were added in the Wards during the course of the seventeenth century. Bell, *Wards*, p. 31. On the equity side of Exchequer, the eight sworn clerks in the king's remembrancer's office acted as attorneys. Bryson, *Equity Side of the Exchequer*, pp. 75–7. In the Exchequer of pleas, practice seems to have been limited to three practitioners in 1560, although the number rose to six by 1640. There are also signs that the office could be passed down from father to son. PRO E 13/254, 260–1, 330, 435–8, 518, 573.

57 Bell, *Wards*, pp. 31–4.
58 Bodl. MS Eng. Hist. c. 304, fols. 265–9. Hunt. Lib. EL. MS 2674. The ultimate power over the appointment of attorneys, however, rested with the lord chancellor. Barnes, 'Due Process and Slow Process', p. 342.
59 John Hare, one of the attorneys in 1589, was a relation of the Tooke family, which for a long period occupied the office of auditor. Later, Hare became clerk of the Wards. Bell, *Wards*, pp. 24–31. Edward Latymer, the personal clerk in the 1590s of the receiver-general, William Fleetwood, became an attorney in 1601. *Ibid.*, p. 17. C. A. F. Meekings, 'Draft of Passages Provided in 1951–52 for Wheatley's Revised Edition of *Edward Latymer and His Foundations*' (typescript) pp. 86–8. I am very grateful to the late Mr Meekings for lending me this typescript.
60 Bodl. MS Eng. Hist. c. 304, fol. 268. In 1597, the Star Chamber clerk William Mill mentioned that two new attorneys in the court had paid dear for their offices. Hunt. Lib. El. MS 2676. There is no direct evidence for the attorneys in Wards, but money changed hands in connection with other offices. Bell, *Wards*, p. 38.
61 PRO WARDS 10–8, transcribed in Meekings, 'Draft passages', p. 86. Bell, *Wards*, p. 30, mentions that suitors had at first not welcomed the emergence in the court of 'officially sponsered attorneys'. W. B. J. Allsebrook, 'The Court of Requests in the Reign of Elizabeth' (London Univ. unpub. M.A. thesis, 1936), pp. 38–41, 47–9.
62 E. W. Ives, 'The Common Lawyers in Pre-Reformation England', *Trans. Royal Historical Soc.*, 5th ser., 8 (1968), 148 n. 7.
63 J. H. Baker, 'Solicitors and the Law of Maintenance 1590–1640', *Cambridge Law Journal*, 32 (1) (1973), 68–9.
64 *Ibid.* W. Harrison, 'The Description of England', in *Holinshed's Chronicles of England, Scotland and Ireland* (6 vols., 1807), i, pp. 304–5. See above, pp. 141–2.
65 Baker, 'Solicitors and the Law of Maintenance', p. 67 n. 52, remarks that many of the 'cases concerning "solicitors" involved attorneys retained to solicit causes in other courts'. PRO E 215/129 gives the name of a clerk in the cursitor's office in Chancery who acted as a solicitor in the 1620s. Even after the Restoration some young barristers acted as solicitors, but in 1594 the judges ruled that it was actionable in slander to call a counsellor at law a solicitor. Baker, 'Solicitors', p. 68. In addition, in 1574 the judicial orders provided that practising solicitors, as well as attorneys, should be excluded from the inns of court, although there is no evidence of barristers being expelled from the inns for soliciting. W. S. Holdsworth, *A History of English Law*, 3rd edn (12 vols., 1945), iv, p. 449. For attempts to regulate solicitors see above, pp. 142–3.
66 Much the same was true in many provincial jurisdictions as well; see above, pp. 37–45.
67 Baker, 'Solicitors and the Law of Maintenance', pp. 56–80, and 'Counsellors and Barristers', *Cambridge Law Journal*, 27 (1969), 214–29. Only in 1592 did the judges finally rule that only men called

by the inns of court to the degree of utter barrister should be allowed the right of audience.

68 Baker, 'Solicitors and the Law of Maintenance', p. 59, and 'The English Legal Profession, 1450–1550', p. 26.

69 R. Abel-Smith and Robert Stevens, *Lawyers and the Courts* (1967), chs. 8 and 9, for an account of lawyers in the eighteenth century and later.

70 Baker, 'The English Legal Profession, 1450–1550', pp. 18–19.

71 There is no completely satisfactory way to calculate the number of senior members of the inns of court in 1560 or to determine how many of them were active practitioners. Guy, *Cardinal's Court*, p. 112, found 69 counsellors active in Star Chamber in the period 1515–29. Lists in the state papers give some guidance for the mid-Elizabethan years. A survey dated 1573 names 96 benchers, readers, and barristers at Lincoln's Inn, but marginal notes suggest that only 29 of them were active as pleaders, although some of those not so noted (for example the future Lord Chancellor Thomas Egerton) clearly were or were soon to become active lawyers (Brit. Lib. Landsdowne MS 106, fol. 91). Another list, believed to date from 1579, gives a total of 176 for the number of benchers and barristers at the four inns of court. However, it also records that only 70 of these men were 'of name for their practise'. Given that there is no reason to assume any great increase in numbers between 1530 and 1560, a total practising bar of 80–90 would seem a reasonable guess for the latter date. The Elizabethan lists are printed in *The Records of the Honourable Society of Lincoln's Inn: The Black Books*, ed. W. P. Baildon and R. F. Roxburgh (5 vols., 1897–1968), i, pp. 456–7, and *A Calendar of the Inner Temple Records*, ed. F. A. Inderwick (5 vols. 1896–1901), i, p. 470.

72 Any figure for the size of this group in 1560 must be something of an estimate, because there are no complete lists of clerks and underclerks for that date. For example, although the six clerks in Chancery are known to have had fifty-four underclerks in 1594, the number in 1560 is unknown, though probably smaller. Hence 130 is likely to be a liberal estimate.

73 PRO CP 40/1187, 1195. KB 27/1194.

74 Baker, 'The English Legal Profession, 1450–1550', p. 24, estimates that the total number of attorneys active in 1480, excluding the officers of the courts, was around 180.

3. THE LEGAL PROFESSION IN THE PROVINCES

1 J. H. Baker, *An Introduction to English Legal History*, 2nd edn (1979), ch. 2.

2 PRO SP 12/224, fols. 138v, 154.

3 A conclusion drawn from a study of the wills of common law attorneys active at the beginning of the reign of Elizabeth.

4 R. Robson, *The Attorney in Eighteenth Century England* (Cambridge, 1959), p. 3.

5 Horses are frequently mentioned in the wills and papers of practitioners, but carriages never.

6 W. S. Holdsworth, *A History of English Law*, 3rd edn (12 vols., 1945), i, p. 187. Baker, *An Introduction*, p. 26.

7 The number of suits commenced each year in King's Bench and Common Pleas may have been in the region of 13,400. The population in 1560 was roughly 2.8 million. Also see above, p. 78.

8 PRO CP 40/1187, 'Roll of Warrants'. Merchants of London were involved in approximately 8 per cent of cases. For more on the nature of litigation see above, pp. 57–71.

9 PRO CP 40/1195, m. viii.

10 In this and all subsequent discussions of provincial attorneys, the names of practitioners are taken from the 'Rolls of Warrants of Attorney'. Lists of names were compiled initially from PRO CP 40/1187, 1753, 2476 and KB 27/1194, 1393, 1649. These were then supplemented by searches in the rolls of various terms around the dates 1560, 1580, 1606, 1625, and 1640. It is hoped that by this method most of the attorneys from any one region have been identified even if some men appear in the documents for one term and not for another. However, it would be beyond expectation to say that these lists are absolutely comprehensive. Some men have no doubt escaped notice, although there is no circumstantial evidence that very many of them have. The other plea rolls consulted include CP 40/1185, 1188, 1198, 1343, 1384, 1439, 1457, 1509, 1769, 1757, 1763, 2175, 2215, 2217, 2303, 2313, 2415, 2462, 2448, 2453 and KB 27/1196.

11 The will of Hawes of Solihull, dated 1574, is in the Lichfield Joint Record Office. Sparrey's will is in PRO PROB 11/101 (17 Bolein). *The Visitation of the County of Warwick in 1619*, ed. J. Featherston (Harleian Soc. xii, 1877), p. 161.

12 For the activities of Warner and Durant in King's Bench see PRO KB 27/1194. The evidence for Warner is not very good. One of this name is mentioned in *The Visitation of Worcestershire, 1634*, ed. A. T. Butler (Harleian Soc., xc, 1938), p. 68, as of Whitting, co. Staffs. In PRO CP 40/1343, m. 79^d, and CP 40/1187, m. 16, he handles a number of cases from that county. See PRO CP 40/1187, mm. 6, 13, for Durant's widespread case load, and CP 40/1187, mm. 21^d–22 for Barnard's. It is of interest that one of Barnard's clients was Ralph Barnard, a citizen and clothier of London.

13 Addresses from wills. PRO PROB 11/48 (19 Crymes), 11/59 (49 Daughtry), and 11/72 (33 Rutland).

14 Sources as in n. 10 above.

15 The eight identified with some certainty are Henry Mynne of Little Farnsham, Thomas Barsham of Oxwich, Christopher Crowe of East Bilney, Thomas Might of Flitchim, Edward Fenne of Gillingham All Saints, Norwich, William Dey of Oxburgh and St Mary Islington, London, and William Bygott of Starston.

16 Sources as in n. 10. The likely Yorkshire practitioners are Wilfrid Brand, Hugh Charnock, Robert Clough, Henry Dyson, Robert Fylmere, and John Jackson.

17 A conclusion based on the study of the published admissions registers of the four inns of court.

18 M. D. Harris, ed., *The Coventry Leet Book or Mayor's Register* (Early English Text Soc., cxxxiv–cxxxv, cxxxviii, cxlvi, 1907–13), pp. 524–5, 635, 642.

19 Thomas Kemp, ed., *The Black Book of Warwick* (Warwick, 1898), p. 331.

20 Forty-four Devon men were called to the bar at the Inner Temple alone between 1550 and 1640. W. K. Willcocks, 'Devonshire Men at the Inner Temple', *Trans. Devon Assoc.*, 17 (1885), 246–65. J. J. Alexander, 'Devon Magnates in 1434', *ibid.*, 72 (1940), 299.

21 G. T. Lapsley, *The County Palatine of Durham: A Study in Constitutional History* (Harvard Historical Studies, viii, 1900). W. J. Jones, 'Palatine Performance in the Seventeenth Century', in *The English Commonwealth 1547–1640*, ed. P. Clark, A. G. R. Smith, and N. Tyacke (Leicester, 1979), pp. 189–204. R. R. Reid, *The King's Council in the North* (1921), pp. 298ff. P. Williams, *The Council in the Marches of Wales Under Elizabeth I* (Cardiff, 1958).

22 There is no comprehensive modern account of all the jurisdictions. See Sir E. Coke, *The Fourth Part of the Institutes of the Laws of England* (1648), for some of them. Also S. and B. Webb, *English Local Government from the Revolution to the Municipal Corporations Act: The Manor and the Borough* (1924 edn), for local courts.

23 R. Houlbrooke, *Church Courts and the People during the English Reformation, 1520–1570* (Oxford, 1979), ch. 1.

24 Although business in hundred and county courts was certainly in general decline, it is clear that as late as the mid seventeenth century county and hundred courts were still active in some areas; for example, papers connected with the activities of local attorneys reveal active jurisdictions in Gloucestershire, Hertfordshire, and Devonshire. Gloucester Co. Rec. Office D 149/B1, fol. 119. HCRO 63849, Court Book of James Willymot. In Devonshire there is much more evidence of the existence of hundred courts than of manor courts. PRO E 215/1455, 1507, Bodl. MS Tanner 287, fol. 102. See also Norfolk Co. Rec. Office, D.S.488, 'County Court Business', fols. 27–40.

25 Holdsworth, *History*, i, pp. 133, 187.

26 F. J. C. Hearnshaw, *Leet Jurisdiction in England* (Southampton Rec. Soc., Southampton, 1908), pp. 19, 34, 37, 75.

27 J. P. Dawson, *A History of Lay Judges* (Cambridge, Mass., 1960), p. 213, estimates that there may have been several thousand manors in sixteenth-century England.

28 Devon Co. Rec. Office, typescript of E. Devon Rec. Office Manor Rolls, CR 100, Culliland, court held 21 August 1601. H. Richardson, ed., 'Court Rolls of the Manor of Acomb', *Yorkshire Archaeological Soc.* 131 (1969), 127. Sir T. Lawson Tancred, ed., *Records of a Yorkshire Manor* (1937), p. 6.

29 C. H. Cooper, *The Annals of Cambridge* (5 vols., Cambridge, 1842), ii, p. 366. D. M. Palliser, *Tudor York* (Oxford, 1979), p. 60. Harris, ed., *Coventry Leet Book*, p. 790. The same was true of Liverpool, Jones, 'Palatine Performance', p. 198.

30 See generally Thomas Emerson, *A Concise Treatise on the Courts of Law of The City of London* (1794).

31 F. F. Foster, *The Politics of Stability: A Portrait of the Rulers of Elizabethan London* (1977), p. 48. For similar ordinances in another town see R. S. Ferguson and W. Nanson, eds., *Some Municipal Records of the City of Carlisle* (Cumb. and Westmor. Antiquarian and Archaeological Soc., extra ser., iv, Carlisle, 1887), pp. 127, 145–7.

32 B. Marsh and J. Ainsworth, eds., *Records of the Worshipful Company of Carpenters*, vol. vi: *Court Book, 1573–1594* (1939), pp. viff. W. W. Greg and E. Boswell, *Records of the Court of the Stationers' Company 1576–1602* (1930), p. xlvi.

33 *CSPD Elizabeth, Addenda*, ix, p. 499.

34 Late-sixteenth-century lawyers argued explicitly that such courts originated in grants from the crown. See above, p. 199.

35 Palliser, *Tudor York*, p. 60.

36 Such fees made up an important part of the income of town clerks and manorial stewards. See above pp. 240–2.

37 See, for example, A. B. Hinds, *A History of Northumberland Issued under the Direction of the Northumberland County History Committe* vol. iii: *Hexamshire, Part I* (Newcastle, 1896), p. 292.

38 Sir Thomas Smith, *De Republica Anglorum*, ed. M. Dewar (Cambridge, 1982), p. 102.

39 See above, p. 97.

40 Dawson, *Lay Judges*, p. 229.

41 Jones, 'Palatine Performance', pp. 193–5. Reid, *Council in the North*, pp. 377–8. Williams, *Council in Wales*, pp. 172–3.

42 Williams, *Council in Wales*, p. 174. Jones, 'Palatine Performance', p. 199. Shropshire Co. Rec. Office, Bridgewater Collection Box 212, Edward Martyn to Earl Bridgewater, 26 July 1640.

43 PRO CHESTER 29/270, 273, 320, 321, 356–7, 355, 406, 420. The Cluttons intermarried with the Wrights and Malbons. An early-seventeenth-century attorney, Richard Werden of Chester, married the daughter of an early Elizabethan practitioner, John Bannester. *The Visitation of Cheshire in 1580*, ed. J. P. Rylands (Harleian Soc., xviii, 1882).

44 Whitby was apparently trained up in the office of the clerk of the peace of Chester. PRO STAC 8/297/15. See also J. Hall, *A History of the Town and Parish of Nantwich* (Nantwich, 1883), pp. 72, 77, 98, 100, 122, 127, 139.

45 Hall, *Nantwich*, p. 123. PRO PROB 11/110 (49 Huddlestone), dated 1608.

46 Reid, *Council in the North*, pp. 469–70. Brit. Lib. Harleian MS 6115, p. 21, a list of officers of the Council in the North, gives fourteen as

the number of attorneys. Leeds City Council Archive Dept, Temple Newsam Collection TN/PO 1/16.

47 Leeds City Council Archive Dept, Temple Newsam Collection TN/PO 1/8. Another example is James Birkeby of York, who practised before the Council and was involved in the city government. Like Lawrence Wright of Nantwich, he profited greatly from this local business. Palliser, *Tudor York*, pp. 109, 142.

48 This was the long-running dispute over a patent granted in 1606 to the courtier John Lepton for making and exhibiting certain procedural instruments connected with business before the Council. Historical MSS Commission, *Hatfield House*, xix, p. 234. Leeds City Council Archive Dept, Temple Newsam Collection TN/PO 1/3, 5–6, 10, 15, 16, 19, 31. On the other hand, in 1606 a case was brought by northern gentry and attorneys of the Common Pleas against the Council for its attempts to prevent practitioners from removing cases from the Council to London. Brit. Lib. Landsdowne MS 1062, fol. 224v. Reid, *Council in the North*, pp. 357, 383–4.

49 Names of practitioners before the Council and palatine courts have been compared with those active in the courts at Westminster.

50 PRO DURHAM 3/218, admissions of attorneys before the chancellor's court, 1660–1723 (no pagination).

51 Holdsworth, *History*, i, p. 185.

52 D. N. J. MacCulloch, 'Power, Privilege and the County Community: County Politics in Elizabethan Suffolk' (Cambridge Univ. unpub. Ph.D. thesis, 1977), p. 64.

53 Dawson, *History of Lay Judges*, p. 224.

54 Webb and Webb, *The Manor and the Borough*, pp. 13–25. J. Kitchin, *Le Covrt Leet et Covrt Baron...* (1581). C. Calthrope, *The Relation betweene the Lord of a Mannor and the Coppyholder his tenant* (1635).

55 Kitchin, *Covrt Leet*, p. 41.

56 E. W. Ives, *The Common Lawyers of Pre-Reformation England* (Cambridge, 1983), pp. 14, 93–100. Dawson, *History of Lay Judges*, pp. 224–5. C. Rawcliffe, *The Staffords, Earls of Stafford and Dukes of Buckingham, 1394–1521* (Cambridge, 1978), p. 56 and ch. 8.

57 The discussion which follows is based on a detailed study of manorial court records for Devonshire, Hertfordshire, and Warwickshire.

58 R. Bearman, *The Gregories of Stivichall in the Sixteenth Century* (Coventry and War. History Pamphlets, no. 8, Coventry, 1972), pp. 19–26.

59 SBT DR 5/2287, 1393, 2671; DR 18; DR 33/59–60; DR 282/3. Green was admitted Middle Temple, 1593; Bencher and Reader, 1621; Treasurer, 1629. James Morley, cursitor in Chancery for Suffolk in 1618, is probably the James Morley who kept courts at Albury and Standon in Hertfordshire. HCRO D/EAp/M6, 65814.

60 For example, Henry Darnell and William Cocke, of Hertfordshire and of Gray's Inn and the Middle Temple respectively. HCRO D/EG/M3 and 65787.

61 For complete references see C. W. Brooks, 'Some Aspects of Attorneys in England during the Late Sixteenth and Early Seventeenth Centuries' (Oxford Univ. unpub. D.Phil. thesis, 1978), p. 170, n. 4.

62 See, for a good example, C. J. Harrison, 'The Social and Economic History of Cannock and Rugeley, 1546–1597' (Keele Univ. unpub. Ph.D. thesis, 1974), p. 120.

63 SBT DR 5/2120, 2197, 2270, 2396, 2382, 2104. DR 18/229, 265. PRO PROB 11/95 (6 Wallopp).

64 SBT DR 17, Alveston and Tiddington. DR 18, Ratley. Kemp, ed., *The Black Book of Warwick*, pp. 295–6. PRO PROB 11/77.

65 PRO E 215/1455, 1474, 1507. Bodl., MS Tanner 287, fol. 102.

66 John Hooker of Exeter described a mid-sixteenth-century mayor of the town as a court holder who had 'good understanding' of the laws of the realm. W. J. Harte, *Gleanings from the Common Place Book of John Hooker, Relating to the City of Exeter 1484–1590* (Exeter, 1920), p. 20. See also E. W. Ives, 'The Common Lawyers in Pre-Reformation England', *Trans. Royal Historical Soc.*, 5th ser., 18 (1968), 148.

67 M. Weinbaum, *British Borough Charters 1307–1606* (Cambridge, 1943), pp. xxiii–xxiv.

68 In many towns the value of this limit was raised in successive charters granted during the late sixteenth and early seventeenth centuries. In some places it was quite high. The Jacobean charter of Tiverton (1616) set a jurisdictional limit of £100. The early-seventeenth-century borough court at Southmolton could entertain cases worth up to £50. W. Barnard Faraday, 'The Recorders of Totnes, and the Courts Civil and Criminal of the Unreformed Borough', *Trans. Devon Assoc.*, 56 (1925), 234.

69 M. Bateson, ed., *Borough Customs* (2 vols., Selden Soc., xviii and xxi, 1904–6), xxi, pp. 10–15.

70 R. Clutterbuck, *History and Antiquities of the County of Hertford* (3 vols., 1815–27), i, Appendix, pp. 23–4.

71 J. M. Guilding, ed., *Reading Records* (4 vols., 1892–6), i, p. 421; ii, pp. 19, 77, 169, 217, 440, 346, 459. Ferguson and Nanson, eds., *Records of Carlisle*, pp. 50, 74. J. Noake, *Worcester in Olden Times* (1849), pp. 124–5. A. J. King and B. H. Watts. *The Municipal Records of Bath, 1189–1604* (1885), p. 44. W. H. Richardson, ed., *The Annalls of Ipswiche: The Lawes, Customes and Governm[ent] of the Same: Collected out of ye Records, Books and Writings of that Towne by Nathanial Bacon Esq. AD 1654* (Ipswich, 1880), pp. 369, 426, 524.

72 Cooper, *Annals of Cambridge*, ii, p. 341; iii, pp. 41, 214.

73 Guilding, ed., *Reading Records*, i, p. 446; ii, pp. 19–20, 459.

74 M. V. Jones, 'The Political History of the Parliamentary Boroughs of Kent, 1642–1660' (London Univ. unpub. Ph.D. thesis, 1967), p. 336.

75 Richardson, ed., *Annalls of Ipswiche*, pp. 369, 524. Cambridge had a similar rule. Cooper, *Annals of Cambridge*, iii, p. 44.

76 PRO E 215/1071, 1454. Another example in Devonshire was the Dartmouth town court. E 215/1431.

77 PRO E 215/1434.
78 Amongst his other activities, Tickett was also an undersheriff of Devon. PRO E 215/1329. These kinds of practitioners do not appear in the Western Circuit *postea* files. PRO ASZ 24/29–30. Trosse was allowed £300 in his father's will. PRO PROB 11/132 (93 Meade).
79 PRO E 215/1423, 1460.
80 See above, pp. 113–14.
81 B. P. Levack, 'The English Civilians, 1500–1750', in W. R. Prest, ed., *Lawyers in Early Modern Europe and America* (1981), p. 112, estimates that there were more than 200 proctors practising throughout England and Wales at the beginning of the seventeenth century. See R. A. Houlbrooke, 'Church Courts and People in the Diocese of Norwich, 1519–1570' (Oxford Univ. unpub. D.Phil. thesis, 1970), pp. 107–15, for insights on the career structure and local activities of the proctors.
82 PRO E 215/1329, fols. 4v, 16, 19. Another common law attorney, Richard Denton, was registrar for the archdeaconry of Coventry. Lichfield Joint Rec. Office, will of Richard Denton, 1593. Edward Harfell, a notary public of Winchester, practised in King's Bench, Common Pleas, Chancery, the Winchester town court, and the bishop's consistory court. A. B. Rosen, 'Economic and Social Aspects of the History of Winchester, 1520–1670' (Oxford Univ. unpub. D.Phil. thesis, 1975), p. 302.
83 W. Holloway, *The History and Antiquities of the Ancient Town and Port of Rye* (1875), pp. 550–1. Lancelot Thorpe, a proctor and official in the bishop's court, was a town clerk of Winchester in the early seventeenth century. Rosen, 'Winchester', pp. 109–10.
84 Bodl. MS Rawlinson, D. 51, transcripts of Scriveners' Company papers made in 1695, fols. 24–9v.
85 *Ibid.*, fol. 15. William Pierson, who was master of the company in 1558 and 1559, is probably the man of that name who had one of the largest practices in the Common Pleas in 1560.
86 D. M. Palliser, 'Some Aspects of the Social and Economic History of York in the Sixteenth Century' (Oxford Univ. unpub. D.Phil. thesis, 1968), p. 324. T. F. Pound, 'The Social and Trade Structure of Norwich, 1525–71', *Past and Present*, 34 (1964), p. 66. Pound also found one court holder in 1525.
87 A scrivener's notebook from the late fourteenth and early fifteenth centuries shows that he drafted conveyances, made wills, and wrote out notes of small debts. A. E. B. Owen, 'A Scrivener's Notebook from Bury St. Edmunds', *Archives*, 14, no. 61 (1979), 16–23. The 'waste' books of two early-seventeenth-century London scriveners contain many bonds, covenants, indentures of bargain and sale, and letters of attorney. PRO WARDS 9/271, 351.
88 W. West, *The First Part of Symbolaeographia. Which May Be Termed the Art or Description or Image of Instruments... Or the Paterne of Praesidents. Or The Notarie or Scrivner* (1590). In the 1740s, there was a dispute between the scriveners of London and attorneys over

the scriveners' claim to a monopoly over conveyancing. E. Freshfield, ed., *The Records of the Society of Gentlemen Practisers* (1897), pp. xiii–lxv.

89 M. Blatcher, *The First Four Hundred: A History of the Firm of Thomson, Snell and Passmore, Solicitors, of Tunbridge, Kent* (1970), pp. 5–8.

90 PRO STAC 8/181/3.

91 *The Reports of Sir Peyton Ventris, Kt.* (1726), p. 11. The judges were uncertain what decision to deliver, and the case was adjourned and then dropped, or so it appears from the printed reports of the period.

92 Coke, *Fourth Institutes*, p. 265.

93 W. R. Prest, *The Inns of Court under Elizabeth I and the Early Stuarts 1590–1640* (1972), ch. VI.

94 L. Stone, *The Crisis of the Aristocracy 1558–1641* (Oxford, 1965), pp. 285–93. M. E. James, *Family, Lineage and Civil Society* (Oxford, 1974), pp. 26–31. E. W. Ives, 'Some Aspects of the Legal Profession in the Late Fifteenth and Early Sixteenth Centuries' (London Univ. unpub. Ph.D. thesis, 1955), pp. 5–9.

95 John Smith, *The Lives of the Berkeleys* (3 vols., Gloucester, 1883–5), ii, pp. 310–12.

96 For instance, two men who eventually became Common Pleas attorneys, John Rosyer of Barnstaple and Stephen Mason of Lincoln, learned their craft and worked in town courts for a number of years before going on to practise at Westminster. PRO E 215/1423, 1575/1–5.

97 C. W. Brooks, 'The Common Lawyers in England c. 1558–1642', in Prest, ed., *Lawyers in Early Modern Europe and America*, p. 43.

98 See references in n. 71 above.

99 See above, pp. 141–3.

100 Sheffield City Lib., Wharncliffe MSS, Wh.M.D. 01.

101 MacCulloch, 'Power, Privilege and the County Community', p. 126. For further examples see M. J. Ingram, 'Communities and Courts; Law and Disorder in Early Seventeenth-Century Wiltshire', in *Crime in England 1550–1800*, ed. J. S. Cockburn (1977), pp. 122–5.

4. THE INCREASE IN LITIGATION

1 F. W. Maitland, 'English Law and the Renaissance', in *Select Essays in Anglo-American Legal History by Various Authors* (3 vols., Boston, 1907), i, p. 195, was an early advocate of the statistical study of the plea rolls. W. S. Holdsworth, *A History of English Law*, 3rd edn (12 vols., 1945), iv, pp. 254–8, detected a take-off in common law business during the Elizabethan period. S. F. C. Milsom, *The Historical Foundations of the Common Law* (1969), p. 58, notes an increase in litigation in the late sixteenth century. For an earlier version of the analysis presented here see C. W. Brooks, 'Litigants and Attorneys in the King's Bench and Common Pleas, 1560–1640', *Legal Records and the Historian*, ed. J. H. Baker (1978), pp. 41–59.

2 Very few Star Chamber records survive for the reign of Charles I. The seventeenth-century history of the Council in the Marches has to be reconstructed from several different kinds of sources. P. Williams, 'The Activity of the Council in the Marches under the Early Stuarts', *Welsh History Review*, 1 (1962), 133–7. For the Council in the North see R. R. Reid, *The King's Council in the North* (1921), pp. 469–70.

3 Quoted in J. H. Baker, 'The Dark Age of English Legal History', *Legal History Studies 1972*, ed. D. Jenkins (Cardiff, 1975), p. 2.

4 Milsom, *Historical Foundations*, p. 45.

5 M. Blatcher, *The Court of King's Bench, 1450–1550: A Study in Self-Help* (1978), pp. 15–19, 165–71.

6 *Ibid.*

7 For the functions of the prothonotaries see M. Hastings, *The Court of Common Pleas in Fifteenth Century England* (Ithaca, N.Y., 1947), pp. 59ff; Blatcher, *The Court of King's Bench*, and her thesis 'The Workings of the Court of King's Bench in the Fifteenth Century' (London Univ. unpub. Ph.D. thesis, 1936); T. Powell, *The Attourneys Academy...* (1623).

8 J. H. Baker, *The Reports of Sir John Spelman* (Selden Soc., xciv, 1978), p. 101, says that 'it seems certain that [the docket rolls] were prepared solely as a means of calculating the fees owed by attorneys for making entries'. However true this may have been for the early Tudor period, it is clear that by the seventeenth century members of the profession used the docket rolls as a means of reference to the plea rolls. By that date the first membrane of the docket rolls for each court contained an alphabetical list of attorneys along with a membrane number which referred to the place in the docket rolls where their entries could be found. These entries in turn refer to membranes in the main series of plea rolls. *The Practick Part of the Law, Shewing the Office of a Complete Attorney* (1658 edn), pp. 29–30, advises practitioners that 'Having youre Declaration drawn, you must enter it upon some roll of the Court... either by your selfe or some Clark of the Office, who must see it put in the Docquet of that Office, and thereto put the number Roll....' PRO STAC 8/132/19 mentions a search made in a docket roll in order to find the membrane in the plea roll on which a writ had been entered. The docket rolls receive scant mention in the printed guides to the Public Record Office, and they are classified in the obscure Index series. A precedent for the use of the docket rolls to measure the volume of business in the King's Bench can be found in E. W. Ives, 'The Common Lawyers in Pre-Reformation England', *Trans. Royal Historical Soc.*, 5th ser., 18 (1968), pp. 165–7.

9 PRO IND 157–65.

10 See above, pp. 15–16 and Blatcher, *King's Bench*, chs. III, VII–VIII. Most docket roll entries refer to writs issued to call jurors or to failures of defendants to enter pleas or to instruct their legal advisors. One major class of entry which has to be excluded are those marked 'Anglia' which denote the enrolement of deeds. A study of the plea rolls indicates that relatively few of the cases which reached advanced

stages ever came to trial at *nisi prius,* and this is confirmed by comparing the approximate number of common law actions in advanced stages from the Western Circuit in 1606 with the number of *posteas* recorded for the Western Circuit in 1611. The total number of actions on the Western Circuit was probably in the region of 3575, but the number of *posteas* in 1611 was 721. See above, p. 64, and J. S. Cockburn, *A History of English Assizes 1558–1714* (Cambridge, 1972), p. 137.

11 Blatcher, *King's Bench,* Ch. II, Appendix. For an explanation of these fluctuations see above, pp. 79–84.

12 Ives, 'The Common Lawyers in Pre-Reformation England', p. 167.

13 See nn. *d* and *e,* Table 4.1. Each prothonotary of the Common Pleas kept his own docket roll. 1563 is the first year for which the rolls of all three offices survive.

14 Brit. Lib. Lansdowne MS 25, fols. 213–16.

15 *Lists of Early Chancery Proceedings Preserved in the Public Record Office, 1386–1558* (PRO *Lists and Indexes,* 10 vols., 1901–36).

16 W. J. Jones, *The Elizabethan Court of Chancery* (Oxford, 1967), p. 304 n. 1.

17 The barrister Timothy Tourner claimed that a Chancery clerk had told him that there were 8000 causes depending in the court in Hilary Term 1617. J. H. Baker, 'The Common Lawyers and the Chancery: 1616', *Irish Jurist* NS, 4 (1969), 386. L. A. Knafla, *Law and Politics in Jacobean England : The Tracts of Lord Chancellor Ellesmere* (Cambridge, 1977), pp. 158, 163, concludes from the order and decree books that the amount of business doubled between 1570 and 1595 and then increased by a further 25 per cent between 1603 and 1610. However, these counts may reflect an increase in procedural paperwork rather than of actual business.

18 C. P. Cooper, *An Account of the Most Important Public Records of Great Britain and the Publications of the Record Commissioners* (2 vols., 1832), i, p. 356, mentions an attempt by the record commissioners to ascertain the number of suits commenced during the periods when More, Bacon, and Nottingham were chancellors. They found that the number commenced under More was 500 p.a., which is a considerable underestimate but of the right order of magnitude. The total number for the reign of James I was put at 32,220.

19 Baker, 'The Common Lawyers and the Chancery', pp. 390–1. Knafla, *Law and Politics,* p. 180, notes that Coventry reduced the level of business to what it had been in the early years of James I. Figures very kindly supplied to me by Dr W. R. Prest, which were compiled from the decree and order books (PRO C 33), show 3454 cases entered in 1616 as against 2256 in 1638.

20 George Norburie, 'The Abuses and Remedies of Chancery', in F. Hargrave, ed., *A Collection of Tracts Relative to the Law of England, from Manuscripts* (1787), pp. 427–31, 433–7. G. W. Thomas, 'Archbishop John Williams: Politics and Prerogative Law 1621–1642' (Oxford Univ. unpub. D.Phil. thesis, 1974), pp. 26, 36–7.

21 J. A. Guy, *The Cardinal's Court: The Impact of Thomas Wolsey in Star Chamber* (Hassocks, 1977), pp. 15, 51.

22 T. G. Barnes, 'Star Chamber Litigants and their Counsel, 1596–1641', in *Legal Records and the Historian*, ed. Baker, p. 8. There was a total of 8228 actions between 1603 and 1625.

23 *Ibid.*, p. 28.

24 H. E. Bell, *An Introduction to the History and Records of the Court of Wards and Liveries* (Cambridge, 1953), ch. v. I. S. Leadam, ed., *Select Cases in the Court of Requests, A.D. 1497–1569* (Selden Soc., xii, 1898). W. B. J. Allsebrook, 'The Court of Requests in the Reign of Elizabeth' (London Univ. unpub. M.A. thesis, 1936), p. 134, counted 264 cases begun in 1597–8 as against 72 in 1561–2. Figures compiled by Prest show an increase in the number of entries in the decree and order books of both Wards and Requests. In the court of Wards the figures rise from 583 in 1616 to 862 in 1636. The increase in Requests from 183 in 1616 to 641 in 1636 is particularly striking even though these figures represent procedural stages in litigation rather than actual numbers of cases. Holdsworth, *History of English Law*, i, p. 415, quotes Nicholas Fuller's comment that in the 1620s the cause list of the court of Requests was as full as that of Chancery.

25 W. H. Bryson, *The Equity Side of the Exchequer* (Cambridge, 1975), pp. 16, 22. An inspection of the plea rolls of the common law side of Exchequer suggests that its business was not very great in volume. PRO E 13/254, 260, 261, 330, 435–8, 518, 573. A. K. Kiralfy, *The Action on the Case* (1951), p. 188, counted twelve cases on the Exchequer of Plea roll for Hilary Term 1563 and 149 on that for Trinity Term 1621.

26 W. J. Jones, 'Palatine Performance in the Seventeenth Century', in *The English Commonwealth 1574–1640*, ed., P. Clark, A. G. R. Smith, and N. Tyacke (Leicester, 1979), p. 192.

27 Reid, *Council in the North*, pp. 362–72.

28 Williams, 'The Activity of the Council in the Marches', pp. 133–60.

29 P. Williams, 'The Attack on the Council in the Marches, 1603–1642', *Trans. Hon. Soc. of Cymmrodorian*, 1961, 1–22.

30 R. Houlbrooke, *Church Courts and the People during the English Reformation, 1520–1570* (Oxford, 1979), pp. 273–4. See also R. A. Marchant, *The Church under the Law: Justice, Administration and Discipline in the Diocese of York 1560–1640* (Cambridge, 1969), p. 62.

31 Hastings, *Court of Common Pleas*, p. 110. Powell, *The Attourneys Academy*, p. 101. For more details see also C. W. Brooks, 'Some Aspects of Attorneys in England during the Late Sixteenth and Early Seventeenth Centuries' (Oxford Univ. unpub. D.Phil. thesis, 1978), pp. 271–3.

32 *The Practick Part of the Law* (1652 edn), pp. 5, 49. G. Jacob, *The Law Dictionary* (1729), 'Misnomer'.

33 G. E. Aylmer, *The King's Servants: The Civil Service of Charles I 1625–1642*, 2nd edn (1974), pp. 326–31.

34 For some estimates of merchant wealth see R. Grassby, 'The Personal Wealth of the Business Community in Seventeenth-Century England', *Economic History Review*, 2nd ser. 23 (1970), 231–2.

35 M. Campbell, *The English Yeoman* (New Haven, 1942), p. 217, although some yeomen could earn as much as £100 p.a. P. Bowden, 'Agricultural Prices, Farm Profits, and Rents', in J. Thirsk, ed., *The Agrarian History of England and Wales*, vol. iv (Cambridge, 1967), p. 657, estimates the income of the subsistence farmer at between £14 and £15 p.a.

36 The fictitious clothier Jack of Newbery was said to have employed 200 men. Thomas Deloney, 'The Pleasant Historie of John Winchcomb, in his Yonguer Yeares called Jack of Newbery', in *Shorter Novels*, vol. i: *Elizabethan and Jacobean* (Everyman, 1929), p. 24. A Jacobean Star Chamber case, PRO STAC 8/300/21, mentions a Devonshire weaver who employed his family and thirty other people.

37 L. Stone, 'Social Mobility in England, 1500–1700', *Past and Present*, 33 (1966), 23.

38 P. Clark and P. Slack, *English Towns in Transition 1500–1700* (Oxford, 1976), pp. 116–21.

39 *Ibid*, ch. 5.

40 J. Thirsk, 'The Farming Regions of England', in Thirsk, ed., *Agrarian History*, vol. iv, pp. 40–9.

41 B. Cozens-Hardy, 'Norfolk Lawyers', *Norfolk Archaeology*, 33 (1965), 267–97, quotes John Morden (1610), who wrote that the inhabitants of Norfolk 'are so skilled in the matter of the Law as many times even the baser sort at the plough-tail will argue *pro et contra* cases in Law, whose cunning and subtilitie hath replenished the shire with more lawyers than any shire whatsoever....' J. H. Baker, 'The Attorneys and Officers of the Common Law in 1480', *Journal of Legal History*, 1 (1980), 186.

42 Thirsk, 'The Farming Regions of England', pp. 71–5. R. S. Schofield, 'The Geographical Distribution of Wealth in England, 1334–1649', *Economic History Review*, 18 (1965), 504, 506.

43 This conclusion arises from attempts to trace the residences of practitioners in both courts in the years around 1606.

44 Clark and Slack, *English Towns*, ch. 5.

45 F. W. Maitland, *The Forms of Action at Common Law* (1969 edn). Milsom, *Historical Foundations*, Chs. 6, 7, 10–12.

46 *The Practick Part of the Law*, pp. 102–4.

47 John Smith, *The Lives of the Berkeleys* (3 vols., Gloucester, 1883–5), ii, pp. 246, 302–3.

48 Maitland, *Forms of Action*, pp. 53–5. Milsom, *Historical Foundations*, ch. 11.

49 Milsom, *Historical Foundations*, ch. 11. *The Practick Part of the Law*, p. 91. Sir A. Fitzherbert, *La Nouvell Natura Brevium* (1616 edn), pp. 92–6.

50 The best modern account of the development of *assumpsit* is Baker, *Reports of Spelman*, pp. 269ff.

51 Milsom, *Historical Foundations*, ch. 10.
52 Kiralfy, *The Action on the Case*, pp. 189–90. Cases of debt on written obligation in the rolls of warrants of attorney can be identified by the inclusion in individual warrants of the 'alias dictus' clause in which the defendant to such an action was styled exactly as he was in the obligation itself. *The Practick Part of the Law*, p. 12. In 1606 some 87 per cent of the warrants filed in the Common Pleas contained this clause. PRO CP 40/1735.
53 A. W. B. Simpson, 'The Penal Bond with Conditional Defeasance', *Law Quarterly Review*, 82 (1966), 392–422. Milsom, *Historical Foundations*, pp. 216–17. As Milsom points out, the exact terms of the conditions of bonds are entered verbatim in the plea rolls and therefore constitute a potentially rich source for social and economic historians. *The Practick Part of the Law*, p. 5. In some cases lenders of money demanded that their debtors sign a bond and confess judgment to a collusive action of debt as an extra guarantee for their loan. For an amusing example of the practice see PRO STAC 8/169/2. Collusive actions of debt of this kind are impossible to identify in the rolls of warrants of attorney, but it is likely that they appear in the docket rolls of the King's Bench as cases in which the defendant confesses or acknowledges the action. The number of such actions in the King's Bench was not insignificant. For an example see PRO IND 1356, Trinity Term, 4 James I, *William Webb* v. *Reginald Tenche*. KB 27/1397, m. 83.
54 PRO CP 40/1195, m. 640, Trinity Term, 1560. See also mm. 643, 664.
55 D. Sutherland, *The Assize of Novel Disseisin* (Oxford, 1973), ch. v.
56 On the other hand, actions of *assumpsit* did in a small number of cases involve sales of land or leases. Kiralfy, *The Action on the Case*, pp. 190–3.
57 Blatcher, *King's Bench*, ch. VII.
58 Kiralfy, *The Action on the Case*, pp. 189–90.
59 W. Sheppard, *The Faithful Councellor; or the Marrow of the Law in English* (1653), p. 280.
60 By movement of business into tribunals such as Star Chamber and Chancery, but this was more likely a feature of the early than the later sixteenth century. See above, pp. 85–90.
61 Guy, *The Cardinal's Court*, pp. 14, 52.
62 Barnes, 'Star Chamber Litigants', pp. 10–22.
63 Holdsworth, *History of English Law*, v, p. 279. T. F. T. Plucknett and J. L. Barton, eds., *St. German's Doctor and Student* (Selden Soc., xci, 1974), pp. 78–9, 97, 103. See also Metzger, 'The Last Phase of the Medieval Chancery', pp. 79–89.
64 Jones, *Chancery*, pp. 418–27, 455–61, 469.
65 *Ibid.*, pp. 425–37. Jones notes that the Chancery jurisdiction which called for the greatest number of injunctions to stay actions or executions in other courts was that which concerned relief in respect of penalties and forfeitures. Simpson, 'The Penal Bond with Con-

ditional Defeasance', pp. 415–21. E. G. Henderson, 'Relief from Bonds in the English Chancery: Mid-Sixteenth Century', *American Journal of Legal History*, 18 (1974), 298–306.

66 For details on costs, see above, pp. 101–5.

67 Bell, *Wards*, pp. 104, 112–13. Leadam, ed., *Court of Requests*, pp. x ff. L. M. Hill, ed., *The Ancient State, Authorities and Proceedings of the Court of Requests, By Sir Julius Caesar* (Cambridge, 1975), pp. xxix–xxxiv, 9.

68 Bryson, *Exchequer*, pp. 10–18.

69 G. T. Lapsley, *The County Palatine of Durham: A Study in Constitutional History* (Cambridge, Mass., 1900), pp. 189–215. Jones, 'Palatine Performance', pp. 189, 196. W. J. Jones, 'The Exchequer of Chester in the Last Years of Elizabeth', in *Tudor Men and Institutions*, ed. A. J. Slavin (Baton Rouge, La., 1972), pp. 124–70. R. Somerville, 'The Palatinate Courts in Lancashire', in *Law-Making and Law-Makers in British History*, ed. Harding, pp. 54–63.

70 P. Williams, *The Council in the Marches of Wales under Elizabeth I* (Cardiff, 1958), p. 27 and ch. II. Williams, 'The Attack on the Council in the Marches', pp. 4–5, 15–16. Reid, *Council in the North*, pp. 343–62.

71 Reid, *Council in the North*, pp. 298–9, 362–3. Williams, 'The Activity of the Council in the Marches', pp. 140–2.

72 The main limitation on the borough court was the ineffectiveness of its writ outside the town precincts. However, outsiders could sue townsmen in the town courts. M. Bateson, ed., *Borough Customs* (2 vols., Selden Soc., xviii and xxi, 1904–6), xviii, pp. 127. In Carlisle, for example, it was held that 'foroners or outmen can sue in the court if they take out surties w[i]thin the liberties'. R. S. Ferguson and W. Nanson, eds., *Some Municipal Records of the City of Carlisle* (Cumb. and Westmor. Antiquarian and Archaeological Soc., extra ser., vol. iv, Carlisle, 1887), p. 75.

73 For further details and some examples see above pp. 98–9.

74 J. H. Baker, *An Introduction to English Legal History*, 2nd edn (1979), p. 22.

75 J. P. Dawson, *A History of Lay Judges* (Cambridge, Mass., 1960), p. 236. Milsom, *Historical Foundations*, p. 60. Kiralfy, *The Action on the Case*, pp. 230ff.

76 There is obviously a need for fuller investigation of the nature of litigants and litigation in many central and local jurisdictions.

77 Reid, *Council in the North*, pp. 298, 363. Relief for the poor was also an aim of the Council in Wales. Williams, *Council in the Marches*, p. 27.

78 In town courts and manorial courts the lower jurisdictional limits were another factor which must have made them less useful to richer men.

79 Bell, *Wards*, p. 104. Kiralfy, *The Action on the Case*, p. 188. Williams, 'The Activity of the Council in the Marches', p. 141. Reid, *Council in the North*, p. 298. Dawson, *History of Lay Judges*, p. 229.

5. THE CAUSES OF THE INCREASE IN LITIGATION

1 For contemporary comments see above, pp. 132–4.
2 See above, pp. 79–83. Figures 5.1 and 5.2.
3 W. S. Holdsworth, *A History of English Law*, 3rd edn (12 vols., 1945), iv, p. 256. For one group of local courts which were important before 1300 see R. C. Palmer, *The County Courts of Medieval England* (Princeton, N.J., 1982).
4 J. S. Cockburn, *A History of English Assizes 1558–1714* (Cambridge, 1972), pp. 138–9. The number of civil cases tried on the Home Circuit declined from 411 in 1673 to 122 in 1713. On the Oxford Circuit there was a decline from 564 in 1661 to 334 in 1697.
5 G. Holmes, *Augustan England: Professions, State and Society, 1680–1730* (1982), p. 130.
6 R. Boote, *An Historical Treatise of an Action or Suit at Law*, 2nd edn (1781), pp. vi, x. M. Miles, '"Eminent Attorneys" – Some Aspects of West Riding Attorneyship, *c.* 1750–1800' (Birmingham Univ. unpub. Ph.D. thesis, 1982), pp. 337, 349.
7 *Parliamentary Papers: First Report of His Majesty's Commissioners (on the) Common Law* (1829), p. 11.
8 Population of England in 1606 is taken to be approximately 4 million. Population in the late 1820s was approximately 12.5 million. E. A. Wrigley and R. S. Schofield, *The Population History of England 1541–1871* (1982), pp. 208–9.
9 *Judicial Statistics Relating to the Judicial Committee of the Privy Council, the House of Lords, the Supreme Court of Judicature, the Crown Court, County Courts and other Civil Courts. For the Year 1975. Compiled by the Lord Chancellor's Department* (HMSO, 1976), pp. 31–2, 34. In 1975 only 4.5 per cent of the 1,815,461 actions commenced in county courts had judgments entered after trial before judges, registrars, or arbitrators. The remainder were by consent, or in default of appearance or defence.
10 Brit. Lib. MS Lansdowne 47, fol. 122, 'Mr Jones Plan to Farm the Seals for Original Writs'. Mr Jones calculated the number of originals as follows: 11 Eliz., 13,512; 14 Eliz., 25,484; 20 Eliz., 18,977; 26 Eliz., 26,321.
11 Early-nineteenth-century figures for bills in Chancery are given in *The Report from the Committee Appointed to Enquire into the Causes that Retard Decisions of Suits in the High Court of Chancery* (1811), p. 956.
12 *Parliamentary Papers* (1829), p. 11.
13 See above, p. 56.
14 *Parliamentary Papers: Second Part of the Appendix to the Fourth Report of the Common Law Commission. 1831–32* (1832), Appendix (I) V, 'Return of All Process Issued from Borough Courts, County Courts, Liberty Courts, Hundred Courts, Manor Courts and Courts of Requests between 12 February 1830 and 12 February 1831'.

15 W. H. D. Winder, 'The Courts of Requests', *Law Quarterly Review*, 52 (1936), 369–94. *Parliamentary Papers 1831–32*, Appendix (I) V. The courts of Requests handled some 202,750 of a total of 297,422 causes heard in local jurisdictions. The Birmingham court of Requests reported 7926 cases; that of Liverpool, 21,334, and that of London (Tower Hamlets), 28,624.

16 *Parliamentary Papers 1831–32*, Appendix (I) V. *Parliamentary Papers* (1829), p. 202, T. W. Snagge, 'Fifty Years of the English County Courts', *Nineteenth Century*, 42 (1895), 562.

17 Snagge, pp. 565–6, 575.

18 For the early twentieth century see the 'Comparative Table' in *Civil Judicial Statistics... for the Year* 1938 (1939), pp. 4–5. *Judicial Statistics 1975*, pp. 5, 34, 36.

19 Snagge, 'English County Courts', pp. 565–6. *Judicial Statistics 1975*, p. 36.

20 I plan in the near future to undertake a more extensive survey of rates of litigation between 1350 and 1980.

21 The number of cases commenced in the major courts is taken from Table 4.3 above. In the case of King's Bench, Common Pleas, Chancery, and the Council in Wales, the figures were doubled in an attempt to convert cases in advanced stages into cases commenced. Then, another 750 have been added to the total to account for the courts of Requests and Wards and the common law and equity sides of Exchequer. The total of all the above, plus 325 for Star Chamber, is 59,075. The numbers of decrees and orders in the chancery courts of the palatinates of Durham and Chester have been tripled in the hope that this might approximate the number of causes commenced and take account of business in their common law jurisdictions. This gives a total of about 1200 cases. Church court litigation must be included in any overall calculation, but is extremely difficult to estimate. Studies of the consistory courts in the dioceses of Norwich and York suggest that 250 cases p.a. might be a reasonable figure for the major diocesan courts. This produces a total for all England of about 5250 cases, but lesser church courts, such as those of archdeaconries, are left completely out of consideration. (R. Houlbrooke, *Church Courts and the People during the English Reformation, 1520–1570* (Oxford, 1979), pp. 273–4. R. A. Marchant, *The Church under the Law : Justice, Administration and Discipline in the Diocese of York 1560–1640* (Cambridge, 1969), p. 62.) The grand total of all the figures above is 65,525.

The most crucial variable in coming to any figure for total litigation is the number of local jurisdictions and the volume of business they entertained. J. P. Dawson, *A History of Lay Judges* (Cambridge, Mass., 1960), p. 213, calculated that there were some 400 manors in Warwickshire in the sixteenth century. L. Stone, *The Crisis of the Aristocracy 1558–1641* (Oxford, 1965), p. 746, found that in 1640 some 3000 manors were held by peerage families, who may be said to have owned roughly 20 per cent of the landed wealth of the nation. Both of these figures suggest that there may have been as many as 12–15,000 manors, say for the sake of argument 12,000, which can also be taken to include all borough, county, and hundred courts. The real difficulty comes in hitting on a reasonable estimate of the volume of litigation. Some manorial courts heard barely a case a year; some, several dozen.

Similarly, we have no guidelines for borough courts or for the very important London tribunals such as the Hustings court. For all of these reasons, I have guessed at a figure of 10 cases p.a. for all local tribunals. This produces a figure of 120,000 cases in local courts and a grand total of 185,525 in all jurisdictions.

22 In 1975, 140,064 divorce proceedings were filed. However, in 1975, as in the 1820s and the early modern period, the vast majority of cases on both the national and local levels had to do with debt collection relating to goods and services. *Judicial Statistics 1975*, pp. 32, 34, 36. Snagge, 'English County Courts', p. 562.

23 V. Aubert, 'Law as a Way of Resolving Conflicts: The Case of a Small Industrialized Society', *Law in Culture and Society*, ed. L. Nader (Chicago, 1969), pp. 282–303. B. Cartwright, M. Galanter, and R. Kidder, 'Introduction: Litigation and Dispute Processing', *Law and Society Review*, 9 (1) (1974) (no pagination). R. A. Kagan, Bliss Cartwright, L. M. Friedman, and S. Wheeler, 'The Business of State Supreme Courts', *Stanford Law Review*, 1977, 121–55.

24 See generally J. Hatcher, *Plague, Population and the English Economy 1348–1530* (1977).

25 The exact state of the fifteenth-century economy is a subject of continuing controversy. The two main starting points in the debate are M. Postan, 'The Fifteenth Century', *Economic History Review*, 9 (1939), 160–7, and A. R. Bridbury, *Economic Growth: England in the Later Middle Ages* (1962). Hatcher, *Plague, Population*, pp. 31, 35, 42, 47, presents a convincing synthesis.

26 Hatcher, pp. 63–5. D. C. Coleman, *The Economy of England 1450–1750* (Oxford, 1977), pp. 48–51.

27 Hatcher, *Plague, Population*, p. 65. I. Blanchard, 'Population Change, Enclosure and the Early Tudor Economy', *Economic History Review*, 2nd ser., 23 (1970), 427–45.

28 C. Phythian-Adams, *Desolation of a City: Coventry and the Urban Crisis of the Late Middles Ages* (Cambridge, 1979), pp. 34–9, 281, 283–7. See also R. B. Dobson, 'Urban Decline in Late Medieval England', *Trans. Royal Historical Soc.*, 5th ser., 25 (1977), 1–22, and D. M. Palliser, *Tudor York* (Oxford, 1979), pp. 51–3, 202–6.

29 M. Blatcher, *The Court of King's Bench 1450–1550: A Study in Self-Help* (1978), pp. 23–4.

30 *Ibid.* Blatcher acknowledged the possible significance of plague in 1517 but did not pursue its importance for the 1520s.

31 *Letters and Papers, Foreign and Domestic, of the Reign of Henry VIII*, vol. ii, ed. J. S. Brewer (2 pts, 1864), pp. 1214, 1247, 1331. *Hall's*

Chronicle ; Containing the History of England during the Reign of Henry the Fourth and the Succeeding Monarchs, ed. H. Ellis (1809), p. 592.

32 PRO E 101/222/13. E 101/222/13/10. *Hall's Chronicle*, p. 592.

33 *Letters and Papers, Foreign and Domestic, of the Reign of Henry VIII*, vol. iii, ed. J. S. Brewer (2 pts, 1867), p. 348.

34 *Hall's Chronicle*, p. 632. *Letters and Papers*, vol. iii, p. 1581. The returns for Michaelmas Term amounted to £9 13s 4d. PRO E 101/220/20.

35 *Hall's Chronicle*, p. 656.

36 *Ibid.*, p. 700. *Letters and Papers, Foreign and Domestic, of the Reign of Henry VIII*, vol. iv, ed. J. S. Brewer (4 pts, 1870), pp. 540, 574, 580–1, 585. It is also worth noticing that there were extremely sharp drops in admissions to the inns of court during the 1510s and early 1520s. W. R. Prest, *The Inns of Court under Elizabeth and the Early Stuarts 1590–1640* (1972), pp. 5–6.

37 *Hall's Chronicle*, p. 707. There are no accounts for incomes from the seals for this term, but the plea roll, PRO CP 40/1048[b], is about one-sixth of the usual size of rolls for this period.

38 *Hall's Chronicle*, pp. 719, 745. There are no accounts for seal income, but evidently the courts were again closed early in June 1528 because of another bout of plague. *Letters and Papers*, vol. iv, p. 1927.

39 The idea that all was not well with the common law in the early sixteenth century was first floated by F. W. Maitland, 'English Law and the Renaissance', in *Select Essays in Anglo-American Legal History by Various Authors* (3 vols., Boston, 1907), i, pp. 185–95, although he noted that a thorough statistical analysis of Tudor judicial records was necessary before various scraps of literary evidence were accepted at face value. Holdsworth, *History of English Law*, iv, pp. 254–8, made a preliminary stab at producing statistics by measuring the size of the plea rolls and came to the conclusion that 'though there was a decline in the business of the common law courts in Henry VIII's reign, owing doubtless to the activities of rival courts and councils, they still had a good deal of business left'. After counting the early Tudor docket roll entries for the King's Bench, E. W. Ives, 'The Common Lawyers in Pre-Reformation England', *Trans. Royal Historical Soc.*, 5th ser., 18 (1968), p. 170, concludes that there was a 'crisis of litigation or jurisdiction betwen Chancery and common law'. Blatcher, *King's Bench*, esp. pp. 20ff, contains the strongest case against the effectiveness of the common law, and her interpretation has been followed by J. A. Guy, *The Public Career of Sir Thomas More* (1980), pp. 38–49. J. H. Baker, *The Reports of Sir John Spelman* (Selden Soc., xciv, 1978), does not confront directly the problem of a decline in business and prefers to emphasize the early Tudor period as one of rejuvenation of the common law (pp. 23, 28).

40 Guy, *Public Career*, p. 48.

41 Blatcher, *King's Bench*, pp. 23–6, 64–77, and ch. v.

42 *Ibid.*, chs. VII and VIII. Guy, *Public Career*, p. 49. This picture of decline followed by reform has recently been summarized in

G. R. Elton, *The Tudor Constitution*, 2nd edn (Cambridge, 1982), p. 149. See also his *English Law in the Sixteenth Century: Reform in an Age of Change* (Selden Soc. Lecture, 1979), and, for a more sophisticated version, E. W. Ives, *The Common Lawyers of Pre-Reformation England* (Cambridge, 1983), ch. 9.

43 N. Pronay, 'The Chancellor, the Chancery, and the Council at the End of the Fifteenth Century', in *British Government and Administration*, ed. H. Hearder and H. R. Lyon (Cardiff, 1974), p. 89. See also Table 4.2 above.

44 J. M. W. Bean, *The Decline of English Feudalism* (Manchester, 1968), ch. III. M. E. Avery, 'Proceedings in the Court of Chancery up to *c.* 1460' (London Univ. unpub. M.A. thesis, 1958), p. 37. Baker, *Reports of Spelman*, pp. 193–9. F. Metzger, 'The Last Phase of the Medieval Chancery', in *Law-Making and Law-Makers in British History*, ed. A. Harding (1980), pp. 84–5.

45 C. M. Gray, *Copyhold, Equity and the Common Law* (1963), pp. 15, 65–6, 92. The number of such cases was never large. A. Savine, 'Copyhold Cases in the Early Chancery Proceedings', *English Historical Review*, 17 (1902), p. 298, discovered eleven cases mentioning copyhold in the fifteenth century. F. Metzger, 'Das Englische Kanzleigericht unter Kardinal Wolsey 1515–1529' (Friedrich-Alexander Universität, Erlangen, unpub. Ph.D. thesis, 1976), p. 152, estimates that there were sixty copyhold cases during the reign of Henry VIII.

46 In general the best guide to the early Tudor Chancery jurisdiction is T. F. T. Plucknett and J. L. Barton, eds., *St. German's Doctor and Student* (Selden Soc., xci, 1974). See also Metzger, 'Das Englische Kanzleigericht', ch. III.

47 Claims of detention were involved in approximately 41 per cent of the Chancery cases heard by Wolsey. Metzger, 'Das Englische Kanzleigericht', p. 333.

48 I. S. Leadam and J. F. Baldwin, *Select Cases before the King's Council 1243–1482* (Selden Soc., xxxv, 1918), pp. xvi–xxxii. Avery, 'Proceedings in Chancery', pp. 12–26.

49 Pronay, 'The Chancellor, the Chancery, and the Council', pp. 92–6. Of 202 cases in a bundle of proceedings from 1474–83, 30 derive from one or the other party being an alien and the transaction having taken place abroad.

50 In Wolsey's time, 28 per cent of Chancery cases referred to debts, bonds, and similar obligations. Metzger, 'The Last Phase', p. 84. It also appears that many cases involving debts were transferred to Chancery from local courts. Metzger, 'Das Englische Kanzleigericht', pp. 173–5.

51 *Ibid.*, pp. 149, 333. Sixty-seven per cent of Chancery suits under Wolsey involved land, and of these about 60–70 per cent concerned the use.

52 See above, p. 51.

53 Blatcher, *King's Bench*, pp. 168–9.

54 Guy, *Public Career*, p. 38, and in particular his *The Cardinal's Court : The Impact of Thomas Wolsey in Star Chamber* (Hassocks, 1977), ch. 2.

55 See Archbishop Wareham's address before parliament in 1510. John Lord Campbell, *The Lives of the Lord Chancellors* (17 vols., 1845), i, p. 427.

56 Baker, *Reports of Spelman*, pp. 77–80. Guy, *Cardinal's Court*, pp. 33–9.

57 Guy, *Cardinal's Court*, pp. 15, 51.

58 Metzger, 'Das Englische Kanzleigericht', ch. III. Guy, *Public Career*, p. 38. I have followed the figures of Metzger and Guy, although Pronay, 'The Chancellor, the Chancery, and the Council', p. 89, gives the slightly different figures of 571 cases p.a. during 1485–1500, 605 p.a. during 1500–15, and 770 cases p.a. under Wolsey. Statistics in Ives, 'The Common Lawyers in Pre-Reformation England', p. 166, agree with those of Metzger and Guy. In any case, it is clear that the most important stage in the growth of Chancery business occurred in the fifteenth century. It is impossible to break down the number of petitions received by each chancellor into figures which reflect annual fluctuations.

59 Ives, 'The Common Lawyers', p. 167.

60 *Pace* Guy, *Public Career*, p. 39, who argues that this is precisely what did happen.

61 Metzger, 'The Last Phase', p. 83.

62 Baker, *Reports of Spelman*, pp. 77–9. The classic, if excessively conservative, critique of Chancery in the 1520s is 'A Replication of a Serjaunt at the Lawes of England, to Certayne Points Alleaged by a Student of the Said Lawes of England' printed in F. Hargrave, ed., *A Collection of Tracts Relative to the Laws of England from Manuscripts* (1787).

63 Blatcher, *King's Bench*, ch. VII.

64 F. W. Maitland, *The Forms of Action at Common Law* (Cambridge, 1936 edn), pp. 55–8.

65 The most comprehensive statement of this view is Baker, *Reports of Spelman*, pp. 23, 53–5, 86–8, 253–97. See also his *An Introduction to English Legal History*, 2nd edn (1979), pp. 38–46, 282–6.

66 Baker, *Introduction*, pp. 38–46, 282–6, and see above, pp. 126–9.

67 A. K. Kiralfy, *The Action on the Case* (1951), p. 187 and Appendix A, 'Analyses of Actions on the Case on the Plea Rolls of the 16th and 17th Centuries'. See above, p. 69. Even in King's Bench, the frequency of actions on the case (not all of which were for *assumpsit*) declined from 19 per cent in 1560 to 13 per cent in 1640.

68 Blatcher, *King's Bench*, pp. 133–7, acknowledges this point.

69 See above, pp. 51, 103.

70 Gray, *Copyhold, Equity and the Common Law*, pp. 16–92.

71 Ejectment never accounted for more than 8 per cent of the business of either bench in the period 1560–1640. See above, p. 69.

72 Baker, *Reports of Spelman*, pp. 192ff.
73 S. F. C. Milsom, *The Historical Foundations of the Common Law* (1969), p. 182.
74 Sir Matthew Hale, *The History of the Common Law*, ed. C. M. Gray (1971), pp. 112–13. F. Bacon, 'Reading on the Statute of Uses', *Works*, ed. J. Spedding *et al.* (14 vols., 1857–74), vii, pp. 395–6.
75 Guy, *Cardinal's Court*, p. 58.
76 A. J. Slavin, 'The Fall of Lord Chancellor Wriothesley: A Study in the Politics of Conspiracy', *Albion*, 7 (1975), 265–87.
77 J. Bellamy, *Crime and the Public Order in England in the Later Middle Ages* (1973), pp. 2–23.
78 Stone, *Crisis of the Aristocracy*, ch. 5.
79 P. Williams, *The Tudor Regime* (Oxford, 1979), pp. 238–41.
80 F. Caspari, *Humanism and the Social Order in Tudor England* (Chicago, 1954), pp. 1–17, 76. F. L. Baumer, *The Early Tudor Theory of Kingship*, 2nd edn (New York, 1966), pp. 85ff.
81 Stone, *Crisis of the Aristocracy*, pp. 240–2. Williams, *Tudor Regime*, p. 241. See also M. E. James, *English Politics and the Concept of Honour 1485–1642* (Past and Present Supplement 3, 1978), and D. M. Loades, *Politics and the Nation 1450–1660* (1974), pp. 298–9.
82 Blatcher, *King's Bench*, pp. 64–77.
83 *Ibid.*, In the Common Pleas in 1827, 18,529 cases were commenced, 5259 appearances were made, 3844 declarations entered, and 1483 records of *nisi prius* returned. *Parliamentary Papers* (1829), Appendix 4, p. 150. See also n. 9 above.
84 R. L. Storey, *The End of the House of Lancaster* (1966), pp. 118–21. J. T. Rosenthal, 'Feuds and Private Peace-Making: A Fifteenth-Century Example', *Nottingham Medieval Studies*, 14 (1970), 84–90. E. Powell, 'Public Order and Law Enforcement in Shropshire and Staffordshire in the Early Fifteenth Century' (Oxford Univ. unpub. D.Phil. thesis, 1979), pp. 318–31, and 'Settlement of Disputes by Arbitration in Fifteenth-Century England', *Law and History Review* 2 (1) (1984), 21–43. I. Rowney, 'Arbitration in Gentry Disputes of the Later Middle Ages', *History*, 67 (1982), 367–76. Storey and Rosenthal associate arbitration with the breakdown of official justice, but, as Powell and Rowney point out, many arbitrations were connected with matters in litigation, were drawn up in the form of conditional bonds, and depended on the courts for their enforcement. Furthermore, arbitration was still an extremely popular method of conflict resolution in the early seventeenth century. J. P. Cooper, 'The Fall of the Stuart Monarchy', in *The Decline of Spain and the Thirty Years War 1609–48/59*, ed. J. P. Cooper (New Cambridge Modern History, iv, 1970), pp. 538–9. M. J. Ingram, 'Communities and Courts: Law and Disorder in Early Seventeenth-Century Wiltshire', in *Crime in England*, ed. J. S. Cockburn (1977), p. 125.
85 K. B. McFarlane, *England in the Fifteenth Century: Collected Essays* (1981), Introduction by G. L. Harriss, pp. xix–xxi.

86 C. Rawcliffe, *The Staffords, Earls of Stafford and Dukes of Buckingham* (Cambridge, 1978), ch. 8. N. Saul, *Knights and Esquires: The Gloucestershire Gentry in the Fourteenth Century* (Oxford, 1981), pp. 90–6, 194–6.

87 A. Herbert, 'Herefordshire 1413–61: Some Aspects of Society and Public Order', in *Patronage, the Crown and the Provinces in Later Medieval England*, ed. R. A. Griffiths (Gloucester, 1981), p. 112.

88 Blatcher, *King's Bench*, p. 87.

89 See above, p. 121.

90 J. P. Cooper, *Land, Men and Beliefs: Studies in Early Modern History* (1983), pp. 78–96.

91 PRO SP 46/15, fol. 266. For other examples see *CSPD 1611–1618*, p. 66, and *CSPD Addenda, 1580–1625*, p. 372.

92 Cockburn, *Assizes*, pp. 144–5. See also SP 12/107, item 96, for a contemporary lament about jurors, and the statute 27 Eliz. c. vi, which raised the property qualification of jurors from 40s. freehold to £4 yearly value of lands. Williams Hudson, 'A Treatise of the Court of Star Chamber', in *Collectanea Juridica: Consisting of Tracts Relative to the Law and Constitution of England*, ed. F. Hargrave (2 vols., 1792), ii, p. 92.

93 Leeds City Council Archive Department, Temple Newsam Collection TN 2/II/34. See above, p. 207.

94 See above, pp. 61–3.

95 A. W. B. Simpson, 'The Penal Bond with Conditional Defeasance', *Law Quarterly Review*, 82 (1966), 392–422.

96 G. Norburie, 'The Abuses and Remedies of Chancery', in Hargrave, ed., *A Collection*, p. 433.

97 Coleman, *Economy of England*, chs. 1–6.

98 R. B. Outhwaite, *Inflation in Tudor and Early Stuart England* (1969).

99 J. Thirsk, ed., *The Agrarian History of England and Wales*, vol. iv: *1500–1640* (Cambridge, 1967), p. 304.

100 *Ibid.* p. 303.

101 Coleman, *Economy of England*, chs. 4 and 5.

102 J. Thirsk, *Economic Policy and Projects: The Development of a Consumer Society in Early Modern England* (Oxford, 1978).

103 Sir John Davies, 'Discourse of the Common Law', *The Complete Works (Including Hitherto Unpublished MSS.) of Sir John Davies*, ed. A. B. Grosart (3 vols., 1869–76), p. 266. Sir E. Coke, *The Fourth Part of the Institutes of the Laws of England* (1648), p. 76.

104 For some particular examples see PRO CP 40/1384, 'Roll of Warrants', mm. 53, 67. KB 27/1397, mm. 83, 238.

105 Coleman, *Economy of England*, pp. 70–1.

106 Thomas Wilson, *A Discourse upon Usury*, ed. R. H. Tawney (1925), Introduction, pp. 19, 28, 36, 46–53, 87–8.

107 For the importance of the development of these facilities in the American context see Kagan, Cartwright, Friedman, and Wheeler, 'The Business of State Supreme Courts', p. 138.

108 Stone, *Crisis of the Aristocracy*, p. 138. B. A. Holderness, 'Credit in English Rural Society before the Nineteenth Century with Special Reference to the Period 1650–1720', *Agricultural History Review*, 24 (1976), 97–109. T. Powell, 'The Mistery and Misery of Lending and Borrowing', in *A Collection of Scarce and Valuable Tracts*, ed. W. Scott, 2nd edn (2 vols., 1812), ii, pp. 211–17. Also, see above, p. 196.

109 Wilson, *Discourse upon Usury*, pp. 89, 98. Brit. Lib. MS Cotton, Titus B, v, 'Gerard Malings discourse for reducing the Lawes into Order', fol. 420.

110 'Malings discourse', fols. 419–21.

111 Wilson, *Discourse*, p. 235.

112 See above, p. 66.

113 Dawson, *A History of Lay Judges*, p. 229, noticed a decline in the number of actions held before the court at Redgrave Manor in Cambridgeshire from forty in the decade 1558–67 to four in the decade 1603–12. The same general trend appears to have existed in the Warwickshire manors I studied. Although their own studies show that there was still a great deal of local variation, S. Webb and B. Webb, *English Local Government from the Revolution to the Municipal Corporations Act : The Manor and the Borough* (1924 edn), p. 31, conclude that by 1689 there was no place where the system of manorial courts was in its 'prime'.

114 The competition for places as attorneys in borough courts might be taken as some evidence of this. See above, p. 41. On the other hand, John Rosyer, the attorney of the town court at Barnstaple, reported to the commission on fees that he 'never kept Clarke nor servant to take money or to write vnder me for my imployment hath bene so little as that I did the same my selfe'. PRO E 215/1423. In general, there is a very great need for further research on the activities of these jurisdictions.

115 See above, p. 34.

116 One of the proposals offered in a set of anonymous law reforms put forward in 1576 was a plan to create commissions of arbitration to hear small cases arising in the same shire. PRO SP 12/107, item 96.

117 43 Eliz. caps. v and vi.

118 Hunt. Lib. El. MS 2847.

119 D. Veall, *The Popular Movement for Law Reform 1640–1660* (Oxford, 1970), ch. VIII. See also the measures recommended by the Hale Committee for creating county courts in 'Several Draughts of Acts heretofore prepared by Persons appointed to consider of the Inconvenience, Delay, Charge and Irregularity in the Proceedings of the Law. Printed by an Order of Parliament... 1653', in W. Scott, ed., *Somers Tracts* (13 vols., 1809–15), iv, p. 212.

120 Thirsk, ed., *Agrarian History*, pp. 649–73, 862–4.

121 Dawson, *Lay Judges*, p. 229. Northumb. Co. Rec. Office, Allendale MSS. P2, Hexham Court Baron, 1624.

122 By a statute of 1278.

123 See above, p. 41. It is said that the Devon borough of Bideford was famous in the reign of Charles I for an action in the mayor's court there for a million pounds. C. Worthy, 'Notes, Genealogical and Historical: Being a Second "Essay towards a History of Bideford"', *Trans. Devon Assoc.*, 16 (1884), 670.

124 Thirsk, ed., *Agrarian History*, pp. 93–6. B. Sharp, *In Contempt of All Authority: Rural Artisans and Riot in the West of England 1580–1661* (1980), chs. I and VII. C. Hill, 'Parliament and People in Seventeenth-Century England', *Past and Present*, 92 (1981), 102.

125 Thomas Ashton of Sheldon. George Averell of Solihull. Simon Blythe of Allesley. William Boothe of Witton. John Corbison of Church Bicknell. Thomas and Martin Holbeache of Meredin. Thomas Jackson of Solihull. George Palmer of Solihull. John Wicksteed of Bagington.

126 V. Skipp, *Crisis and Development: An Ecological Case Study of the Forest of Arden 1570–1674* (Cambridge, 1978). A. L. Hughes, 'Politics and Society and Civil War in Warwickhire, 1620–1650' (Liverpool Univ. unpub. Ph.D. thesis, 1979), pp. 12–17.

127 Thirsk, ed., *Agrarian History*, p. 308.

128 *Ibid.*, p. 340.

129 P. Clark and P. Slack, *English Towns in Transition 1500–1700* (Oxford, 1976), ch. 7.

130 Clark and Slack, *English Towns*, ch. 9.

131 Star Chamber cases provide some examples. PRO STAC 8/300/21, 8/206/21, 8/201/4, 8/233/20. See also PRO E 215/1329, fols. 20, 47, 92–3, for complaints by various citizens of Exeter against their town clerk, Samuel Isacke, and R. Carew, *A Survey of Cornwall* (1602), p. 86v, for a lengthy criticism of borough courts.

132 *Journals of the House of Commons, 1547–1714* (17 vols., 1742), i, p. 490.

133 See above, p. 97.

134 A point made by Boote, *An Historical Treatise of an Action or Suit at Law*, p. 47.

135 W. J. Jones, *The Elizabethan Court of Chancery* (Oxford, 1967), pp. 487–8.

136 F. J. C. Hearnshaw, *Leet Jurisdiction in England* (Southampton Record Soc., 1908), pp. 19–75. J. Kitchin, *Le Covrt Leet et Covrt Baron...* (1581), Preface.

137 Hale, *History of the Common Law*, p. 112.

138 L. A. Knafla, *Law and Politics in Jacobean England: The Tracts of Lord Chancellor Ellesmere* (Cambridge, 1977), p. 305.

139 See above, pp. 112–18.

140 Thomas Powell, *The Attornies Almanacke* (1627).

141 See, for example, Stone, *Crisis of the Aristocracy*, p. 242. C. Russell, *The Crisis of Parliaments: English History 1509–1660* (Oxford, 1971), p. 53. In fact there has never been any systematic study of legal costs in the early modern period.

142 See above, p. 147.

143 Court procedure is outlined in works such as T. Powell, *The Attour-neys Academy*...(1623).
144 *Ibid.*, p. 138.
145 *Ibid.*, p. 146.
146 These fees are calculated at the increased rates presented to the commissions on fees and acknowledged by Prothonotary Brownlow, PRO E 215/9/694.
147 Powell, *Academy*, p. 142. On the expense of counsellors' services see above, p. 192.
148 For King's Bench costs see PRO E 215/11/849. Powell, *Academy*, pp. 165–6, confirms that there was little difference between the cost of litigation in King's Bench and Common Pleas.
149 Powell, *Academy*, p. 138.
150 For the charges in King's Bench see PRO E 215/11/849.
151 Jones, *Chancery*, chs. IV, VII.
152 Powell, *Academy*, pp. 75–6.
153 *Ibid.* The standard fee was 10s., but bills of costs show both that larger fees were sometimes paid and that on occasion more than one counsellor was consulted.
154 Powell, *Academy*, pp. 75–6.
155 *Ibid.*, p. 76.
156 See above, p. 24.
157 Bills of costs suggests that 6s. 8d. was the usual fee.
158 Jones, *Chancery*, pp. 309–14. Norburie, 'The Abuses and Remedies of Chancery', p. 437, complained that the increased use of motions in his day made litigation both longer and more expensive.
159 W. R. Prest, 'Counsellors' Fees and Earnings in the Age of Sir Edward Coke', in *Legal Records and the Historian*, ed. J. H. Baker (1978), pp. 165–84. Holmes, *Augustan England*, pp. 130–2.
160 Roger North, *Autobiography*, ed. A. Jessopp (1887), p. 168.
161 Quoted by G. W. Thomas, 'Archbishop John Williams: Politics and Prerogative Law 1621–1642' (Oxford Univ. unpub. D.Phil. thesis, 1974), p. 37, from Williams' essay on reform in Chancery. Cambridge Univ. Lib. Gg 2/31.
162 D. D. Hopkins, 'Three Early Solicitor's Bills', *Notes and Queries*, 2nd ser., 12 (1861), p. 355, Michaelmas Term, 1564. Bill for returning a *postea* and entering a judgment after trial, 32s. 10d. Shelagh Bond, ed., *The Chamber Order Book of Worcester 1602–1650* (Worcs. Historical Soc., NS, viii, 1974), p. 134, £6 due as costs for suits on a bond in 1626. PRO KB 27/1397, m. 109. Gregory Mileham sues for £7 5s. due to him for legal fees. PRO SP 46/72, fols. 112, 122, 169. Legal costs of William Carensew, 1616–17. Termly bills from common law actions of from 12s. to 16s. per term. Essex Co. Rec. Office, D/D. B9. A19. Legal costs of Sir Francis Barrington in the first decade of the seventeenth century (a good series, which covers a number of cases). Fees for a term's work range from as little as 8s. 8d. to as much as £14 1s. 10d. for a term in which declarations were drawn and pleas entered (40s. of this went for counsellors' fees

and another 83s. for copies of the pleadings). I am very grateful to Dr W. R. Prest for lending me transcripts of the Barrington papers.

163 Durham Univ. Lib., Mickleton and Spearman MS 87. 'The Account Book of George Draper', MS in possession of Hawkins and Co., Portmill Lane, Hitchin. See also PRO E 101/526/20, which is apparently the account book of an Exchequer attorney, 15 James 1.

164 'Account Book of George Draper', fols. 7, 11, 8v, 15, 19.

165 *Ibid.*, fols. 4, 6v, 8, 33. Miscellaneous bills give the same impression. Bond, ed., *Worcester Chamber Order Book*, pp. 226–7. Nearly £94 laid out by the city for a Chancery suit concerning charitable uses. SBT DR 37/Box 83. Costs of £2 11s. for starting a Chancery suit. SBT DR 10/1826. £6. 13s. fees in Chancery for one term's work. Hunt. Lib. EL. MS 8004 (facsimile). Fees for one term's work filing a petition in Chancery come to £3 1s. 4d. On the other hand, some Chancery cases evidently got off the ground relatively cheaply. The Countess of Kent paid termly bills of costs over four terms in the late 1650s which ranged from 10s. to £1. Bedford Co. Rec. Office, L 24/414.

166 PRO WARDS 10/14.

167 The 'Rules and Orders' for the Common Pleas frequently remind attorneys that they should pay fees due to clerks of the court by the end of each term. See for example PRO E 215/756, fol. 2v. A document entitled 'An Account of What Warrantes are in each Clerkes Numberes since Pas. 31 Car. 2nd Regis, A°. Dom. 1679', PRO KB 139/120, shows clearly that some attorneys owed large debts to the clerk of the warrants.

168 Technically, an attorney who used his own money to pay for a client's case committed the offence of maintenance. However, when the issue arose in a Star Chamber case in 1607, the judges concluded that 'If a man wryte vnto an attornie to instructe or reteyne couselle, or take out proces for him, it is so Common *and* necessary for the poore of *the* Cuntrye that, albeit yt be an offence...this Cowrte will not sentence yt.' John Hawarde, *Les Reportes del Cases in Camera Stellata, 1593–1609*, ed. W. P. Baildon (1894), p. 331.

169 'Account Book of George Draper'. Also see above, p. 248.

170 See, for examples, PRO/215/1420 A and E 215/847.

171 See above, p. 140.

172 SBT DR 10/1934. 'Account Book of George Draper', loose sheet.

173 A. Fletcher, *A County Community in Peace and War: Sussex 1600–1660* (1975), pp. 54–5.

174 SBT DR 10/1859, legal expenses of Coventry in the 1550s. D. M. Livock, ed., 'Bristol City Chamberlain's Accounts in the Sixteenth and Seventeenth Centuries', *Bristol Record Soc.*, 24 (1966), p. 126. York City Archives, Chamberlain's Accounts. Bodl. MS All Souls' College, C. 291. I owe the last two of these references to Dr W. R. Prest.

175 Stone, *Crisis of the Aristocracy*, p. 485, mentions only one case of an already impoverished nobleman, Lord Cromwell, whose downfall was accelerated by long and costly lawsuits. See also Appendix XXIII for

the relative importance of legal costs in the annual expenditure of members of the aristocracy.

176 L. A. Clarkson, *The Pre-Industrial Economy in England* (1971), p. 222. For a list of wage assessments by justices of the peace in the early seventeenth century see R. H. Tawney *et al.*, *English Economic History: Select Documents* (1913), pp. 345–50.

177 See above, p. 146.

178 Snagge, 'Fifty Years of the English County Courts', p. 562. In the 1820s it was said that an attempt to recover £20 in the royal courts would require the expenditure of four times that amount.

179 M. Zander, *The State of Knowledge about the English Legal Profession* (1980), p. 24. *Legal Services and Lawyers: A Summary of the Report of the Royal Commission on Legal Services* (HMSO, 1979).

180 C. Wilson, *England's Apprenticeship 1603–1763* (1965), ch. 3. B. Supple, *Commercial Crisis and Change 1600–1640* (1959), chs. 1–6. Wrightson, *English Society*, pp. 142–5.

181 PRO IND 1361, 1363. Dr W. R. Prest informs me that the number of entries in the Chancery Decree and Order Books (PRO C 33) actually declines from 3454 in 1616 to 2256 in 1638.

182 Ingram, 'Communities and Courts', p. 118.

183 Saul, *Knights and Esquires*, pp. 186–94. Anthropologists have noticed similar tendencies in non-European societies. M. Gluckman, 'The Judicial Process among the Barotse of Northern Rhodesia', in *The Sociology of Law*, ed. V. Aubert (1969), p. 167.

184 Anthony Cade, *A Sermon of the Nature of Conscience which May Well Be Termed, A Tradgedy of Conscience... Preached before... Assizes at Leicester 1620* (1621), p. 16. Immanuel Bourne, *The Anatomie of Conscience... Preached at Darby Assizes, Lent 1623* (1623), Dedication. *Opinion Diefied: Discovering the Ingins, Traps, and Traynes that Are Set in this Age, Whereby to Catch Opinion by B[read] R[yce]; gent., Servant to the King* (1613), p. 21. 'The Essays of Sir Anthony Benn, Knt, Recorder of London', Bedford Co. Rec. Office, L28/46, fols. 17v–18.

185 'Memorialles for Iudicature. Pro Bono Publico' (*c.* 1609), in Knafla, *Law and Politics in Jacobean England*, p. 274.

186 F. Bacon, 'Maxims of the Law', *Works*, ed. Spedding, vii, pp. 315, 319.

187 This is a view advanced by T. G. Barnes, 'Star Chamber Litigants and their Counsel, 1596–1641', in *Legal Records and the Historian*, ed. Baker, p. 8.

188 *Ibid.*, p. 12.

189 J. P. Cooper, ed., *Wentworth Papers 1597–1628* (Royal Historical Soc., Camden 4th ser., vol. xii, 1973), pp. 17, 320–1. P. Q. Karkeck, 'Extracts from a Memorandum Book Belonging to Thomas Roberts and Family of Stockleigh Panery, 1621–1644', *Trans. Devon Assoc.*, 10 (1878), 315–29. J. A. Sharpe, 'Litigation and Human Relations in Early Modern England – Defamations... the Church Courts at York' (typescript paper, Past and Present Soc. Conference, 1980), 2–3.

190 P. F. Carter-Ruck, *Libel and Slander* (1972), pp. 39–41. See also J. A. Sharpe, *Defamation and Sexual Slander in Early Modern England : The Church Courts at York* (Borthwick Papers no. 58, 1981).

191 Ingram, 'Communities and Courts', pp. 119–20, reaches similar conclusions.

192 G. Mynshull, *Essays and Characters of a Prison and Prisoners* (1618), p. 9. Alexander Harris, *The Economy of the Fleete*, ed. A. Jessopp (Camden Soc., NS, xxv, 1879). William Fennor, 'The Counter's Commonwealth' in *The Elizabethan Underworld*, ed. A. V. Judges (1930), pp. 432ff.

193 William Shakespeare, *The Merchant of Venice*. John Day, *Law Tricks* (1608) (Malone Soc. Reprints, Oxford, 1949). Ben Jonson, *The Staple of the News* (1631). D.S., *The Honest Lawyer* (1616).

6. THE INCREASE IN LITIGATION AND THE LEGAL PROFESSION

1 W. R. Prest, *The Inns of Court under Elizabeth I and the Early Stuarts 1590–1640* (1972), pp. 7, 52–3.

2 W. R. Prest, 'The English Bar, 1550–1700', in Prest, ed., *Lawyers in Early Modern Europe and America* (1981), p. 67. Exact figures for calls to the bar and the number of active practitioners have been supplied to me by Dr Prest. They represent his most up-to-date counts.

3 In the 1620s the number of underclerks to the six clerks totalled 100, and some, possibly all, of these men had underclerks of their own. PRO E 215/498 and 632. Brit. Lib. Lansdowne MS 163, fols. 242–6. J. S. Wilson, 'The Administrative Work of the Lord Chancellor in the Early Seventeenth Century' (London Univ. unpub. Ph.D. thesis, 1927), p. 142. H. E. Bell, *An Introduction to the History and Records of the Court of Wards and Liveries* (Cambridge, 1953), p. 31. T. G. Barnes, 'Due Process and Slow Process in the Late Elizabethan – Early Stuart Star Chamber, Part II', *American Journal of Legal History*, 6 (1962), 341. In 1615, the four attorneys of Star Chamber had eight clerks each.

4 Hunt. Lib. EL. MS 1762.

5 For sources see above, p. 295 n. 61. H. A. C. Sturgess, ed., *Register of Admissions to the Honourable Society of the Middle Temple* (3 vols., 1949).

6 Darcies, the court of Edward Scroggs, and Waters, alias Mardock, the court of John Watts. HCRO 65946 and 10824.

7 This generalization should, of course, exclude Yorkshire, where there were always large numbers of practitioners. See above, pp. 33, 113.

8 See Table 4.1 above.

9 Prest, *Inns of Court*, p. 30.

10 For the social origins of practitioners see above, p. 243.

11 E. R. Foster, ed., *Proceedings in Parliament 1610* (2 vols., New Haven, 1966), ii, p. 405.

12 J. Kitchin, *Le Covrt Leet et Covrt Baron...* (1581), Preface.

13 Sir George Cooke, *Rules, Orders and Notices in the Court of King's Bench and Common Pleas* (1747), item 2, Michaelmas Term 1573.
14 See above, p. 142.
15 T. Clay, *A Chorologicall Discourse of the Well Ordering, Desposing and Gouerning an Honorable Estate...* (1619), pp. 2–4.
16 *Ibid.*, pp. 17–18.
17 PRO E 215/1069, 1071, 1072, 1423, 1434, 1454, 1460.
18 That is including amateur court holders and solicitors who had no connections with any court of law.
19 See C. W. Brooks, 'Some Aspects of Attorneys in England during the late Sixteenth and Early Seventeenth Centuries' (Oxford Univ. unpub. D.Phil. thesis. 1978), pp. 250–2, for a demonstration that the majority of the early-seventeenth-century King's Bench attorneys spent all of their working lives in the profession.
20 The form of the oath was certainly well known. Many copies of it survive in printed and manuscript manuals of practice. For example, Bodl. MS Rawlinson C. 65, 'Instructions for an Attorney', fol. 2v. Gloucs. Co. Rec. Office D 149/B1, p. 187, papers of John Clifford of Frampton.
21 Cooke, *Rules, Orders, passim*; and PRO E 163/16/17 for orders not given by Cooke.
22 Cooke, *Rules, Orders*, Common Pleas, 6 Eliz.
23 *Praxis Utriusque Banci : The Ancient and Modern Practice of the Two Superior Courts...* (1674), pp. 40–5.
24 *The Reports of Sir Edward Coke*, ed. J. H. Thomas (13 parts in 7 vols., 1826), vi, p. 263. G. O. Sayles, *Select Cases in the Court of King's Bench under Edward III*, vol. vi (Selden Soc., lxxxii, 1965), p. xxxix.
25 Bodl. MS Rawlinson, D. 1123, presentment of the attorney jurors for Common Pleas, 3 Charles I. PRO E 215/11/849, presentment of the jurors for King's Bench, 22 April 1630. Northants. Co. Rec. Office, Finch-Hatton MS 43, presentment of attorney-jurors for Common Pleas, 1623.
26 Bodl. MS Rawlinson D. 1123, fol. 30.
27 Sir C. Carr, *Pension Book of Clement's Inn* (Selden Soc., lxxviii, 1960), p. 222. H. Pugh, 'Origin and Progress of Barnard's Inn', *Notes and Queries*, 7th ser., 2 (1886), 301.
28 Ambrose Mudford invited all his 'brethren' in the King's Bench office to attend his funeral. For other examples see PRO PROB 11/229 (1649/259), 11/126 (83 Rudd), 11/77 (32 Sainberbe), 11/126 (96 Rudd).
29 PRO PROB 11/61 (21 Bakon).
30 PRO PROB 11/118 (86 Wood).
31 PRO PROB 11/48 (5 Crymes).
32 H. Ellis, ed., *The Obituary of Richard Smyth, Secondary of the Poultry Compter, London : Being a Catalogue of All Such Persons as he Knew in their Life : Extending from A.D. 1627 to A.D. 1674* (Camden Soc., os, xliv, 1849).
33 R. Hine, 'Records of the Firm of Hawkins and Co', MS in possession of Hawkins and Co., 7/8 Portmill Lane, Hitchin, p. 1.

34 For this and a number of other interesting legal epitaphs see B. Cozens-Hardy, 'Norfolk Lawyers', *Norfolk Archaeology*, 33 (1965), 266–79.

35 Brooks, 'Some Aspects of Attorneys', pp. 20–4, 28–30.

36 The phrase comes from G. E. Aylmer, 'Attempts at Administrative Reform, 1625–1640', *English Historical Review*, 72 (1957), 259.

37 See generally J. E. Neale, 'The Elizabethan Political Scene', *Proc. British Academy*, 34 (1948), 4–23.

38 5 & 6 Edw. VI c. xvi, 'An Acte againste buying and sellinge offices'. It specifically mentions officers of the courts of justice and clerkships in any court of record.

39 The classic treatment of this subject is G. E. Aylmer, *The King's Servants: The Civil Service of Charles I 1625–1642* (1961), pp. 225–39.

40 *Ibid.*, pp. 69–73, 96–106. W. J. Jones, *Politics and the Bench: The Judges and the Origins of the English Civil War* (1971), pp. 110–11. Hunt. Lib. EL. MSS 2964–8, papers relating to the controversy surrounding John Elphenstone's petition for an office for receiving and returning writs in Common Pleas. Historical Manuscripts Commission, *Hatfield House*, xix, p. 298, October 1607, petition of Sir Robert Carye craving the office for the sole making of *latitats* in King's Bench; xvii, p. 13, for the hostile response of Sir John Popham, CJKB, to an earlier proposal for the same office, 1605. *CSPD, 1603–1610*, pp. 10, 115, 188, 231, 335, 362, 366, 397, 422; *CSPD 1611–18*, pp. 14, 60, 78, 206, 284, 299, 415, 419, 431, 498, for various grants in the time of James I.

41 Aylmer, *King's Servants*, pp. 95–223.

42 Hunt. Lib. EL. MSS 2669–70, 2672–7, 2680, 2682, 2686, 2688.

43 Barnes, 'Due Process and Slow Process', p. 342.

44 Jones, *Chancery*, pp. 70ff, 136–43.

45 John Trye, *Jus Filizarii: or, the Filacer's Office in the Court of King's Bench* (1684), 'To the reader', p. 3. Bodl. MS Bankes 24, 24/2, memoranda concerning the abuses of Robert Henley, chief prothonotary of King's Bench, 1638.

46 *CSPD 1611–1618*, p. 75, September 1611.

47 Bodl. MS North b.1, fol. 145.

48 Aylmer, *King's Servants*, pp. 125–36, 213.

49 J. H. Baker, 'Sir Thomas Robinson (1618–83) Chief Prothonotary of the Common Pleas', *Bodleian Lib. Rec.*, 10 (1978), 27–40. PRO SP 12/224, fol. 154. Brownlow was an exigenter of C.P. in 1589. William Nelson, prothonotary at that date, acted as an attorney in 1560. Gulston and Waller were active in 1606. CP 40/1187, 1735.

50 Aylmer, *King's Servants*, p. 229. S. D. White, *Sir Edward Coke and 'The Grievances of the Commonwealth', 1621–1628* (Chapel Hill, N.C., 1979), p. 58.

51 PRO E 215/629; STAC 8/204/8.

52 PRO E 215/696/1–5.

53 PRO STAC 8/9/4. Oaths were administered to the underclerks of the six clerks in Chancery but not to the underclerks of the prothonotaries of the Common Pleas. See above, p. 17.

54 See above, p. 20.
55 *Praxis Utriusque Banci.* PRO E 215/756. It is certain that the prothonotaries made notes of the men who became attorneys. Their remembrance rolls usually contain lists of names of men sworn each term. See for example PRO CP 45/125, Hilary 45 Eliz., which records the admission of five attorneys. Elias Ashmole carefully kept the ticket from a prothonotary which verified that he had been sworn as an attorney in 1641. Bodl. MS Ashmole 1136, fol. 9v. The earliest known roll of attorneys dates from 1657. PRO IND 4603. However, although none are at present known to exist for earlier periods, the judges certainly thought that the clerk of the warrants kept one. PRO E 163/16/17, p. 16. In the mid-to-late Elizabethan period the cost of admission included the payment of 2s. to the judges, but by the 1620s this fee had risen to £1. In addition, the attorney owed 12d. to the clerk of the warrants for entering him and 4d. each term for keeping him on the roll. Bodl. MS Rawlinson C. 65, fol. 2v. Northants. Co. Rec. Office, Finch-Hatton MS 43.
56 PRO E 163/16/17, p. 21.
57 Lincoln's Inn Lib., MS Misc., 586, pp. 37–8. The agreement specified that no attorney should be admitted as an entering clerk unless he had been 'brought up' in a prothonotary's office. In addition, no clerk of an attorney was to be allowed to work in an office unless the attorney himself was a clerk to one of the prothonotaries. Finally, if there was a falling out between an attorney and one of the prothonotaries, then neither of the other two prothonotaries was to allow the attorney to do business in his office.
58 *Ibid.*, p. 38.
59 See above, p. 238.
60 PRO E 215/599.
61 Northants. Co. Rec. Office, Finch-Hatton MS 43.
62 Given their connections with the chief prothonotary, it is not surprising that the attorney-jurors of the King's Bench had no criticisms to make. PRO E 215/11/849.
63 Lincoln's Inn Lib., Misc. MS 586. Described as 'Robert Moyles' Practice of the Courts', this MS in fact contains notes on practice by several early-seventeenth-century prothonotaries, including Thomas Corey, John Gouldesborough, and Richard Brownlow. The essay on 'The Abuse of suing writs of trespass where *the* cause of accon is debt...', fols. 35–7, follows a copy of a court order against the abuse dated 1623 and refers to the volume of business in the court twelve or thirteen years previous. Handwriting and internal evidence in fols. 37–8 make Moyle the most likely author, but the attribution is uncertain. For a list of the seventeenth-century prothonotaries see Baker, 'Sir Thomas Robinson', pp. 39–40.
64 Lincoln's Inn Lib., Misc. MS 586.
65 *Ibid.*
66 *Ibid.*
67 *Ibid.*, p. 38. PRO STAC 8/9/4, *Hele* v. *Coke*, 1604.

68 Cooke, *Rules, Orders*, Hilary Term, 1626. Ellesmere, 'Memorialles for Iudicature. Pro Bono Publico', in L. A. Knafla, *Law and Politics in Jacobean England : The Tracts of Lord Chancellor Ellesmere* (Cambridge, 1977), p. 278.

69 T. Powell, *The Attourneys Academy...* (1623), p. 97. *The Practick Part of the Law, Shewing the Office of a Complete Attorney* (1658 edn), pp. 10, 77. Cooke, *Rules, Orders*, Michaelmas, 15 Eliz.; Michaelmas 1654.

70 D. Veall, *The Popular Movement for Law Reform 1640–1660* (Oxford, 1970), *passim*. M. Cotterell, 'Interregnum Law Reform: The Hale Commission of 1652', *English Historical Review*, 83 (1968), 689–92.

71 *Certaine Proposals of Divers Attorneys of the Court of Common Pleas, For the regulating the proceedings at Law, and remedying some inconveniences : whereby the Clyent will be much secured, the Process shortened, the greatest part of the charge of most Suits abated, many unnecessary Suits in Law and Equity prevented, and the Creditor and Purchaser well provided for : and thereby Lending, Trade and Commerce advanced : which is the end desire of the Proposers* (5, December 1650), 'Epistle' and p. 1.

72 *Ibid.*, 'Epistle'.

73 *Ibid.*

74 *Ibid.*, pp. 1, 3, 6, 8, 11, 12.

75 Cotterell, 'Interregnum Law Reform', pp. 701, 703. B. Worden, *The Rump Parliament* (Cambridge, 1977 edn), pp. 111–12.

76 Ellesmere, 'Memorialles for Iudicature', pp. 275–80. *Coke's Reports*, part iv, 'Epistle'. White, *Sir Edward Coke*, p. 50.

77 'Severall Draughts of Acts heretofore prepared by Persons appointed to consider of the Inconvenience, Delay, Charge, and Irregularity in the Proceedings of the Law. Printed by an Order of Parliament of the 12th of July 1653, for the Members of the House', in *Somers Tracts* (13 vols., 1809–15), vi, pp. 177ff. Cotterell, 'Interregnum Law Reform', p. 697.

78 R. Boote, *An Historical Treatise of an Action or Suit at Law*, 2nd edn (1781), p. 25. S. F. C. Milsom, *The Historical Foundations of the Common Law* (1969), pp. 57–8.

7. THE ATTITUDES OF LAYMEN AND ATTEMPTS AT REFORM

1 See, for example, J. S. Cockburn, *A History of English Assizes 1558–1714* (Cambridge, 1972), pp. 145–9, and M. Birks, *Gentlemen of the Law* (1960), pp. 87–90.

2 Sir John Fortescue, *De Laudibus Legum Angliae*, ed. S. B. Chrimes (Cambridge, 1942), p. 31. H. Finch, *Law or a Discourse Thereof in Foure Bookes* (1627), p. 1.

3 W. Fulbecke, *A Direction or Preparative to the Study of the Lawe* (1603), p. 2.

4 C. Brooks and K. Sharpe, 'History, English Law and the Renaissance: A Comment', *Past and Present*, 72 (1976), 138–9. T. Mun,

'Englands Treasure by Forraign Trade', in J. P. McCulloch, ed., *A Select Collection of Early English Tracts on Commerce* (Cambridge, 1970 edn), p. 179. For the views of Sir Edward Coke and Sir John Davies, see above, pp. 94–5.

5 PRO SP 12/107, item 96. R. Parsons, 'A Memorial of the Reformation in England', in *The Jesuit's Memorial*, ed. Edward Gee (1690), p. 244.

6 Sir John Davies, 'A Discourse of Law and Lawyers' (1615), *The Complete Works (Including Hitherto Unpublished MSS.) of Sir John Davies...*, ed. A. B. Grosart (3 vols., 1869–76), iii, 259.

7 Vexatious litigation was criticized on these grounds. See above, pp. 108–9. For interesting comments on 'neighbourliness' see K. Wrightson, *English Society 1580–1680* (1982), pp. 51–9.

8 S. A. H. Burne, ed., *The Staffordshire Quarter Sessions Rolls 1598–1602* (Staffs. Rec. Soc., iv, 1936), p. xx n. 1.

9 Hunt. Lib. EL. MS 1762.

10 Bodl. MS Ashmole 1159, fol. 78v.

11 R. Burton, *The Anatomy of Melancholy...* (2 vols., 1813 edn), ii, p. 86.

12 'Britannia Languens, or a Discourse of Trade' (1680), in McCulloch, ed., *A Select Collection*, pp. 302, 375.

13 See also, for example, John Day, *Law Tricks* (1608) (Malone Soc. Reprints, Oxford, 1949), sig. C3v:

> 'Lord what a broaking Advocate is this?
> He was some Squier's Scrivenor, and hath
> Scrapt
> Gentilitie out of Atturneys fees....'

and William Fennor 'The Counter's Commonwealth', in *The Elizabethan Underworld*, ed. A. V. Judges (1930), pp. 432ff. The most famous of the satires on lawyers was George Ruggle, *Ignoramus* (1630), which was first performed before James I at Cambridge University.

14 Sir Roger Wilbraham, 'Diary and Commonplace Books, 1593–1646', Folger Lib., Washington, D.C., microfilm of typescript copy of MS M. b. 42, p. 22. *The Lord Coke his Speeche and Charge* (1607), [sig. c. iv].

15 See above, pp. 201–3, for more on this.

16 Brit. Lib. Lansdowne MS 99, fol. 134, letter from Barlee to William, Lord Burghley, November 1578. W. Barlee, *A Concordance of All Written Lawes Concerning Lords of Mannours, theire Free Tenetes, and Copieholders* (Manorial Soc., 1911).

17 Barlee, *A Concordance*, p. 1.

18 [John Earle], *Micro-cosmographie; or, A Peece of the World Discovered* (1628), sig. C3v.

19 'The Essays of Sir Anthony Benn, Knt, Recorder of London', Bedford Co. Rec. Office, L28/46, fols. 18v–19v.

20 D. Veall, *The Popular Movement for Law Reform 1640–1660* (Oxford, 1970), *passim*.

21 'The Essays of Sir Anthony Benn', fol. 19.

22 *Aristotle's Politics and the Athenian Constitution*, ed. J. Warrington (1959), pp. 21 n. 3, 74.

23 E. W. Ives, 'The Reputation of the Common Lawyer in English Society, 1450–1550', *Univ. of Birmingham Historical Journal*, 7 (1959–60), 130–61.

24 See above, p. 256.

25 William West, *The First Part of Symbolaeographia. Which May Be Termed the Art or Description or Image of Instruments.... Or the Paterne of Praesidents. Or The Notarie or Scrivner* (1590), p. 352.

26 Sir George Cooke, *Rules, Orders and Notices in the Courts of King's Bench and Common Pleas* (1747). There are, for example, many more orders for the period 1550–1650 than for the years between 1650 and 1750. See also PRO E 163/16/17, 'Copies of Orders touching the practice of divers courts in the reigns of Elizabeth and James I', which includes a number of orders which are not printed by Cooke.

27 For a guide to the application of the law of slander to the attorneys see W. Sheppard, *Action upon the Case for Slander or a Methodical Collection...* (1662). PRO CP 40/2636, Mich. 1653, m. 1517. See also R. Brownlow and J. Goldesborough, *Reports of Divers Choice Cases in Law* (1651), p. 44: attorney put out of the roll for trying to influence a sheriff's selection of jurors. It is likely that a thorough search of the Prothonotaries' Remembrance Rolls (Common Pleas) would yield important evidence about the discipline of attorneys. PRO CP 45. E. H. Bodkin, *The Law of Maintenance and Champerty and the Lawful Financing of Actions by Solicitors, Legal Aid and Trade Protection Societies and Others* (1935), pp. 3–4, 7, 11–15, 39, 49–50.

28 W. Lambarde, *Archion or a Commentary upon the High Courts of Justice in England* (1635), p. 102. Lambarde thought that the Star Chamber jurisdiction over malpractice and abuses of justice was one of the most important justifications for its existence. John Hawarde, *Les Reportes del Cases in Camera Stellata, 1593–1609*, ed. W. P. Baildon (1894), pp. 61, 70, 89, 91, 230, 280, 302, 331, which includes an account of two attorneys being hurled over the bar of the court and restricted from practice for professional misconduct. Many Jacobean Star Chamber cases (PRO STAC 8) have provided evidence for this book. They have recently been made much more accessible by the publication of T. G. Barnes, ed., *List and Index to the Proceedings in Star Chamber for the Reign of James I, 1603–1625...* (3 vols., Chicago, 1975).

29 *CSPD 1581–1590*, p. 69.

30 Brit. Lib. Lansdowne MS 46, fol. 90.

31 Brit. Lib. Lansdowne MS 44, fol. 2, Francis Alford to Burghley on the reform of expenses of lawsuits, 9 November 1585.

32 Brit. Lib. Lansdowne MS 46, fol. 90.

33 S. D'Ewes, *The Journals of All the Parliaments during the Reign of Elizabeth*, rev. R. Bowes (1882), p. 437. William Monson and Heyward Townshend, *Megalopschy. A Particular and Exact Account of the Last XVII Years of Queen Elizabeth's Reign* (1682), part II, p. 17.

Neither of these accounts sheds any light on whatever discussion of the bill might have occurred in either the House of Commons or in committee.

34 The council was instrumental in provoking the expulsion of attorneys from the inns of court. H. H. Bellot, 'The Exclusion of Attorneys from the Inns of Court', *Law Quarterly Review*, 26 (1910), 138. Brit. Lib. MS Cotton Vesp. c. xix, vol. 2, fol. 15, 'The Some of the Commission for Reformation of Officers towardes bothe Lawes'.

35 Monson and Townshend, *A Particular and Exact Account*, part ii, p. 178. L. A. Knafla, *Law and Politics in Jacobean England : The Tracts of Lord Chancellor Ellesmere* (Cambridge, 1977), p. 274.

36 The only known copy of a set of judges' orders dated 6 May 1597, which seem to form the basis of the act, is found in Egerton's papers in Hunt. Lib. EL. MS 2982.

37 *Ibid*. The Bill was entrusted to a committee which included, amongst other lawyers, John Hoskins, Thomas Hedley, and William Noy, three barristers who were associated with other aspects of the law reform movement. *Commons Journals*, 1, p. 444. Committed on 12 June 1604.

38 See *Notes and Queries*, 2nd ser., 12 (1861), 245, 355, for examples of early Elizabethan bills. Though many bills of charges survive from the early seventeenth century, I have never found the prescribed receipt from counsel. The reason for this is more likely to have been the resistance of barristers than the negligence of the lower branch. At about the same time as this act was being passed, money paid to a barrister in return for his services was beginning to be classified as a gratuity or honorarium rather than as a set fee. A 'ticket' from a counsellor for money laid out by an attorney would have put this fee in the same category as other fees charged for legal business. It would also have destroyed the fiction that the fee was an honorarium and might ultimately have opened the door to control over barristers' fees. Instead, these fees increased steadily over the course of the seventeenth century. *The English Reports*, ed. M. Robertson (1914), cxliii, pp. 268ff, *Kennedy* v. *Brown and Wife*, January 1863. See also p. 104 above. It is worth reporting that late Elizabethan and early Stuart concern about reform of the legal profession extended to the fees of counsel and barristers. One reason for the failure of such measures must be that the barristers and serjeants constituted an important interest group both inside and outside of parliament. See also *The Anti-Levellers Antidote* (1652), p. 25, which alleges that counsellors did not give notes of their fees because they were 'ashamed' of their high charges. I owe this last reference to Dr W. R. Prest.

39 See above, p. 20.

40 E. R. Foster, ed., *Proceedings in Parliament 1610* (2 vols., New Haven, 1966), i, pp. 144–5; ii, pp. 278–9.

41 In 1625 an act for 'Abridging the Number of Unskillfull attorneys and reducing them to an orderly practice' was read in the House of Commons, and in 1629 a similar measure is listed in a set of

government proposals for legislation. *Commons Journals*, 1, p. 837. PRO SP 16/124/10.

42 C. Russell, *Parliaments and English Politics 1621–1629* (Oxford, 1979), *passim*.

43 See above, p. 204.

44 Francis Bacon, *Works*, ed. J. Spedding *et al.* (14 vols., 1857–74), v, pp. 14–15.

45 Cooke, *Rules, Orders*, Michaelmas 1564. J. H. Baker, 'Solicitors and the Law of Maintenance 1590–1640', *Cambridge Law Journal*, 32 (1973), 71.

46 Baker, 'Solicitors', p. 73.

47 Monson and Townshend, *A Particular and Exact Account*, p. 178, William Hudson, 'A Treatise of the Court of Star Chamber', *Collectanea Juridica*, ed. F. Hargrave (2 vols., 1792), p. 95.

48 Baker, 'Solicitors and the Law of Maintenance', p. 76.

49 Monson and Townshend, *A Particular and Exact Account*, p. 178.

50 *Ibid.*, p. 200.

51 Baker, 'Solicitors and the Law of Maintenance', p. 75.

52 *Ibid.*, p. 80.

53 See, for example, PRO STAC 8/90/20 and 8/267/8.

54 That is, such men were neither attorneys, clerical officials, nor men called to the bar at one of the inns of court.

55 PRO STAC 8/202/34. In 1616, Humphrey Perrot of Bellhall, co. Worcester was accused of soliciting causes even though he was 'noe attorney or Clarke in anie of your Ma[jes]t[ie]s courts nor otherwise trayned up or experienced in the lawes of this land'.

56 See above, p. 114.

57 PRO E 215/11/848 is a series of depositions to the commissions of fees by fifty-four attorneys of King's Bench and Common Pleas. Almost all of them describe themselves as both attorneys and solicitors. It may be that the solicitors who were neither attorneys, officials, nor men called to the bar had a revival with the decentralization of the profession in the late seventeenth and early eighteenth centuries.

58 PRO E 215/756, fol. 1.

59 In May 1633, the privy council asked the judges for estimates of the number of attorneys active in King's Bench and Common Pleas. Once again, the concern was that attorneys were 'conceived to be a principal cause of the stirring up and multiplying of suits', and the government's aim was 'suppression' of the excess. PRO PC 2/43, fol. 115. *CSPD 1633–34*, p. 251.

60 Brit. Lib. Add. MS 25,232, fol. 122.

61 *Rules and Orders for the Court of Common Pleas at Westminster* (1654), pp. 2, 4, 8, 10–11. Cooke, *Rules, Orders*, Upper Bench, 1655.

62 PRO IND 4603, 'Book of Attornies. Common Pleas 1656–1761'. This document is an important starting point for the post-Restoration history of the profession. In 1673, the judges reported that there were 1392 Common Pleas attorneys. Historical Manuscripts Commission, *9th Report, Part II: Manuscripts of the House of Lords* (1884), p. 20.

63 The statute 2 Geo. II c. 23 (1728) stipulated that only attorneys who had been bound apprentices by contracts in writing should be sworn to practise in the courts. A continuation act of 1749 required that affidavits relating to the contracts should be filed by the courts at Westminster.

64 For earlier use of juries of attorneys see above, pp. 119 and 126, for attacks by practitioners on office holders. Veall, *The Popular Movement for Law Reform*, p. 195. M. Cotterell, 'Interregnum Law Reform: The Hale Commission of 1652', *English Historical Review*, 83 (1968), 689–703. Any definitive conclusions about the fate of these reforms must of course await the badly needed study of the late-seventeenth-century profession.

65 For the commissions of the Elizabethan period see *Praxis Utriusque Banci: The Ancient and Modern Practice of the Two Superior Courts at Westminster...Together with the Rules and Orders of the Said Courts...* (1674), p. 40. The 1567 investigations may not have been a royal commission, since the only evidence is the appointment of jurors by Chief Justice Dyer to inquire into misdemeanors committed by officers of the Common Pleas. Brit. Lib. Lansdowne MS 44, fols. 25, 27–9, a schedule of fees established for the Star Chamber by the council and judges, 1585, and papers setting tasks for investigation in 1585; marginalia in Burghley's hand. Brit. Lib. MS Cotton, Vesp. c. xiv, vol. II, fol. 2, 'The Some of the Commission for Reformation of officers towardes bothe Lawes, 1594'. In addition, Lord Keeper Egerton appointed commissions in 1597 to inquire into problems in Chancery and Star Chamber. W. J. Jones, *The Elizabethan Court of Chancery* (Oxford, 1967), pp. 86–7. T. G. Barnes, 'Due Process and Slow Process in the Late Elizabethan – Early Stuart Star Chamber', *American Journal of Legal History*, 6 (1962), 342. For the Stuart commissions see generally G. E. Aylmer, 'Charles I's Commissions on Fees, 1627–40', *Bull. Institute of Historical Research*, 31 (1958), 59, and W. J. Jones, *Politics and the Bench: The Judges and the Origins of the English Civil War* (1971), pp. 108–20. Copies of the commissions for 1610, 1623, and 1631 are preserved in the Ellesmere MSS. Hunt. Lib. EL. MSS 2941, 12,001, 7928.

66 Aylmer, 'Commissions on Fees', pp. 59–60.

67 Brit. Lib. MS Cotton Vesp. c. xix, vol. II, fol. 2. Hunt. Lib. EL. MS 12,001, fols. 2–3.

68 Aylmer, 'Commissions on Fees', p. 58. Hunt. Lib. EL. MS 2994, information of Thomas Morley, woodmonger of London to the House of Lords concerning increased fees in Common Pleas (no date, but early-seventeenth-century).

69 Hunt. Lib. EL. MS 2874, 1602 suit by the filazers of Common Pleas for increased fees. Bodl. MS Tanner 169, 'Sir Fran. Bacons Arguments against ye Bill of Sheets 1605', fol. 42. Also printed in Bacon, *Works*, iii, pp. 285–7. Bacon pointed out that whilst gentlemen had raised their rents to compensate for inflation, fees had remained the same. Aylmer, 'Commissions on Fees', p. 59.

70 Aylmer, 'Commissions on Fees', p. 60. W. H. Richardson, ed., *The Annalls of Ipswiche* (1880), p. 408. There is also some evidence of pressure from court officials in other towns for increased fees. In 1617, the attorneys and steward of the borough court of Reading petitioned for increases and some were in fact allowed. J. M. Guilding, ed., *Reading Records* (4 vols. 1892–6), i, p. 73. Attorneys' fees were doubled in Cambridge in 1560. C. H. Cooper, *Annals of Cambridge* (5 vols., Cambridge, 1842), ii, p. 163.

71 Brit. Lib. Lansdowne MS 23, item 70, John Lennarde to Sir William Cecil. R. Zaller, *The Parliament of 1621* (Berkeley, Calif., 1971), pp. 47, 90–7. Aylmer, 'Commissions on Fees', p. 63.

72 PRO E 215/2/147. It was alleged that pleadings in the Common Pleas were drawn to an extraordinary length. The old rate for pleadings was 8d. a sheet for the first three sheets and 'something less' for the rest. The new rate was 8d. a sheet for the first three and 12d. a sheet for the rest. Moreover, before 1569, the prothonotaries had charged 6s. 8d. a roll (membrane in the plea rolls) for entering pleas, and each roll contained about twenty-one sheets. After that, however, they no longer charged by the roll but took 2s. for the first three sheets enrolled and 12d. for additional sheets. Prothonotary Brownlow confessed to these increases in November 1635. PRO E 215/9/694A. For the calculation of the cost of a suit, see above, pp. 101–3.

73 Bodl. MS Rawlinson D. 1123, certificate of fees taken in the Common Pleas presented by the jury of attorneys, 1628, fols. 4v–13.

74 PRO E 215/857; E 215/1417; E 215/1420A.

75 See above, pp. 101–3, and M. Hastings, *The Court of Common Pleas in Fifteenth Century England* (Ithaca, N.Y., 1947), pp. 247–55.

76 Bacon, *Works*, iii, p. 287. Thomas, Lord Ellesmere, 'Memorialles for Iudicature. Pro Bono Publico' (1609), in Knafla, *Law and Politics in Jacobean England*, p. 275. In 1614, 'An Act for Manifestation of all fees due or payable by the King's Subjects in all Courts of ecclesiastical and temporal jurisdiction' was introduced into the House of Commons. *Commons Journals*, 1, p. 489.

77 T. Powell, *The Attourneys Academy* (1623), p. 5.

78 Bacon, *Works*, iii, p. 286.

79 J. E. Neale, *Elizabeth I and her Parliaments 1584–1601* (1957), pp. 207, 417.

80 See above, p. 123. *Commons Journals*, 1, pp. 259–68.

81 Zaller, *Parliament of 1621*, p. 97.

82 For the Star Chamber dispute see above, p. 122. However, it is true that the commission was directed towards the investigation of abuses in all courts.

83 Jones, *Chancery*, pp. 86–7. Barnes, 'Due Process and Slow Process', p. 342.

84 Most King's Bench practitioners at this date were clerks of the prothonotary and not attorneys according to statutory regulations. See above, p. 21. Hunt. Lib. EL. MS 2941. For a printed version of the

commission see Historical Manuscripts Commission, *Knole*, i, pp. 221–2.

85 Aylmer, 'Commissions on Fees', pp. 59, 61. Jones, *Politics and the Bench*, pp. 108–20.

86 Jones, *Politics and the Bench*, pp. 63–7.

87 For hostility between and amongst these various groups see above, pp. 122–3.

88 Brit. Lib. Lansdowne MS 23, item 70, May 1576. T. Barrett-Lennard, *An Account of the Families of Lennard and Barrett* (1908), p. 15. Lady Elizabeth Cust, *Records of the Cust Family* (3 vols., 1909), ii, p. 40.

89 The words of J. P. Cooper in Cooper, ed., *The Decline of Spain and the Thirty Years War 1609–48/49* (New Cambridge Modern History, iv, 1970), p. 542.

8. CLERKSHIP, THE INNS OF CHANCERY, AND LEGAL EDUCATION

1 See generally W. R. Prest, *The Inns of Court under Elizabeth I and the Early Stuarts 1590–1640* (1972).

2 Elijah Williams, *Early Holborn and the Legal Quarter of London* (2 vols., 1927), i, p. 44. T. F. Tout, 'The Household of the Chancery and its Disintegration', in *Essays in History Presented to Reginald Lane Poole*, ed. H. W. C. Davis (Oxford, 1927), p. 76. W. J. Jones, *The Elizabethan Court of Chancery* (Oxford, 1967), pp. 120–1, 159.

3 PRO E 215/756.

4 *The Practick Part of the Law, Shewing the Office of a Complete Attorney* (1658 edn), p. 3.

5 Sir George Cooke, *Rules, Orders and Notices in the Courts of King's Bench and Common Pleas* (1747), for example orders dated Michaelmas 1564 and Michaelmas 1573.

6 PRO STAC 8/86/5. Needler's father was an acquaintance of Harrison's. PROB 11/51 (22 Sheffield).

7 E. Turner, 'History of John Rowe', *Sussex Archaeological Collections*, 24 (1872), 85ff. PRO STAC 8/9/4, *Hele* v. *Coke*, 1604. This case gives many examples of careers in the clerical underworld (fols. 105, 109, 116). See also, PRO E 215/1575/1–5, and Historical Manuscripts Commission, *Hatfield House*, part xxiii (1973), p. 153.

8 PRO PROB 11/43 (39 Mellrish), will dated 1559.

9 PRO PROB 11/126 (96 Rudd), dated 1615. PRO PROB 11/254 (1656/150).

10 Lichfield Joint Rec. Office, will of Richard Denton, proved 1593.

11 PRO PROB 11/159 (27 St John).

12 H. Ellis, ed., *The Obituary of Richard Smyth, Secondary of the Poultry Compter, London : Being A Catalogue of All Such Persons as he Knew in their Life : Extending from A.D. 1627 to A.D. 1674* (Camden Soc., os, xliv, 1849), p. 7.

13 L. B. Osborn, *The Life, Letters and Writings of John Hoskyns, 1566–1638* (New Haven, Conn., 1937), pp. 65–7.

14 See O. J. Dunlop, *English Apprenticeship and Child Labour* (1912), p. 55.
15 PRO Prerogative Court of Canterbury (108 Barrington). Borthwick Institute, York, Prerogative Court of York, Doncaster D.: Executor's Accounts, 1652. I owe both of these references to Dr W. R. Prest.
16 See generally PRO IR 1/1. An analysis of premiums for the county of Surrey shows that of forty valued at above £200, seven related to attorneys, two to barber-surgeons, and the rest to merchants and other miscellaneous trades. [H. Jenkinson, ed.], *Surrey Apprenticeships from the Registers in the Public Record Office 1711–1731* (Surrey Rec. Soc., xxx, 1929), p. xv.
17 PRO CP 5, articles of clerkship for attorneys, 1730–1838.
18 W. Cunningham, *The Growth of English Industry and Commerce in Modern Times* (Cambridge, 1921), pp. 321–3. Dunlop, *English Apprenticeship*, p. 119.
19 *Journals of the House of Commons*, 21, p. 267.
20 Turner, 'History of John Rowe', pp. 85ff. PRO STAC 8/65/5.
21 Barnard's Inn Admissions Book (MS in possession of Gray's Inn). Names in the register have been compared with the plea rolls and docket rolls of the King's Bench and Common Pleas in the PRO.
22 W. P. Baildon, ed., *The Records of the Honourable Society of Lincoln's Inn: The Black Books* (4 vols., 1897–1907), i, pp. vii, xiii, xxiv, 253.
23 F. A. Inderwick, ed., *A Calendar of the Inner Temple Records* (5 vols., 1896–1901), i, p. xxxv. C. T. Martin, ed., *Minutes of Parliament of the Middle Temple* (3 vols. plus index, 1904–5), i, p. 640.
24 Inner Temple Lib., Misc. MS. 32, fol. 25.
25 Bedford Co. Rec. Office, L 26/270 (no pagination).
26 *Ibid.*
27 Prest, *Inns of Court*, p. 27.
28 Bedford Co. Rec. Office, L 26/270.
29 Sir C. Carr, *The Pension Book of Clement's Inn* (Selden Soc., lxxviii, 1960), pp. lxi–lxvii.
30 D. S. Bland, *A Bibliography of the Inns of Court and Chancery* (Selden Soc. Supplement, no. iii, 1965), introduces the material in print. The most serious difficulties arise from the fact that no records of the governing bodies of any of the inns of chancery survive for the period between 1500 and 1640. The admissions register of Barnard's Inn (Gray's Inn Lib.), which covers the period from 1620 up to the Restoration, is the only official guide to membership, but lists of members of Barnard's Inn and Staple Inn in 1585 are found in the papers of William Cecil, Lord Burghley. Brit. Lib. Lansdowne MS 47, fols. 119–21. In addition, it is now emerging that the names of members of the inns are sometimes given in lawsuits, the records of which survive in the plea rolls. The use of this source was pioneered by J. H. Baker, and for his exploitation of it in connection with the fifteenth century see his 'The English Legal Profession, 1450–1550', in *Lawyers in Early Modern Europe and America*, ed. W. R. Prest

(1981), pp. 16–41, and 'The Attorneys and Officers of the Common Law in 1480', *Journal of Legal History*, 1 (1980), 182–93. For the later period, lists of members of Furnival's Inn, New Inn, and Clifford's Inn can be found in PRO CP 40/1145, mm. 85, 267, and 938 (1553). PRO CP 40/1553, m. 1680, contains a list of members of Staple Inn (1595).

31 For more speculation on the early history of the inns see C. W. Brooks, 'Some Aspects of Attorneys in England during the Late Sixteenth and Early Seventeenth Centuries' (Oxford Univ. unpub. D.Phil. thesis, 1978), pp. 102–5.

32 Sir John Fortescue, *De Laudibus Legum Angliae*, ed. S. B. Chrimes (Cambridge, 1942), pp. 118–19.

33 *Ibid.*, pp. 116–17.

34 Baker, 'The English Legal Profession, 1450–1550', pp. 31–5.

35 D. S. Bland, *The Early Records of Furnival's Inn* (Newcastle upon Tyne, 1957), pp. 23, 25, 35. Bland prints extracts relating to Furnival's Inn which are contained in a Middle Temple manuscript which also deals with the history of Lincoln's Inn and Thavies Inn. A typescript of the entire manuscript, which was transcribed by W. P. Baildon, is in Lincoln's Inn Lib., Misc. MS 720.

36 Lincoln's Inn Lib., Misc. MS 720.

37 Carr, *Pension Book of Clement's Inn*, pp. 218–39.

38 Inner Temple Lib., Misc. MS 186, 'Statutes of Clifford's Inn'. The statutes, written on vellum panels in law French, are at present hanging in the library. I have used a typescript translation of them which is in the possession of the librarian.

39 Baker has found that one-third of a sample of attorneys active in 1480 were members of either an inn of court or an inn of chancery. He believes that, given the poor survival rate of membership records, this is consistent with all practitioners having been members. This hypothesis may well prove to be correct, but my own comparisons of the names of attorneys active in the reigns of Henry IV and Henry VI with the early membership of Furnival's Inn suggest that no member of that inn was an active attorney of the Common Pleas. Furthermore, Baker does have lists of names of members of six inns of chancery within ten years on either side of 1480. Consequently, his figures of one-third may in fact be taken to suggest that not all practitioners joined an inn. Baker, 'English Legal Profession, 1450–1550', p. 26, and 'Attorneys and Officers of the Common Law in 1480', pp. 186–203. The lists of members of the inns of chancery can be deduced from the references in his biographical index. My comparison used Bland, *Early Records of Furnival's Inn*, pp. 21–9, and PRO CP 40/598, 646–7.

40 Early-sixteenth-century records of the inns of court note attorneys who served as assistant stewards at Christmas revels, and they are also mentioned in various levies on members of the societies. Baildon, ed., *Black Books of Lincoln's Inn*, i, pp. xvi–xvii, 318. Clerical officials were frequently made members of the inns of court by virtue of their offices.

Baker, 'English Legal Profession, 1450–1550', p. 22. Prest, *Inns of Court*, p. 57.

41 Carr, *Pension Book of Clement's Inn*, p. 200.

42 Compare the list of members given in CP 40/1145, mm. 85, 264, and 938, with the roll of warrants of attorney in the same plea roll.

43 Bland, *Early Records of Furnival's Inn*, p. 43. Four of eleven names mentioned, including that of the principal, Bateman, were admitted to Lincoln's Inn. *The Records of the Honorable Society of Lincoln's Inn : Admissions, 1420–1893, and Chapel Registers* (2 vols., 1896).

44 Sir Thomas Elyot, *The Boke Named the Governour*, ed. H. H. S. Croft (2 vols., 1880), i, pp. 141–2, 144, 154–5.

45 R. M. Fisher, 'Thomas Cromwell, Humanism and Educational Reform', *Bull. Institute of Historical Research*, 50 (1977), 151–63.

46 Prest, *Inns of Court*, pp. 23–4.

47 For the status of entrants to the lower branch see above, pp. 243–7.

48 Versions of these orders can be found in the printed editions of the inns of court records. The provisos were that attorneys and solicitors could remain in the inns if they were approved individually or if they kept the learning exercises. Inderwick, *Inner Temple Records*, p. 190. Baildon, ed., *Black Books*, i, p. 315. On the subject of attorneys at the inns of court see H. H. Bellot, 'The Exclusion of Attorneys from the Inns of Court', *Law Quarterly Review*, 26 (1910), 137–45.

49 R. J. Fletcher, ed., *The Pension Book of Gray's Inn 1569–1669* (3 vols., 1901–10), i, pp. 212–13.

50 Brit. Lib. Lansdowne MS 47, fols. 114, 119–21. PRO CP 40/1439, 1443, 1453, 1457, 1495, 1501, 1503, 1509, 1520. KB 27/1292, 1307. Gray's Inn Lib., 'Barnard's Inn Admissions Book'. PRO CP 40/2251, 2257. KB 27/1649. IND 293(2), 328, 353–7, 1360, 1370.

51 Baildon, ed., *Black Books*, i, pp. 366, 381. An order of May 1569 specified that 'Fellows of Furnival's Inn and David's Inn...who have been allowed Utter Barresters there, and have mooted there two vacations at the Utter Bar shall pay 13s. 4d. only for admission to the Fellowship of this House....'

52 Of 112 men listed as members of Barnard's Inn in 1585, only 24 stayed on during the learning vacations. At Staple Inn 60 out of a total of 145 continued on during the vacations. However, only 12 of these men ever entered Gray's Inn, the inn of court to which Staple Inn was connected, and only 2 of these were called to the bar. Searches in the plea rolls indicate that very few of them became practitioners. Brit. Lib. Lansdowne MS 47, fols. 114, 119–21. For admissions to Gray's Inn see J. Foster, ed., *Register of Admissions to Gray's Inn* (1889).

53 Carr, *Pension Book of Clement's Inn*, p. xix.

54 Foster, *Register of Admissions to Gray's Inn*. See also Prest, *Inns of Court*, p. 129.

55 Prest, *Inns of Court*, p. 129.

56 Baildon, ed., *Black Books*, ii, pp. 265, 270, 281. For the nature of the learning exercises see Prest, *Inns of Court*, pp. 124–36.

57　H. Pugh, 'Origins and Progress of Barnard's Inn', *Notes and Queries*, 7th ser., 2 (1886), 223. This series of articles is based on a manuscript history of the inn which was written at a time when the records of the governing body of the house still survived. Carr, *Pension Book of Clement's Inn*, pp. xx, 226.

58　Bland, *Records of Furnival's Inn*, p. 35. Baildon, ed., *Black Books*, i, p. 292.

59　H. H. Bellot, 'The Jurisdiction of the Inns of Court over the Inns of Chancery', *Law Quarterly Review*, 26 (1910), 384–99.

60　*Ibid.* But Bellot underestimated the amount of control exercised by the inns of court during the late sixteenth and early seventeenth centuries. See, for example, Baildon, ed., *Black Books*, i, p. 391; ii, p. 454.

61　See generally L. Stone, 'The Educational Revolution in England, 1560–1640', *Past and Present*, 28 (1964), 41–80.

62　Baildon, ed., *Black Books*, i, p. 315.

63　L. A. Knafla, 'The Matriculation Revolution and Education at the Inns of Court in Renaissance England', in *Tudor Men and Institutions*, ed. A. J. Slavin (Baton Rouge, La., 1972).

64　Brit. Lib. Lansdowne MS. 47, fol. 114. The numbers given for each of the inns of chancery in term time were as follows: Clement's Inn, 100; Clifford's Inn, 110; Lyon's Inn, 80; Newe Inn, 80; Thavyes Inn, 40; Furnival's Inn, 80; Barnard's Inn, 112; Staple Inn, 145. By comparison, Gray's Inn, the largest of the inns of court, accommodated 356, whilst the other inns of court held 200 each. Since the number of men admitted to the inns may well have been larger than the number accommodated, these figures cannot be taken as anything other than minimums for the total numbers of members of the inns of court and chancery.

65　*Ibid.*, fols. 114, 119–21. These figures are an extrapolation based on what is known about the percentage of active practitioners at Barnard's Inn and Staple Inn.

66　For the size of the profession in 1585 see above, pp. 112–13. The figure for the number of practitioners at the inns of court is probably an underestimate, since there were 31 attorneys resident at the Middle Temple as late as 1635. Martin, ed., *Minutes of Parliament of the Middle Temple*, ii, p. 837.

67　PRO SP 12/224, fol. 154, dated June 1589.

68　Sir George Buc, 'The Third Universitie of England or A Treatise of the Foundation of All the Colleges... in London', appendix to John Stow, *The Annales or Generall Chronicle of England*, ed. Edmund Howes (1615), p. 976. Bland, *Early Records of Furnival's Inn*, p. 14. PRO 30/26/74/3 gives a great deal of information about agreements for the erection of chambers at Clement's Inn. Robert Willett built chambers at Staple Inn late in the reign of Elizabeth. PRO PROB 11/81 (16 Neville). On the other hand, the will of Alen Hendre suggests that Davies' (or Thavies) Inn may have been in decline. PROB 11/118 (86 Wood).

69 The surviving records of Clement's Inn suggest that at least seventy new double rooms were erected between 1593 and 1640. PRO 30/26/74/3.

70 During the two decades before 1642, the average entry was 13.2 men each year. Gray's Inn Lib., 'Barnard's Inn Admissions Book'.

71 PRO E 215/756, fol. 1. *Rules and Orders for the Court of Common Pleas at Westminster* (1654), p. 2.

72 R. Robson, *The Attorney in Eighteenth Century England* (Cambridge, 1959), p. 3.

73 Carr, *Pension Book of Clement's Inn*, p. 229.

74 For example, in the second decade of the seventeenth century, Rowland Hall, a Common Pleas attorney, kept a room for himself and his clients in the Flying Horse in the parish of St Dunstan's. PRO STAC 8/180/3.

75 Gray's Inn Lib., 'Barnard's Inn Admissions Book'. William Harris admitted April 1621; John Harris, January 1627. *The Visitation of Cambridge in 1575 and 1619*, ed. J. W. Clay (Harleian Soc., xli, 1897), p. 107. PRO PROB 11/302 (1660), will of John Harris of Milton, gent. In general, extensive attempts to trace biographical details of those admitted to Barnard's Inn who did not take up legal careers have produced very little information. This can only be taken to mean that the entrants were relatively obscure men even in their own localities.

76 For the greater houses see Prest, *Inns of Court*, pp. 153–67.

77 PRO PROB 11/81 (16 Neville). PROB 11/112 (109 Windebank). PROB 11/234 (1654/26). Roberts was granted a Special Admission to Barnard's Inn in 1623. Another similar example is John Stephens, citizen and tallowchandler of London and member of Staple Inn in the 1580s. PRO CP 40/1553, m. 1680. PROB 11/72 (20 Rutland).

78 Gray's Inn Lib., 'Barnard's Inn Admissions Book', Feb.–May 1622.

79 Chambers were normally shared between two men, and they apparently shared the costs of furnishing them. See, for example, the wills of William Death of Staple Inn and Edmund Ashfield of Barnard's Inn. PRO PROB 11/77 (32 Saintberbe), and PROB 11/101 (29 Bolein). At Clement's Inn the rent for one-half a chamber was £13 5s. 8d. PRO 30/26/74/3, fol. 24.

80 Carr, *Pension Book of Clement's Inn*, p. xlii.

81 PRO 30/26/74/3.

82 Brit. Lib. Lansdowne MS 47, fol. 119. Gray's Inn Lib., 'Barnard's Inn Admissions Book'. *The Visitations of Hertfordshire in 1572 and 1634*, ed. W. C. Metcalfe (Harleian Soc. xxii, 1886), pp. 60, 107.

83 Gray's Inn Lib., 'Barnard's Inn Admissions Book', June 1623. C. H. Cooper, *Annals of Cambridge* (5 vols., Cambridge, 1842), iii, pp. 53, 181.

84 Cooper, vol. iii, pp. 41, 244. Gray's Inn Lib., 'Barnard's Inn Admissions Book', Nov. 1627–Nov. 1629.

85 Carr, *Pension Book of Clement's Inn*, p. lvi.

86 See for example, PRO STAC 8/90/25, which names a number of Devon and Somerset attorneys resident at Lyon's Inn.

87 Gray's Inn Lib., 'Barnard's Inn Admissions Book'.

88 Prest, *Inns of Court*, ch. IV.

89 Pugh, 'Barnard's Inn', pp. 221–2.

90 Fletcher, ed., *Pension Book of Gray's Inn*, i, p. 124. Lincoln's Inn Lib., Misc. MS 720 [p. 254]. Baildon, ed., *Black Books*, ii, p. 111.

91 Carr, *Pension Book of Clement's Inn*, p. xlvii n. 1. Godfrey Maydwell, principal in 1632, was a six clerk. Another principal, Rowland Fryth, was a six clerk's clerk, as was Richard Kelway. PRO E 215/498, list of the six clerks and their underclerks, 1629. In 1618 Maydwell bought a lease for sixty years on a new building with twelve chambers for £380. PRO 30/26/74/3, fol. 9.

92 Lincoln's Inn Lib., Misc. MS 720, [p. 254]. PRO E 215/1069, CP 40/1757, 'Roll of warrants', m. 28. Baildon, ed., *Black Books*, ii, p. 111. For Plombe's practice see, for example, PRO CP 40/1753, mm. 22–2v. For Alexander's, PRO IND 1356, m. 1v.

93 Carr, *Pension Book of Clement's Inn*, p. xxxvi. For more on Holbeache and Prescott see above, pp. 185, 273.

94 Carr, *Pension Book of Clement's Inn*, pp. 218–29. Inner Temple Lib., 'Statutes of Clifford's Inn'. Pugh, 'Barnard's Inn', p. 301, quotes an ordinance of 1594 'that no great Ruff should be worn, nor any white color in doublets or hosen, nor any facing of Velvet in Gowns, and that no Gentleman should walk in the Streets in their Cloaks but no Gowns'.

95 Pugh, 'Barnard's Inn', p. 142. This John Wilkinson was very likely the author of a leading manual on local government. John Wilkinson of Barnards Inne, Gent., *A Treatise Collected Ovt of the Statvtes of This Kingdom... concerning the Office and Authoritie of Coroners and Sheriffs* (1st edn, 1618, and others in 1618, 1620, 1628, 1638).

96 Pugh, 'Barnard's Inn', p. 142.

97 *Ibid.*, p. 223.

98 Carr, *Pension Book of Clement's Inn*, p. xxxvi. Baildon, ed., *Black Books*, ii, p. 62.

99 Baildon, ed., *Black Books*, ii, p. 356.

100 Ibid., p. 62. Fletcher, ed., *Pension Book of Gray's Inn*, i, p. 126.

101 Fletcher, ed., *Pension Book*, i, p. 126.

102 For some examples see above, p. 222.

103 Pugh, 'Barnard's Inn', p. 302. These were disapproved of in 1659.

104 See, for example, the wills of Henry Farmer and Richard Barton of Staple Inn. PRO PROB 11/127 (3 Cope) and PROB 11/114 (58 Dorset).

105 Baildon, ed., *Black Books*, ii, p. 111.

106 Pugh, 'Barnard's Inn', p. 222. PRO PROB 11/118 (86 Wood).

107 PRO PROB 11/127 (3 Cope). Farmer's will, which was written in 1615, also mentions his 'loving friends' Thomas Pope, principal of Staple Inn, and Stephen Herenden, Christopher Hodesdon, and Nicholas Foxley, ancients. PROB 11/114 (58 Dorset). Richard Barton's will mentions a large number of friends, including William Death, another prominent member of the inn.

108 Interestingly, both Barton and Farmer were bachelors. So, too, was

a sometime principal of Barnard's Inn, Edmund Ashfield, who left £6 to the society. PRO PROB 11/101 (29 Bolein).

109 The vast majority of the wills of practitioner members of the inns never mention them. However, it is often clear from other sources that they were active members.

110 Inner Temple Lib. MS 32, fol. 15.

111 Townesend appears in the plea rolls for 15 Chas. I. PRO CP 40/2448. His daughter, Elizabeth, married Robert Kenwrick of King's Sutton, Northants., whose brother, Raphael, was an attorney. *The Visitation of the County of Northampton in 1681*, ed. H. I. Longden (Harleian Soc., lxxxvii, 1935), p. 97.

112 Townesend, *A Preparative*, p. 4.

113 *Ibid.*, p. 16. *The Practick Part of the Law* (1658 edn), p. 1.

114 Reproduced as the frontispiece in M. Birks, *Gentlemen of the Law* (1960).

115 Bodl. MS Rawlinson C. 64. Folger Shakespeare Lib., Washington, D.C., MS x d 483 (196). This copy belonged to John Mulys of Hulmpston, Devon and Lyon's Inn. Lincoln's Inn Lib., Misc. MS 586, fols. 9ff. SBT DR 10/1813. In addition, there are the copies of the guides owned by John Clifford, Elias Ashmole, and Christopher Mickleton, which are mentioned below.

116 Inner Temple Lib., Barrington MS 29, pp. 687ff. It is likely that 'The Perfect Instruction' was designed to be used in conjuction with the same author's 'A Brief Collection of the Queenes Ma[jes]ties most high and most honourable Courts of Record'. Bodl. MS New College D. 325.

117 T. Powell, *The Attourneys Academy or the Manner and Some of Proceeding Practically upon any Suit, Plaint or Action Whatsoever in Any Court of Record...* (1623), p. 111.

118 *Ibid.* (1630 edn), pp. i–iv.

119 *The Practick Part of the Law*, p. 1.

120 Gloucs. Rec. Office, D 149/B.

121 *Ibid.*

122 *A Booke of Entries: Containing Perfect and Approved Presidents of Courts, Declarations, Informations, Pleints, Inditements, Barres...* (1614), preface by Sir E. Coke. W. Rastell, *An Exposition of Certain Difficult and Obscure Words and Terms* (1579). J. Cowell, *A Law Dictionary or the Interpreter* (Cambridge, 1607).

123 Gloucs. Rec. Office, D 149/B1, p. 188.

124 N. L. Matthews, *William Sheppard, Cromwell's Law Reformer* (Cambridge, 1984), pp. 19, 70.

125 C. H. Josten, ed., *Elias Ashmole (1617–1692): His Autobiographical and Historical Notes* (5 vols., Oxford, 1966), ii, p.312.

126 *Ibid.*, pp. 329, 334. Ashmole was admitted to Clement's Inn five days before being sworn as an attorney.

127 Bodl. MSS Ashmole 1147, 1156, 1159, 1151.

128 *Ibid.*, 1151 (III), fols. 1–1v, 9, 13.

129 W. West, *The First Part of Symbolaeographia. Which May Be Termed the Art or Description or Image of Instruments.... Or the Paterne of Praesidents. Or The Notarie or Scrivner* (1590).

130 Durham University Lib., Mickleton–Spearman Collection MSS vols. 1, 15, 17, 18, 60, 81. See also F. J. W. Harding, 'Mickleton and Spearman MSS', *Durham Philobiblon*, I (1949–50), pp. 40ff. Mickleton died in 1669. He was a member of Clifford's Inn until 1635, when he entered the Inner Temple, but was never called to the bar.

131 P. Styles, 'The Social Structure of Kineton Hundred in the Reign of Charles II', *Trans. and Proc. Birmingham Archaeological Soc.*, 78 (1962), 115. Turner, 'History of John Rowe', *Sussex Archaeological Collections*, 24 (1872), 92. *Essex Journal* (Spring 1973), 2. C. J. Palmer, ed., *The History of Great Yarmouth by Henry Manship, Town Clerk* (Yarmouth, 1854). C. Kerry, 'Anthony Bradshaw of Duffield and the Alms Houses Founded by Him at That Place', *The Reliquary*, 23 (1882–3), 137–9. A. Atkinson, 'The Trussel Manuscripts', *Papers and Proc. Hampshire Field Club*, 29 (3) (1957), 290–8. R. Izacke, *Antiquities of the City of Exeter* (1677). I owe several of these references to Dr W. R. Prest.

132 [John Earle], *Micro-cosmographie; or, a peece of the World Discovered* (1628), p. sig. [C3v].

133 Buc. 'The Third Universitie', p. 969.

134 W. Dugdale, *Origines Juridicales or Historical Memorials of the English Laws...* (1666), p. 242. Prest, *Inns of Court*, p. 42. See above, p. 000.

135 Bodl. MS New College D. 325 [fol. 2].

136 On Roman attitudes towards lawsuits see J. M. Kelly, *Studies in the Civil Judicature of the Roman Republic* (Oxford, 1976), pp. 97–8. On the attitudes of sixteenth- and seventeenth-century Englishmen see above, p. 133.

137 *The Complete Works of Sir Thomas More*, ed. E. Surtz and J. H. Hexter (5 vols., New Haven, Conn., 1965), iv, p. 490, for the quotation from Quintilian.

138 Elyot, *The Gouernour*, i, pp. 154–5, 157. For Servius see *The Oxford Classical Dictionary*, ed. N. Hammond and H. Scullard, 2nd edn (Oxford, 1970).

139 Historical Manuscripts Commission, *Hatfield House*, part i (1883), p. 163.

140 L. G. Schowoerer, 'Roger North and his Notes on Legal Education', *Huntington Lib. Quarterly*, 22 (1958), 76.

141 T. G. Barnes, 'Star Chamber Litigants and their Counsel, 1596–1641', in *Legal Records and the Historian*, ed. J. H. Baker (1978), pp. 24–5.

142 L. Stone, *The Crisis of the Aristocracy 1558–1641* (Oxford, 1965), pp. 672–85.

143 Elyot, *The Gouernour*, i, p. 139.

144 Sir Thomas Smith, *De Republica Anglorum* (1583), ed. Mary Dewar (Cambridge, 1982), p. 76. J. Ferne, *The Blazon of Gentrie Devided into Two Parts the First Named the Glorie of Generositie* (1586), pp. 7–9, 32–4, 70ff. E. Bolton, *The Cities Advocate: In This Case or Question of Honour and Armes; Whether Apprenticeship Extinguisheth Gentry?* (1618).

9. PRIVATE PRACTICE

1 *The Visitation of the County of Warwick in 1619*, ed. J. Featherston (Harleian Soc., xii, 1886), p. 275.
2 Shapcott was clerk of the peace for Devon. PRO SP 23/183, p. 1255. Eveleigh served as mayor and MP for Totnes in the 1650s. C. F. Rea, 'The Bastewells of Totnes', *Trans. Devon Assoc.*, 56 (1925), 204–5.
3 For details see C. W. Brooks, 'Some Aspects of Attorneys in England during the Late Sixteenth and Early Seventeenth Centuries' (Oxford Univ. unpub. D.Phil thesis, 1978), p. 169 n. 2.
4 Humfrey Turnor of Devon owned a house in the parish of St Andrew's Undershaft and in Kent. Thomas Bland of Tunbridge in Kent held property near St Paul's. Michael Mosely of Staffordshire also owned the Blue Anker in the parish of St Clement's. Ambrose Mudford of Halberton in Devon owned property in Milford Lane, parish of St Clement Dane's. William Crosse owned a manor in Somerset, lands in Essex, and a house in Orchard Street in the City of Westminster. Simon Bunce of Linsted, Kent held lands in the parish of St Clement Dane's. Francis Martyn of Devon owned property in Goswell Street, parish of St Giles Cripplegate. PRO PROB 11/126 (83 Rudd), 131 (47 Meade), 160 (103 St John), 265 (1657/217), 276 (1658/245), 119 (44 Fenner), 240 (1654, 385).
5 PRO PROB 11/128 (85 Cope). Lichfield Joint Rec. Office, will of Richard Denton, 1593. Birmingham Reference Lib., Gregory–Hood Deeds, Nos. 184–5, gives the address of Tyllesley as Coventry, where he had a large number of cases in PRO CP 40/1457. W. G. Hoskins, ed., *Exeter in the Seventeenth Century: Tax and Rate Assessments* (Devon and Cornwall Rec. Soc., NS, ii, 1957), p. 5. J. L. Vivian, *Devon Pedigrees* (Exeter, 1898), pp. 526, 729. PRO PROB 11/132 (126 Audley).
6 J F. Pound, 'The Social and Trade Structure of Norwich, 1525–1575', *Past and Present*, 34 (1966), 66, mentions eighteen scriveners amongst the freemen in 1569, but no attorneys. Of six Norfolk attorneys active in 1560, only one, Edward Fenne, lived in Norwich. Norfolk Consistory Court (183 Cowells). The others were Christopher Crowe of East Bilney: PRO PROB 11/120 (106 Fenner); Thomas Might of Castle Rising: PROB 11 (62 Woodhole); Thomas Payne of Castleacre: PROB 11/55 (3 Peter); Thomas Barsham of Oxwich: PROB 11/55 (52 Windebank); and William Bygott of Starstone: Norfolk Consistory Court (97 Moyse). By contrast, in 1660 a Norwich tax assessment listed fourteen lawyers. J. T. Evans, *Seventeenth-Century Norwich* (Oxford, 1979), p. 6. For York see D. M. Palliser, *Tudor York* (Oxford, 1979), pp. 142, 147.
7 See above, pp. 253–4.
8 Sources for the residences of attorneys include wills, heraldic visitations, the Victoria County Histories, local histories, lay subsidy rolls, and hearth tax returns. For attorneys in the town of Warwick see also P. Styles, 'The Social Structure of Kineton Hundred in the

Reign of Charles II', *Trans. and Proc. Birmingham Archaeological Soc.*, 78 (1962), 96–117.

9 Thomas Shapcott, John Wootton, George Izacke, George Moncke, Nicholas Street, Richard Tickell, Nicholas Weare, Richard Long, John Tucker, and German Shapcott are known to have lived in Exeter. Francis Giles lived about two miles away in Pynhaw. Christopher Potter, George Richards, and Henry Skybowe lived six miles up the river Exe at Silverton.

10 See above, p. 313 n. 125.

11 Francis Eades, John Halford, Thomas Hunt, Henry Makepeace, James Prescott, Edward Rainsford, Richard and John Yardley.

12 K. R. Adey, 'Seventeenth-Century Stafford: A Country Town in Decline', *Midland History*, 2 (3) (1973), 153.

13 PRO PROB 11/133 (18 Parker), will of William Clarke. *The Visitation of the County of Warwick in 1682 and 1683*, ed. W. H. Rylands (Harleian Soc., lxii, 1911), pp. 28, 89. *The Visitations of Hertfordshire in 1572 and 1634*, ed. W. C. Metcalfe (Harleian Soc., xxii, 1886), pp. 65, 104.

14 Jackson was the son-in-law of Hawes. Lichfield Joint Rec. Office, will of Thomas Hawes. PRO PROB 11/89 (40 Cobham). George Averell was George Palmer's grandfather. *Visitation of the County of Warwick in 1619*, p. 239.

15 The Holbeaches had ancient ties with Coventry. Coventry City Rec. Office, Leech Miscellanea C215, mortgage deed between William and Thomas Holbeache of Filongley and several citizens of Coventry, 28 Hen. VIII.

16 See above, pp. 246–7.

17 PRO PROB 11/81 (39 Nevell). PROB 11/130 (82 Weldon).

18 PRO PROB 11/130 (82 Weldon), will of Thomas Ashton of Sheldon. PROB 11/128 (85 Cope), will of Hugh Willington of Coventry.

19 R. Hine, 'Records of the Firm of Hawkins and Co.', typescript in possession of Hawkins and Co., 7/8 Portmill Lane, Hitchin, whom I thank for giving me permission to consult it.

20 This seems an obvious conclusion to draw from the names of the following King's Bench practitioners: M. Bland and T. Bland; S. Bunce sen. and S. Bunce jun.; J. Sharpe sen. and J. Sharpe Jun.; Stamp sen. and Stamp jun., Wend sen. and Wend jun.; Yardley sen. and Yardley jun. PRO IND 1356 (King's Bench Docket Roll, 1606).

21 W. Dugdale, *Antiquities of Warwickshire* (1656), p. 650a. Hine, 'Records of Hawkins and Co.', p. 1.

22 Bodl. MS Ashmole 1537 (I), 'Attorneys in Parte Anatomized...', fol. 4.

23 J. A. Chartres, 'The Place of Inns in the Commercial Life of London and Western England, 1660–1760' (Oxford Univ. unpub. D.Phil. thesis, 1973), pp. 83–95.

24 PRO PROB 11/289 (1659/199), 48 (5 Crymes), 312 (1663/138). Though Waller lived at Ashwell, he owned the Chequers at Royston.

25 The wills of a number of practitioners mention 'studies'. The inventory of William Foster of Warwick includes a study with

lawbooks, a little cupboard, and a little table. Worcester Co. Rec. Office, BA 3585, 233.

26 MS in possession of Hawkins and Co., 7/8 Portmill Lane, Hitchin. Hereafter referred to as Draper MS. For a closer analysis of this document see Brooks, 'Some Aspects of Attorneys', pp. 173–6.

27 PRO CP 40/1384 (Hil. 28 Eliz.), 'Roll of Warrants', mm. 15, 20, 97. CP 40/1187 (East. 2 Eliz.), 'Roll of Warrants', mm. 3^d, 16.

28 Draper MS, fol. 281, letter from Jane Baldock to George Draper, 20 May 1673. Gloucs. Rec. Office, D149/81, notebooks of John Clifford of Frampton, pp. 93, 95–6, 122, 131–2.

29 See, for example, a letter from George Palmer to Edmund Ferrers. SBT DR 3/634.

30 Sir G. Cooke, *Rules, Orders and Notices in the Courts of King's Bench and Common Pleas* (1747) (no pagination). In fact this also appears to have been the practice before the order was issued. J. H. Baker, *The Reports of Sir John Spelman* (Selden Soc., xciv, 1978), p. 89.

31 Corpus Christi College, Oxford, MS B/20/1, letters dated February 1602 and February 1603.

32 PRO STAC 5, F 17/36.

33 Bodl. MS Rawlinson C. 65, 'Instructions for an Attorney' (no pagination), [fols. 20–2v].

34 See, for example, SBT DR 10/1952, letter from John Smith to Arthur Gregory of Stivichall, March 1599; SBT DR 10/1709, letter from James Prescott to Arthur Gregory.

35 For a good account of the functions of the attorneys in preparing cases for assize see Powell, *The Attourneys Academy...* (1623), pp. 134–5.

36 Lists of attorneys who were receiving *posteas* from the clerk of assize on the Western Circuit have survived for the early years of the seventeenth century in the PRO. See, for example, ASZ 24/29.

37 HCRO 63849, Court Book of James Willymott, fol. 77, mentions a meeting of the Odsey hundred court (p. 119). Notes of cases handled by John Clifford of Frampton at 'the County Court at Shroud', October 1642. For town courts see above, pp. 41–3.

38 See, for example, S. C. Ratcliff and H. C. Johnson, eds., *Quarter Sessions Records, Easter 1674 to Easter 1682* (Warwick Co. Records, vii, 1946), p. 1. B. W. Quintrell, 'The Government of the County of Essex, 1603–1642' (London Univ. unpub. Ph.D. thesis, 1965), p. 346. Lawyers also appeared for individuals and groups at assizes on matters relating to county administration. T. G. Barnes, ed., *Somerset Assize Orders* (Somerset Rec. Soc., lxv, Frome, 1959), p. xxxiii.

39 J. H. Baker, 'Criminal Courts and Procedure at Common Law 1550–1800', in *Crime in England 1550–1800*, ed. J. S. Cockburn (1977), pp. 28–30, 37. J. H. Langbein, *Prosecuting Crime in the Renaissance: England, Germany, France* (Cambridge, Mass., 1974), pp. 5, 10, 20, 104. The use of counsel to represent defendants to felony came into use only in the eighteenth century.

40 Quintrell, 'Government of Essex', p. 74.

41 PRO STAC 8/69/22. The case in question involved a defendant accused of riot. Although the wording is slightly ambiguous, it is interesting that Brere makes no distinction between felonies and misdemeanours. Pleas of the crown involved both kinds of offence.

42 Hants. Rec. Office, Quarter Sessions Order Book, 1628–49, fol. 50, dated 8 January 1633. I thank Dr J. S. Cockburn for giving me a photocopy of this document.

43 B. Abel-Smith and Robert Stevens, *Lawyers and the Courts* (1967), pp. 237, 457.

44 J. H. Baker, 'Counsellors and Barristers: An Historical Study', *Cambridge Law Journal*, 27 (1969), 208.

45 *Ibid.*, p. 224. *The Lives of the Right Hon. Francis North, Baron Guildford...By the Hon. Roger North...*, ed. A. Jessopp (3 vols., 1890), i, p. 40. *The Autobiography of Roger North*, ed. A. Jessopp (1887), p. 141.

46 I owe these points to Mr J. P. Cooper and Dr W. R. Prest.

47 Draper MS, fols. 4v, 6, 11, 12, 17, 18v, 30, 48.

48 Birmingham Reference Lib., Hagley Hall MS 358304, Misc. Vol. II, fol. v. (I am grateful to Mr J. Tonks for this reference.) Corpus Christi College, Oxford, MS B/20/1, letter dated 24 October 1599.

49 Powell, *Attourneys Academy*, p. 120.

50 Draper MS., fols. 4v, 6, 11, 12, 17, 18v, 30, 48.

51 SBT DR 3/634.

52 Corpus Christi College, Oxford, MS B/20/1, letter dated 24 October, 1599.

53 The Gregory papers at SBT contain an unusually large number of such letters. See, for example, DR 10/1491, 1670, 1709, and 1934.

54 PRO SP 46/72, fols. 30, 35.

55 See above, pp. 105–6.

56 John Hawarde, *Les Reportes del Cases in Camera Stellata, 1593–1609*, ed. W. P. Baildon (London, 1894), p. 230. Other examples of charges of maintenance can be found in the Star Chamber records. For example, PRO STAC 8/204/8 contains a charge against an attorney for contracting 'for the benefit of the thing to be recovered'. See also STAC 8/90/20; 8/181/11.

57 PRO E 215/857/1.

58 PRO E 215/752.

59 PRO E 215/1530. Squire was an attorney of the Stannery Court at Chagford.

60 Bodl. Tanner MS 287, fol. 72. PRO E 215/1329, fols. 3–4v, and E 215/1587 c, fol. 3.

61 PRO STAC 8/88/1, *Peter* v. *Calmady*. The attorney, Thomas Peter of Okehampton, was accused of making changes in a *latitat*. It is also of interest that the warrants were drawn up in this case by the brother of the deputy sheriff of Devon, John Rattenbury, who was away at the time. For Lashbrooke see Barnes, ed., *Somerset Assize Orders*, pp. xix, 20, and P. W. Hasler *The House of Commons, 1558–1603* (3 vols., 1981).

62 See in general J. S. Cockburn, *A History of English Assizes 1558–1714* (Cambridge, 1972), ch. v, for examples of the corrupt practices of attorneys. However, I disagree with his conclusions.

63 See above, p. 137. In general, the very existence of a large number of Star Chamber cases about alleged malpractice is proof that some means existed for controlling it.

64 SBT DR 10/1951, 1723.

65 M. Zander, *The State of Knowledge about the English Legal Profession* (1980), p. 19. Conveyancing provides 55.6 per cent of income; court work, only about 13.7 per cent.

66 Fees for writing legal instruments appear to have been quite high in comparison with those for litigation. See above, p. 241.

67 *The Tenours and Fourme of Indenture, Obligations, Quitaunces, Bylles of Paymente, Letters of Sale and Letters of Exchauncy, Protections, Supplications, Complaints...* (printed by John Tysdale, 1541). *A Newe Boke of Presidents Exactly Written in Maner of a Register Newly Imprinted Augmented and Corrected...* (1543). There are many subsequent editions.

68 William West, *The first Part of Symbolaeographia. Which May Be Termed the Art or Description or Image of Instruments.... Or the Paterne of Praesidents. Or The Notarie or Scrivner* (1590), sect. 352.

69 H. Winch, *Reports in the Last Years of the Reign of King James* (1657), p. 40, Mich. 20 Jac. I.

70 Brit. Lib. Lansdowne MS 569 includes, fol. 61v, the certificate for the election of a constable. Bodl. MS Rawlinson C. 271, esp. fols 32v ff. Gloucs. Rec. Office, D 149/B1, notebook of John Clifford, pp. 9–60. D 2375/1 14, 'A Lawyer's Precedent Book'.

71 Styles, 'The Social Structure of Kineton Hundred', p. 115.

72 North, *Autobiography*, p. 141. Although there may have been some changes in the relative proportions of contentious versus non-contentious business over the years from 1660 to 1800, I cannot agree with M. Miles, '"Eminent Attorneys" – Some Aspects of West Riding Attorneyship, *c.* 1750–1800' (Birmingham Univ. unpub. Ph.D. thesis, 1981), pp. 134–52, that non-contentious business was a feature of practice particularly characteristic of the eighteenth century.

73 J. A. R. Abbott, 'Robert Abbott, City Money Scrivener, and his account book 1646–1652', *Guildhall Miscellany*, 7 (1956), 31–3.

74 Guildhall Lib., London, MS 2931, 'Account book of Robert Abbott, Citizen of London', fols. 5, 23v–24. Abbott also acted as a real-estate broker (fol. 66v).

75 SBT DR 10/1870, memoranda and accounts of Thomas Gregory of Coventry, Easter 1551–1573/4, fols. 16, 39. Bodl. MS Dugdale 50, transcript by F. Maddon of Dugdale's diary for 1656, p. 10. In February 1656 Dugdale gave a bond to Prescott for £50 borrowed. He repaid £52 10s. (p. 12).

76 Bodl. MS Dugdale 50, p. 11. In June 1656 Dugdale gave Prescott £53 which Dugdale owed to a Mrs Dean of Barford on a bond.

77 Devon Co. Rec. Office, 'Enrolled Deeds, Calendar and Introduction', by J. C. Tingley (typescript), nos. 1462, 1475.

78 L. Stone, *The Crisis of the Aristocracy 1558–1641* (Oxford, 1965), p. 183. B. A. Holderness, 'Credit in English Rural Society before the nineteenth Century with Special Reference to the Period 1650–1720', *Agricultural History Review*, 24 (1976), 97–109.

79 Devon Co. Rec. Office, 'Enrolled Deeds'. These have been searched for all references involving the Devonshire practitioners in my sample.

80 J. Cowell, *A Law Dictionary or the Interpreter* (Cambridge, 1607), *sub.* 'Distress'.

81 The survival and importance of manorial courts varied from region to region. P. Clark, *English Provincial Society from the Reformation to the Revolution: Religion, Politics and Society in Kent 1500–1640* (Hassocks, 1977), pp. 113, 116. Pages 142–8 argue that in Kent quarter and petty sessions had begun by the end of the reign of Elizabeth to take over most of the functions of the court leet. However, studies by Emmison and Harrison of manorial courts in Essex and Staffordshire agree that the courts leet were still quite active in the late Elizabethan period. Harrison finds that between 1584 and 1602 justices of the peace handled only a handful of cases of assault, theft, and poaching involving the men of the manor of Cannock and Rugeley while the manorial court heard hundreds of similar cases. F. G. Emmison, *Elizabethan Life: Home, Land and Work* (Chelmsford, 1976), pp. 197ff. C. J. Harrison, 'The Social and Economic History of Cannock and Rugeley, 1546–1597' (Keele Univ. unpub. Ph.D. thesis, 1974), p. 155. My own cursory study of the manorial records of Warwickshire tends to support the conclusions of Emmison and Harrison.

82 Before roughly the 1580s, it seems to have been rare for the steward of a manorial court to give his name in the records. Stone, *Crisis of the Aristocracy*, ch. VI, introduces the subject of estate management but has little to say about legal personnel or the manorial courts.

83 See, for example, HCRO 63849, the early-seventeenth-century court book of James Willymot of Kelshall.

84 The *Modus Tenendi Cûr Barôn Cum Visu Franci Plegii*, published in 1510 by Wynkyn de Worde, was undoubtedly the descendant of an earlier manuscript tradition. F. J. C. Hearnshaw, *Leet Jurisdiction in England* (Southampton Rec. Soc., Southampton, 1908), pp. 19–156.

85 Hearnshaw, *Leet Jurisdiction*, p. 75. J. Kitchin, *Le Covrt Leet et Covrt Baron*... (1581). Sir E. Coke, *The Complete Copyholder* (1641). C. Calthrope, *The Relation betweene the Lord of a Mannor and the Coppyholder his Tenant* (1635).

86 See generally E. Kerridge, *Agrarian Problems in the Sixteenth Century and After* (1969), and P. F. W. Large, 'Economic and Social Change in North Worcestershire during the Early Seventeenth Century' (Oxford Univ. unpub. D.Phil, thesis, 1980), pp. 10–30. Also see above, pp. 201–3.

87 See above, pp. 116–17. Kitchin, *Le Covrt Leet et Covrt Baron*, p. 1.
88 Calthrope, *The Relation*, pp. 1–6.
89 SBT DR 10/1815, fol. 1.
90 SBT DR 10/1813, fols. 3v–4v.
91 See above, p. 178.
92 C. Kerry, 'Anthony Bradshaw of Duffield and the Alms Houses Founded by him at That Place', *The Reliquary*, 23 (1882–3), 137, 171. Bradshaw also thought that rhythmic repetition might help the less well educated to remember their rights.
93 M. E. James, 'The Concept of Order and the Northern Rising of 1569', *Past and Present*, 60 (1973), 57–83.
94 HCRO 63849.
95 Birmingham Reference Lib., Hagley Hall MS 358304, Misc. Vol. II, fols. 10–10v.
96 Devon Co. Rec. Office, Petre MS 123M/1040.
97 J. T. Cliffe, *The Yorkshire Gentry* (1969), p. 120.
98 Hence the remarks of Thomas Clay advising landlords to hire well-trained men as stewards. See above, pp. 117–18.
99 I owe this information to Mr Julian Tonks.
100 See below, p. 260.
101 *Lives of the Norths*, ed. Jessopp, i, p. 31.
102 PRO E 215/1587c, presentments of the commissioners for Surrey, 1628–9, fol. 4
103 M. Campbell, *The English Yeoman* (New Haven, Conn., 1942), p. 133. But she also points out that copyholders could use the law (p. 124). Cliffe, *Yorkshire Gentry*, p. 41.
104 Kerridge, *Agrarian Problems*. My own reading supports Kerridge's conclusions about the legal position after 1550.
105 Birminham Reference Lib., Hagley Hall, Box 72, dispute between the tenants of the manor of Cradley and Sir Thomas Littleton, 1630–3. War. Rec. Office, 'Catalogue of Maxstoke Castle MS', item 56. Bedford Co. Rec. Office, L 24/419, letter from John Chemocke to his neighbours in Clophill about a joint suit.
106 T. Barrett-Lennard, 'Two Hundred Years of Estate Management at Horsford during the Seventeenth and Eighteenth Centuries', *Norfolk and Norwich Archaeological Soc.*, 20 (1) (1919), 69. See also C. Holmes, *Seventeenth-Century Lincolnshire* (History of Lincolnshire, vii, Lincoln, 1980), pp. 12–13.
107 See above p. 135.
108 Mill Stephenson, *A List of Monumental Brasses in the British Isles* (1926), p. 121.
109 M. Spufford, *Contrasting Communities: English Villagers in the Sixteenth and Seventeenth Centuries* (Cambridge, 1974), ch. 2 and pp. 165–7. However, a great deal of allowance has to be made for regional variations.

10. PUBLIC OFFICE AND POLITICS

1 C. W. Brooks, 'The Common Lawyers in England, *c.* 1558–1642', in W. R. Prest, ed., *Lawyers in Early Modern Europe and America* (1981), pp. 57–60. S. D. White, *Sir Edward Coke and 'The Grievances of the Commonwealth', 1621–1628* (Chapel Hill, N.C., 1979).

2 Of Elizabethan practitioners, Lewis Lashbrook, Richard Sparry, Thomas Goddard, and William Badger are known to have gained places in the House of Commons thanks largely to their connections with the town governments of Totnes, Southampton, and Winchester. P. W. Hasler, *The House of Commons, 1558–1603* (3 vols., 1981). In general the presence of members of the lower branch in parliament during the early seventeenth century does not seem to have increased in proportion to the increase in their numbers. Of the practitioners in the three-county sample, only Gilbert Eveleigh of Totnes is known to have been an MP (in the 1650s). I am grateful to Dr B. Clendenin for giving me a copy of his list of MPs, 1604–10, against which I have checked my lists of attorneys and clerks. B. Clendenin, 'The Common Lawyers in Politics and Society: A Social and Political Study of the Common Lawyers in the First Jacobean Parliament' (Univ. of North Carolina unpub. Ph.D. thesis, 1975).

3 In a letter to Sir Francis Walsingham, dated 1582, the Earl of Leicester called for a revision of the commissions of the peace and claimed that 'even attorneys, and no better, are by heaps put into the commission'. *CSPD, 1581–1590*, p. 69. However, I have found no evidence that practitioners of the lower branch were ever regularly appointed to the commissions.

4 T. G. Barnes, *The Clerk of the Peace in Caroline Somerset* (Univ. of Leicester Department of English Local History, Occasional Papers 14, 1961), gives the history and discusses the duties of the office. For clerks of assize see J. S. Cockburn. *A History of English Assizes 1558–1714* (Cambridge, 1972), ch. 5.

5 Barnes, *Clerk of the Peace*, pp. 20, 29.

6 *Ibid.*, p. 14.

7 S. A. H. Burne, ed., *The Staffordshire Quarter Sessions Rolls*, vol. i: *1581–1589* (Wm Salt Archaeological Soc., 1929), p. xxix. J. E. Neale, 'The Elizabethan Political Scene', *Proc. British Academy*, 34 (1948), 113.

8 Historical Manuscripts Commission, *Hatfield MSS*, part xxii, pp. 86–7.

9 J. P. Cooper, ed., *Wentworth Papers 1597–1628* (Royal Historical Soc., Camden, 4th ser., xii, 1973)), pp. 85–6, 255.

10 Barnes, *Clerk of the Peace*, p. 7.

11 S. C. Ratcliff and H. C. Johnson, eds., *Quarter Sessions Order Book: Easter 1625 to Trinity 1637* (Warwick Co. Records, vol. i, 1935), p. xxiv.

12 J. J. Bagley, 'Kenyon vs. Rigby: The Struggle for the Clerkship of the Peace in Lancashire in the Seventeenth Century', *Historic Soc. of Lancashire and Chester*, 106 (1955), 34–5. B. W. Quintrell, 'The

Government of the County of Essex, 1603–1642' (London Univ. unpub. Ph.D. thesis, 1965), p. 68, notes that Edward Eldred of Stebbing was clerk in Essex from 1611 to 1624, but adds that not all clerks enjoyed long tenures in office.

13 Bagley, 'Kenyon vs. Rigby', pp. 35–7.

14 See. A. Hassell Smith, *County and Court: Government and Politics in Norfolk, 1558–1603* (Oxford, 1974), ch. VII, for a good account of the office.

15 Cooper, ed., *Wentworth Papers*, pp. 12–13. Smith, *County and Court*, ch. VII. Quintrell, 'Government of Essex', pp. 91–2, found little enthusiasm for the office.

16 1 Hen. V caps. 3–6.

17 There were many Star Chamber cases alleging malpractice by under-sheriffs. PRO STAC 5/P/19/10, 5/A/41/30, 5/K/8/11, 5/A/2/17. I owe these references to E. Skelton, 'The Court of Star Chamber in the Reign of Elizabeth' (London Univ. unpub. M.A. thesis, 1931).

18 Cooper, ed., *Wentworth Papers*, p. 13.

19 Smith, *County and Court*, p. 151.

20 Cooper, ed., *Wentworth Papers*, pp. 13, 41. PRO SP 46/72, fol. 212. See also T. E. Hartley, 'Under-Sheriffs and Bailiffs in Some English Shrievalties, *c.* 1580 to *c.* 1625', *Bull. Institute Historical Research*, 47 (1974), 164–85.

21 Hartley, 'Under-Sheriffs and Bailiffs', pp. 164–5. M. Dalton, *Officium Vicecomitum: The Office and Authoritie of Sherifs* (1623).

22 SBT DR 98/1267.

23 SBT DR 98/1117, 1118.

24 Hartley, 'Under-Sheriffs and Bailiffs', Appendix A.

25 See, for example, Shelagh Bond, ed., *The Chamber Order Book of Worcester 1602–1650* (Worcs. Historical Soc., NS, viii, 1974), p. 29. Recorders will be treated in more detail by Dr W. R. Prest in his forthcoming book on the upper branch of the legal profession.

26 Coventry City Rec. Office, A. 34, Book of Humphrey Burton, fol. 94. Historical Manuscripts Commission, *Exeter* (1916), p. 124.

27 Coventry City Rec. Office, A. 34, fol. 94.

28 P. Styles, 'The Corporation of Warwick, 1660–1835', *Trans. and Proc. Birmingham Archaeological Assoc.*, 59 (1935), 22. J. Roberts 'Reflections on Elizabethan Barnstaple Politics and Society', *Trans. Devon Assoc.*, 103 (1971), 143.

29 In large towns in particular, town clerks might well have been called to the bar at one of the inns of court. This was true of both Worcester and Bristol. Bond, ed., *Chamber Order Book of Worcester*, p. 29. John Latimer, *The Annals of Bristol in the Sixteenth Century* (Bristol, 1900; repr. 1970), p. 79.

30 Devon Co. Rec. Office, Exeter City Book 51, John Hooker's Commonplace Book, fol. 175.

31 *Ibid.* Some of Hooker's views on this office and others were published in John Vowell, alias Hooker, *A Pamphlet of the Offices and Duties of Everie Particular Sworne Officer of the Citie of Excester* (1584).

32 Thomas Kemp, ed., *The Book of John Fisher, 1580–1588* (Warwick, 1900), provides insights into the activities of a sixteenth-century town clerk.

33 Devon Co. Rec. Office, Exeter City Book 51, fol. 175.

34 Vowell, alias Hooker, *A Pamphlet of the Offices*, fol. i.

35 See in general R. Tittler, 'The Incorporation of Boroughs 1540–1558', *History*, 62 (1977), 24–42 and esp. Appendix A.

36 Bideford (1574), Southmolton (1590), Tiverton (1616), Torrington (1618), Okehampton (1624).

37 M. Weinbaum, *The Incorporation of Boroughs* (Manchester, 1936), p. xxiii.

38 Styles, 'The Corporation of Warwick', 14. For many detailed examples see D. Hirst, *The Representative of the People?* (Cambridge, 1975).

39 *Victoria County History of Warwickshire*, iii (1945), p. 250.

40 Kemp, ed., *The Book of John Fisher*, p. 2.

41 E 215/1069. Noyes was town clerk in 1634. He already had a large practice in Common Pleas in 1606.

42 Coventry City Rec. Office A 14, Council Minute Book (b), fol. 240v. *VCH Warwickshire*, viii (1969), p. 267.

43 J. Foster, *Alumni Oxonienses: The Members of the University of Oxford 1500–1714* (1891–2). Another father-and-son combination, Richard and Edward Hext, held the Exeter town clerkship from 1538 to 1620. W. T. MacCaffrey, *Exeter 1540–1640: The Growth of an English County Town* (Cambridge, Mass., 1958), p. 46. Yet another comes from Reading, where Edward Wylmer junior succeeded his father in 1652. J. M. Guilding, ed., *Reading Records* (4 vols., 1892–6), iv, p. 444.

44 See above, p. 241.

45 Devon Co. Rec. Office, Exeter City Book 51, fol. 175.

46 Coventry City Rec. Office A 14 (b), p. 249.

47 W. H. Richardson, ed., *The Annals of Ipswiche...Collected...by Nathaniel Bacon...* (1880), p. 367, for regulations governing the activities of the town clerk.

48 C. F. Rea, 'The Bastewells of Totnes', *Trans. Devon Assoc.*, 56 (1925), 204.

49 The clerk was elected at Coventry, Exeter, Warwick, Worcester, Bristol, Rye, Reading, Newcastle upon Tyne, Cambridge, and Northampton. Bond, ed., *Chamber Order Book of Worcester*, p. 31. William Barrett, *History and Antiquities of Bristol* (1789), p. 115. William Holloway, *The History and Antiquities of the Ancient Town and Port of Rye* (1857), pp. 550–1. Guilding, ed., *Reading Records*, i, pp. 323, 459. John Brand, *History and Antiquities of the Town and County of the Town of Newcastle upon Tyne* (London, 1789), p. 215. C. H. Cooper, *Annals of Cambridge* (5 vols., Cambridge, 1842), iii, p. 41. J. Charles Cox, ed., *The Records of the Borough of Northampton* (2 vols., Northampton, 1898), i, pp. 67–70.

50 For faction fights related to the appointment of clerks see, for example, M. V. Jones, 'The Political History of the Parliamentary Boroughs of Kent 1642–1660' (London Univ. unpub. Ph.D. thesis, 1967), pp. 332–8.

51 M. Bateson, ed., *Records of the Borough of Leicester* (3 vols., Cambridge, 1905), iii, p. 278.

52 PRO CHESTER 14/6, fol. 11

53 Cooper, *Annals of Cambridge*, ii, pp. 41, 211, 220, 244.

54 See above, pp. 221–2.

55 See above, pp. 184–6.

56 War. Rec. Office, W 21/6, fols. 60, 68, 127.

57 *VCH Warwickshire*, ii, p. 257.

58 In Worcester, attorneys apparently had to become freemen. John Noake, *Worcester in Olden Times* (1849), pp. 124–5. The Somerset practitioner William Harvey was a Jacobean mayor of Bridgwater and a great power in the town. PRO STAC 8/233/20. Bartholemew Cox was town clerk and mayor of Wells in 1624, 1632, 1636, and 1648. M. Birks, *Gentlemen of the Law* (1960), p. 122. John Wickstead was an alderman of Cambridge in 1612. Cooper, *Annals of Cambridge*, iii, p. 53.

59 K. R. Adey, 'Aspects of the History of the Town of Stafford 1590–1710' (Keele Univ. unpub. M.A. thesis, 1971), p. 65.

60 *Ibid.*, p. 60.

61 See in general P. Borsay, 'The English Urban Renaissance: The Development of Provincial Urban Culture c. 1680–c. 1760', *Social History*, 5 (1977), 581–605.

62 In Coventry, Henry Tadlow, George Palmer, and Hugh Willington. In Exeter, Thomas Osmund, Thomas Shapcott, John Wootton, George Izacke, George Moncke, Richard Long, Nicholas Weare, German Shapcott, Philip Biggleston, John Tucker. Devon Co. Rec. Office, Exeter City Book, 51, fol. 351v.

63 W. B. Stephens, 'Merchant Companies and Commercial Policy in Exeter 1625–1655', *Trans. Devon Assoc.* 86 (1954), 136. The same author's *Seventeenth Century Exeter* (Exeter, 1958), p. 43, points out that Thomas Shapcott, the attorney, who was assessed at a capital value of £3280 by the committee for compounding, was one of the richest men in the city. However, the richest was a merchant worth £15,572. For London see F. F. Foster, *The Politics of Stability: A Portrait of the Rulers of Elizabethan London* (1977), p. 62. Latimer, *Annals of Bristol*, and Barrett, *History and Antiquities of Bristol*, *passim*. J. T. Evans, *Seventeenth-Century Norwich* (Oxford, 1979), pp. 31–3. Brand, *History and Antiquities of Newcastle*, *passim*.

64 W. G. Hoskins, *Devon and its People* (1968). Roberts, 'Reflections on Elizabethan Barnstaple Politics and Society', pp. 137–47. W. G. Hoskins and H. P. R. Finberg, *Devonshire Studies* (1952), p. 230.

65 Hugh North of Hertford was rated at two hearths; William Ellis of St Albans at five (PRO E 179/248/23, m. 149). On the other hand,

James Willymott of Kelshall was valued at twelve, as was Jonathon Waller of Ashwell. William Houlker of King's Langley was listed at ten. PRO E 179/248/23, m. 172.

66 R. L. Hine, *The History of Hitchin* (2 vols. 1928–9), i, 52.

67 PRO E 179/375/30, Herts. Hearth Tax Return, Michaelmas 1662.

68 William Bulworthie, Thomas Stephens, John Rosyer, and William Warman lived in Barnstaple. Daniel Sloleigh and Thomas Prideaux lived in the nearby village of Fermington.

69 In Tiverton, Henry Newte and Joseph Skinner; but Hugh Canworthy, Phineaus May, and Thomas Osmund (all of Halberton), and George Salter (of Cruse Morchant) lived nearby. In Totnes, Gilbert Eveleigh and Richard Wolfe. In Plympton, Thomas Avent and Christopher Martin. In Okehampton, John Rattenbury. In Ashburton, John Ford.

70 H. J. Hanham, 'Ashburton as a Parliamentary Borough, 1640–1866', *Trans. Devon Assoc.*, 98 (1966), 207–9.

71 See, for example, W. S. Holdsworth, *The Influence of the Legal Profession on the Growth of the English Constitution* (Creighton Lecture, Oxford, 1924), pp. 6–29.

72 Sir John Fortescue, *De Laudibus Legum Angliae*, ed. S. B. Chrimes (Cambridge, 1942), p. 25.

73 For a more detailed discussion see C. W. Brooks, 'Law, Politics and the Ancient Constitution in Sixteenth-Century England (Forthcoming). See also Brit. Lib. Harleian MS 361, fol. 68, the charge of the judges to the jurors in the Marprelate case. And [Sir William Cecil], *The Execution of Justice in England for Maintenaunce of Publique and Christian Peace...* (1583).

74 William Lambarde, *Archion or a Commentary upon the High Courts of Justice in England* (1635, but written during the reign of Elizabeth), pp. 1–5.

75 R. Crompton, *L'Authoritie et Iurisdiction des Covrts de la Maiestie de la Roygne* (1594), Preface. J. Kitchin, *Le Covrt Leet et Le Covrt Baron...* (1581), pp. 2–3. Ferdinando Pulton, *De Pace Regis et Regni: viz. A Treatise Declaring Which Be the Great and Generall Offences of the Realme and the Chiefe Impediments of the Peace of the King and Kingdome...* (1609), Preface. William Fulbecke, *A Direction or Preparative to the Study of the Lawe* (1603), p. 2.

76 *The Reports of Sir Edward Coke*, ed. J. H. Thomas (13 parts in 7 vols., 1826), i, part II, pp. v–x. Sir John Davies, *Le primer report des cases et matters en ley resolues et adiudges en les courts de roy en Ireland* (Dublin, 1615; London, 1617), 'Epistle', J. G. A. Pocock, *The Ancient Constitution and the Feudal Law* (Cambridge, 1957), chs. II and III. C. Brooks and K. Sharpe, 'History, English Law and the Renaissance: A Comment', *Past and Present*, 72 (1976), 133–42. E. R. Foster, ed., *Proceedings in Parliament 1610* (2 vols., New Haven, Conn., 1966), ii, pp. 170–224. C. Russell, *Parliaments and English Politics 1621–1629* (Oxford, 1979), ch. VI. Brooks, 'The Common Lawyers in England', pp. 57–60.

77 For some interesting contemporary answers to this question see Russell, *Parliaments and English Politics*, p. 348.

78 See above, pp. 198–203.

79 W. Cobbett, T. B. Howell, *et al.*, eds., *A Complete Collection of State Trials* (42 vols., 1816–98), ii, p. 416, and above, p. 127.

80 Brooks, 'The Common Lawyers in England', p. 58. See also J. H. R. Dias, 'Politics and Administration in Nottinghamshire and Derbyshire 1590–1640' (Oxford Univ. unpub. D.Phil thesis, 1973). A. L. Hughes, 'Politics and Society and Civil War in Warwickshire, 1620–1650' (Liverpool Univ. unpub. Ph.D. thesis, 1979). Quintrell, 'The Government of the County of Essex'.

81 Bond, ed., *The Chamber Order Book of Worcester*, p. 30. Wm Salt Lib., Stafford, MS 369, Notebook of Thomas Worwicke, sometime mayor of Stafford, fol. 143. W. J. Connor, ed., *The Southampton Mayor's Book of 1606–8* (Southampton Rec. Soc., 1978), p. 100. C. J. Palmer, ed., *The History of Great Yarmouth by Henry Manship, Town Clerk* (Yarmouth, 1854), pp. iv–v. R. W. Greaves, ed., *The First Ledger Book of High Wycombe* (Bucks. Rec. Soc., xi, 1956), pp. 170–1. H. J. Moule, *Descriptive Catalogue of the Charters, Minute Books and Other Documents of the Borough of Weymouth and Melcombe Regis* (Weymouth, 1883), p. 50. A. B. Rosen, 'Economic and Social Aspects of the History of Winchester, 1520–1670' (Oxford Univ. unpub. D.Phil. thesis, 1975), pp. 109–10. Bodl. MS Top. Hants. c. 5, John Trussell's MS on Winchester, pp. 83ff. T. Kemp, ed., *The Black Book of Warwick* (Warwick, 1898), pp. 99–104.

82 Moule, *Descriptive Catalogue*, p. 50. Connor, ed., *Southampton Mayor's Book*, p. 100.

83 Palmer, ed., *History of Great Yarmouth*, pp. iv–v. Wm Salt Lib., Stafford, MS 369, fol. 143.

84 Bodl. MS Top. Hants. c. 5, pp. 83ff.

85 Styles, 'Corporation of Warwick', p. 14. P. Williams, 'Government and Politics in Ludlow, 1590–1642', *Trans. Shropshire Archaeological Soc.*, 56 (1957–60), 283.

86 See, for example, Coventry City Rec. Office A 34, Book of Humphrey Burton, fol. 151. Charges for obtaining a new charter in 1623 came to £180 2s 6d.

87 In Hilary Term 1637, Coventry spent £100 on such lawsuits. *Ibid.*, W 571/1. Styles, 'Corporation of Warwick', p. 14.

88 Coventry City Rec. Office, A 34. Rea, 'The Bastewells of Totnes', pp. 204–5. Richardson, ed., *Annals of Ipswiche*, pp. 405, 449.

89 C. Holmes, *Seventeenth-Century Lincolnshire* (History of Lincolnshire, vii, Lincoln, 1980), p. 51. War. Rec. Office W 21/6, fols. 259–60.

90 Williams, 'Government and Politics in Ludlow', p. 285.

91 John Smith, *The Lives of the Berkeleys* (3 vols., Gloucester, 1883–5), ii, pp. 296, 302–3, 310, 313.

92 As we have seen already, three attorneys served as chief burgesses of the corporation (above, p. 214). Another practitioner, James Prescott,

was related by marriage to Rainsford and served as steward on the estates of Sir Thomas Lucy, a member of the faction opposed to Sir Thomas Leigh. War. Rec. Office CR 258/84, fol. 10. D. Mosler, 'A Social and Religious History of the English Civil War in the County of Warwick' (Stanford Univ. unpub. Ph.D. thesis, 1974), pp. 17–19.

93 Bodl. MS Top. Hants. c. 5, fols. 88–91. Palmer, ed., *History of Great Yarmouth*, pp. 24–6, 62, 191–2.

94 Bodl. MS Top. Hants. c. 5, fol. 83. Manship stressed the need for magistrates to put the law into service, for 'if they be both compared together, of the two, good magistrates be more needful, a great deal, than good laws....' Palmer, ed., *History of Great Yarmouth*, p. 191.

95 For Case see *Dictionary of National Biography* and C. B. Schmitt, 'John Case and Machiavelli', in *Essays Presented to Myron P. Gilmore*, ed. Sergio Bertelli and G. Ramakus (Florence, 1978), pp. 231–40.

96 C. M. Ingleby, ed., *Shakespeare and the Enclosure of Common Fields, Being a Fragment of the Private Diary of Thomas Greene, Town Clerk of Stratford 1614–1617* (Birmingham, 1885), pp. 3–6. Kemp. ed., *Black Book of Warwick*, pp. 295–6.

97 D. Underdown, *Somerset in Civil Wars and Interregnum* (Newton Abbot, 1973), pp. 124–5, 157–8. J. S. Morrill, *Cheshire 1630–1660* (Oxford, 1974), pp. 182, 224.

98 K. Lindley, *Fenland Riots and the English Revolution* (1982), pp. 140–1. Daniel Noddel, *To the Parliament of the Commonwealth of England and Every Individual Member Thereof the Declaration of Daniel Noddel, Solicitor for the Freeholders and Commoners within the Mannor of Epworth...* (1653), is an eloquent statement of the legal case of the freeholders and commoners. For Harrison see H. Ellis, ed., *The Obituary of Richard Smyth, Secondary of the Poultry Compter...* (Camden Soc., os, xliv, 1849), p. 52. Another practitioner, Thomas Malbon of Nantwich, seems to have supported the parliamentary cause at least partly because he considered the parliamentary forces less rapacious than the royalists. J. Hall, *A History of the Town and Parish of Nantwich* (Nantwich, 1883), pp. 140ff.

99 Jones, 'The Political History of the Parliamentary Boroughs of Kent', pp. 76, 89, 190, 338. M. A. E. Green, *Calendar of the Proceedings of the Committee for Compounding 1642–1656* (5 vols., 1889–92), checked for men who called themselves legal practitioners and against lists of attorneys from the three-county sample. Green notes that lawyers were fined more heavily than laymen because it was thought that lawyers should have been capable of making rational political choices. However, although it is true that practitioners were fined more heavily, the claim that this was because of their legal knowledge is not well documented (part v, p. xiv).

100 C. H. Firth and R. S. Rait, eds., *Acts and Ordinances of the Interregnum 1642–1660* (3 vols., 1911). A similar picture emerges from study of R. H. Silcock, 'County Government in Worcestershire, 1603–1660' (London Univ. unpub. Ph.D. thesis, 1974), and M. D. G. Wanklyn, 'Landed Society and Allegiance in Cheshire and

Shropshire in the First Civil War' (Victoria Univ. of Manchester unpub. Ph.D. thesis, 1976).

101 Hughes, 'Politics and Society and Civil War in Warwickshire', p. 329.

102 It is of interest that Thomas Shapcott of Exeter told the committee for compounding that he could not take up arms by reason of his profession, and Richard Williams of Chichester claimed that limits on his freedom of movement as a result of the wars hindered his professional activity. PRO SP 23/183, p. 587. SP 23/223, p. 865.

103 D. M. Palliser, 'Some Aspects of the Social and Economic History of York in the Sixteenth Century' (Oxford Univ. unpub. D.Phil. thesis, 1968), p. 326. C. A. Markham and J. C. Cox, eds., *The Records of the Borough of Northampton* (2 vols., Northampton, 1898), i, p. 197.

104 This was certainly the case in both Ludlow and Warwick.

105 P. Clark and P. Slack, *English Towns in Transition 1500–1700* (Oxford, 1976), ch. 9.

106 C. Holmes, *Seventeenth-Century Lincolnshire*, pp. 47–52, and, more generally, his 'The County Community in Stuart Historiography', *Journal of British Studies*, 19 (1980), 54–73.

107 F. J. C. Hearnshaw, *Leet Jurisdiction in England* (Southampton Rec. Soc., Southampton, 1908), pp. 174–5. P. Clark, *English Provincial Society from the Reformation to the Revolution: Religion, Politics and Society in Kent 1500–1640* (Hassocks, 1977), p. 298.

108 PRO STAC 8/233/20. Bond. ed., *Chamber Order Book of Worcester*, p. 30.

109 The long tenures in office of individuals and of families are one illustration of this. In Essex, Quintrell notes that the appointment of a new clerk of the peace had an 'individualistic' impact on the records. 'The Government of the County of Essex', p. 58. See also Barnes, *Clerk of the Peace in Caroline Somerset*, pp. 6, 19, 33.

110 Barnes, *Clerk of the Peace*, pp. 15–17. Barnes notes that many fifteenth-century clerks were holders of other offices and members of the royal household.

11. FEES AND INCOMES

1 PRO SP 12/224, fol. 139v. Richard Read, cursitor for Oxfordshire and Rutland, was described as a 'poor man and a poor office'. Thomas Albery (Devon and Kent) had only a small living and little land. At least fourteen cursitors were described as living entirely from the profits of their offices. G. E. Aylmer, *The King's Servants: The Civil Service of Charles I 1625–1642*, 2nd edn (1974), pp. 221–2, for the value of this and a number of other offices in the 1620s and 1630s.

2 W. J. Jones, *The Elizabethan Court of Chancery* (Oxford, 1967), p. 135. The minimum income of a six clerk in the late 1590s was probably £750 p.a.

3 *Ibid.* Aylmer, *King's Servants*, pp. 221–2, 294ff. As a means of comparison at this point and later on in this chapter, it is worth noting

that marriage portions for knightly families in the period 1551–1600 averaged £859, and that those of the greater gentry rose to something in the region of £2500 in the early seventeenth century. By this later date many marriage portions offered by peers were worth as much as £5000. J. P. Cooper, 'Patterns of Inheritance and Settlement by Great Landowners from the Fifteenth to the Eighteenth Centuries', in *Family and Inheritance: Rural Society in Western Europe 1200–1800*, ed. J. Goody, J. Thirsk, and E. P. Thompson (Cambridge, 1976), pp. 306–11. L. Stone, *The Crisis of the Aristocracy 1558–1641* (Oxford, 1965), pp. 638–9.

4 PRO PROB 11/203 (203 Fines). M. Campbell, *The English Yeoman under Elizabeth and the Early Stuarts* (New Haven, Conn., 1942), p. 238.

5 PRO E 215/631.

6 PRO PROB 11/179 (34 Harvey); 169 (99 Sadler); 183 (105 Coventry).

7 Aylmer, *King's Servants*, pp. 221–2.

8 H. E. Bell, *An Introduction to the History and Records of the Court of Wards and Liveries* (Cambridge, 1953), pp. 28–9. A. L. Hughes, 'Politics and Society and Civil War in Warwickshire, 1620–1650' (Liverpool Univ. unpub. Ph.D. thesis, 1979), pp. 66, 71.

9 C. A. F. Meekings, 'Draft of Passages Provided in 1951–52 for Wheatley's Revised Edition of *Edward Latymer and His Foundations*' (typescript).

10 PRO E 215/629.

11 *Ibid.*

12 PRO PROB 11/92 (79 Lewyn); 128 (96 Cope).

13 PRO E 215/629.

14 T. Barrett-Lennard, *An Account of the Families of Lennard and Barrett* (1908), pp. 6–8, 15, 31, 148. PRO PROB 11/77 (27 Sainberbe).

15 Lady Elizabeth Cust, *Records of the Cust Family* (3 vols., 1909), ii, pp. 19, 22, 33–41, 49–50.

16 Richard Colchester and Edward Latymer also had relations within the profession.

17 Aylmer, *King's Servants*, pp. 221–2. Compared with land, the purchase prices of offices were low in proportion to their annual value.

18 See above, pp. 123–4.

19 Cust, *Records*, ii, p. 35.

20 PRO PROB 11/77 (27 Sainberbe). Barrett-Lennard, *An Account*, p. 7.

21 Cust, *Records*, ii, p. 40.

22 By way of comparison, the usual counsellor's fee appears to have been 10s., although they were sometimes given as much as £1 for argument before the judges or for speaking at trials. Serjeants and counsellors were also sometimes paid according to the 'pains' they took. PRO E 215/11/849, fol. 9. PRO E 215/750, fol. 3.

23 The 'Roll of Warrants' is in PRO KB 27/1395.

24 A directory of attorneys with notes on their case loads has been compiled from the plea rolls for 1606–7. PRO CP 40/1735, 1763, 1757, 1769.

25 'Account Book of George Draper', manuscript in possession of Hawkins and Co., Portmill Lane, Hitchin. Gloucs. Rec. Office, D 149/B1–3.

26 *Parliamentary Papers : First Report of His Majesty's Commissioners (on the) Common Law* (1829), p. 690.

27 For a more detailed account of the relationship of the attorneys to the court bureaucracies, see above, pp. 23–4.

28 PRO E 215/11/849, fol. 11, presentment of the attorney-jurors of King's Bench to the commissioners of fees for this and other fees due to practitioners.

29 *Ibid.*

30 PRO E 215/629, fol. 2.

31 PRO PROB 11/114 (99 Dorset).

32 PRO PROB 11/265 (1657/217); 276 (1658/245).

33 PRO PROB 11/152 (180 Skynner); 131 (47 Meade); 161 (9 Audley); 121 (18 Capell).

34 See above, p. 189

35 T. Powell, *The Attourneys Academy...* (1623), p. 142.

36 *Ibid.*, chapters on litigation in Chancery, Star Chamber, etc.

37 PRO E 215/1454.

38 R. Bearman, *The Gregories of Stivichall in the Sixteenth Century* (Coventry and War. History Pamphlets No. 8, 1972), p. 12.

39 Draper MS, fols. 3v, 31.

40 PRO SP 23/183, p. 582 (papers of the committee for compounding).

41 J. S. Cockburn, *A History of English Assizes 1558–1714* (Cambridge, 1972), p. 82.

42 See above, p. 212.

43 C. A. Markham and J. C. Cox, eds., *The Records of the Borough of Northampton* (2 vols., Northampton, 1898), ii, p. 71.

44 A. L. Merson, ed., *The Third Book of Remembrance of Southampton 1514–1602* (2 vols., Southampton, 1955), ii, p. 125 n. 1. Goddard is an interesting example of an attorney who was the son of a merchant (p. 34 n. 1).

45 Coventry City Rec. Office, A 14(a), Council Minute Books, fol. 198v.

46 *Victoria County History of Warwickshire*, iii, p. 250.

47 Coventry City Rec. Office, A 14(b), fol. 353.

48 A number of lists of fees due to town clerks are in PRO E 215.

49 Norfolk Co. Rec. Office, Norfolk Consistory Court Wills, 380 Clearke.

50 SBT DR 10/1870, fol. 61.

51 E. A. Buckland, *The Rainsford Family* (Worcester, n.d. [*c.* 1939]), p. 136.

52 SBT DR 3/204. For Knight's court keeping see DR 5/2205, 3301, 2306. Francis North claimed to have made £5–£7 clear profit from one of the manorial courts he kept during the second half of the seventeenth

century. Roger North, *The Lives of the Norths*, ed. A. Jessopp (3 vols., 1890), i, p. 109.

53 This negative conclusion has been reached by checking the Victoria County Histories of Warwickshire and Hertfordshire, W. Dugdale, *Antiquities of Warwickshire* (1656), H. Chauncy, *The Historical Antiquities of Hertfordshire* (1700), and various local sources for Devonshire in the search for the manorial holdings of practitioners and their fathers.

54 M. Spufford, *Contrasting Communities: English Villagers in the Sixteenth and Seventeenth Centuries* (Cambridge, 1974), p. 173.

55 W. G. Hoskins and H. P. R. Finberg, *Devonshire Studies* (1952), p. 334.

56 A. Welsford, 'Mr Newte's Library in St Peter's Church, Tiverton', *Trans. Devon Assoc.*, 106 (1974). W. H. Wilkin, 'Some Axminster Worthies', *ibid.*, 61 (1934), 239. The attorney John Risdon was probably a brother of Tristram Risdon, author of *The Geographical Description or Survey of the County of Devon* (1811). For Shapcott see Hoskins and Finberg, *Devonshire Studies*, p. 347.

57 J. Burman, *Solihull and its School* (Birmingham, 1939), p. 4. S. C. Ratcliff and H. C. Johnson, eds., *Quarter Sessions Order Book: Easter 1625 to Trinity 1637* (Warwick Co. Records, i, Warwick, 1935), p. xxiv. One Richard Hawes was clerk of the peace in Warwickshire from 1516 to 1549. It is unclear whether Thomas was related to him.

58 R. Pemberton, *Solihull and its Church* (Exeter, 1905), p. 55.

59 T. W. Hutton, *King Edward's School Birmingham 1552–1952* (Oxford, 1952), pp. 6–7.

60 F. J. Fisher, ed., 'The State of England. Anno Domini 1600 by Thomas Wilson', *Camden Miscellany*, 3rd ser., 16 (1936), 24.

61 *The Visitations of Hertfordshire in 1572 and 1643*, p. 93.

62 *The Visitation of the County of Gloucester Taken in the Year 1623*, ed. J. Maclean and W. C. Hearne (Harleian Soc., xxi, 1885), p. 111.

63 *The Visitation of the County of Warwick in 1619*, p. 377.

64 *Staffordshire Pedigrees*, ed. G. J. Armytage and W. H. Rylands (Harleian Soc., lxiii, 1912), p. 99.

65 PRO SP 23/183, p. 582. Hoskins and Finberg, *Devonshire Studies*, p. 334.

66 *VCH Warwickshire*, iii, p. 214.

67 *The Visitation of the County of Warwick in 1682–83*, p. 89. Worcs. Rec. Office, will of Edmund Rawlins of Dorington, 28 February 1662.

68 *The Visitations of the County of Leicester in 1619*, ed. J. Featherston (Harleian Soc., ii, 1870), p. 145. PRO PROB 11/351, fol. 378; proved 1672.

69 PRO SP 23/279, p. 483.

70 PRO SP 23/190, p. 121.

71 PRO PROB 11/116 (98 Wingfield), will of William Booth of Witton, proved 1610.

72 PRO SP 23/223, p. 865.

73 PRO SP 23/183, p. 583.

74 Will proved in 1633. PRO PROB 11 (65 Scroope). For the son see J. Venn and J. A. Venn, *Alumni Cantabrigienses... from the Earliest Times to 1900* (Cambridge, 1922).

75 PRO PROB 11/159 (27 St John), will dated 1636.

76 *Ibid.* For another similar case see Norfolk Consistory Court Wills, 115 Trotter, will of Henry Skarburgh of Walsham, proved 1617.

77 PRO PROB 11/130 (82 Weldon).

78 PRO SP 23/185, pp. 225, 261.

79 PRO SP 23/184, p. 743. SP 23/183, p. 583.

80 Again, a negative conclusion based on the sources in Table 11.3. Of course, the value of manors varied.

81 HCRO 87625, 87630, 87650, 87666, 87685, 87688.

82 J. A. Bradney, ed., *The Diary of Walter Powell of Llantilio Crossenny in the County of Monmouth, Gentleman, 1603–1654* (Bristol, 1907), pp. iii, 11.

83 PRO SP 23/182, p. 341.

84 PRO SP 23/185, p. 327.

85 Hoskins and Finberg, *Devonshire Studies*, p. 353.

86 M. A. E. Green, *Calendar of the Proceedings of the Committee for Compounding 1643–1660* (5 vols., 1889–92), i, p. viii, for the penalties. It is interesting that no allowance for fees was made in the valuations compiled by the committee. Members of the legal profession were fined more heavily than laymen, however.

87 Stone, *Crisis of the Aristocracy*, pp. 132–3, discusses the problems involved in using the composition papers. He warns that the particulars 'only give the bare rental, which might be substantially increased by fines, sales of woods, and other casualties', but concludes, after comparing the composition papers with other evidence of the income of individuals, that the estimates produced for the committee 'were not too hopelessly remote from the truth'.

88 PRO SP 23/175, p. 1047. SP 23/184, p. 743. SP 20/205, p. 139. SP 23/179, p. 483. SP 23/220, p. 137, SP 23/190, pp. 121, 1183. SP 23/182, p. 341. SP 23/185, pp. 173, 191, 261, 327. SP 23/221, p. 563. SP 23/183, p. 582. SP 23/223, pp. 861, 865.

89 PRO SP 23/179, p. 483.

90 PRO SP 23/183, p. 582.

91 See in general P. H. Ramsey, ed., *The Price Revolution in Sixteenth-Century England* (1971).

92 G. O. Sayles, *Select Cases in the Court of King's Bench under Edward I* (Selden Soc., lv, 1936), p. lxxxvii.

93 E. H. Phelps-Brown and S. V. Hopkins, 'Seven Centuries of Prices of Consumables', in Ramsey, ed., *The Price Revolution*, p. 23, fig.1.

94 J. E. Cussans, *History of Hertfordshire* (3 vols., 1870–81), parts III and IV, p. 7, assessment of gentlemen in Hertfordshire in 1593.

95 Lichfield Joint Record Office, will of Thomas Hawes of Solihull.

96 V. H. T. Skipp, 'Economic and Social Change in the Forest of Arden, 1530–1649', *Agricultural History Review*, 18 (1970), 104–5.

97 PRO PROB 11/81 (39 Nevell), will proved in 1593.

98 SBT DR 10/1870, accounts of Thomas Gregory of Coventry, 1551–73/4. The accounts show Gregory's considerable interest in agriculture.
99 Thomas Hanchett was a member of Clifford's Inn. PRO PROB 11/59 (49 Daughtry). PROB 11/48 (19 Crymes).
100 H. J. Carpenters, 'Furse of Moreshead: A Family Record of the Sixteenth Century', *Trans. Devon. Assoc.*, 26 (1894), 168–84.
101 *Ibid.*, p. 253.
102 *Ibid.*, p. 176.
103 See above, pp. 178–9.
104 Lichfield Joint Record Office, will of Thomas Hawes.
105 PRO PROB 11/72 (33 Rutland).
106 J. L. Vivian, *The Visitations of the County of Devon* (Exeter, 1889), pp. 224, 535, 624.
107 J. Foster, *Alumni Oxonienses : The Members of the University of Oxford 1500–1714* (1891–2).
108 Vivian, *The Visitations of Devon*, p. 624.
109 Norfolk Consistory Court, 380 Clearke.
110 PRO PROB 11/55 (52 Windebank). PROB 11/55 (3 Peter).
111 PRO PROB 11/120 (106 Fenner). Norfolk Consistory Court, 97 Moyse alias Spicer.
112 PRO PROB 11/61 (21 Bakon).
113 PRO PROB 11/49 (11 Stonnarde).
114 PRO PROB 11/89 (40 Cobham), will of Thomas Jackson.
115 Lichfield Joint Record Office, will of Richard Denton, 1593.
116 Foster, *Alumni Oxonienses*. William was called to the bar at the Middle Temple in 1614 and was Autumn Reader in 1633.
117 *Ibid.* This William was called to the bar in 1647. He was a notable antiquary. See Dugdale, *Antiquities*, p. 878.
118 Worcs. Rec. Office, BA 3585233, inventory of William Foster, gent., of Warwick, dated June 1640.
119 PRO SP 23/179, p. 483. SP 23/220, p. 137.
120 PRO PROB 11/303 (1661, 14).
121 PRO PROB 11/229 (1653, 259).
122 PRO PROB 11/289 (1659/199).
123 War. Rec. Office, CR 258/84, will of James Prescott, dated 1659.
124 PRO PROB 11/330 (1669/62).
125 PRO PROB 11/130 (82 Weldon). PROB 11/159 (27 St John). PROB 11/189 (74 Campbell).
126 PRO PROB 11/160 (105 St John). Norfolk Consistory Court, 115 Trotter. PRO PROB 11/302 (1660/294).
127 PRO PROB 11/168 (73 Sadler), will of Richard Wolfe of Totnes; proved 1634.
128 For example, PRO SP 46/72, fol. 72, is a letter, dated 1603, from a solicitor to his client, Richard Carnsew, which expresses confidence in a King's Bench attorney. On the other hand, in 1662 William Booth of Witton told a client that 'You have this trouble by reason Mr Leight is no great experienced Lawyer.' Wm Salt Library, Stafford, MS SMS 28, 'William Booth's Clients' Cawses. 1662–1663', fol. 299.

129 T. G. Barnes, *The Clerk of the Peace in Caroline Somerset* (Univ. of Leicester Dept of English Local History Occasional Papers No. 14, Leicester, 1961), p. 36.

130 PRO SP 23/190, p. 121. Cockburn, *History of English Assizes*, pp. 76–7.

131 J. J. Bagley, 'Kenyon vs. Rigby: The Struggle for the Clerkship of the Peace in Lancashire in the Seventeenth Century', *Historic Soc. of Lancs. and Chester*, 106 (1955), 59. This valuation was made for use in a lawsuit.

132 See above, p. 205

133 Ratcliff and Johnson, eds., *Quarter Sessions Order Book : Easter 1625 to Trinity 1637*, p. xxiv. Hunt was clerk in 1604 and again from 1618 to 1625. B. W. Quintrell, 'The Government of the County of Essex, 1603–1642' (London Univ. unpub. Ph.D. thesis, 1965), p. 75, notes that Edward Eldred, clerk of the peace of Essex from 1611 to 1624, did not die a particularly rich man.

134 Prescott is known to have held courts for the Hales family at Smitterfield during the 1630s. SBT DR 38/1454. He was steward for Sir Thomas Lucy from 1626 until at least 1645. War. Rec. Office, L 6/29, 40. Eades held courts at Hanbury for the Earl of Leicester in 1657 (MR 4) and at Kington Parva (SBT DR 98/919). James Willymott kept the records of the manorial courts for which he was steward in a single bound volume which has survived in HCRO 63849.

135 A negative conclusion based on the published admissions registers of the inns of court.

136 Foster, *Alumni Oxonienses*.

137 PRO PROB 11/159 (27 St John).

138 PRO PROB 11/310 (1663, 51).

139 *Visitation of the County of Warwick in 1682–83*, p. 28.

140 On the wealth of the richer London merchants see R. G. Lang, 'The Greater Merchants of London in the Early Seventeenth Century' (Oxford Univ. unpub. D.Phil. thesis, 1963), ch. 5. It is interesting that Lang found that the merchants in his sample sprang largely from men of middling wealth – middling gentry, provincial tradesmen, and prosperous Londoners – men quite similar to the attorneys (p. 8).

12. CONCLUSION

1 M. S. Larson, *The Rise of Professionalism : A Sociological Analysis* (Berkeley, Calif., 1977), J. Ben-David, 'Professions in the Class System of Present-Day Societies', *Current Sociology*, 12 (1963–4), 247–96. A. M. Carr-Saunders and P. A. Wilson, *The Professions* (Oxford, 1933). T. Parsons, 'The Professions and Social Structure', *Essays in Sociological Theory* (Glencoe, Ill., 1954), p. 34.

2 T. E. Johnson, *Professions and Power* (1972), p. 51. Larson, *Rise of Professionalism*. pp. xii, 2, 68.

3 See the informative table in D. Podmore, *Solicitors and the Wider Community* (1980), p. 14, which lists the relationship between the number of solicitors and population from 1729 to 1977.

4 In the case of the lower branch of the legal profession, I see no reason to agree with Holmes' claim that the half-century or so beginning in the last years of Charles II's reign witnessed changes 'more remarkable in themselves and far-reaching in their implications, both for the state and for society, than anything which had taken place in comparable areas before the Civil Wars or the Restoration'. G. Holmes, *Augustan England: Professions, State and Society, 1680–1730* (1982), pp. x–xi and esp. ch. 5.

5 For some very brief comments on the lower branch in the early Tudor period see E. W. Ives, *The Common Lawyers in Pre-Reformation England* (Cambridge, 1983), ch. 1.

6 R. Robson, *The Attorney in Eighteenth Century England* (Cambridge, 1959), ch. 1.

7 *Ibid.*, chs. 1–2. See also M. Miles, '"Eminent Attorneys" – Some Aspects of West Riding Attorneyship, *c.* 1750–1800' (Birmingham Univ. unpub. Ph.D. thesis, 1982), pp. 331ff.

8 Robson, *The Attorney*, ch. 3–4.

9 J. W. Reader, *Professional Men: The Rise of the Professional Classes in Nineteenth-Century England* (1966), p. 25.

10 P. Elliot, *The Sociology of the Professions* (1972), p. 5.

11 See above, p. 144.

12 K. Charlton, 'The Professions in Sixteenth-Century England', *Univ. of Birmingham Historical Journal*, 12 (1969–70), 35.

13 Ives, *The Common Lawyers*, p. 17.

14 J. H. Baker, 'Solicitors and the Law of Maintenance, 1590–1640', *Cambridge Law Journal*, 32 (1) (1973), 56–80.

15 J. H. Baker, *An Introduction to English Legal History*, 2nd edn (1979), pp. 135–8.

16 See above p. 179.

17 Carr-Saunders and Wilson, *The Professions*, pp. 19, 53.

18 Reader, *Professional Men*, p. 25.

19 G. Unwin, *Industrial Organization in the Sixteenth and Seventeenth Centuries* (repr. 1957).

20 *Oxford English Dictionary*.

21 W. Perkins, 'A Treatise of Vocations or Callings of Men', *The Works...of Mr William Perkins* (3 vols., Cambridge, 1612), i, pp. 741ff.

22 PRO PROB 11/120 (106 Fenner); 310 (1663/51).

23 See, for a few of many examples, the wills of Emor Bilcliff, John Rosyer jun., Josias Bull, and Richard Yardly. PRO PROB 11/167 (9 Saddler), 289 (1659/199), 378, fol. 6, and 189 (74 Campbell).

24 PRO PROB 11/111 (5 Windebank); 11/254 (1656/148); 121 (59 Capell); 11/130 (82 Weldon).

25 See, for example, Thomas Nash, *Quaternio: or A Fourefold Way to a Happie Life, Set Forth in a Dialogue betweene a Countryman and a Citizen, a Divine and a Lawyer* (1633), 'To the Reader'. William Martin, *Youth's Instruction* (1612). Martin was recorder of Exeter. R. Brathwait, *The English Gentleman* (1630), pp. 107, 136ff.

26 Perkins, 'A Treatise of Vocations', p. 758.
27 H. Winch, *Reports in the Last Years of the Reign of King James* (1657), p. 40.
28 W. Sheppard, *Action upon the Case for Slander or a Methodical Collection under Certain Heads of Thousands of Cases...* (1662), p. 3.
29 Perkins, 'Treatise of Vocations', p. 759.
30 See N. Denholm-Young, *The Country Gentry in the Fourteenth Century* (Oxford, 1969). Sir George Sitwell, 'The English Gentleman', *The Ancestor*, 1 (April 1902), 58–103, and K. B. McFarlane, *The Nobility of Later Medieval England* (Oxford, 1973), ch. 1.
31 R. Kelso. *The Doctrine of the English Gentleman* (Urbana, Ill., 1929), pp. 23, 27, 37, 43, 49, 51.
32 Gray's Inn Lib., Barnard's Inn Admissions Book.
33 See above, pp. 249–51. G. E. Aylmer, *The King's Servants : The Civil Service of Charles I 1625–1642* (1961), p. 331.
34 L. Stone and J. F. C. Stone, 'Country Houses and their Owners in Hertfordshire, 1540–1879', in *The Dimensions of Quantitative Research in History*, ed. W. O. Aydelotte *et al.* (1972), p. 63. P. Styles, 'The Social Structure of Kineton Hundred in the Reign of Charles II', *Trans. and Proc. Birmingham Archaeological Soc.*, 78 (1962), 98, 105–6.
35 Stone and Stone, 'Country Houses', p. 100.
36 War. Rec. Office, QS 11/1, 3, 4, 5, Hearth Tax Returns 1662. PRO E 179/375/30, Hertfordshire Hearth Tax Returns, Michaelmas 1662.
37 PRO E 179/375/30.
38 War. Rec. Office, QS 11/1, 3, 4, 5.
39 Styles, 'Kineton Hundred', p. 116.
40 R. Grassby, 'The Personal Wealth of the Business Community in Seventeenth-Century England', *Economic History Review*, 2nd ser., 23 (1970), 220–33.
41 See above, pp. 186, 258.
42 PRO PROB 11/302 (1660/294).
43 PRO PROB 11/128 (85 Cope), 159 (27 St John).
44 L. Stone, 'Social Mobility in England, 1560–1640', *Past and Present*, 33 (1966), 27–8, 34, although he adds that very little is known about people like attorneys.
45 R. Grassby, 'Social Mobility and Business Enterprise in Seventeenth-Century England', in *Puritans and Revolutionaries*, ed. K. Thomas and D. Pennington (Oxford, 1978), pp. 355–82.
46 R. Finlay, *Population and Metropolis : The Demography of London 1580–1650* (Cambridge, 1981), pp. 63–7. For more on this subject see also C. W. Brooks, 'Guilds, Professions and the Middling Sort of People', in *Professions in Early-Modern England*, ed. W. R. Prest (forthcoming).
47 See above, pp. 132–5.
48 Bodl. MS Ashmole 1537 I, 'The Attorneys in parte Anatomized... By a Christian Hand', fols. 2–15.

49 S. A. Strong, *Catalogue of Letters and Other Historical Documents Exhibited in the Library at Welbeck* (1903), Appendix I: the Duke of Newcastle's advice to Charles II as he was about to take the throne (p. 192).

50 See above, p. 130.

51 Strong, *Catalogue of Letters*, p. 200.

52 See, for example, K. Wrightson, 'Two Concepts of Order: Justices, Constables, and Jurymen in Seventeenth-Century England', in *An Ungovernable People*, ed. J. Brewer and J. Styles (1980), p. 21–46.

53 J. Kent, '"Folk Justice" and Royal Justice in Early Seventeenth-Century England: A "Charivari" in the Midlands', *Midland History*, 8 (1983), 68–85. University of Durham, Department of Diplomatic and Paleography, Weardale Chest MSS 113–16.

54 D. Veall, *The Popular Movement for Law Reform 1640–1660* (Oxford, 1970).

SELECT BIBLIOGRAPHY

A. MANUSCRIPTS

Public Record Office, London

ASZ 24/29–30 *Posteas* files, Western Assize Circuit, 11–12 Jac. I
CHESTER 29 Palatinate of Chester, Exchequer court plea rolls
CP 11/2 Roll of attorneys, 1732
CP 40 Common Pleas plea rolls
CP 45 Common Pleas, Prothonotaries' remembrance rolls
DURHAM 3/218 Admissions of attorneys before the Chancellor's court, 1660–1723
E 13 Exchequer of pleas, plea rolls
E 101 Exchequer, King's Remembrancer accounts
E 163/16/17 Exchequer attorney's account book, 15 Jac. I
E 179 Lay taxation rolls (includes subsidy and hearth tax returns)
E 215 Papers of the early Stuart commissions on fees
IND 20–1, 23, 54–6, 157–65, 293, 328, 353–8, 1336, 1339, 1346–7, 1356–7, 1361, 1363, 1360, 1369–70 King's Bench and Common Pleas docket rolls
IND 4603 Book of attorneys, 1656–*c.* 1740
IR 1 Apprenticeship books
KB 27 King's Bench plea rolls
KB 139/120 Account book of clerk of the warrants, 1679
KB 150 Warrants of attorney files
PROB 11 Wills proved in the Prerogative Court of Canterbury
PC 2 Privy Council registers, Jac. I and Chas. I
SP 12, 14, 16 Elizabethan, Jacobean, and Caroline state papers, domestic
SP 23 Papers of the parliamentary committee for compounding
SP 46 State papers, supplementary
STAC 5, 8 Eizabethan and Jacobean Star Chamber proceedings
WARDS 9/271, 351 Scriveners' 'waste books'
    10/6 List of officials in the court of Wards. Undated, but between 1590 and 1594
    10/24 Bills of costs
30/26/74/3 Agreements for the erection of chambers at Clement's Inn

British Library, London

Additional MS 25,232 Judges' orders for Common Pleas, 1633
Cotton Titus B, iv, fol. 419 Gerard Malines discourse for reducing the laws to order
Cotton Titus F, iv Proceedings in parliament during the reign of James I
Cotton, Vespasian C, xix, vol. ii, fol. 2 'The Some of the Commission for the Reformation of Officers towards both Lawes', 1594
Hargrave 491, fol. 5v Post-Restoration reading on the statute 3 Jac. I c. 7
Lansdowne 23, 25, 44, 46, 47, 49, 106, 163, 1062 Burghley state papers. Papers of Sir Julius Caesar
Stowe 153 Critique of the reports of Sir Edward Coke

Gray's Inn Library, London

Barnard's Inn Admissions Book

Inner Temple Library, London

Miscellaneous 32 Collection relating to the antiquities of the Inner and Middle Temples
  62 Items touching the courts of Chancery and King's Bench
  186 Statutes of Clifford's Inn
Barrington 29 Miscellaneous legal tracts and documents

Lincoln's Inn Library, London

Miscellaneous 586 'Robert Moyle's Practice of the Courts'
  720 Baildon's transcript of the Middle Temple manuscript history of Lincoln's Inn and Furnival's Inn

Guildhall Library, London

Manuscript 2931 Account book of Robert Abbot, citizen of London

Bodleian Library, Oxford

All Souls' College, C. 291 Accounts
Ashmole 1136, 1144, 1147, 1151 (III), 1156, 1159, 1137 (I) Miscellaneous legal tracts and papers
Bankes 6/25, 11/51, 16/40, 16/54, 24, 37/55 Petitions and papers concerning officers in King's Bench and Common Pleas
Dugdale 50 Transcript of Sir William Dugdale's diary for 1656
English History b. 117 Contemporary copies of English state papers, *c.* 1580–90
  c. 304 Answer of clerk of Star Chamber to accusations made against him
New College D. 325 Robinson's tract on courts of record
North b. 1, b. 19 Miscellaneous legal and state papers

Rawlinson D. 51, fols. 24ff Transcripts of Scriveners' Company papers
  C. 65 Instructions for an attorney
  C. 271 Attorney's note-book
  C. 798 Notebook of Thomas Ravenhill
  D. 1123 Certificate of fees in the Common Pleas, 1627/8
Tanner 169 Miscellaneous letters and papers collected by Stephen Powle, clerk of the crown
  287 Returns to the commissioners on fees, 1623
Top. Hants. c. 5 John Trussell's MS on Winchester

Bedford County Record Office

Earl of Kent papers L24/347–355 Papers concerning Giles Blofield's work for the Earl of Kent
L24/414 Bills of legal costs
L26/270 Account book of Giles Blofield
L28/46 Essays of Sir Anthony Benn, Knt, Recorder of London
L28/47 Essay on the court of Chancery

Birmingham Reference Library

Gregory-Hood Deeds 184 and 185
Hagley Hall 358304 Misc., Littleton estate papers, vol. II

Corpus Christi College, Oxford

B/20/1 Letters between the president of the college and John Stampe, early seventeenth century

Coventry City Record Office

A 14 (a, b) Council Minute Books, 1557–1696
A 25 Court Book, 1584–1824
A34 Humphrey Burton's Book
Leech Miscellanea Deeds
'W' Collection 560–95 Bills of legal costs

Devon County Record Office

CR 52, 69–70, 89, 94–5, 98–9, 100–1, 115, 118, 153, 159, 1073–4, 1077–9, 1086, 1111, 1113, 1171, 1188, 1194 Transcripts of manorial and hundred court rolls
123 M/1040 Petre manuscripts
Exeter City Book 51 John Hooker's Common-place Book
J. C. Tingley, 'Enrolled Deeds Calendar and Introduction' (typescript)

Durham University Library

Mickleton-Spearman vols. 1, 15, 17, 18, 60, 81, 87 Manuscripts of Christopher Mickleton

Essex County Record Office

Barrington papers

Folger Library, Washington, DC

Mb. 42 Diary of Sir Roger Wilbraham, 1593–1646 (microfilm)
xd. 483 (196) The office of an attorney

Gloucestershire Record Office

D 149/B1–3 Papers of John Clifford of Frampton
D 149/81 Lawyer's precedent book

Hertfordshire Record Office

Accession 87625, 87630, 87650, 87666, 87685, 87688, 87698, 87701, 87707–9 Deeds involving John Skinner of Hitchin
6398–401, 6583–90, 7117–60, 9437–63, 47587, 57518, 65648, 65787, 65814, 65946, D/E6/E13, D/E6/M3, D/EAp/M6 Manorial court rolls
63849 Court book of James Willymott

Hawkins and Co., 7/8 Portmill Lane, Hitchin

Account book of George Draper
R. Hine, 'Records of the Firm of Hawkins and Co.' (typescript)

Henry E. Huntington Library, San Marino, California

Ellesmere manuscripts

Leeds City Council Archive Department

Temple Newsam Collection

Lichfield Joint Record Office

Wills and administrations in the Consistory Court of Coventry and Lichfield

Norfolk and Norwich Record Office

D.S. 488 'County Court Business'
Norfolk Consistory Court Wills

Northamptonshire Record Office

Finch-Hatton 43 Presentment of attorney-jurors to the commission on fees, 1623

2794 'Cases wherein there is no helpe in Chancery'

Northumberland Co. Record Office

Allendale MSS P2 Hexam Court Baron, 1624

Shakespeare's Birthplace Trust, Stratford-upon-Avon

DR 3 Ferrers of Baddesley Clinton papers

DR 5/1393, 2120, 2161-2, 2197, 2270, 2287, 2396, 2382, 2671; 17/2; 282/1-8 Manorial court rolls

DR 10 Gregory of Stivichall papers

DR 17 Alveston and Tiddington court rolls

DR 18 Stoneleigh manuscripts

DR 33/54, 57, 59-60 Clifford Chambers manorial court rolls

DR 37 Archer Collection

DR 38/1444-61 Smitterfield manorial court rolls

DR 98 Willoughby de Brooke papers

BRU 2 Stratford Corporation minute books

ER 1/132; 24/4/1-5; 24/11/15; 24/14/1-3; 24/22/2; 24/40/2, 6; 24/42; 28/1; 58/6-8; 65/22; 87/3-5; 109/16-20; 119/24 Manorial court rolls

Sheffield City Library

Wh.M.D. 01 Notebook of Edmund Cundy

Shropshire County Record Office

Bridgewater Collection

William Salt Library, Stafford

SMS 28 William Booth's Clients' Causes, 1662-3

SMS 369 Notebook of Thomas Worwick, sometime mayor of Stafford

Staffordshire Co. Record Office

D 661/11 Dyott Collection

Warwickshire Record Office

QS 11/1, 3, 4, 5 Hearth tax returns 1662

W 9/1 Minute book of the Warwick borough court of record, 1657-8

W 11/1 Warwick borough court leet book
W 21/6 Warwick town council minute book
CR 136 Newdigate family papers
CR 258/84 Will of James Prescott the elder
CR 26/7a and b; 284/37, 39, 136; 299/2/1–21; 440; 450; 544/206–15; 623; 1115; 1122; 1291/8/1–7 Manorial court rolls
L 6/29, 40
MR 1, 2, 4, 9, 13, 14, 19, 21/1–5

Worcestershire Record Office

Wills and inventories in the Episcopal Consistory Court of Worcester

B. PRIMARY PRINTED SOURCES AND CALENDARS

Unless otherwise stated, the place of publication for printed books is London.

The Anti-Levellers Antidote, 1652.
Aristotle's Politics and the Athenian Constitution, ed. J. Warrington, 1959.
Bacon, Francis, *Works*, ed. J. Spedding *et al.*, 14 vols., 1857–74.
Baildon, W. P., ed., *The Records of the Honourable Society of Lincoln's Inn : The Black Books*, 4 vols., 1897–1902.
Barlee, W., *A Concordance of All Written Lawes Concerning Lords of Mannours, theire Free Tenetes, and Copieholders*, Manorial Society, 1911.
Barnes, T. G., ed., *List and Index to the Proceedings in Star Chamber for the Reign of James I, 1603–1625...*, 3 vols., Chicago, 1975.
Somerset Assize Orders, Somerset Record Society, vol. lxv, Frome, 1959.
Bateson, M., ed., *Records of the Borough of Leicester*, 3 vols., Cambridge, 1905.
Borough Customs, 2 vols., Selden Society, vols. xviii, xxi, 1904–6.
Bland, D. S., *The Early Records of Furnival's Inn*, Newcastle upon Tyne, 1957.
Bond, Shelagh, ed., *The Chamber Order Book of Worcester 1602–1650*, Worcestershire Historical Society, NS, vol. viii, 1974.
A Booke of Entries : Containing Perfect and Approved Presidents of Courts, Declarations, Informations, Pleints, Inditements, Barres..., 1614. Preface by Sir E. Coke.
Boote, R., *An Historical Treatise of an Action or Suit at Law*, 2nd edn, 1781.
Bourne, Immanuel, *The Anatomie of Conscience...Preached at Derby Assizes, Lent 1623*, 1623.
Bradney, J. A., ed., *The Diary of Walter Powell of Llantilio Crossenny in the County of Monmouth, Gentleman, 1603–1654*, Bristol, 1907.
Brathwait, R., *The English Gentleman*, 1630.
British Parliamentary Papers : The Report from the Committee Appointed to Enquire into the Causes That Retard Decisions of Suits in the High Court of Chancery, 1811.

First Report of His Majesty's Commissioners (on the) Common Law, 1829.

Second Part of the Appendix to the Fourth Report of the Common Law Commission, 1831–32, 1832.

Brownlow, R., and J. Goldesborough, *Reports of Divers Choice Cases in Law*, 1651.

Buc, Sir George, 'The Third Universitie of England or A Treatise of the Foundation of All the Colleges...in London'. Appendix to John Stow, *The Annales or Generall Chronicle of England*, ed. Edmund Howes, 1615.

Burne, S. A. H., ed., *The Staffordshire Quarter Sessions Rolls*, vol. i: *1581–1589*, William Salt Archaeological Society, i, 1929.

    The Staffordshire Quarter Sessions Rolls 1598–1602, Staffordshire Record Society, vol. iv, 1936.

Burton, R., *The Anatomy of Melancholy...*, 2 vols., 1813 edn.

Cade, Anthony, *A Sermon of the Nature of Conscience Which May Well Be Termed, A Tradgedy of Conscience... Preached before... Assizes at Leicester 1620*, 1621.

Calendars of State Papers Domestic, Elizabeth I, James I, Charles I.

Calthrope, C., *The Relation betweene the Lord of a Mannor and the Coppyholder his Tenant*, 1635.

Carr, Sir Cecil, *The Pension Book of Clement's Inn*, Selden Society, vol. lxxviii, 1960.

[Cecil, Sir William], *The Execution of Justice in England for Maintenaunce of Publique and Christian Peace...*, 1583.

Certaine Proposals of Divers Attorneys of the Court of Common Pleas, for the Regulating the Proceedings at Law..., 1650.

Chauncy, H., *The Historical Antiquities of Hertfordshire*, 1700.

Civil Judicial Statistics... for the Year 1938, HMSO, 1939.

Clay, T., *A Chorologicall Discourse of the Well Ordering, Desposing and Gouerning an Honorable Estate...*, 1619.

Clutterbuck, R., *History and Antiquities of the County of Hertford*, 3 vols., 1815–27.

Cobbett, W., T. B. Howell, *et al.*, eds., *A Complete Collection of State Trials*, 42 vols., 1816–98.

Coke, Sir E. *The Complete Copyholder*, 1641.

    The Fourth Part of the Institutes of the Laws of England, 1648.

    The Second Part of the Institutes of the Laws of England, 1717.

    The Reports of Sir Edward Coke, ed. J. H. Thomas, 13 parts in 7 vols. (1826).

    The Lord Coke his Speeche and Charge, 1607.

The Complete Sollicitor Performing his Duty..., 1672.

Connor, W. J., ed., *The Southampton Mayor's Book of 1606–8*, Southampton Record Society, 1978.

Conway Davies, J., *Catalogue of Manuscripts in the Library of the Honourable Society of the Inner Temple*, 3 vols., Oxford, 1972.

Cooke, Sir George, *Rules, Orders and Notices in the Courts of King's Bench and Common Pleas*, 1747.

Cooper, J. P., ed., *Wentworth Papers 1597–1628*, Royal Historical Society, Camden, 4th ser., vol. xii, 1973.

Cowell, J., *A Law Dictionary or the Interpreter*, Cambridge, 1607.

Crompton, R., *L'Authoritie et Iurisdiction des Covrts de la Maiestie de la Roygne*, 1594.

D. S., *The Honest Lawyer*, 1616.

Dalton, M., *Officium Vicecomitum: The Office and Authoritie of Sherifs*, 1623.

Davies, Sir John, 'Discourse of the Common Law' (1615), in *The Complete Works (Including Hitherto Unpublished MSS.) of Sir John Davies...*, ed. A. B. Grosart, 3 vols., 1869–76.

Day, John, *Law Tricks*, 1608; Malone Society Reprints, Oxford, 1949.

Deloney, Thomas, 'The Pleasant Historie of John Winchcomb, In his Yonguer Yeares called Jack of Newbery', *Shorter Novels*, vol. i: *Elizabethan and Jacobean*, Everyman, 1929.

D'Ewes, S., *The Journals of All the Parliaments during the Reign of Elizabeth*, rev. R. Bowes, 1882.

D[oddridge], J[ohn], *The Lawyers Light or A Due Direction for the Study of Law*, 1629.

Dugdale, W., *Origines Juridiciales or Historical Memorials of the English Laws, Courts of Justice, Forms of Tryall...Also a Chronology of the Lord Chancellors Justices* [etc.], 1666.
  Antiquities of Warwickshire, 1656.

[Earle, John], *Micro-cosmographie; or, A Peece of the World Discovered*, 1628.

Ellis, H., ed., *The Obituary of Richard Smyth, Secondary of the Poultry Compter, London: Being a Catalogue of All Such Persons as He Knew in their Life: Extending from A.D. 1627 to A.D. 1674*, Camden Society, os, xliv, 1849.

Elyot, Sir Thomas, *The Boke Named the Gouernour*, London, 1531; ed. H. H. S. Croft, 2 vols., 1880.

Fennor, William, 'The Counter's Commonwealth', in *The Elizabethan Underworld*, ed. A. V. Judges, 1930.

Ferguson, R. S., and W. Nanson, eds., *Some Municipal Records of the City of Carlisle*, Cumberland and Westmorland Antiquarian and Archaeological Society, extra ser., vol. iv, Carlisle, 1887.

Finch, H., *Law or a Discourse Thereof in Foure Bookes*, 1627. First printed in French in 1613.

Firth, C. H., and R. S. Rait, eds., *Acts and Ordinances of the Interregnum 1642–1660*, 3 vols., 1911.

Fisher, F. J., ed., 'The State of England. Anno Domini 1600 by Thomas Wilson', *Camden Miscellany*, 3rd ser., 16 (1936).

Fitzherbert, Sir A., *La Nouvell Natura Brevium*, 1616 edn.

Fletcher, R. J., ed., *The Pension Book of Gray's Inn 1569–1669*, 3 vols., 1901–10.

Fortescue, Sir John, *De Laudibus Legum Angliae*, ed. S. B. Chrimes, Cambridge, 1942.

Foster, E. R., ed., *Proceedings in Parliament 1610*, 2 vols., New Haven, Conn., 1966.

Foster, J., *Alumni Oxonienses: The Members of the University of Oxford 1500–1714*, 1891–2.

Foster, J., ed., *Register of Admissions to Gray's Inn*, 1889.

Fraunce, A., *The Lawiers Logicke*, 1588.

Freshfield, E., ed., *The Records of the Society of Gentlemen Practisers*, 1897.

Fulbecke, William, *A Direction or Preparative to the Study of the Lawe*, 1603.

Greaves, R. W., ed., *The First Ledger Book of High Wycombe*, Buckinghamshire Record Society, vol. xi, 1956.

Green, M. A. E., *Calendar of the Proceedings of the Committee for Compounding 1643–1660*, 5 vols., 1889–92.

Greg, W. W., and E. Boswell, *Records of the Court of the Stationers' Company, 1576–1602*, 1930.

Guilding, J. M., ed., *Reading Records*, 4 vols., 1892–6.

Hale, Sir Matthew, *The History of the Common Law*, ed. C. M. Gray, 1971.

Hall's Chronicle; Containing the History of England during the Reign of Henry the Fourth and the Succeeding Monarchs, ed. H. Ellis, 1809.

Hargrave, F., ed., *A Collection of Tracts Relative to the Laws of England, from Manuscripts*, 1787.

Harris, Alexander, *The Economy of the Fleete*, ed. A. Jessopp, Camden Society, NS, vol. xxv, 1879.

Harris, M. D., ed., *The Coventry Leet Book or Mayor's Register*, Early English Text Society, nos. cxxxiv–cxxxv, cxxxviii, cxlvi, 1907–13.

Harrison, W., 'The Description of England', in *Holinshed's Chronicles of England, Scotland and Ireland*, 6 vols., 1807.

Harte, W. J., *Gleanings from the Common Place Book of John Hooker, Relating to the City of Exeter 1484–1590*, Exeter, 1920.

Hasler, P. W., ed., *The House of Commons, 1558–1603*, 3 vols., 1981.

Hawarde, John, *Les Reportes del Cases in Camera Stellata, 1593–1609*, ed. W. P. Baildon, 1894.

Hearne, T., *A Collection of Curious Discourses*, 2 vols., 1773.

Herrtage, S. J., ed., *England in the Reign of King Henry the Eighth*, part 1: *Starkey's Life and Letters*, 1828.

Hill, L. M., ed., *The Ancient State, Authoritie and Proceedings of the Court of Requests, by Sir Julius Caesar*, Cambridge, 1975.

Historical Manuscripts Commission, *Hatfield House*.
    Exeter.
    Hertford.
    St Albans.
    House of Lords.

Hoskins, W. G., ed., *Exeter in the Seventeenth Century: Tax and Rate Assessments*, Devon and Cornwall Record Society, NS, vol. ii, 1957.

Hudson, William, 'A Treatise of the Court of Star Chamber', *Collectanea Juridica: Consisting of Tracts Relative to the Law and Constitution of England*, ed. F. Hargrave, 2 vols., 1792.

Inderwick, F. A., *A Calendar of the Inner Temple Records*, 5 vols., 1896–1901.

Ingleby, C. M., ed., *Shakespeare and the Enclosure of Common Fields, Being a Fragment of the Private Diary of Thomas Greene, Town Clerk at Stratford 1614–1617*, Birmingham, 1885.

Izacke, R., *Antiquities of the City of Exeter*, 1677.

Jacob, G., *The Law Dictionary*, 1729.

Jonson, Ben, *The Staple of the News*, 1631.

Josten, C. H., ed., *Elias Ashmole (1617–1692): His Autobiographical and Historical Notes*, 5 vols., Oxford, 1966.

Journals of the House of Commons, 1547–1714, 17 vols., 1742.

Judicial Statistics.... For the year 1975, HMSO, 1976.

Kemp, Thomas, ed., *The Book of John Fisher, 1580–1588*, Warwick, 1900.

The Black Book of Warwick, Warwick, 1898.

King, A. J., and B. H. Watts, *The Municipal Records of Bath, 1189–1604*, 1885.

Kitchin, J., *Le Covrt Leet et Covrt Baron...*, 1581.

Lambarde, W., *Eirenarcha: or the Office of the Justices of the Peace*, 1582 plus at least 13 later editions.

Archion or a Commentary upon the High Courts of Justice in England, 1635.

Leadam, I. S., ed., *Select Cases in the Court of Requests, A.D. 1497–1569*, Selden Society, vol. xii, 1898.

Leadam, I. S., and J. F. Baldwin, *Select Cases before the King's Council 1243–1482*, Selden Society, vol. xxxv, 1918.

Letters and Papers, Foreign and Domestic, of the Reign of Henry VIII, vols. i–iv, ed. J. S. Brewer, 1862–76.

McCulloch, J. P., ed., *A Select Collection of Early English Tracts on Commerce*, Cambridge, 1970 edn.

Markham, C. A., and J. C. Cox, eds., *The Records of the Borough of Northampton*, 2 vols., Northampton, 1898.

Marsh, B., and J. Ainsworth, eds., *Records of the Worshipful Company of Carpenters*, vol. vi: *Court Book, 1573–1594*, 1939.

Martin, C. T., ed., *Minutes of Parliament of the Middle Temple*, 3 vols. plus index, 1904–5.

Martin, William, *Youth's Instruction*, 1612.

Merson, A. L., ed., *The Third Book of Remembrance of Southampton 1514–1602*, 2 vols., Southampton, 1955.

Modus Tenendi Cûr Barôn Cum Visu Franci Plegii. Published by Wynkyn de Worde, 1510.

Monson, William, and Heyward Townshend, *Megalopschy. A Particular and Exact Account of the Last XVII Years of Queen Elizabeth's Reign*, 1682.

More, Sir Thomas, *The Complete Works*, ed. E. Surtz and J. H. Hexter, 5 vols., New Haven, Conn., 1965.

Mynshull, G., *Essays and Characters of a Prison and Prisoners*, 1618.

Nash, Thomas, *Quaternio: or A Fourefold Way to a Happie Life, Set Forth in a Dialogue betweene a Countryman and a Citizen, a Divine and a Lawyer*, 1633.

A Newe Boke of Presidents Exactly Written in Maner of a Register, 1543.

Noddel, Daniel, *To the Parliament of the Commonwealth of England and Every Individual Member Thereof the Declaration of Daniel Noddel, Solicitor for the Freeholders and Commoners within the Mannor of Epworth...*, 1653.

North, Roger, *Autobiography*, ed. A. Jessopp, 1887.

The Lives of the Right Hon. Francis North, Baron Guilford; the Hon. Sir Dudley North; and the Hon. and Rev. Dr. John North. By the Hon. Roger North. Together with the Autobiography of the Author, ed. A. Jessopp, 3 vols., 1890.

Notestein, W., *et al.*, *Commons Debates 1621*, New Haven, Conn., 1935.

Noy, W., *A Treatise of the Principall Grounds and Maximes of the Lawes of this Kingdom*, 1641.

Opinion Diefied: Discovering the Ingins, Traps, and Traynes that Are Set in This Age, Whereby to Catch Opinion by B[read] R[yce]; Gent, Servant to the King, 1613.

Palmer, C. J., ed., *The History of Great Yarmouth by Henry Manship, Town Clerk*, Yarmouth, 1854.

Parsons, R., 'A Memorial of the Reformation in England', in *The Jesuit's Memorial*, ed. Edward Gee, 1690.

Perkins, W., 'A Treatise of Vocations or Callings of Men', *The Works... of Mr William Perkins*, Cambridge, 1612.

Plucknett, T. F. T., and J. L. Barton, eds., *St. German's Doctor and Student*, Selden Society, vol. xci, 1974.

Powell, T., *The Attourneys Academy or the Manner and Some of Proceeding Practically upon Any Suit, Plaint or Action Whatsoever in Any Court of Record...*, 1623.

The Attornies Almanacke, 1627.

'The Mistery and Misery of Lending and Borrowing', in W. S. Scott, ed., *q.v.*, 2nd edn, vol. ii.

The Practick Part of the Law, Shewing the Office of a Complete Attorney (1652 and 1658 edns).

Praxis Utriusque Banci: The Ancient and Modern Practice of the Two Superior Courts..., 1674.

Pulton, Ferdinando, *De Pace Regis et Regni: viz. A Treatise Declaring Which Be the Great and Generall Offences of the Realme and the Chiefe Impediments of the Peace of the King...*, 1609.

Rastell, W., *An Exposition of Certain Difficult and Obscure Words and Terms*, 1579.

Ratcliff, S. C., and H. C. Johnson, eds., *Quarter Sessions Order Book: Easter 1625 to Trinity 1637*. Warwick Co. Records, vol. i, 1935.

Quarter Sessions Records, Easter 1674 to Easter 1682, Warwick Co. Records, vol. vii, 1946.

The Reports of Sir Peyton Ventris, Kt., 1726.

Richardson, H., ed., 'Court Rolls of the Manor of Acomb', *Yorkshire Archaeological Society*, 131 (1969).

Richardson, W. H., ed., *The Annalls of Ipswiche: The Lawes, Customes and Governm[ent] of the Same Collected Out of ye Records, Books and*

Writings of That Towne by Nathanial Bacon, Esq. AD 1654, Ipswich, 1880.

Robinson, Richard, 'A Briefe Collection of the Queenes Majesties Most High and Most Honourable Courtes of Recordes', ed. R. L. Rickard, *Camden Miscellany*, 3rd ser., 20 (1953).

Ruggle, George, *Ignoramus*, 1630.

Rules and Orders for the Court of Common Pleas at Westminster, 1654.

Sanders, G. W., *Orders in Chancery*, 1845.

Sayles, G. O., *Select Cases in the Court of King's Bench under Edward I.* Selden Society, vol. lv, 1936.

Scott, W., ed., *A Collection of Scarce and Valuable Tracts...Selected from...Public as Well as Private Libraries, Particularly That of the Late Lord Somers*, 13 vols., 1809–15; 2nd edn, 2 vols., 1812.

Sheppard, W., *Action upon the Case for Slander or a Methodical Collection...*, 1662.

The Faithfull Councellor; or the Marrow of the Law in English, 1653.

Smith, John, *The Lives of the Berkeleys*, 3 vols., Gloucester, 1883–5.

Smith, Sir Thomas, *De Republica Anglorum* (1583), ed. Mary Dewar, Cambridge, 1982.

Staffordshire Pedigrees, ed. G. T. Armytage and W. H. Rylands, Harleian Society, vol. lxiii, 1912.

Statutes of the Realm, ed. A. Luders, T. E. Tomlins, J. Raith, *et al.*, 11 vols., 1810–28.

Staunford, W., *An Exposition of the King's Prerogative Collected Out of the Great Abridgement of Iustice Fitzherbert...*, 1586.

Staunford, Sir William, *Les Plees del Coron*, ed. P. R. Glazebrook, Classical English Law Texts, 1971.

Stephenson, Mill, *A List of Monumental Brasses in the British Isles*, 1926.

Strong, S. A., *Catalogue of Letters and Other Historical Documents Exhibited in the Library at Welbeck*, 1903.

Sturgess, H. A. C., ed., *Register of Admissions to the Honourable Society of the Middle Temple*, 3 vols., 1949.

Tancred, Sir T. Lawson, ed., *Records of a Yorkshire Manor*, 1937.

Tawney, R. H. *et al.*, *English Economic History: Select Documents*, 1913.

The Tenours and Fourme of Indenture, Obligations, Quitaunces, Bylles of Paymentes, Letters of Sale..., 1541.

Townesend, G., *A Preparative to Pleading... [Being] a Work Intended for the Instruction and Help of Young Clerks of the Common Pleas*, 1675.

Trye, John, *Jus Filizarii: or, the Filacer's Office in the Court of King's Bench*, 1684.

Venn, J., and J. A. Venn, *Alumni Cantabrigienses...from the Earliest Times to 1900*, Cambridge, 1922.

The Visitation of Cambridge in 1575 and 1619, ed. J. W. Clay, Harleian Soc., vol. xli, 1897.

The Visitation of Cheshire in 1580, ed. J. P. Rylands, Harleian Soc., vol. xviii, 1882.

The Visitation of the County of Gloucester Taken in the Year 1623, ed. J. Maclean and W. C. Hearne, Harleian Society, vol. xxi. 1885.

The Visitations of Hertfordshire in 1572 and 1634, ed. W. C. Metcalfe, Harleian Soc., vol. xxii, 1886.

The Visitations of the County of Leicester in 1619, ed. J. Featherston, Harleian Society, vol. ii, 1870.

The Visitation of the County of Northampton in 1681, ed. H. I. Longden, Harleian Soc., vol. lxxxvii, 1935.

The Visitation of the County of Warwick in 1619, ed. J. Featherston, Harleian Soc., vol. xii, 1877.

The Visitation of the County of Warwick in 1682 and 1683, ed. W. H. Rylands, Harleian Soc., vol. lxii, 1911.

The Visitation of Worcestershire, 1634, ed. A. T. Butler, Harleian Soc., vol xc, 1938.

Vivian, J. L., *The Marriage Licenses of the Diocese of Exeter*, Exeter, 1887. *Devon Pedigrees*, Exeter, 1898.

The Visitations of the County of Devon, Exeter, 1889.

Vowell (alias Hooker), John, *A Pamphlet of the Offices and Duties of Everie Particular Sworne Officer of the Citie of Excester*, 1584.

Warwick County Records: Hearth Tax Returns, vol. i, ed. M. Walker, Warwick, 1957.

West, W., *The First Part of Symbolaeographia. Which May Be Termed the Art or Description or Image of Instruments...Or The Paterne of Praesidents. Or The Notarie or Scrivner*, 1590 and several later editions.

Wilkinson, John, *A Treatise Collected Out of the Statutes of This Kingdom... Concerning the Office and Authoritie of Coroners and Sheriffs*, 1st edn, 1618; others in 1618, 1620, 1628, and 1638.

Wilson, Thomas, *A Discourse upon Usury*, ed. R. H. Tawney, 1925.

Winch, H., *Reports in the Last Years of the Reign of King James*, 1657.

C. SECONDARY SOURCES

Books and articles

Abbott, J. A. R., 'Robert Abbott, City Money Scrivener, and his Account Book 1646–1652', *Guildhall Miscellany*, 7 (1956).

Abel-Smith, B., and Robert Stevens, *Lawyers and the Courts*, 1967.

Atkinson, A., 'The Trussel Manuscripts', *Papers and Proceedings of Hampshire Field Club*, 19 (3) (1957).

Aubert, V., 'Law as a Way of Resolving Conflicts: The Case of a Small Industrialized Society', in *Law in Culture and Society*, ed. L. Nader, Chicago, 1969.

Aylmer, G. E., 'Attempts at Administrative Reform, 1625–1640', *English Historical Review*, 72 (1957).

'Charles I's Commissions on Fees', *Bulletin of the Institute of Historical Research*, 31 (1958).

The King's Servants: The Civil Service of Charles I, 1625–1642, 1961; 2nd edn, 1974.

Bagley, J. J., 'Kenyon vs. Rigby: The Struggle for the Clerkship of the Peace in Lancashire in the Seventeenth Century', *Historic Society of Lancashire and Chester*, 106 (1955).

Baker, J. H., 'Counsellors and Barristers: An Historical Study', *Cambridge Law Journal*, 27 (1969).
'The Status of Barristers: An Historical Study', *Law Quarterly Review*, 85 (1969).
An Introduction to English Legal History, 1971; 2nd edn, 1979.
'Solicitors and the Law of Maintenance 1590–1640', *Cambridge Law Journal*, 32 (1) (1973).
'The Dark Age of English Legal History', in *Legal History Studies 1972*, ed. D. Jenkins, Cardiff, 1975.
'Criminal Courts and Procedure at Common Law 1550–1800', in *Crime in England 1550–1800*, ed J. S. Cockburn, 1977.
The Reports of Sir John Spelman, Selden Society, vol. xciv, 1978.
'Sir Thomas Robinson (1618–83) Chief Prothonotary of the Common Pleas', *Bodleian Library Record*, 10 (1978).
'The Attorneys and Officers of the Common Law in 1480', *Journal of Legal History*, 1 (1980).
'The English Legal Profession, 1450–1550', in *Lawyers in Early Modern Europe and America*, ed. W. R. Prest, 1981.
Barnes, T. G., 'Due Process and Slow Process in the Late Elizabethan – Early Stuart Star Chamber, Part II', *American Journal of Legal History*, 6 (1962).
The Clerk of the Peace in Caroline Somerset, University of Leicester Department of English Local History, Occasional Papers, No. 14, 1961.
'Star Chamber Litigants and their Counsel, 1596–1641', in *Legal Records and the Historian*, ed. J. H. Baker, 1978.
Baumer, F. L., *The Early Tudor Theory of Kingship*, 2nd edn, New York, 1966.
Bell, H. E., *An Introduction to the History and Records of the Court of Wards and Liveries*, Cambridge, 1953.
Bellamy, J., *Crime and the Public Order in England in the Later Middle Ages*, 1973.
Bellot, H. H., 'The Exclusion of Attorneys from the Inns of Court', *Law Quarterly Review*, 26 (1910).
'The Jurisdiction of the Inns of Court over the Inns of Chancery', *Law Quarterly Review*, 26 (1910).
Birks, M., *Gentlemen of the Law*, 1960.
Bland, D. S., *A Bibliography of the Inns of Court and Chancery*, Selden Society, Supplement Series, No. 3, 1965.
Blatcher, M., 'Touching the Writ of Latitat: An Act of No Great Moment', in *Elizabethan Government and Society*, ed. S. T. Bindoff, J. Hurstfield, and C. H. Williams, 1961.
The Court of King's Bench, 1450–1550: A Study in Self-Help, 1978.
The First Four Hundred: A History of the Firm of Thomson, Snell and Passmore, Solicitors, of Tunbridge, Kent, 1970.
Bodkin, E. H., *The Law of Maintenance and Champerty and the Lawful Financing of Actions by Solicitors, Legal Aid and Trade Protection Societies and Others*, 1935.

Borsay, P., 'The English Urban Renaissance: The Development of Provincial Urban Culture, c. 1680–c. 1760', *Social History* 5 (1977).

Bouwsma, W. J., 'Lawyers in Early Modern Culture', *American Historical Review*, 78 (1973).

Bridbury, A. R., *Economic Growth: England in the Later Middle Ages*, 1962.

Brooks, C., and K. Sharpe, 'History, English Law and the Renaissance: A Comment', *Past and Present*, 72 (1976).

Bryson, W. H., *The Equity Side of the Exchequer*, Cambridge, 1975.

Campbell, John, Lord, *The Lives of the Lord Chancellors*, 17 vols., 1845.

Carr-Saunders, A. M., and P. A. Wilson, *The Professions*, Oxford, 1933.

Cartwright, B., M. Galanter, and R. Kidder, 'Introduction: Litigation and Dispute Processing', *Law and Society Review*, 9 (1974).

Charlton, K., 'The Professions in Sixteenth-Century England', *University of Birmingham Historical Journal*, 12 (1969–70).

Christian, E. B. V., *A Short History of Solicitors*, 1896.

Leaves of the Lower Branch: The Attorney in Life and Letters, 1909.

Clark, P., *English Provincial Society from the Reformation to the Revolution: Religion, Politics and Society in Kent 1500–1640*, Hassocks, 1977.

Clark, P., and P. Slack, *English Towns in Transition 1500–1700*, Oxford, 1976.

Cockburn, J. S., *A History of the English Assizes 1558–1714*, Cambridge, 1972.

Cohen, H., *History of the English Bar and Attornatus to 1450*, 1929.

Cooper, C. P., *An Account of the Most Important Public Records of Great Britain and the Publications of the Record Commissioners*, 2 vols., 1832.

Cooper, J. P., 'The Social Distribution of Land and Men in England 1436–1700', *Economic History Review*, 2nd ser., 20 (1967).

Land, Men and Beliefs: Studies in Early-Modern History, 1983.

Cotterell, M., 'Interregnum Law Reform: The Hale Commission of 1652', *English Historical Review*, 83 (1968).

Cozens-Hardy, B., 'Norfolk Lawyers', *Norfolk Archaeology*, 33 (1965).

Cussans, J. E., *History of Hertfordshire*, 3 vols., 1870–81.

Cust, Lady Elizabeth, *Records of the Cust Family*, 3 vols., 1909.

Dawson, J. P., *A History of Lay Judges*, Cambridge, Mass., 1960.

Dunlop, O. J., *English Apprenticeship and Child Labour*, 1912.

Elton, G. R., *English Law in the Sixteenth Century: Reform in an Age of Change*, Selden Society Lecture, 1979.

The Tudor Constitution, 2nd edn, Cambridge, 1982.

Emerson, Thomas, *A Concise Treatise on the Courts of Law of the City of London*, 1794.

Emmison, F. G., *Elizabethan Life: Home, Land and Work*, Chelmsford, 1976.

Evans, J. T., *Seventeenth-Century Norwich*, Oxford, 1979.

Everitt, A., 'Social Mobility in England 1500–1700', *Past and Present*, 33 (1966).

The Community of Kent and the Great Rebellion, Leicester, 1973.

Faraday, W. Barnard, 'The Recorders of Totnes, and the Courts Civil and Criminal of the Unreformed Borough', *Transactions of the Devon Association for the Advancement of Science, Literature and Art*, 56 (1925).

Fisher, R. M., 'Thomas Cromwell, Humanism and Educational Reform', *Bulletin of the Institute of Historical Research*, 50 (1977).

Foss, E., *A Biographical Dictionary of the Judges of England*, 1870.

Gleason, J. H., *The Justices of the Peace in England 1558–1640*, Oxford, 1969.

Grassby, R., 'The Personal Wealth of the Business Community in Seventeenth-Century England', *Economic History Review*, 2nd ser., 23 (1970).

'Social Mobility and Business Enterprise in Seventeenth-Century England', in *Puritans and Revolutionaries*, ed. K. Thomas and D. Pennington, Oxford, 1978.

Gray, C. M., *Copyhold, Equity and the Common Law*, 1963.

Guy, J. A., *The Cardinal's Court: The Impact of Thomas Wolsey in Star Chamber*, Hassocks, 1977.

The Public Career of Sir Thomas More, 1980.

Hamilton, B., 'The Medical Professions in the Eighteenth Century', *Economic History Review*, 2nd ser., 4 (1951).

Harding, A., *A Social History of English Law*, 1966.

Harding, F. J. W., 'Mickleton and Spearman MSS', *Durham Philobiblon*, 1 (1949–55).

Hartley, T. E., 'Under-Sheriffs and Bailiffs in Some English Shrievalties, c. 1580–c. 1625', *Bulletin of the Institute of Historical Research*, 47 (1974).

Hastings, M., *The Court of Common Pleas in Fifteenth Century England*, Ithaca, N.Y., 1947.

Hatcher, J., *Plague, Population and the English Economy 1348–1530*, 1977.

Hearnshaw, F. J. C., *Leet Jurisdiction in England*, Southampton Record Society, Southampton, 1908.

Henderson, E. G., 'Relief from Bonds in the English Chancery: Mid-Sixteenth Century', *American Journal of Legal History*, 18 (1974).

Hill, C., *Change and Continuity in Seventeenth Century England*, 1974.

Hine, R. L., *The History of Hitchin*, 2 vols., 1927–9.

Holderness, B. A., 'Credit in English Rural Society before the Nineteenth Century with Special Reference to the Period 1650–1720', *Agricultural History Review*, 24 (1976).

Holdsworth, W. S., *A History of English Law*, 3rd edn, 12 vols., 1945.

The Influence of the Legal Profession on the Growth of the English Constitution, Creighton Lecture, Oxford, 1924.

Holmes, C., 'The County Community in Stuart Historiography', *Journal of British Studies*, 19 (1980).

Holmes, G., *Augustan England: Professions, State and Society, 1680–1730*, 1982.

Hopkins, D. D., 'Three Early Solicitor's Bills', *Notes and Queries*, 2nd ser., 12 (1861).

Hoskins, W. G., *Devon and its People*, 1968.

Hoskins, W. G., and H. P. R. Finberg, *Devonshire Studies*, 1952.

Houlbrooke, R., 'The Decline of the Ecclesiastical Jurisdiction under the Tudors', in *Continuity and Change: Personnel and Administration of the Church of England, 1500–1642*, ed. R. O'Day and F. Heal, Leicester, 1976.

Church Courts and the People during the English Reformation, 1520–1570, Oxford, 1979.

Ingram, M. J., 'Communities and Courts: Law and Disorder in Early Seventeenth-Century Wiltshire', in *Crime in England 1550–1800*, ed. J. S. Cockburn, 1977.

Ives, E. W., 'The Reputation of the Common Lawyer in English Society, 1450–1550', *University of Birmingham Historical Journal*, 7 (1959–60).

'The Common Lawyers in Pre-Reformation England', *Transactions of the Royal Historical Society*, 5th ser., 18 (1968).

The Common Lawyers of Pre-Reformation England, Cambridge, 1983.

James, M. E., 'The Concept of Order and the Northern Rising of 1569', *Past and Present*, 60 (1973).

English Politics and the Concept of Honour 1485–1642, Past and Present Supplement 3, 1978.

Johnson, T. E., *Professions and Power*, 1972.

Jones, W. J., *The Elizabethan Court of Chancery*, Oxford, 1967.

'The Exchequer of Chester in the Last Years of Elizabeth', in *Tudor Men and Institutions*, ed. A. J. Slavin, Baton Rouge, La., 1972.

'The Crown and the Courts', in *The Reign of James VI and I*, ed. A. G. R. Smith, 1973.

Politics and the Bench: The Judges and the Origins of the English Civil War, 1971.

'Palatine Performance in the Seventeenth Century', in *The English Commonwealth 1547–1640*, ed. P. Clark, A. G. R. Smith, and N. Tyacke, Leicester, 1979.

Kelso, R., *The Doctrine of the English Gentleman*, Urbana, Ill., 1929.

Kerridge, E., *Agrarian Problems in the Sixteenth Century and After*, 1969.

Kerry, C., 'Anthony Bradshaw of Duffield and the Alms Houses Founded by him at That Place', *The Reliquary*. 23 (1882–3).

Kiralfy, A. K., *The Action on the Case*, 1951.

Knafla, L. A., 'The Matriculation Revolution and Education at the Inns of Court in Renaissance England', in *Tudor Men and Institutions*, ed. A. J. Slavin, Baton Rouge, La., 1972.

Law and Politics in Jacobean England: The Tracts of Lord Chancellor Ellesmere, Cambridge, 1977.

Langbein, J. H., *Prosecuting Crime in the Renaissance: England, Germany, France*, Cambridge, Mass., 1974.

Lapsley, G. T., *The County Palatine of Durham: A Study in Constitutional History*, Harvard Historical Studies, vol. viii, 1900.

Larson, M. S., *The Rise of Professionalism: A Sociological Analysis*, Berkeley, Calif., 1977.

Legal Services and Lawyers: A Summary of the Report of the Royal Commission on Legal Services, HMSO, 1979.

Levack, B., *The Civil Lawyers in England 1603–1641*, Oxford, 1973.

MacCaffrey, W. T., *Exeter 1540–1640: The Growth of an English County Town*, Cambridge, Mass., 1958.

McFarlane, K. B., *The Nobility of Later Medieval England*, Oxford, 1973. *England in the Fifteenth Century: Collected Essays*, 1981.

Maddicott, J. R., *Law and Lordship: Royal Justices as Retainers in Thirteenth- and Fourteenth-Century England*, Past and Present Supplement 4, 1978.

Maitland, F. W., *The Forms of Action at Common Law*, Cambridge, 1909; later edns.
    'English Law and the Renaissance', in *Select Essays in Anglo-American Legal History by Various Authors*, 3 vols., Boston, 1907.

Marchant, R. A., *The Church under the Law: Justice, Administration and Discipline in the Diocese of York 1560–1640*, Cambridge, 1969.

Meekings, C. A. F., 'Draft of Passages Provided in 1951–52 for Wheatley's Revised Edition of *Edward Latymer and His Foundations*' (typescript).

Metzger, F., 'The Last Phase of the Medieval Chancery', in *Law-Making and the Law-Makers in British History*, ed. A. Harding, 1980.

Milsom, S. F. C., *The Historical Foundations of the Common Law*, 1969.

Neale, J. E., 'The Elizabethan Political Scene', *Proceedings of the British Academy*, 34 (1948).

Ogborn, M. E., *Staple Inn*, 1964.

Osborn, L. B., *The Life, Letters and Writings of John Hoskyns, 1566–1638*, New Haven, Conn., 1937.

Owen, A. E. B., 'A Scrivener's Notebook from Bury St. Edmunds', *Archives*, 14 (1979).

Palliser, D. M., *Tudor York*, Oxford, 1979.

Palmer, R. C., *The County Court of Medieval England*, Princeton, N.J., 1982.

Pocock, J. G. A., *The Ancient Constitution and the Feudal Law*, Cambridge, 1957.

Podmore, D., *Solicitors and the Wider Community*, 1980.

Pollock, F., and F. W. Maitland, *The History of English Law*, 2nd edn, ed. S. F. C. Milsom, 2 vols., Cambridge, 1968.

Post, J. B., 'King's Bench Clerks in the Reign of Richard II', *Bulletin of the Institute of Historical Research*, 47, no. 116 (1974).

Postan, M., 'The Fifteenth Century', *Economic History Review*, 9 (1939).

Prest, W. R., *The Inns of Court under Elizabeth I and the Early Stuarts 1590–1640*, 1972.
    'Counsellors' Fees and Earnings in the Age of Sir Edward Coke', in *Legal Records and the Historian*, ed. J. H. Baker, 1978.

Prest, W. R., ed., *Lawyers in Early Modern Europe and America*, 1981.

Pronay, N., 'The Chancellor, the Chancery, and the Council at the End of the Fifteenth Century', in *British Government and Administration*, ed. H. Hearder and H. R. Lyon, Cardiff, 1974.

Pugh, H., 'Origins and Progress of Barnard's Inn', *Notes and Queries*, 7th ser., 2 (1886).

Pulling, A., *The Order of the Coif*, 1884.

Reader, J. W., *Professional Men: The Rise of the Professional Classes in Nineteenth-Century England*, 1966.

Reid, R. R., *The King's Council in the North*, 1921.

Robson, R., *The Attorney in Eighteenth Century England*, Cambridge, 1959.

Rosenthal, J. T., 'Feuds and Private Peace-Making: A Fifteenth-Century Example', *Nottingham Medieval Studies*, 14 (1970).

Rowney, I., 'Arbitration in Gentry Disputes of the Later Middle Ages', *History*, 67 (1982).

Roxburgh, R., *The Origins of Lincoln's Inn*, Cambridge, 1963.

Russell, C., *Parliaments and English Politics 1621–1629*, Oxford, 1979.

Samaha, J. B., 'The Recognizance in Elizabethan Law Enforcement', *American Journal of Legal History*, 25 (1981).

Savine, A., 'Copyhold Cases in the Early Chancery Proceedings', *English Historical Review*, 17 (1902).

Schowoerer, L. G., 'Roger North and his Notes on Legal Education', *Huntington Library Quarterly*, 22 (1958).

Sharpe, J. A., *Defamation and Sexual Slander in Early Modern England: The Church Courts at York*, Borthwick Papers, No. 58, 1981.

'Litigation and Human Relations in Early Modern England – Defamations...The Church Courts at York', typescript paper, Past and Present Society Conference, 1980.

Simpson, A. W. B., 'The Penal Bond with Conditional Defeasance', *Law Quarterly Review*, 82 (1966).

'The Early Constitution of Gray's Inn', *Cambridge Law Journal*, 34 (1975).

Sitwell, Sir George, 'The English Gentleman', *The Ancestor*, 1 (April 1902).

Skipp, V., *Crisis and Development: An Ecological Case Study of the Forest of Arden 1570–1674*, Cambridge, 1978.

Slavin, A. J., 'The Fall of Lord Chancellor Wriothesley: A Study in the Politics of Conspiracy', *Albion*, 7 (1975).

Smith, A. Hassell, *County and Court: Government and Politics in Norfolk, 1558–1603*, Oxford, 1974.

Snagge, T. W., 'Fifty Years of the English County Courts', *Nineteenth Century*, 42 (1895).

Somerville, R., 'The Palatine Courts in Lancashire', in *Law-Making and Law-Makers in British History*, ed. A. Harding, 1980.

Stone, L., *The Crisis of the Aristocracy 1558–1641*, Oxford, 1965.

'The Educational Revolution in England, 1560–1640', *Past and Present*, 28 (1964).

'Social Mobility in England, 1500–1700', *Past and Present*, 33 (1966).

Styles, P., 'The Corporation of Warwick, 1600–1835', *Transactions and Proceedings of the Birmingham Archaeological Society*, 59 (1935).

'The Social Structure of Kineton Hundred in the Reign of Charles II',
Transactions and Proceedings of the Birmingham Archaeological Society,
78 (1962).

Sutherland, D., *The Assize of Novel Disseisin*, Oxford, 1973.

Thirsk, J., ed., *The Agrarian History of England and Wales*, vol. iv:
1500–1640, Cambridge, 1967.

Thorne, S. E., 'The Early History of the Inns of Court with Special
Reference to Gray's Inn', *Graya*, 50 (1959).

Tittler, R., 'The Incorporation of Boroughs 1540–1558', *History*, 62
(1977).

Tout, T. F., 'The Household of the Chancery and its Disintegration', in
Essays in History Presented to Reginald Lane Poole, ed. H. W. C. Davis,
Oxford, 1927.

Veall, D., *The Popular Movement for Law Reform 1640–1660*, Oxford,
1970.

Victoria County Histories: Warwickshire.
Hertfordshire.

Webb, S., and B. Webb, *English Local Government from the Revolution to the
Municipal Corporations Act: The Manor and the Borough*, 1924 edn.

Weinbaum, M., *The Incorporation of Boroughs*, Manchester, 1936.

White, S. D., *Sir Edward Coke and 'The Grievances of the Commonwealth'*,
1621–1628, Chapel Hill, N.C., 1979.

Willcocks, W. K., 'Devonshire Men at the Inner Temple', *Transactions
of the Devon Association for the Advancement of Science, Literature and
Art*, 17 (1885).

Williams, Elijah, *Early Holborn and the Legal Quarter of London*, 2 vols.,
1927.

Williams, P., *The Council in the Marches of Wales under Elizabeth I*,
Cardiff, 1958.

  'Government and Politics in Ludlow, 1590–1642', *Transactions of the
  Shropshire Archaeological and Natural History Society*, 56 (1957–60).

  'The Activity of the Council in the Marches under the Early Stuarts',
  Welsh History Review, 1 (1962).

  'The Attack on the Council in the Marches, 1603–1642', *Transactions
  of the Honourable Society of Cymmrodorian*, 1961.

  The Tudor Regime, Oxford, 1979.

Winder, W. H. D., 'The Courts of Requests', *Law Quarterly Review*, 52
(1936).

Wrightson, K., *English Society 1580–1680*, 1982.

Zaller, R., *The Parliament of 1621*, Berkeley, Calif., 1971.

Zander, M., *The State of Knowledge about the English Legal Profession*,
1980.

Unpublished theses

Adey, K. R., 'Aspects of the History of the Town of Stafford 1590–1710'
(Keele M.A., 1971).

Allsebrook, W. B. J., 'The Court of Requests in the Reign of Elizabeth'
(London M.A., 1936).

Avery, M. E., 'Proceedings in the Court of Chancery up to *c.* 1460' (London M.A., 1958).

Clendenin, B., 'The Common Lawyers in Politics and Society: A Social and Political Study of the Common Lawyers in the First Jacobean Parliament' (Univ. of North Carolina Ph.D., 1975).

Chartres, J. A., 'The Place of Inns in the Commercial Life of London and Western England, 1660–1760' (Oxford D.Phil., 1973).

Dias, J. H. R., 'Politics and Administration in Nottinghamshire and Derbyshire 1590–1640' (Oxford D.Phil., 1973).

Harrison, C. J., 'The Social and Economic History of Cannock and Rugeley, 1546–1597' (Keele Ph.D., 1974).

Hughes, A. L., 'Politics and Society and Civil War in Warwickshire, 1620–1650' (Liverpool Ph.D., 1979).

Jones, M. V., 'The Political History of the Parliamentary Boroughs of Kent 1642–1660' (London Ph.D., 1967).

Kew, J., 'The Land Market in Devon, 1536–1558' (Exeter Ph.D., 1967).

Lang, R. G., 'The Greater Merchants of London in the Early Seventeenth Century' (Oxford D.Phil., 1963).

Large, P. F. W., 'Economic and Social Change in North Worcestershire during the Early Seventeenth Century' (Oxford D.Phil., 1980).

MacCulloch, D. N. J., 'Power, Privilege and the County Community: County Politics in Elizabethan Suffolk' (Cambridge Ph.D., 1977).

Metzger, F., 'Das Englische Kanzleigericht unter Kardinal Wolsey 1515–1529' (Friedrich-Alexander Universität, Erlangen, Ph.D., 1976).

Miles, M., '"Eminent Attorneys" – Some Aspects of West Riding Attorneyship, *c.* 1750–1800' (Birmingham Ph.D., 1982).

Mosler, D., 'A Social and Religious History of the English Civil War in the County of Warwick' (Stanford Ph.D., 1974).

Powell, E., 'Public Order and Law Enforcement in Shropshire and Staffordshire in the Early Fifteenth Century' (Oxford D.Phil., 1979).

Quintrell, B. W., 'The Government of the County of Essex, 1603–1642' (London Ph.D., 1965).

Rosen, A. B., 'Economic and Social Aspects of the History of Winchester, 1520–1670' (Oxford D.Phil., 1975).

Silcock, R. H., 'County Government in Worcestershire, 1603–1660' (London Ph.D., 1974).

Skelton, E., 'The Court of Star Chamber in the Reign of Elizabeth' (London M.A., 1931).

Thomas, G. W., 'Archbishop John Williams: Politics and Prerogative Law 1621–1642' (Oxford D.Phil., 1974).

Wanklyn, M. D. G., 'Landed Society and Allegiance in Cheshire and Shropshire in the First Civil War' (Victoria Univ. of Manchester Ph.D., 1976).

Wilson, J. S., 'The Administrative Work of the Lord Chancellor in the Early Seventeenth Century' (London Ph.D., 1927).

INDEX

Abbott, Robert, 196
actions on the case: *see* forms of action at common law
affinities, magnate, 84; *see also* retainers and retaining
Albery, Thomas, 351n1
alehouses, 166, 188
Alexander, Jerome, 169
Alford, Francis, 139
All Souls College, Oxford, 107
allegiance: *see* civil wars of 1642–60
Allen, Nicholas, 153, 156
amateur lawyers: *see* lawyers
Andover, 42, 120, 169, 212
antiquarian interests of practitioners, 178, 200, 223
apothecaries, 266, 275
apprentices at law: *see* barristers
apprenticeship, 136, 187, 218, 260, 269, 276; attitudes towards, 161–2, 179–81; indentures, 155; premiums, 154; and the sons of practitioners, 261–2; and the training of practitioners, 152–8
arbitration, 91, 194, 310n84, 312n116
Archer, Sir Simon, 178
Arden, forest of, 7, 98
aristocracy, the, 90–1, 107, 270
Aristotle, 136, 180
Ashburton, 216, 253, 348n69
Ashfield, Edmund, 333n79, 334n108
Ashmole, Elias, 176–7, 178, 186
Ashton, Thomas, 185, 248, 270, 313n125
assizes, 92, 102, 128, 184, 187, 188, 192, 236, 238–9; Northern Circuit, 115; Western Circuit, litigation from, 63; functions of attorneys at, 189–90; see also *nisi prius*

assumpsit: *see* forms of action at common law
Astree, William, 153
Atterbury, Lewes, 258
attorneys: acting as solicitors, 27, 141–3; as a profession, 119–21; attitudes of laymen towards, 132–7, 178–81, 278; contentious v. non-contentious work of, 165, 195–6, 240; as deputy sheriffs, 189; division of labour with barristers, 190–2; exclusion from the inns of court, 162–3, 179–80; fees of, 102, 104–6, 118, 147, 236–40, 240–2; friendships outside the profession, 274–5; functions of, 17–19, 25–6, 27; image of, 268–9; increase in number of, 112–14, 116, 124–5; intellectual interests of, 177–8; juries of, 119–20, 144–5, 146, 266; and law reform, 129–31; life styles of, 258, 274–5; and litigiousness, 75, 115–16; litigious work in the country, 188–91; location of offices of, 188; number of (1560–1640), 28, 112–14, 264; number of compared to population, 113, 264; oath of, 119, 125, 264; places of residence of, 30, 32, 98, 182–6; and procedural innovation, 126–31; and provincial jurisdictions, 100–1; qualifications for admission as, 119, 124–5, 143–5; reform of, 138–40; regulation of, 19–20; regulation of numbers of, 138–41, 143–5, 149; training of, 151–81; *see also* books; clients; fees; incomes; inns of chancery; inns of court; legal profession; malpractice;

CAMBRIDGE STUDIES
IN ENGLISH LEGAL HISTORY